BETTING FOR AND AGAINST EMU

Betting For and Against EMU

Who wins and who loses in Italy and in the UK
from the process of European monetary integration

LEILA SIMONA TALANI

Ashgate

Aldershot • Brookfield USA • Singapore • Sydney

© Leila Simona Talani 2000

Published by
Ashgate Publishing Ltd
Gower House
Croft Road
Aldershot
Hants GU11 3HR
England

Ashgate Publishing Company
Old Post Road
Brookfield
Vermont 05036
USA

Ashgate website: http://www.ashgate.com

British Library Cataloguing in Publication Data
Talani, Leila Simona
    Betting for and against EMU : who wins and who loses in Italy
    and in the UK from the process of European monetary
    integration
        1.Monetary policy - Great Britain 2.Monetary policy - Italy
        3.Europe - Economic integration
        I.Title
        332.4'94

Library of Congress Catalog Card Number: 99-75560

ISBN 0 7546 1054 3

Printed in Great Britain

Contents

v

List of Graphs

List of Tables

INTRODUCTION

Interests or Expectations? A Political Economy Analytical Approach to Exchange Rate Commitments

Setting the Problem

Only recently, and thanks to the seminal work of Susan Strange (1971, 1986 and 1998), have social scientists turned to devote more attention to the issue of international financial and monetary arrangements from an integrated political economy perspective.

However, notwithstanding the many and precious contributions to the development of this branch of international political economy (IPE) (see, for example, Underhill and Coleman, 1998; Underhill, 1997), it seems to the author that there is still some scope for speculation on the relation between sociopolitical and economic accounts of financial phenomena. There is, in a few words, the possibility of finding a convincing 'synthesis' of the two cognitive and interpretative models and this is, ultimately, the aim of this book.

The broad theoretical context in which this contribution is to be inserted is given by the debate going on in IPE on the nature and sources of financial markets' behaviour with a particular reference to foreign exchange markets. In the approach of both the economists and political scientists to the issue there is indeed a discussion going on as to whether financial markets' behaviour should be considered as perfectly rational or absolutely illogical.[1]

This book will argue in favour of the rational behaviour of foreign exchange markets, but within a more structural definition of the credibility of exchange rate commitments which links together economic and political science perspectives. Indeed, when dealing with the problem of the reasons underlying a government's commitment to a pegged or fixed exchange rate regime, economic and political science analyses tend to differ consistently.

While political scientists focus primarily on a sociopolitical analysis aimed at tracing back the 'interests' underlying exchange rate policy-making, economists tend to give importance to purely financial and economic variables as connected to the 'expectations' of the markets.

In this book it is argued that both perspectives, if taken separately, can account only for a partial representation of reality and do not prove exhaustive of the many implications arising from the process of European monetary integration.

It becomes thus important to underline that the study of such an issue needs an integrated political economy approach in order to bring together in the discussion the two poles of the question.

The theoretical aim of this book is that of confronting the economists' and political scientists' approaches to exchange rate commitments and trying to reconcile them in an integrated political economy approach, where 'interests' and 'expectations' do appear as the two sides of the same coin.

In particular, this contribution seeks to explain why a country commits itself to fix its exchange rate, and why, at a certain point, the credibility of this commitment may fade triggering the rational expectations of the financial markets to re-orient towards a realignment of the exchange rate eventually, producing speculative attacks.

Thus, the following research question will be addressed: Why does a government decide to commit itself to fixed exchange rates? On what is the credibility of this commitment based? Why and when do the markets decide to bet on the lack of credibility of a similar commitment?

The analysis will be conducted on the cases of Italy and the United Kingdom and their experience in the exchange rate mechanism of the European monetary system. The period considered ranges from the decision of the two governments to peg their currencies in the ERM of the EMS to their departure on September 1992.

This is clearly an economic object of analysis with many economic consequences, but, according to the author, its political economy aspects should not be underestimated and may be fully understood by adopting a more sociological definition of credibility.

However, before doing so, it is worth having a look at the concurrent economic and political science contributions to the explanation of the issue of exchange rate commitments to see to what extent they leave room for an integrated political economy approach.

'Interests': Political Scientists' Approaches to Exchange Rate Commitments

The social science background in which to insert the issue of exchange rate commitment is represented by those IR/IPE approaches concerned with the sources of a government's commitment to international agreements, with particular reference to economic ones.

In this context the first relevant stream of theorising is represented by the literature on European integration and on EMU.

The theoretical debate over the issue of the European integration is characterised by the dichotomy between the neo-functionalist approach and the intergovernmental one (see Sandholtz, 1993).

The neo functionalist integration theory finds direct expression in the European Community since the community itself in its early stage was the inspiration for the thesis in the form in which it was originally offered by E.B. Haas in his study 'The Uniting of Europe' (1958).

Neo-functionalist explanations of integration rest on the argument of spill-overs, that is that integration in one issue area will reveal functional linkages to other issue areas. As a result, the desire to obtain the full benefits of integration in the first area would lead to pressures for integration in a second linked area.

In fact, neo-functionalists identify two sorts of spill-overs, each of which deepens and widens integration by working through interest group pressure, public opinion, elite socialisation or other domestic actors and processes. The first, functional spill-over, is economic and occurs when incomplete integration undermines the ability to achieve all the benefits of the existing policies, both in the areas that are already integrated and in related sectors of economy, thus automatically creating the need for further cooperation among the EC countries. The second, political spill-over, is linked to the fundamental role of existing EC institutions in giving impetus to a self-reinforcing process of institution building.

If applied to the issue of European Economic and Monetary Union, the spill-over proposition implies that the 1992 single-market process increased the level of support among the public opinion and the EC governments for all those EC initiatives that could enhance the gains coming from the single-market programme.

On the other hand, the intergovernmentalist integration theory postulates that nation states dominate EC politics and that outcomes directly reflect the interests and relative power of the member states. Bargaining at the European level results from strategies pursued by rational governments acting on the basis of their preferences and power, with the weakest states being induced to accept undesired policies through 'side-payments'.

A meaningful example of the intergovernmentalist view is given by Andrew Moravcsik in 'Negotiating the Single European Act' (1991), in which he proposes an intergovernmental institutional approach to European integration.

As Moravcsik himself claims (ibid., p. 27), intergovernmental institutionalism is founded on realist assumptions. States are the principal actors of the international system; interstate bargains reflect national interests and relative power; international regimes shape interstate politics by providing a common framework that reduces the uncertainty and transaction costs of interstate interactions.

An attempt to explain the negotiations over the EMU from an intergovernmental point of view has been recently made by David Andrews (1993; see also Andrews, 1994), who traces back the origins of the Maastricht agreement to a confluence of interests between the French and the German governments.

The debate between neo-functionalist and intergovernmentalist theories of European integration reflects the long-standing one between neo-institutionalist and neo-realist explanation of international events and agreements.

As Hix (1994) points out, both neo-functionalist and neo-realist approaches provide for agent-based accounts of international commitments, the main differences being in the identification of the agents of integration.

Indeed, where neo-functionalists trace back the origins of international and supranational commitments in the interests of national and European level interest groups,[2] intergovernmentalists emphasise the interests of the states in a state-centric, systemic study of international events (see Moravcsik, 1991).

However, the state-centric assumption of realist approaches has become particularly difficult to sustain in the light also of the revival of domestic approaches, or inside-out approaches to international phenomena.

In recent days, many scholars come to believe that a more comprehensive and complete explanation of international events must imply the analysis of the domestic process of interests' formation.

Indeed, the almost exclusive international focus of the systemic approaches is problematic because it rests upon a series of unexamined assumptions about domestic politics that are crucial to the result (see Milner, 1992; see also Milner 1993).

Important assumptions are made mainly about three areas: the determination of the pay-off structures, or national interests of states, the strategies available to states to alter systemic conditions, and the capacity of states to ratify and implement cooperative arrangements.

Considerations of domestic politics help to solve the problem of unfounded assumptions on these areas in the following three important respects.

First, a domestic politics approach allows us to determine how preferences are aggregated and national interests defined since, whether the focus is on absolute gains or on relative gains, a theory of domestic politics is the only means to calculate gains and losses.

Second, an analysis of the domestic situation can help explain the strategies that states adopt to realise their goals. It is true that strategies may be suggested by a state's structural position in the international environment, but the nature of its political system, bureaucratic politics, the influence of special interest and pressure groups and, in some issues, even public opinion may ultimately determine which strategies states can pursue internationally.

Third, internationally agreed terms must always be enforced internally to become effective. Thus, since domestic ratification is essential, when negotiating internationally, policy makers must always anticipate domestic reactions: international agreements can always be reached, but they can only be implemented if the domestic actors concur.

For these reasons domestic politics are essential in order to understand international cooperation and international economic cooperation in particular.

Moving out of US academic circles toward the European debate over the issue of European integration it is necessary to give an account of the attempt made by Simon Bulmer (1983) to transfer Katzenstein's integrated international-domestic politics approach from foreign economic policy issues to the problems of European policy (see also Rosamund, 1995).

This need has also been recently addressed by Moravcsik himself who has built on his preceding institutional intergovernmentalist approach to create a new 'liberal intergovernmentalism'. The latter refines the theory of interstate bargaining and institutional compliance and adds an explicit theory of national preference formation grounded in liberal theories of international interdependence (see Moravcsik, 1993a).

At the core of liberal intergovernmentalism are three essential elements: the assumption of rational state behaviour, a liberal theory of national preference formation, and an intergovernmentalist analysis of interstate negotiation.

The model of rational state behaviour, on the basis of domestically constrained preferences, implies that international conflict and cooperation can be modelled as a process that takes place in two successive stages. First governments define a set of interests, then bargain among themselves in an effort to realise those interests.

This shift towards a two-level approach to the study of international relations is completed by Moravcsik (1993b) in his introduction to Evans, Jacobson and Putnam's recent book *Double Edged Diplomacy: International bargaining and domestic politics.*

Here the author acknowledges that the question facing international relation theorists today is no longer whether to combine domestic and international explanations into a theory of double-edged diplomacy, but how best to do it, and the answer to this question is found in Putnam's two-level games theory (ibid., p. 9).

Indeed, Putnam (1988), in his article 'Diplomacy and Domestic Politics', provided for one of the most well-known attempts to find an integrated domestic-international politics approach to international agreements

Putnam's approach to the problem rests on the metaphor of the two-level game for domestic-international relations. At a national level, domestic groups pursue their interests by pressuring the governments to adopt favourable policies, and politicians seek power by constructing coalitions among these groups. At the international level, national governments seek to maximise their own ability to satisfy domestic pressures, while minimising the adverse consequences of foreign developments. Since each national political leader appears at both game boards, international relations scholars can ignore neither of the two games.

However, it is Jeffrey Frieden (1991), in his 'Invested interests: the politics of national economic policies in a world of global finance' to provide for the application of Putnam's two-level game to the issue of international exchange rate commitments (see also Frieden, 1994). In particular, he identifies the main domestic interests at stake in the two interrelated issues of exchange rate level and regimes, thus proposing the bases for a socioeconomic definition of the sources of exchange rate commitments credibility.

According to Frieden, two interrelated dimensions of policy choice are especially important in an environment of increasing capital mobility as in the European Community over the last 20 years:[3] the degree of exchange rate flexibility and the level of the exchange rate itself.

With regard to the first dimension, in a Mundell-Fleming world,[4] with full capital mobility, a country faces something of a trade-off between exchange rate stability and monetary policy autonomy (see also Padoa-Schioppa, 1988).

Thus, while some actors will favour a low degree of exchange rate flexibility, others will be willing to accept a higher degree of exchange rate flexibility, ranging from a freely floating rate solution to a two-tier EMU.

With respect to the second dimension, which is the preferred level of exchange rates itself, some fixing of exchange rate is assumed, as in the EMS before the crisis. However, some actors will prefer a high, more appreciated, exchange rate, while others will prefer a low, more depreciated, one.

The constellation of interests involved in the negotiation and implementation phases of exchange rate commitments according to Frieden's model can be simplified as follows:

Table 1   Freiden's model

	Floating exchange rates	Fixed exchange rates	
Depreciation of the currency	Manufacturing, small companies	Export-oriented, big companies	Manufacturing, small companies + export oriented, big companies
Appreciation of the currency	Public sector	Financial and banking sector	Public sector + financial and banking sector
	Manufacturing, small companies, + public sector	Export-oriented, big companies + financial and banking sector	

The evidence collected in this book shows that Frieden's model is not exhaustive of the complex political issues arising at the domestic level from the international economic phenomena nor does it succeed in predicting the actual positions adopted by the domestic economic interest groups.

No doubt Frieden proposes economically plausible hypotheses on economic sectors' exchange rate preferences. Those hypotheses in the absence of any kind of power struggle in the political arena among different social and economic actors, would prove effective in explaining and even predicting interest groups' positions towards the issue of exchange rate level and regime. However, when inserted in the historical reality of the internal debate taking place in a particular country and in a particular historical moment, these hypotheses do not prove to be adequate.

The main reason for this is that the model is a static one, which does not even contemplate the possibility of a modification in the actors' attitudes and, consequently, it is not capable of explaining why change occurs. Frieden's contribution is however quite significant because he provides a basis for the reconciliation between the political scientists' approach to exchange rate commitments, based on the identification of the socioeconomic interests involved, and the economists' one, based on the concepts of credibility and market expectations.

However, before going on to the identification of a more integrated political economy approach to the issue of exchange rate commitments it would be worth having a look at the economists' side of the coin.

'Expectations': How do Economists Cope with the Problem of Credibility[5]

In the recent debate, economic approaches to exchange rate commitments are focusing on the concept of markets' expectations about the credibility of exchange rate pegs.

There are two problems that need to be tackled when talking about the economic interpretation of the concept of credibility. One is the problem of the context in which to use it. The second is the way to measure it, which is, in turn, connected to the definition of the concept itself.

As regards the first issue, a possibility is to apply the notion of credibility to the policy-makers, as in the case of the public choice approach or of game theory models.[6] The problem then becomes to define the nature of the policy-maker's objective function, which implies making arbitrary assumptions on the nature of the utility he/she wants to maximise. It also poses some problems in terms of identifying the policy-maker's freedom of manoeuvre in complex economic policy issues like implementing a pegged exchange rate agreement.[7]

However, in this contribution the concept of credibility is applied to the policies themselves, and in particular to the likelihood that the commitment to fixed exchange rates will in fact be maintained, as viewed by the markets.[8] The problem becomes thus to see how and with which success economists have measured the credibility of a government's exchange rate commitment, particularly in relation to the Exchange Rate Mechanism (ERM) issue.

The majority of economists give a narrow definition of the concept of credibility as applied to exchange rate regimes. They interpret it as the 'level of realignment expectations' of the financial markets, usually associating low credibility with high expectations of currency realignment. This, in turn, has been measured in a variety of ways.[9]

The easiest way to measure realignment expectations is raw interest differentials. Svensson's (1990) 'simplest test' of target zone credibility, for example, is founded on the consideration that if a fluctuation band is imposed on the exchange rate there is an implicit band on the rate of return of foreign investment as well. This is due to the relation linking the rate of return on foreign investment to the actual and the future spot exchange rate.[10] Thus, given free capital mobility, in a credible target zone domestic interest rates must move within this 'rate of return band', otherwise there would be completely safe arbitrage. Therefore, if indeed the domestic interest rate is outside this 'rate of return band', the no-arbitrage assumption implies that the target zone is not credible and that the expected future spot exchange lies outside the exchange rate bands.[11]

Some other economists adjust interest rates differentials for the expected drift in the exchange rate,[12] which is particularly important in a system like the ERM, allowing for some flexibility of exchange rates around central parities (see Rose and Svensson, 1993). This method is the so-called 'drift adjusted method' and the drift can be measured in different ways (see Artis and Fratianni, 1996).

When applied to the case of the pound and lira's experiences within the ERM before their departure in September 1992, these measures of credibility give contrasting results. Indeed, the application of these methods leads to the conclusion that while the British government's commitment to the ERM was fairly credible up to the very last minute before the currency crisis, the Italian one was not sustainable throughout the whole of 1992 (ibid.).

This result is puzzling because both currencies were indeed involved in a major wave of speculation in September 1992 and both governments were forced not only to devalue their currency, but also to leave the system altogether. There must therefore be an explanation, which can give account of the similarities between the countries' experience in the ERM. It must be possible therefore to trace back 'the common nature of ERM credibility' (see Rose and Svensson, 1993).

Artis and Fratianni (1996) have found a solution to this problem by broadening the definition of credibility of the exchange rate commitment to include its sustainability in terms of fundamentals. Thus, even if financial indicators like interest rate differentials or forward exchange rates did not enshrine the lack of credibility of the British government's commitment to the ERM, a closer look at the fundamentals might signal the unsustainability of the currency peg.

Indeed, according to Artis and Fratianni, the markets form their exchange rate expectations not only on financial variables but also on their understanding of the 'average' response of the authorities to the performance of business cycle factors, in particular, inflation and output rates.[13] The argument then runs as follows: the British commitment to the ERM became incredible because the markets knew that the UK authorities would respond to the performance of the inflation and output rates in a way which was inconsistent with the maintenance of the pound in the system.

However, in Britain the recession started much before that in the other ERM countries. Therefore, if the markets based their assessment of exchange rate credibility on monetary authorities' response to the performance of the leading business cycle indicators, they should have attacked the pound within the ERM much before they attacked the lira and the franc.

On the contrary, Sterling's performance within the ERM was by no means disastrous. Although it had been given the facility to fluctuate against other ERM currencies within a 6 per cent margin, for most of its experience in the ERM it had moved safely within the 2.25 per cent band accorded to the core EMS countries, without interest rates being forced up. Instead, UK nominal interest rates showed a clear downward trend in the period Sterling remained in the ERM, while the inflation rate fell drastically from 9.5 in 1990 to 5.9 in 1991 and 3.7 in 1992 (see OECD, 1991).

Moreover, British authorities had justified British entry in the ERM mainly on business cycle considerations, namely the necessity to reduce inflation rates and to keep interest rates in line with the needs of an economy in recession (see Major, 1990b). This was actually what happened in the course of British permanence in the exchange rate mechanism.

This conclusion would be consistent with the idea that the markets considered the British government's commitment to the ERM credible up to the very last minute before the British decision to leave the ERM.

Yet we shall argue that this is not true, and that, however paradoxical this claim may seem, British commitment to the ERM was much less credible than the Italian one. Of course, however, the definition of credibility on which this claim is based is different from the economic ones given so far.

De Grauwe (1996, ch. 3) has provided far the most useful contribution to the identification of a broader definition of credibility from an economic standpoint. He traces back the origins of a speculative crisis to a dissolution of the *consensus* on the exchange rate commitment (ibid., pp. 26–27). The problem, then, becomes the identification of the basis of this *consensus*.

According to Prof. De Grauwe, the first, and fundamental source of this consensus is not endogenous to the country, but exogenous, or, better, systemic. A fixed exchange rate system necessitates a systemic consensus, that is, a consensus among the participant nation states about the stance of monetary policy for the system as a whole, what economists call the 'n-1 problem'. Consequently, it is the dissolution of this systemic consensus, represented by the rise of a conflict between the monetary policy objectives of the 'n-1 country' and the ones of the other participants to the system, which triggers the reaction of the markets and, eventually, the speculative crisis.

This approach leaves unsolved the problem of the identification and sources of the monetary policy objectives of both the 'n-1' country and the other ones.

However, even if at a subordinate level of explanation, De Grauwe considers also the endogenous sources of the dissolution or 'death' of consensus identifying them in the conflict between a country's exchange rate commitment and its domestic economic objectives, the so-called 'adjustment problem' (ibid., 1996, pp. 59–60).

What this contribution tries to identify is exactly the basis of this domestic consensus on a certain level of fixed exchange rates. In other words, it looks for the sources of the objectives pursued by a country at the moment in which it commits itself to a fixed exchange rate, and the sources of the dissolution of this consensus.

The definition of the credibility of a government's exchange rate commitment that is adopted here is thus that it depends on the existence of a social 'consensus' to such a commitment within the domestic arena, and, in particular, among the leading socioeconomic groups (see, for example, Eichengreen and Frieden, 1994).

Here credibility is linked to something 'more fundamental than the fundamentals'. It is linked to the structure of capitalism itself and to the power relations between socioeconomic groups in a certain historical moment.

Of course, however, this interpretation of credibility needs a framework in which to analyse socioeconomic behaviour. This framework is the subject of the next section of this introduction.

An Alternative Political Economy Analytic Framework

In accounting for the analytic framework of this book it is important to underline that the study has been conducted at three different levels of analysis which correspond to three different levels of explanation.

The first level of analysis is what might be called the '*political economy analysis*' and is represented by the analysis of the domestic structure of capital and of power relations between the various socioeconomic actors as historically developed. It represents the limits within which further developments must necessarily take place. This first level of analysis allows for the identification of the power relations between the social forces under consideration as related to the structure of a certain economy in a certain historical moment and to compare them with a different set of power relations in a different country. It is in this context that the theories on the diversity of capitalist economies acquire an important explanatory value.

However, these kinds of structural considerations cannot account for the whole history of Italian and British stances in the process of European monetary integration. Neither can they represent the basis for reliable predictions of future behaviour, as it is necessary to connect this first level of analysis with the second and the third ones to have a dynamic picture of the phenomenon under consideration.

The second level of analysis, '*pure economic analysis*', is given by the identification of the concrete interest groups' preferences. It allows one to focus on the concrete struggle for economic power, on the interest groups' competition to obtain the kind of economic measures necessary for their economic strengthening. It is at this level that Frieden's classification on socioeconomic preferences towards exchange rate levels and regimes may be tested on the empirical evidence.

Finally, the third level, '*pure political analysis*', is given by the analysis of the day to day political struggle, of the way in which economic interests become politics and are processed through the political and institutional system. It is here where the political bargaining process, the role of political parties and leaders and the incentive/disincentive mechanism are taken into consideration.

Of course, in a concrete explanatory effort, each of these levels of analysis concurs to give the most reliable possible picture of the phenomenon under analysis. This reflects the fact that in the real world there is an osmotic relation between the economic structure, the economic interests promoted by socioeconomic groups and the political and institutional life.

Thus, for example, the Italian decision to enter the ERM is, of course to be analysed as a political decision in the framework of the day to day political life. However, it has also much deeper roots in the underlying struggle for power among the different Italian economic interest groups, mainly trade unions and the employers' organisations. On the other hand, the British decision to enter the ERM has much more to do with the day to day political life and the need to gain political consensus on the eve of a general election.

More important for the purposes of this book, from the analytic framework above it is possible to infer a 'phenomenology of credibility' of the international economic commitments and, in particular of exchange rate commitments. This is not based on pure economic expectations, but on a much more complex set of political economy considerations.

In particular, it is possible to hypothesise that the more foreign economic commitments in general, and exchange rate policies in particular, are rooted in the economic and social structure of the country, the more these commitments are credible. That is, in the case of fixed exchange rates or target zone commitments, the more they can count in the 'consensus' of the most powerful sections of society, the less they are likely to be put under discussion by the mighty, impersonal forces of the markets.

Thus, more than contrasting interests and expectations it would be worth hypothesising a dynamic relation between the two, since the expectations of the markets are deeply influenced by the interests and preferences of the leading socioeconomic sectors of the country under consideration. In a few words, this approach postulates that market expectations, and thus also markets behaviour, are crucially affected by considerations about something 'more fundamental than the fundamentals': the economic structure and the way in which it is reflected in economic and political life.

This definition is perfectly consistent with the political scientists' view that exchange rate commitments are international agreements and therefore need to be based on the existence of a domestic 'consensus' rooted in the 'interests' of domestic actors.

From the economists' standpoint, this approach to the credibility of exchange rate pegs could help in reconciling the two opposing theories on speculative attacks. The contemporary debate in exchange rate economics is in fact characterised by the opposition between 'fundamentalists', i.e. supporters of the thesis that real exchange rate fluctuations largely reflect changes in macroeconomic fundamentals,[14] and those who believe that:

> Foreign exchange markets behave more like the unstable and irrational asset markets described by Keynes than the efficient markets described by modern finance theory (see Krugman, 1989).

The latter approach characterises speculative attacks as self-fulfilling, by that meaning that, in a multiple equilibria environment, the markets produce their own exchange rate expectations without any intelligible connection with fundamentals.[15] In turn, these expectations produce speculative attacks, which ultimately compel governments to abandon the exchange rate peg and to adopt *ex-post* softer monetary stances.

Some compromise approach has been proposed which allows for multiple equilibria only within a certain range of fundamentals' performance (see Flood and Marion, 1996). Alternatively, economists tend to overcome the problem by lifting the assumption of market participants' complete information on the performance of economic fundamentals.[16]

What this books suggests is that the failure of the fundamentals to explain speculative attacks does not necessarily imply that exchange rate markets act 'irrationally' or 'inefficiently' or that they are constrained by the lack of information. It can also mean that the markets, in deciding which of the multiple equilibria is more likely to be adopted by the government after a speculative attack, evaluate a wide range of events, including sociopolitical and structural ones. Thus the credibility of an exchange rate commitment is crucially depending on the behaviour and interests of socioeconomic actors in a particular historical moment.

Adopting a similar broad, sociological definition of credibility, Italian commitment to the ERM may be considered very credible. Indeed, it was rooted not only in the pure economic interests of the socioeconomic dominant group, but also in their political-economy need to shift the balance of power from the national to the European level in order to maintain their leading position. When, then, this consensus faded, the only obvious conclusion that the markets could draw, was to attack the lira in the ERM. However, that the consensus had faded only at the second level of analysis, that is, at the level of pure economic considerations and not of structural ones, is demonstrated by the fact that Italian commitment to the realisation of Economic and Monetary Union (EMU) did not disappear despite the ERM crisis.

On the contrary, the British decision to enter the ERM was far less credible because it was in contrast with the more structural interests of its leading fraction which were then reaffirmed in the British government's opposition to EMU. Of course, this analytic framework is not static and changes may occur at each level of analysis.

At the first level of analysis, changes are certainly long-term ones and are represented by substantial changes in the structure of the economy under consideration. In Italy an example is given by the decline in the power of trade unions and in the strengthening in the power of the industrial and banking organisations from the second half of the 1980s onwards. In Britain, a change in power relationship among economic interest groups was, for example, that happening during the First World War aftermath when the City lost, temporarily, part of its economic power on behalf of the industrial sector to regain it from the Second World War aftermath till the 1960s

At the second level of analysis, the preferences of the socioeconomic groups considered may vary from time to time and from country to country. Indeed, in 1979 neither of the British economic sectors showed an overwhelming enthusiasm for the making of the European Monetary System (EMS). However, by 1985 the British industrial sector, as represented by the Confederation of British Industry (CBI), had, completely changed its mind and started to push for British entry in the ERM, while the British trade unions are nowadays definitely in favour of further progress on the way to EMU. Similarly, the Italian CGIL, once one of the most convinced opponents of the European monetary integration process, has, in recent years, completely endorsed the goal of fulfilling the Maastricht criteria, despite their evident social consequences.

Finally, at the third level, changes are linked to the decline of the leadership of a political party/ies or a political leader/s. The end of the Thatcher era or the '*tangentopoli*' revolution in Italy are clear examples of changes at the third level of analysis. Their importance, however, must not be overestimated since, in the lack of more structural roots, their consequences appear rather superficial.

Indeed, each of the third level change may, but also may not, spill over the second level and produce changes in it which, may, or may not, produce changes at the first level of analysis.

Having clarified the analytic context in which to read them, it is worth reviewing from this perspective the outcomes of the analysis on the concrete cases of Italian and British interest groups attitudes towards the process of European monetary integration.

Notes

1 For an exhaustive account of this debate see Strange, 1998, URL: http://www.warwick.ac.uk/fac/soc/CSGR; see also Strange, 1998.
2 In Haas's conception interest groups are more important than parties: they are the dynamic element of political process in advanced pluralist democracies, and this is especially true of the groups which operate in the economic sector. See Haas, 1958, p. 5.
3 Incidentally, the issue of European Monetary Union was addressed for the first time in the context of the European community exactly at the beginning of the 1970s, with the Werner

plan, since the Treaty of Rome, in its original version, did not contain any reference to the goal of monetary union. Although many authors, like Padoa Schioppa (1988), claim that this was due to the collapse of the Bretton Wood system, some evidence may be found that this debate over monetary arrangements was urged by the growing impact of greater capital mobility. See, for references on this subject, Bank for International Settlement (BIS), 1990.

4   The Mundell-Fleming model is a macroeconomic model which links together the monetary equilibrium, that is, the equilibrium of monetary set of variables, given by the equilibrium between the money supply and demand, summarised in the so-called LM curve, and the real variables equilibrium, the equilibrium between investments and savings, summarised by the so-called IS curve. The model does include also the equilibrium of the external economic relationships in the form of the balance of payments equilibrium, summarised in the so-called BP curve. For further explanation of the model see Gandolfo, 1989, ch. 18.

5   It would certainly not be the case to address here the issue of methodological individualism as the most suitable approach to explain collective action and, in particular, state action. It is just important to point out that in complex issues like the ones arising from the process of European Monetary Integration it is simply not possible to hypothesise that there is a single decision-maker for all the policy issues implied. Neither it is thinkable that this decision-maker is free to make the choice according exclusively to his/her preferred utility function. On the contrary, one of the most interesting political economy questions is given precisely by the identification of the sources of real, not formal, decision-making power. That is why in this article it is not the credibility of the policy maker but that of the policy itself, which is taken into consideration. For a detailed explanation of methodological individualism at the root of rational choice and game theory models see Buchanan and Tullock, 1962.

6   For the application game theory to the issue of the credibility of exchange rates see Avesani, Gallo and Salmon, 1995a and 1995b; Artis, Gallo and Salmon, 1998.

7   For a similar criticism of the adoption of an approach based on the credibility of the policy maker see Drazen Masson, 1994.

8   For a similar interpretation of credibility see Masson, 1994.

9   See, for example, Rose and Svensson, 1994; Fratianni and Artis, 1996.

10 Indeed, the rate of return of a foreign investment after 'τ' months (R_t, τ) depends on both the actual (S_t) and the future spot exchange (S_t,τ) according to the following relation:

$$R_t, τ = [(1 + i^*_t, τ) . (S_t,τ/S_t)] - 1$$

Therefore, if the spot exchange rate (S_t) can fluctuate between a minimum ($\underline{S}_t$) and a maximum ($\bar{S}_t$) also the rate of return (R_t) will fluctuate between a minimum ($\underline{R}_t$) and a maximum ($\bar{R}_t$).

11 The expected spot exchange rate is then defined according to uncovered interest rate parity as:

$$eS_t,τ = S_t(1 + i_t, τ/1 + i^*_t, τ)$$

where 'eS_t,τ' is the expected spot exchange after 'τ' months, 'S_t' is the spot exchange rate, 'i_t, τ' is the domestic interest rate after 'τ' months and 'i^*_t, τ' is the foreign interest rate after 'τ' months.

12 The total rate of expected depreciation ($E_t(\Delta s_t)/\Delta_t$) can be separated into two parts:

$$E_t(\Delta s_t)/\Delta_t \equiv E_t (\Delta x_t)/\Delta_t + E_t (\Delta c_t)/\Delta_t$$

where x_t denotes the deviation of the spot rate from the central parity (c_t).

The object of interest is the expected rate of change of the central parity $E_t(\Delta c_t)/\Delta_t$, which can actually be measured by using the interest rate differential (δ_t) under the assumption that $E_t(\Delta x_t)/\Delta_t = 0$. However the economists have devised a number of methods to measure the drift. See Lindberg, Svensson and Soderlind, 1991; Rose and Svensson, 1993; Svensson, 1991.

13 Artis and Fratianni propose the following testable equation:

$$i_{j,t} - id,t = f(A(L)\,\pi_{j,t},\, B(L)\,\pi_{d,t},\, C(L)y_{j,t},\, D(L)y_{d,t})$$

where π stands for the rate of inflation, y for the deviation of output from the trend, L for the lag operator, and A, B, C, and D for functional operators.

14 For more details see De Grauwe, 1996, p. 71.
15 For a detailed account of the approach see De Grauwe, 1996, p. 75.
16 For an application of this approach to the 1987 crash see Romer, 1993.

PART I
THE BIRTH OF CONSENSUS

1 Italy and Entry into the ERM: Shifting the Domestic Power Struggle to the European Level

Domestic Versus European Politics: The Italian Government's Contradictory Behaviour

The first striking characteristic of the Italian government's behaviour during the negotiations of July to December 1978 is that, although at home it had made entry in the European Monetary System (EMS) conditional on the achievement of some 'minimal requirements',[1] its attitude abroad was much less tough and clear cut.

As a premise it must be noted that the decision to establish the European Monetary System was a political decision taken exclusively by the German Chancellor, Schmidt, and the French President, Giscard d'Estaing. Even the role played by Jenkins, who, at that time, was President of the European Commission and who had put forward the issue of further European Monetary integration in a lecture given to the European University Institute in October 1977 (see Jenkins, 1977), was only a marginal one.

The Franco-German plan was communicated to the other European Prime Ministers during the European Council in Copenhagen, on 7–8 April 1978.

Since the determination of Chancellor Schmidt and President d'Estaing was to keep out of the political decision everyone but the other European Heads of State or Government, the first day of the Copenhagen summit was organised by the Danes in a way that minimised even the participation of Foreign Ministers. Indeed, the most of the discussions went on between the Prime Ministers in informal talks and dinner meetings.

It is worth pointing out that, during the Copenhagen meeting, Andreotti, then Italian Head of Government, played no significant role in the discussion. Observers underline that he was hardly heard to utter a word.

Furthermore, finance ministers and central bankers were not involved in any stage of the political process leading to the decision to establish the EMS. They did not even play a role in the definition of the project which took place between April and July 1978, that is, between the Copenhagen and the Bremen European Councils. It is, thus possible to infer that neither the Italian Finance Minister, Pandolfi, nor the Governor of the Bank of Italy, Baffi, had any say in it.

In fact, the definition of the plan was attributed to a very small group of persons. This included Clappier, a man very close to the French Prime Minister, Schulmann, a man very close to the German Prime Minister, and Couzens, a British Treasury man who was 'not very close' to Callaghan, the British Prime Minister. Thus Callaghan's move was interpreted in diplomatic circles as a demonstration of the fact that the British would not take part actively in the definition of the EMS because of the lack of support to the project by the British domestic actors. Regarding this, it is worth noting that the position of the British Treasury towards the whole project had been extremely negative from the very beginning of the talks. However, UK participation to the system was considered particularly important by the two leading partners of the EEC, and the negotiations with the British delegation went on until the Brussels summit of December 1978.

Turning to the behaviour of the Italian delegation during the negotiations, the overall feeling is that the Italians never had any serious intention to reject the new system despite the multitude of issues and problems that they were raising especially at the national level, issues that sometimes annoyed their European counterparts.

In order to prove how rigid and firm was the attitude of the Italian government towards the conditions of entry in the EMS in the *internal debate*, reference can be made to three separate declarations released by the Minister of Treasury, Pandolfi.[2]

On 9 September, at a conference held by the Christian Democrat group, AREL, Pandolfi said:

> One thing is certain as far as the position of the Italian government is concerned: we cannot and will not be satisfied by formal changes hardly sufficient to conceal a reality which would be that of the Snake. It is essential for us to achieve a symmetry of intervention obligations between strong and weak currencies; it is further essential that the system fits all community currencies and is therefore endowed with adequate elements of flexibility, one of which is certainly the width of the margin [...]. On the issue of parallel measures we obtained an

important result yesterday [...]; we secured the French support to our proposal that the Community should finance large-scale national development projects.[3]

There was then a short statement in the same vein at the Finance and Treasury Committee of the Chamber of Deputies on 27 September.

Finally, on 10 October, Pandolfi, in his introduction to the Budget debate, devoted part of his speech to the Italian position towards the EMS, saying:

> We fought to obtain that the negotiations [...] would progress simultaneously along three lines: the exchange rate agreements, the European Monetary Fund, the measures in favour of the less prosperous economies: *with the warning that there are minimal requirements which, if not satisfied in one of these three sectors, cannot be compensated by concessions in the other two.*[4]

Such minimal requirements appeared to be the following. In the exchange rate field, a substantial difference of the new system from the snake and conditions ensuring symmetry of obligations; in particular, sufficiently wide generalised margins and compulsory action when the signal of the early warning system had flashed. For the European Monetary Fund, pending its institution, an immediate activation of adequate credit facilities. In the field of development, expansive policies on the part of stronger countries and sizeable transfers of resources to the less prosperous economies.

On the monetary side, the Italian effort to design the new system as a consistent whole differing from the old snake had already been made public in the *Blueprint for the European Monetary System*, a thorough document by the Bank of Italy which was submitted to the EEC Monetary Committee and to the Committee of the European Governors (see Banca d'Italia, 1978).[5] Its major features were:

- the acceptance of the Belgian compromise;[6]
- new criteria to define the initial weight of European currencies in the ECU and to revise the amount of each currency in case of realignment;
- a general band of bilateral intervention limits wider than the snake band;
- narrow ECU margins for the early-warning system, with definition of the consultation procedures and intervention rules such as to ensure symmetry when the alarm goes off;
- a project for the European Monetary Fund in its definitive form.[7]

The key element in the exchange rate agreement was the combination of the wider bilateral band with the much narrower ECU band whose purpose was to make the system more flexible and durable without making it looser, especially if obligations in case of early warning were accepted.[8]

At the Committee of Governors, however, it became clear that no other country was interested in a wider band system, although there was some readiness to grant Italy a wider band. Therefore, the Italian government confined itself to a rearguard semantic action to assure that the wider band would be considered a theoretical option for all the former snake floaters and not merely a special concession to Italy. An agreement along these lines received the consensus of Chancellor Schmidt at the meeting with prime minister Andreotti in Siena on 1 November. It was then approved by the Monetary Committee on 6 and 7 November and by the Committee of Governors on 11 November and received a final sanction at the Council of Economic and Finance ministers on 21 November.

Although the likelihood of creating a truly new system had, by that time, completely vanished, a number of individual questions were still open where Italian interests were at stake. These were: the size of the credit facilities; the terms of the settlement of the very short-term support; a generally accepted interpretation of the Belgian compromise. Among this set of issues, only the one relating to short-term credit facilities was settled satisfactorily at the ECOFIN Council of 21 November. Support facilities would amount to 25 billion ECU, instead of the smaller figure proposed by the Germans and the Dutch. Moreover, at the European Council of December in Brussels, the Germans accepted the majority's wish to allocate more to the short- than to the medium-term support[9] and a compromise was reached for the settlement of the very short-term support.[10]

Whereas in the monetary field the Italian negotiators succeeded in obtaining some concessions, the chapter of the 'parallel measures' (concerning further integration of the less developed countries) was almost ignored by the Italian delegation throughout the whole period of the negotiations. This happened despite the great importance which had been given to this issue in the internal debate.

Unlike the other two Committees[11] involved in the making of the EMS, the Economic Policy Committee, the one responsible for the definition of the chapter of parallel measures, never recovered from the stalemate that had characterised its working from the outset. The only conclusion that it was possible to infer from its Report (submitted to the Council on 13 November) was that the matter had not received consideration at the political level. As a result, there was complete disagreement on all the questions concerned.

In this respect, it is particularly interesting to look at the 'widely different approaches of the three less prosperous countries' (Ludlow, 1982, p. 254), namely, Italy, United Kingdom and Ireland, which were the most interested by the discussion on the transfer of resources.

Of the three governments, the British, since it was clear that they were not going to enter the system immediately, had the simplest task: to secure the maximum number of propaganda points. An aim which they eventually succeeded in achieving.

The Irish government's tactics were also relatively straightforward, since they focused their requests on a set of aids in the form of loans and grants, whose amount was clearly stated from the beginning of the negotiations.

On the contrary, despite many warnings, the Italians remained very evasive and vague in the definition of the content and amount of their requests. It is true that Pandolfi spoke on several occasions of a project to clean up the Bay of Naples, and that there was some talk about a major hydraulic scheme in the Apennines. However, neither of these plans, nor others that were raised and then dropped, seem to have gone much beyond the stage of rhetoric.

As a result, the agreement reached in Brussels on 4–5 December, only marginally covered the issue of Community help to the less developed member states. The measures decided by the European Council provided only for a five year 1 bn loan for structural interventions to be granted to the less prosperous countries participating to the ERM with, as the only facility, the possibility for the Commission to decide a support on interest payments no higher than 3 per cent.

The Domestic Political Debate: A Preliminary Level of Explanation

Many hypotheses have been put forward to explain this 'peculiar' attitude of the Italian government towards the issue of 'parallel measures' to further the economic integration of the less developed regions.

According to the approach adopted in this book, the first level of explanation of the Italian government's behaviour is given by the underlying domestic political debate. This, in turn, reflects the conflict of the economic interests involved in the issue of joining the ERM and the broader issue of power relationships among these groups.

Indeed, analysing the sources on the subject, it seems clear that the question of parallel measures was a main concern of the Communist Party. According to the Italian Communist Party (PCI), this transfer of real resources to the weakest members of the Community should not be conceived as a mere financing of 'special projects' to be realised in Italy. On the contrary, it was to be pursued through the revision of some Community policies, such as the Common Agricultural Policy (CAP),[12] the regional policy or the budgetary policy, associated with the coordination of member states' economic policies.

Since the coalition that sustained Andreotti's government during the negotiations relied on the external support of the Communist Party ('governo di solidarieta' nazionale'[13]), the government had nothing to gain by isolating the PCI, unless this was absolutely inevitable. Therefore, the government was ready to grant, theoretically, additional concessions on the measures to which the communists attached more importance. In relation to the ERM issue, these measures were, on the one hand, the linkage between monetary integration and further economic integration within the EEC and, on the other hand, the consequent emphasis on the need for parallel measures.

Thus, the Italian government's insistence on a set of minimal requirements for Italy to enter the ERM was mainly an instrumental device designed to keep the PCI's support to the governmental coalition.

On the other hand, despite Andreotti's 'Colpo di scena' on 5 December, when the Prime Minister announced the Italian government's decision not to join the EMS to reverse his position only a week later, Italian determination to enter the system was unarguable from the outset. This may explain why Italians obtained very little from the negotiations, not only in the economic field, where Italian government requests were purely instrumental ones, but also in the monetary field.

Particularly revealing on this respect is the parliamentary debate which took place in the week immediately following the Brussels Summit and, then, the one which followed Andreotti's announcement of Italian entry in the ERM. In his speech to the Italian Republican Senate on 7 December 1978, Andreatta, Senator of the Christian Democratic Party, openly reassured Prime Minister Andreotti, and, indirectly, the markets, about the genuine will of Italian political and economic forces to implement policies consistent with the pegging of the lira to a fixed exchange rate regime (see Andreatta, 1978a). Indeed, these policies had already been enshrined in the so-called '*piano* Pandolfi'.[14]

Thus, for the Christian Democratic Party, Italy had only one choice to make: to join the ERM immediately. This was what punctually happened on 12 December, when Andreotti (1978) announced to the Chamber of Deputies the Italian government's decision to enter the new European monetary arrangements from the outset.

The politically strategic nature of Andreotti's delay in joining the ERM appears clearly in almost all the declarations to the Chamber of Deputies.

They all noted how the delay responded to the need to verify the opportunity to break the governmental majority on the specific issue of the EMS.[15] Eventually, the outcome of the parliamentary discussions was the de facto opening of the political crisis within the governmental majority with the adoption by its constituents of absolutely inconsistent positions over the most important resolution on the EMS, the so-called 'Risoluzione Galloni'.[16] The declarations of vote, undertaken by secret ballot, registered the consensus of the Christian Democratic Party (DC),[17] the Italian Social Democratic Party (PSDI), the Italian Liberal Party (PLI),[18] and the right wing parties Costituente di Destra-Democrazia Nazionale[19] and Movimento Sociale Italiano-destra nazionale.[20] The resolution could also clearly count on the support by the Italian Republican Party (PRI),[21] while Pannella's Radical Party (PR), though explicitly in favour of Italian participation to the ERM to the extent that presented and voted a parallel, favourable resolution, decided not to vote the 'Risoluzione Galloni'.[22] On the other hand the Italian Communist Party[23] rejected the central part of the resolution, which asked for immediate Italian entry in the ERM of EMS, while declaring its abstention on the first and third sections, which contained a more general commitment to the process of European integration and defined the political lines of action for the implementation of the agreement on the ERM. Finally, the Italian Socialist Party declared its abstention on all the sections of the resolution,[24] while the extreme left groups rejected it entirely.[25]

In his intervention to the Chamber of Deputies on 12 December, Spaventa highlighted the negative economic consequences deriving from joining the ERM (see Spaventa, 1978c). They ranged from the loss of competitiveness, to the decrease in the growth rate and the increase in unemployment. These implications were particularly unwelcome in a moment in which Italy needed expansionary macroeconomic policies to overcome its backwardness in terms of income pro capita, unemployment rates, and the development gap between the South and the North.[26] Thus, according to Spaventa, the Italian government's decision to enter the system was not determined by the consideration of the economic interests of the nation as a whole, but by the 'political' will of some economic and political sectors.[27] Moreover, this 'political' will was only instrumentally linked to the need for Italy to strengthen its commitment to the European project, while its true aim was to overcome the existing balance of power among the political parties.

What Spaventa failed to point out is that the credibility of Italian commitment to the set of deflationary measures consistent with the maintenance of quasi-fixed and overvalued exchange rates, was guaranteed by the existence of a strong consensus among certain political and economic actors. These, in turn, were the same actors who supported the shift of power relationships eventually leading to the withdrawal of the Communist Party from the government majority.

Indeed, the most likely explanation of the reasons why there was little doubt about Italian government's eventual determination to enter the ERM is that the government was increasingly supported by those economic and political groups which gained the most by fixing the exchange rates. Moreover, these groups were, at that time, achieving a more powerful position in relation to those doomed to lose from joining the system.

To test this hypothesis it is necessary to move from the political analysis to an economic one, and to have a look at the interests and preferences of the Italian socioeconomic groups in the debate over the making of the EMS.

An Analysis of Domestic Interest Groups' Preferences with Reference to Frieden's Model

As already pointed out in the introduction, political scientists' approach to the issue of foreign economic commitments rest on the notion of 'interests'. In particular, with reference to exchange rate commitment, Frieden put forward a model to predict and explain the preferences and interests of domestic socioeconomic actors towards the two interrelated issues of exchange rate level and regime.

According to this model, pegging the lira to the ERM implied a quasi fixed and relatively appreciated real exchange rate against the Deutschmark (DM), since the inflation differential of Italy with Germany was a positive one.

Moving from flexible to more rigid exchange rates provided greater predictability in foreign trade and exchange. However, it made it much more difficult for the government to use exchange rate policies to alter domestic macroeconomic conditions and relative prices. It also involved the commitment to the implementation of monetary policies consistent with fixed exchange rates.

On the other hand, the level of the exchange rates had relative price implications. An appreciated, or 'strong' currency, enhanced the domestic prices of non-tradable goods and services relative to the domestic prices of tradeables, but it also decreased the competitiveness of domestic tradable goods relative to foreign ones.

On the basis of these considerations, Frieden projects the position of socioeconomic groups towards fixing the lira.

A fixed and relatively appreciated exchange rate is considered favourable to those heavily involved in international trade and payments, mainly big firms and the banking and financial sector. Non-tradeable producers, such as those in the public sector, are expected to hold an ambiguous position. A strong currency is positive for them, while foregoing national monetary autonomy is unattractive to the extent that they depend upon national economic conditions; on the other hand, they are not affected by the stability of exchange rates. Producers of tradeable goods, like producers of standardised manufactures that compete primarily on price, are assumed to be hostile to both a strong currency, causing them substantial difficulties in competing with imports and in maintaining export markets, and its being fixed, inasmuch as they are interested in keeping their internal markets.

Thus, following Frieden's scheme, the big firms and the banking and financial sector should be favourable to a strong, fixed currency, the traditional import competing manufacturing sector, namely, small firms should be hostile, while non-tradeable producers, namely the public sector, should be ambivalent.

These hypotheses will be tested with reference to the internal debate going on between the Italian socioeconomic actors at the eve of Italian entry in the ERM. The final aim is to assess whether and to what extent Italian government decision to enter the ERM from the outset may be explained on the basis of *purely economic* considerations, or it is necessary to adopt a *political economy* point of view.

1   Italian Industrial Capital Support to the ERM: Short-term Economic Interest Versus Long-term Political Economy Ones

Italian entry in the ERM was endorsed with true enthusiasm by Italian big companies to the extent that De Benedetti, Agnelli and Pirelli were its most active supporters. Umberto Agnelli, in a speech to the AREL meeting on 9 September 1978, welcomed with 'great pleasure' the Bremen agreement of 6–7 July 1978 which made public the EC member states' commitment to establish a new European Monetary System by the beginning of 1979. According to Agnelli, in a moment in which the Italian industrial sector was experiencing a relatively favourable moment, Italian industrial macroeconomic preferences moved towards the need to cut production costs, mainly by cutting wages, and to reduce public deficit. Thus Agnelli considered the so-called '*piano triennale*' (or '*piano* Pandolfi'), as the Italian response to the Bremen agreement thanks to the commitment it implied to reduce Italian public deficit to a level consistent with European inflation rates and to limit wage increases in order to preserve industrial sector competitiveness.[28]

Regarding the issue of Italian entry into the ERM, Agnelli's position was clear-cut. Italy's foremost industrialist rejected completely the need of flexibility and of mechanisms which preserved value of the weakest currencies. On the contrary, he included among 'minimum requirements' for Italian entry, the commitment by the union movement to the implementation of the measures required by the '*piano* Pandolfi'. Agnelli's support for the creation of a European Monetary System, and for its linkage with the adoption of severe macroeconomic policies, was reiterated several times in the course of the negotiations. At the British Foreign Trade Convention held in London in mid-November he said that the weaker nations were 'to accept fewer jobs for their workers and less popularity for their governments, as the price for entering a more stable world'.

In the opinion of Antonio Mosconi (1978), director of the Fiat study office, the opposition to early Italian entry in the ERM came from those sectors of Italian economy which rejected wage cuts as the means to sustain the exchange rate commitment, namely, the trade unions. Moreover, Mosconi did not consider it legitimate to define the then existing inflation differentials as the indicators of future ERM problems, as it was claimed by most Italian and foreign economists. Indeed, according to the FIAT manager, on the one hand, Italy would join the system with the initial advantage of having an undervalued currency and of presenting a huge surplus in the current account, and, on the other hand, Italian inflation was expected to be reduced exactly by its commitment to the new European monetary arrangements.

Turning to the position of Confindustria, its commitment to the project of the creation of a more stable European currency area may be traced back to the period preceding the Bremen agreement of 6–7 July 1978. Guido Carli, President of Confindustria, had already put forward a 'plan for currency stabilisation'[29] at the UNICE meeting on 25 May 1978. During this meeting a 'task force' was established within the UNICE, chaired by Carli himself, and responsible for the elaboration of a European monetary strategy to be presented at the Bremen and Bonn summits. The content of this European monetary strategy should ensure that 'Brussels influence on single member states' economies resulted enhanced' and that 'the supranational considerations in the development of member states' macroeconomic policies increased' in the name of the 'free market' philosophy (see *il Sole 24 ore*, 1978; Spinelli, 1978a).

After the publication of the Bremen meeting proposal on the EMS, Carli reiterated his commitment to the establishment of an area of exchange rate stability within Europe. He claimed that the European countries had to realise the aim to limit infra European fluctuation bands by adopting two strategies. Firstly, by coordinating the exchange rate policies of the member states vis-à-vis the dollar. Secondly, by coordinating national macroeconomic policies through the implementation of domestic economic policies consistent with the commitment to the ERM. However, that the preferences of Carli were for the second strategy was demonstrated by the fact that he soon dropped the first strategy. Indeed, during the Forex international meeting in London on 21 November, he even claimed that the EMS could have had a major role in the stabilisation of financial markets 'independently' of any linkage with the dollar. Moreover, after the Brussels meeting and still pending Italian decision, he declared himself satisfied by the Brussels agreement paragraphs 3.6 and 5.1 merely mentioning the need of coordination procedures between the Community exchange rate policies and those of 'third countries', particularly the USA.

Also the Confindustria clearly favoured the second option, namely, the strategy to limit, through the imposition of an 'external constraint', the government's power to determine macroeconomic policies. This was clearly stated in the first report of Confindustria on the economic performance of the Italian industrial sector, where it was claimed:

> The way in which strict interdependence among the different sectors of the Italian economic system is interwoven with huge independence of the decision-making centres' policies producing economic results almost by chance but always in the direction of a decrease in the economic growth, has become one of the central subjects of the economic policy and perhaps also of the politics tout court in our country. Italy's entry in the ERM is to be intended as a way to change this situation and to modify these attitudes in order to render them consistent with the economic and productive events (Confidustria, 1978a, p. 54).

More specifically, Confindustria described Italian political and economic situation as being characterised by: '… a progressive paralysis of the state institutions' tools to determine and control economic activities' (ibid.).

Therefore, Confindustria urged a transfer of macroeconomic decision-making power from the state to the market through the entry in the ERM. According to the report of Confindustria, industrial competitiveness, only temporarily enhanced by the 1976 devaluation, was threatened by the dynamics of the 'Scala Mobile'. The latter was also considered responsible for the increase of external finances needed by Italian companies, particularly private companies, and, thus, for the decrease of investments. Consequently, the primary goal of Confindustria in that period was that of loosening the constraints imposed to the industrial and productive sector by both the public sector and the trade unions. This could easily be achieved by joining the ERM of EMS with all that it meant in terms of reducing state autonomy in taking macroeconomic policy decisions.[30]

The tension between private capital, the state and the trade unions, was a major concern of the President of Confindustria too (see Confindustria, 1978b). In his opinion, the solution to this problem was given by the adoption of neo-liberal policies in the context of open economy and free markets.

Concluding, in the domestic debate over the EMS, Confindustria did not focus on the issue of Italian entry in the system. The necessity of a similar decision was never put under discussion and was given for granted even before the Brussels meeting.[31] However, the Italian industrial employers' organisation repeatedly emphasised the linkage between entry in the ERM and the need to implement macroeconomic policies consistent with a reduction of the economic role of the state and of the trade unions.

Contrary to what could be expected following Frieden's model, also Italian small companies were definitely favourable to joining the ERM. This clearly appears from the declarations released by Gianni Castiglioni, vice-president of the API (Associazione Piccole Imprese – Small Companies' Association) in the immediate aftermath of the Brussels Summit of 5–6 December 1978, in which he claimed: '... our interest is to have the most fixed exchange rate possible' (see Galvani, 1978).

Similar statements were reiterated, after Italian entry in the EMS, by the General Secretary of the CONFAPI (Confederazione delle Associazioni delle Piccole Imprese – Confederation of Small Companies' Associations) who believed it essential to link the provisions of the Pandolfi's Plan and Italian acceptance of the Exchange Rate Agreement.

Finally, true enthusiasm was expressed by the Italian Association of Commerce at the announcement of the Andreotti government's decision to join the system (see Ferrari, 1978).

A major inconsistency with Frieden's hypotheses is that state-owned companies, which traditionally had showed only a limited interest in European subjects,[32] in the debate over the making of the EMS, took a very clear-cut and strong position in favour of Italian early entry into the system. This much is clear from the declarations released by Giuseppe Petrilli, IRI President, in a very politically oriented speech held at the meeting organised in Madrid on 30 May–2 June 1978 by the European Public Company Centre:

... It is impossible to have a true European industrial policy and a true European industrial reorganisation policy without moving towards European economic and monetary union (Petrilli, 1978a, p. 15).

His intervention to the AREL meeting of 9 September 1978 was along the same line:

... the achievement of European economic and monetary union is an inescapable goal which does not allow for alternatives ... [European economic and monetary union] is an issue presently affecting our country. The 'Piano Pandolfi', now under discussion, represents the most important effort carried out up to now by Italy to be ready to participate to this new phase of European integration [the European Monetary System] (Andreatta et al., 1978).

Consistently, Italian government's decision to join immediately the Exchange Rate Mechanism of the EMS, was welcomed with nothing but great enthusiasm by the IRI President who defined it: '... an important step forward on the way to the building of Europe ...' (Petrilli, 1978b).

The favourable position of the Italian public industrial sector towards the establishment of the EMS was not limited to the IRI but also included the INTERSIND as a whole. In meetings organised by the Italian Council of the European Movement in Rome, on 26–27 January 1979, Sampietro, General Vice-Director of the INTERSIND, underlined how the 'Italian way' to the reduction of Italian economic unbalances was perfectly coincident with the 'Community way' embedded in the European Monetary System. Both implied curtailing public debt and labour costs[33] and assumed the abandonment of the exchange rate policy based on competitive devaluations (see Sampietro, 1979).

Similar arguments were put forward by a smaller and less significant public companies' association called ASAP[34] to justify its support to Italian entry in the ERM.

2 The Banking Sector and the ERM: Sharing the Preferences of the Industrial Capital

Coming to the financial sector, the almost unconditionally favourable position of the Italian banking sector towards the establishment of an area of monetary stability within the European Community is clear in all the official declarations of the Italian Banking Association (ABI), as well as in the articles published by the ABI official review, 'Bancaria', and of the review of the Ordinary

Credit Companies National Association and of the Banks and Bankers Central Institute (Rivista della Associazione Nazionale Aziende Ordinarie di Credito e dell' Istituto Centrale di Banche e Banchieri), 'Banche e Banchieri'.

In the immediate aftermath of the European Council in Copenhagen, an article was published in the review 'Banche e Banchieri' which contained an explicit commitment to the project of the European Monetary Union and to all the intermediary monetary arrangements leading to its gradual establishment. Perhaps more meaningful for the identification of the position of the Italian banking sector towards the EMS, is the declaration contained in the ABI 1978 Report. In this declaration, the initiatives regarding the establishment of new European monetary arrangements were explicitly urged and supported. Moreover, the monetary markets analyses, published by the ABI review, showed that Italian economy needed a general exchange rate and trade stability and had to actively pursue these aims without paying too much attention to the protection of short term national interests (see Bancaria, 1978).

Thus, the Italian Banking Association (ABI), in its report released on 5 July 1979, gave a favourable assessment of the European Monetary System as defined by the Brussels agreement. It underlined how the new European Monetary arrangements overcome the weaknesses of the previous attempts to link European currencies in a fixed exchange rates regime. This was possible because the strict observance of the constraints imposed by the participation in the ERM implied the convergence in the management of national economies by member states' governments, particularly in relation to the implementation of deflationary policies, thus eliminating the main sources of trouble for the stability of exchange rates (see Associazione Bancaria Italiana, 1979, p. 250). The need to give the highest priority to the objectives of the reduction of inflation rate and of public deficit was, then, the central subject of the ABI President 1980 annual speech (Associazione Bancaria Italiana, 1980, p. 33).

Regarding the other institutions of the financial sector, it is worth mentioning the favourable position of the vice president of the FIME (Finanziaria Meridionale – Southern Financial Company), Olivetti. He argued that Italian participation to the ERM from the beginning (with all that it implied in terms of the implementation of deflationary macroeconomic policies) was a necessary precondition to induce foreigners to invest in southern Italy.

On the other hand, the interventions of the President of the Forex Club (Associazione dei Cambisti – Exchange Rates Agents Association), Perticone, were much more cautious. He declared himself against early Italian entry in the system, even if he favoured an active role of Italy in the process leading to its establishment (see Perticone, 1978).

It is clear, at this point, that an early Italian entry in the ERM was favoured by both the banking capital and the industrial one, both private and public. In other words, it is possible to claim that the industrial and banking capital represented the socioeconomic basis of the consensus on which the credibility of the Italian government's commitment to the ERM was founded.

This conclusion already contrasts with Frieden's hypotheses on socioeconomic interest groups preferences over the degree of stability and strength of the national currency's exchange rate. However, the analytical model conceived by Frieden proves inadequate to explain Italian reality also because it does not take into account of one of the fundamental constituents of the Italian economic, social and political systems, namely, organised workers as represented by the trade unions.

3 Italian Trade Unions and the ERM: Fragmented Interests and Political Divisions

Turning to the position of Italian trade unions on the ERM issue, Italian CGIL, the left Italian trade union, actively supported the European Confederation of trade unions' declaration on the Bremen Council preparatory works. The latter stated that, though acceptable, the establishment of a more stable exchange rates system could not be considered an objective in itself without substantial structural interventions in the industrial, regional and development policies, explicitly aimed at the creation of employment (see Confederazione Europea dei Sindacati, 1978).

That the CGIL position towards EMS was not one of total opposition is demonstrated by the articles published by its political review, 'Rassegna sindacale'. There it was claimed that it was indeed in the interest of the trade unions to have a stable monetary system given, however, the guarantee of a certain degree of flexibility. This, in practice, meant the acceptance of some conditions necessary to cope with the wide economic divergences existent within the European community (see Bonaccini, 1978a).

The Bremen agreement seemed to the Italian trade unions to fulfil these requirements, to the extent that the Executive Committee of the CGIL, CISL, UIL federation expressed its unanimous interest in the project (ibid.). However, as the negotiations went on at the European level and as the political significance acquired by the issue at the domestic level broadened, the different trade union organisations took increasingly different positions. This eventually led to a serious breakdown in their relations.

In particular, the CGIL, composed of a communist majority and a socialist minority, considered unacceptable the consequences that a monetary agreement based exclusively on an exchange rate mechanism could have had on Italian economy. Consequently, it required, in exchange for its consensus to the entry in the ERM, the adoption of economic measures in favour of less-developed European regions together with a reform of the CAP (see Tropea, 1978). Meanwhile the UIL, the socialist trade union, linked its support to Italian entry in the ERM to the acceptance of a domestic economic planning aimed at increasing industrial productivity (see Cicala, 1978). Both the CGIL and the UIL however, expressed their open opposition to the Andreotti government's acceptance of the Brussels terms to enter the ERM. This decision was perceived as a means to pave the way, through the external constraint of the EMS, to a renewed attack on the 'Scala Mobile'. On the contrary, the catholic component of the Italian Trade Union Federation, the CISL, expressed its favourable position to an immediate Italian entry in the ERM. The grounds on which this position was based were that a rejection of the ERM would mean the disintegration of the free trade area, and would imply competitive devaluations, protectionism and trade wars, eventually leading to the collapse of the European integration process (see Orlando, 1978).

Thus, given the dissociation of the CISL, and given the uncertainties of the New Craxi Socialist Party (PSI), trade unions and left political groups' position on the issue of Italian entry in the ERM was not as clear-cut and cohesive as the one of Italian capital.

In conclusion, it is possible to claim that the mere analysis of the position of political parties and institutions towards the ERM is not enough to explain the contradictions of the Italian government's behaviour in the course of the negotiations over the making of the EMS. A more detailed analysis of the socioeconomic interest groups' preferences is required. However, the analytic framework put forward by social scientists, and, in particular, by Frieden, to identify such socioeconomic preferences over the issue of the exchange rate level and regime does not explain the Italian case. This happens because first, it fails to take into consideration the interests of important sectors of Italian economy, such as the trade unions. Second, it fails to identify the real stances adopted by the categories under consideration.

It seems therefore appropriate to broaden the analysis and to insert the behaviour of the socioeconomic actors into the context of the structure of Italian capitalist economy and of the power relations between its components.

This is a subject on which attention will be focused in the next section of this chapter.

Macroeconomic Issues During the Early 1980s

Summing up, Italian entry in the Exchange Rate Mechanism of the European Monetary System, as agreed upon in Brussels, meant the following:

- the loss of monetary policy instruments, mainly the nominal interest rates, and thus of the ability to decide both the economy growth rate, at least in the short run, and the level of employment;
- losing control of the exchange rate instrument and, thus, of the ability to respond with exchange rate movements to balance of payments disequilibria;
- the lack of guarantees, at least in the short term, to achieve a lower inflation rate;
- an appreciation of the real exchange rate and, thus, in the long run, the loss of competitiveness of the industrial sector.

Why, then, were Italian banking and industrial sectors so anxious to enter the system?

The reasons were clearly political, but not so much in the ideological sense of stating Italian commitment to the ideal of European integration. They were political in the political economy sense of making some particular interests prevail both in the daily political struggle and in the longer term definition of power relationships between different economic and social groups.[35]

However, the interesting questions in relation to Italian position in the EMS, do not end with its entry. On the contrary, far more important problems arose in the implementation phase, when it was actually necessary to implement macroeconomic policies, mainly counter inflationary ones, consistent with the maintenance of the parities in the ERM.

As a matter of fact, in the first four years of its operation, there were seven realignments of EMS currency values which brought a devaluation of the lira vis-à-vis the DM of 27 per cent. However, over the following four years, between April 1983 and January 1987, there were only four more realignments, with a devaluation of the Lira of only 13 per cent vis-à-vis the DM. Moreover, after 1983, exchange rate variability within the EMS declined substantially, while monetary policies converged on virtually every dimension.[36]

It is generally agreed that the decisive turning point in the evolution of the EMS came between 1981 and 1985, when the French and the Italian

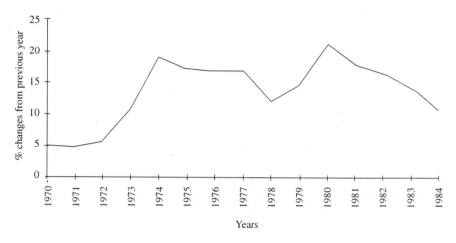

Graph 1   Italian consumer prices % changes 1970–84

Source: *OECD Economic Outlook*, No. 38, December 1985.

governments changed course to bring their inflation rates in line with the EC average (see IMF, 1988, p. 48).

This implied the adoption by the Italian government of economic policies aimed at the reduction of inflation rates by acting on labour costs and on the public deficit side. On the implementation of these measures, there was a widespread consensus precisely by those interest groups which had supported early Italian entry in the ERM (see, for example, Confindustria, 1978a, p. 4).

There are two events which are traditionally considered the major steps in reorienting monetary policy. The first is the so-called 'Divorce' of the Banca d'Italia from the Treasury, which happened when the Governor of the Central Bank indicated that he would no longer be guided by the 1975 commitment to purchase unsold Treasury securities. The second is the 1985 curtailing of the 'Scala Mobile' after a long political conflict which started in 1983 and ended with the PCI and the CGIL losing the referendum on this subject on 9 June 1985.

These two events were just the final result of a change in power relationships among the Italian socioeconomic groups dating back to the second half of the 1970s. The beginning of this power shift had been represented by the Italian government's decision to join the ERM, with all that it implied in terms of more severe economic policies. Its outcome would be the end of the 'Era of Union centrality' (see Lange, 1986, p. 29).

1   The Political Economy of the 'Divorce'

The shift of the monetary policy instruments managed by the Bank of Italy from those under a certain control of the state to those acting only throughout the market was not a sudden event which happened in the immediate aftermath of Italian entry in the ERM. Instead, it was a gradual and silent process through which a substantial reform of the system was made possible.[37]

The introduction of the free auction to sell Treasury securities, the equalisation of the compulsory reserve quotas for all types of credit institution, the abolition of the commitment of the Bank of Italy to buy all unsold Treasury securities, the issue of new Treasury securities with a wider range of expiration dates and rents such as the CCT, the increase in the frequency of the auctions, the reform of the financing system for the credit institutions with the substitution of discount operations with temporary public securities sales and purchases: all these measures (which built up a new institutional system allowing monetary management through open market operations) were justified on the basis of technical reasons but their political aspect, concerning power allocation, is unarguable.[38]

It is in this context that the issue of Italian acceptance of the ERM arrangements should be considered as a moment of this process leading to the detachment of monetary policy from public control. The importance of these institutional changes from a political point of view can be assessed by recalling that the government, at the end of this process, was no longer able to use freely monetary policy instruments to bargain with social partners. Nor was it able to implement an expansive monetary policy to stimulate employment in exchange of wage-cuts, or to allow exchange rates depreciation in exchange for fewer workers being dismissed.

A political economy model of interpretation of the independence of the Central Bank has been put forward by Epstein and Schor. It is worth recalling here some of the main elements of this model to explain how the process leading to a greater independence of the Italian central bank may be linked to the underlying struggle for power between social and political actors.

From the empirical evidence, Epstein and Schor derive three main elements characterising the relationships between Central Bank independence and the underlying social relations. First, the independence of a Central Bank is influenced by the relationship between productive and financial capital, since, where this relationship is not strong, as in the UK, the Central Bank is usually linked to the interests of the financial community and more favourable to the implementation of stricter monetary policies.[39] Second, the independence of the Central Bank is related to the position of the country in international economy, being likely that the Central Bank of a small and open country is more independent than that of a bigger one. Finally, and perhaps more importantly for the analysis of the Italian case, the policies of the Central Bank are influenced by the relations between capital and labour. Regarding this, empirical evidence shows that in the countries where trade unions and left political parties are more powerful, the independence of the Central Bank, as well as its capacity to implement deflationary policies, may be structurally limited to render it accountable to democratic bodies like the parliament (see Epstein and Schor, 1987, p. 179). Furthermore, the existence of strong linkages between the working class and the political system, capable of pushing through institutional channels working class demands for the rigidity of real wages, the stability of employment, and the implementation of social policies, further influence Central Bank autonomy of manoeuvre.

The Italian Central Bank at that time might be defined as an integrated (ibid., p. 150) Central Bank, in the sense that its policies were not independent from political considerations and actors. In particular, scholars tend to link the policies pursued by the Bank of Italy, especially when Carli was Governor,[40] to the interests of the Italian industrial sector, given the great stress that the Central Bank traditionally put on the objectives of the maintenance of industrial profitability and of capital accumulation. In the 1950s this concern was not considered inconsistent with the adoption of Keynesian policies, and state intervention, aimed at the increase of productive investments, was even regarded as essential.[41] However, in the course of the 1960s and, to a greater extent, during the 1970s, the Bank of Italy increasingly urged the separation of the roles of the Monetary Authority and the government and supported, as a condition necessary for the development of Italian economy, the maintenance of the balance between costs and profits of the enterprises in a context of stricter wage policies (see Balducci and Marconi, 1981, p. 87).[42]

In the pursuance of these objectives the Bank of Italy could count on the neutrality, if not support of the banking and financial community, given the strict relations between Italian productive and financial capital. However, the relative weakness of Italian capital during the late 1960s and early 1970s compared to the high level of organisation[43] and political power of the working class,[44] limited its capacity to achieve these aims and even compelled it to accept both a widening of the 'Scala Mobile' and the institutionalisation of the obligation to buy unsold Treasury securities.[45]

The 'external constraint', as we have seen in analysing the debate over the Italian entry in the EMS, was thus considered a useful tool to impose deflationary policies on the domestic social and political actors in the lack of independence of the Central Bank. This explains why the coalition of interests supporting early Italian entry in the EMS coincided with the one urging the implementation of these policies.

By the end of the 1970s, however, the situation was already more favourable to a shift in power relationship among Italian socioeconomic actors. The decision itself to enter the EMS was a reflection of this change which sharply contrasted with Italian previous inability to maintain any pegged exchange rate commitment. However, the remaining power of the trade unions deferred the solution of two more important Italian macroeconomic problems, the 'Scala Mobile' and the public deficit monetisation, to the first half of the 1980s.

The need to eliminate the 1975 commitment of the Bank of Italy to the Treasury was already implicitly urged in the 1979 Report of the Bank where the Governor claimed that '… public expenses and the means chosen to finance it contributed to provoke the high level of inflation rates' (Bank of Italy, 1980, p. 378). However the explicit request to the government was formulated only in the 1980 Report, where the Bank asked insistently for:

> … a re-examination of the means through which, in our system, the Issuing Institute finances the Treasury: the overdraft in the Treasury Current Account, the practice of buying unsold Treasury bills in the auctions, the subscription by the Bank of Italy of other government securities. In particular it is urgent that the Bank of Italy ceases to buy unsold BOTs (Bank of Italy, 1981, p. 384).

All this was required in the name of Central Bank independence (ibid., p. 386).

In July 1981, the Bank of Italy and the Treasury eventually concluded a 'Divorce' which eliminated Central Bank obligation to buy all unsold Treasury bills. The grounds on which the 'Divorce' was motivated by the Bank of Italy's experts were the traditional monetarist linkages between government deficits, money creation and inflation. In particular, it was claimed that excessive public deficits financed through the Central Bank purchasing of unsold Treasury bills added to money creation and produced inflation.

It is true that the Italian Public deficits grew at a higher rate in the period between 1970 and 1982. However, a study by Spaventa shows that the debt with the Bank of Italy, the one which might have caused money creation, and, thus, higher inflation rates, even decreased at constant 1970 prices in the period between 1976 and 1982 (Spaventa, 1984, p. 119).

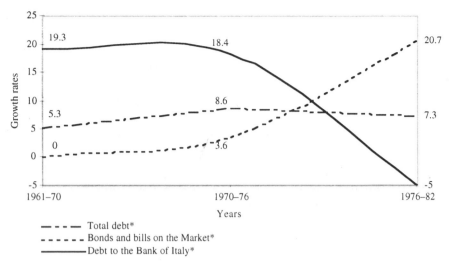

Graph 2   Italian public debt growth rates at constant prices 1970–82

Source: Spaventa, 1984.

Indeed, while in the period preceding 1975 government bills could only be purchased by the Bank of Italy, the 1975 decision to sell public securities to the private sector[46] in the market produced a considerable reduction of the need for a Bank of Italy intervention,[47] though this intervention had achieved an almost compulsory nature.[48]

The other reason put forward by the experts to justify the 'Divorce' was the crowding out of the private sector. The term 'crowding out' can be generally related to the displacement that private economic activity suffers as a result of that of the public sector. More precisely, in the economic policy debate reference is made both to real crowding out and to financial one. Real crowding out refers to the crowding out of private investment and expenditure by public expenditure, and to the substitution of credit to the private sector by the financing of public expenditure. Financial crowding out can be related both to a rise in interest rates and to the existence of limits on credit, and is represented by the substitution of the state to the credit system in its traditional functions.

In the Italian political debate of the early 1980s both forms of crowding out, being clearly connected, were discussed. However, with regard to the 'Divorce', the financial crowding out was considered of prevailing importance.

Those who blamed state intervention in the economy, claimed not only that there did exist a financial crowding out of the credit system but also that it spilled over in a real crowding-out, which means that it severely constrained the investment and production capacity of the private sector.

However, this approach ignored public sector spending in favour of the private sector. In particular it ignored public sector transfers to the private corporate sectors in the forms of production subsidies,[49] investment subsidies,[50] credits and participations[51] and others.[52]

Table 2   Estimates of enlarged public sector transfer payments to the corporate sector in Italy (bn lire)

Years	Total	Production subsidies	Investment subsidies	Credits and participations
1970	1,572	657	601	314
1971	1,757	735	300	722
1972	2,058	926	300	802
1973	2,147	916	360	871
1974	1,979	994	604	381
1975	3,068	1,500	839	729
1976	5,058	2,098	1,070	1,890
1977	5,701	2,672	1,217	1,812
1978	8,697	3,369	2,481	2,847
1979	12,390	3,829	2,954	5,607

Source: Monti and Siracusano, 1979.

Thus, while the public expenditures compensated, at least to some extent, the shortage of total domestic credit to the private sector, the real problem appeared to be the financial crowding out of the credit system[53] operated by the state. This phenomenon is commonly known as '*disintermediazione*', and is a phenomenon in which the state acts, using a famous definition of Monti, as an 'hidden banker' (*banchiere occulto*) by financing the private sector through the expansion of public expenditures.

The extent to which this intervention of the state in the functions traditionally performed by the credit system was a substantial and worrying phenomenon or only a normal adjustment, was a very controversial issue in the economic debate of the period. The figures put forward by the different scholars interested in the problem diverge somehow (see Monti and Siracusano,

1979; see also Nardozzi and Onado, 1980; Nardozzi, 1980). However, they all agree that it was possible to note a decrease in the intermediation of the credit system and an increase in the public support to the private sector in various forms.

In the analysis carried out by Monti and Siracusano (1979; see also 1980) and discussed also in the official sites of the Bank of Italy and of the Directorate General of the Treasury, the trend towards '*disintermediazione*' appeared clear and posed serious problems for the credit system as a whole. In contrast, Onado and Nardozzi concluded their study claiming that the phenomenon of the reduction of the recourse of enterprises to Bank credit was to be regarded as normal (Nardozzi and Onado, 1980, p. 370).

However, there are clear indications that the credit system cared about '*disintermediazione*', which was seen as a usurpation by the state of the traditional functions of the banking sector by competing for deposits and directly financing firms.

In expressing its concerns over the economic and financial conditions of the Italian corporate sector, for example, the Administrative Committee of Mediobanca, in its 1978 Report, stressed the responsibilities of the '... abundant flow of facilitated credit to particular entrepreneurs, both private and public' (Mediobanca, 1978, p. 10) in the persistence of that situation. In a market characterised by high interest rates and by the almost nonexistence of firm self-financing, facilitated credit influenced the development of investment decisions which were subtracted to the markets and attributed to sociopolitical dynamics and assessments with distorted and suboptimal results (ibid., p. 11). The financial crowding out of the credit system by the public sector was, then, explicitly denounced by Mediobanca in its 1980 Report. The latter underlined how Mediobanca had to operate '... in a market in which the investment in short and medium term public securities offered interest rates with which it was impossible to compete' (ibid., p. 9).

Even more explicit was the position of the Italian Banking Association. In his relation of 21 June 1978, the President of the ABI, Golzio, denounced the unsustainable behaviour of the public sector on both the supply and the use of savings and proposed as objectives (whose achievement was linked to 'difficult political choices' of the 'utmost responsibility') to put an end to public intervention (Associazione Bancaria Italiana, 1978, p. 35). Clearly this position could not be and, actually, was not, separated from a broader criticism of the whole system of public constraints on banking intermediation, represented, at that time, by the portfolio constraint and by the ceiling on banking lending. Their elimination or, at least, substantial cut, constituted for the ABI '... an objective to be tenaciously pursued and obtained as soon as possible' (ibid., p. 40). The linkage to the 'Divorce' is evident in the calls for Italian monetary policy to be increasingly detached from short-term considerations, that is, from the need to finance public deficits through the compulsory purchasing of unsold Treasury Bills by the Bank of Italy. Furthermore, the increase in the demand of public securities by the families produced the phenomenon of '*disintermediazione*' on the supply side, and undermined the availability of savings to the credit system as a whole.

Similar concerns were expressed by the Bank of Italy whose 1979 Report underlined how the decline in intermediation could lead to negative conseque-nces for companies (Bank of Italy, 1980, p. 97) and that the Banks had focused 'concern and attention to "*disintermediazione*"'. It was further noted that:

> the shift in the demand from deposits to securities did not have any adverse effect on Bank's profits since it occurred at a time when the size of the demand for credit and the banks' predominant role in short-term financing of firms allowed them to widen the spread between lending and deposit rates. However, the circumstances described above, which led to a widening of the spread between bank rates, might not occur again. If they do not, disintermediation will have adverse effects on banks' profits (ibid.).

More clearly, in his conclusive remarks Ciampi claimed that: '... the publicising of credit through the growing intermediation role pursued by the Treasury does not benefit resource allocation' (ibid., p. 383). He also affirmed the need '...to give again to the banking system the serenity and the degree of certainty necessary to its normal working'. All this was essential because 'the transformation of public financial intermediaries in institutional instruments of specific economic policy objectives would imply a de-legitimising of the banking management principles' and, in particular, of the principle of profitability of the intermediation system (ibid., p. 390).

A second possibility is that the process of '*disintermediazione*' hurt some powerful banks.

The 1980 Bank of Italy Annual Report noted that: 'the process of disintermediation affected most of all the three major commercial banks and the two largest savings banks' (ibid., p. 102).

In any case, the authorities were concerned about excessive levels of '*disintermediazione*', which explains the link with the divorce. The ostensible purpose of the divorce was, in fact, to make it more difficult for the state to raise funds, thereby leading to expenditures reductions. This would then allow a lifting of loan ceilings and portfolio constraints and help eliminate the activity of the 'hidden banker'.

It is important to note that the cleavages between those in favour or against the introduction of these innovative measures are also to be found inside governing parties, while opposition parties focused their attention on the content and not on the methods through which monetary policies were being implemented (for further details, see Epstein and Schor, 1987, p. 197). In fact, from the first steps taken in 1975 until the final decision of the 'Divorce', the Bank of Italy encountered no significant opposition on its path to greater independence, not even from the Communist Party, while Andreatta, the Treasury minister, explicitly favoured it.

The explanation for the lack of public and political debate, apart from the interventions reported above by those sectors which actually urged the divorce, may be easily found in the extreme technicality of the issue, whose implications were very difficult to figure out for the non-experts. However, when the effects of the move became clear, political parties, and the PCI in particular, eventually opened up the public debate (for further details, see ibid.).

The reasons why these interests were successful in passing these measures are related, again, to the shift in the allocation of power defined by Peter Lange (1986) as 'the end of the Union Centrality Era'. This is a process which took place in Italy from the second half of the 1970s onwards and whose implications are more evident when analysing the second important political economy decision taken in the aftermath of Italian entry in the ERM: the abolition of the 'Scala Mobile'.

2   The Struggle Over the 'Scala Mobile'

In the opinion of scholars (see Lange, Ross and Vannicelli, 1982, p. 97; see also Giugni, 1981, p. 341; Regini, 1981), the 'hot autumn' of 1969 marked the beginning of the 'era of Union Centrality'. This was an era in which Italian economic policy was characterised by prevailing concerns for the maintenance of the purchasing power of wages, the institutionalisation of workers' rights and the leading role played by the trade unions and their political counterparts in Italian socioeconomic policy-making. The growing strength of trade unions during this period is reflected clearly in the ascending slope of its membership parabola whose density rates increased constantly from 1969 onwards reaching their peak in 1978 (with 49 per cent of total employed, an 18.2 per cent increase with respect to the 1969 figure).

Table 3   Italian trade union membership 1969–85

Years	Density rates (employed)	Total members* (x100)
1969	30.8	4,050.6
1970	34.8	4,646.1
1971	37.6	5,059.9
1972	39.3	5,327.5
1973	40.8	5,630.2
1974	44.2	6,233.1
1975	46.0	6,519.2
1976	48.4	6,930.3
1977	48.6	7,000.5
1978	49.0	7,104.5
1979	48.6	7,148.1
1980	48.6	7,226.0
1981	46.9	7,005.9
1982	45.5	6,793.1
1983	44.4	6,572.1
1984	44.0	6,484.1
1985	41.4	6,155.8

* Excluded self-employed and retired workers

Source: Centro Studi Economici Sociali e Sindacali, (CESOS), *Le Relazioni Sindacali in Italia*, Reports, various issues.

The era of union centrality reached its political apex in 1975, with the signing of an agreement between the union confederations and Confindustria to upgrade the 'Scala Mobile', a system protecting workers' wages against inflation. The agreement provided for a three months' payment of a fixed amount for each unit increase in the inflation rate, the so-called 'punto di contingenza'.[54] The main features of the agreement, which was the product of collective bargaining and not the result of a parliamentary process,[55] were the relatively high and immediate degree of inflation protection paying equal amounts to all workers, and thus reducing wage differentials, and the automatic character of the system. These elements rendered the agreement a powerful means to protect workers' purchasing power marking a major victory for the union movement. However, the defence of this victory proved to be very problematic and eventually led, with the beginning of the late 1970s–early

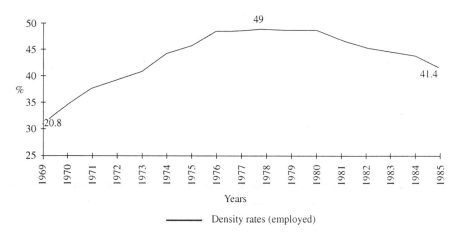

Graph 3   Density of union membership in Italy 1969–85

Source: Centro Studi Economici Sociali e Sindacali, (CESOS), *Le relazioni sindacali in Italia*, Reports, various issues.

1980s economic crisis, to major conflicts not only between the unions and their social and political referents, but also within the unions themselves.

In the face of the growing economic problems and, particularly, growing unemployment, the Italian Union Federation[56] adopted in 1978 a new strategic orientation, the so-called EUR strategy. This was based on a trade-off between less guarantees to the workers and more participation in investment decisions, and it was aimed at increasing employment through the new instrument of triangular negotiations with the government and employer representatives. Given the increasing involvement of the Italian Communist Party in the governmental area, thanks to the pacification process between the PCI and the DC (the so-called 'historic compromise'), this 'new course' of Italian unions appeared to secure their participation in the official sites of Italian economic policies' decision-making. On the contrary, in the light of the following, tragic end of 'national solidarity', the EUR strategy marked the beginning of a descending parabola of union bargaining power and political influence (see Accornero, 1994).

As already noted, the dismantling of the 'Scala Mobile', or, at least, the substantial reform of its mechanisms, together with the reduction of the state intervention in the economy, constituted the main issues at stake in the domestic debate over the establishment of the European Monetary System. Indeed, it was precisely in the course of this debate that the differences within the governmental majority and within the union federations over the future of the 'Scala Mobile' became unbridgeable.

Within the union movement itself, the 'automatic' increases of the 'Scala Mobile' were increasingly blamed. This is true especially for the UIL, which in this period was beginning to be controlled by the new PSI of Craxi,[57] and for the CISL, traditionally linked to the catholic interests and to the DC. By 1982, for instance, both Pierre Carniti, secretary general of the CISL and Giorgio Benvenuto, secretary general of UIL, were favourable to a major reform of the wage indexation mechanism within the context of triangular negotiations. On the other hand, the Communist component of the CGIL was far less ready than the others to modify the system. The inconsistencies in the positions of the different unions eventually led to the first major blow to the 'Scala Mobile' represented by the accord of 22 January 1983.[58] With this accord, for the first time since 1975, the unions accepted the reduction of the automatic inflation-indexed payments coupled with an 18-month freeze of wage bargaining with the private corporate sector. This constituted a major defeat whose significance should not be underestimated, even if the government agreed to protect the real purchasing power of workers wages by cutting the incidence of certain taxes, limiting the rise of government controlled prices and changing the family allowance system.

Given the compromise nature of the 1983 accord, and the fact that the balance of power between unions and employers was still shifting towards the latter, in late 1983 the unions agreed to pursue a possible revision of the 1983 accord. The issues at stake were still wages and job flexibility and, above all the 'Scala Mobile', but this time Confindustria was taking a much tougher position and the unions reached the negotiation table without having achieved a joint position. The CISL and the UIL, were favourable to further reduction in the 'Scala Mobile', while the CGIL made the reform of the system conditional on a government's commitment not to distribute the costs of further economic growth and employment exclusively among the working class. The situation was further complicated by the governmental leadership of Bettino Craxi, which was characterised by a strong claim of the executive autonomy in taking hard economic policy decisions (*decisionismo*) and by an even stronger opposition to the Communist Party. The atmosphere was so heated that in early February 1984, the communist and the socialist factions of the CGIL split assuming different positions on the 'Scala Mobile' and on the need to consult the workers before signing any agreement, a step which slowed, if not prevented, CGIL participation in any compromise. On 12 February the

Minister of Labour, Gianni De Michelis, presented a draft accord which maintained the trade-off nature of the 1983 accord. It proposed a limitation of the number of units to be paid every three months during 1984, but it also promised that, in case of higher inflation rates, the following year fiscal policy interventions would compensate any unforeseen losses. The CISL and the UIL promptly declared their willingness to conclude negotiations, while the CGIL, after a moment of hesitation, declared its unwillingness to accept it, thus joining the PCI in its negative assessment of the manoeuvre. Open conflict broke out between the government on one side, and the PCI and the communist component of the CGIL on the other side, when Craxi translated the basic terms of the 14 February protocol in a decree to be converted in law. Despite the obstructive campaign of the communists and their parliamentary allies, especially the deputies of the 'Democrazia Proletaria', and the massive popular demonstrations throughout Italy, this eventually happened on 12 June 1984. In June, the PCI decided to pursue the referendum on Art. 3 of the decree, the one concerning the cuts to the 'Scala Mobile' and by late September, more than the required number of signatures had been submitted. On 7 December 1984 the referendum was declared constitutionally legal by the Central Office of the Corte di Cassazione. On 9 and 10 June 1985, after a long and bitter referendum campaign further complicated by the administrative elections of 12 May 1985, Italian voters finally defeated the PCI effort to overturn Art. 3 when 54.3 per cent voted 'no' and only 46.7 per cent voted 'yes'.

The long battle over the 'Scala Mobile' and its outcome made it manifestly clear, that an era of Italian political economy, characterised by the market and political power of the Union movement and by the PCI's ability to act as a political 'guarantor' of union cooperation with government policy, had come to an end. The battle over the 'Scala Mobile', transcending its economic meaning, became a struggle over the political economic balance of power within the different Italian sociopolitical and economic actors. The issue at stake was the control of the pattern of growth and distribution in the Italian political economy. With its conclusion, the outline of the political economy had fundamentally changed and the era of union centrality had ended with the labour movement and the PCI as net losers.

What were the reasons for such a change?

Analysts of industrial relations in Italy identify some tendencies in the union organisation development during the late 1970s and early 1980s which might help to explain this phenomenon.[59] On the one hand there was a renewed dependency of Italian industrial relations on the party system, after their relative autonomy during the early 1970s (see Lange and Regini, 1989). This is demonstrated by the shift from the centralised political negotiations of the 1960s and early 1970s to the new triangular agreements of the late 1970s and 1980s in which the political parties and the government played a much more important and active role. On the other hand, unions found it increasingly difficult to perceive which interests to represent. A real representation crisis occurred during this period and this, together with the new linkages with the political parties, led to a growing division within the union movement and to a progressive decline of their political and bargaining power.[60]

These factors, however, are not enough to explain the change in power allocation and greater attention must be paid to the fact that the phenomena under analysis took place in a period of deep economic changes and crises.[61]

Table 4   Italian macroeconomic indexes 1970–84

Years	Consumer prices % changes	Unemployment rates	Real GDP growth
1970	5.0	5.3	5.3
1971	4.8	5.3	1.6
1972	5.7	6.3	3.2
1973	10.8	6.2	7.0
1974	19.1	5.3	4.1
1975	17.0	5.8	-3.6
1976	16.8	6.6	5.9
1977	17.0	7.0	1.9
1978	12.1	7.1	2.7
1979	14.8	7.6	4.9
1980	21.2	7.5	3.9
1981	17.8	8.3	0.2
1982	16.6	9.0	-0.5
1983	14.6	9.8	-0.4
1984	10.8	10.2	2.6

Source: *OECD Economic Outlook*, No. 38, December 1985.

After the recession of 1970–71, Italy experienced a moderate recovery led by the depreciation of the Lira after the abandonment of the European snake in the spring of 1973. This, however, proved to be only a palliative measure, to the extent that in late 1974, early 1975, economic crisis broke out in all its severity.[62] Italian unemployment started to grow almost constantly from 1974 onwards reaching a double digit figure, 10.2 per cent, in 1984

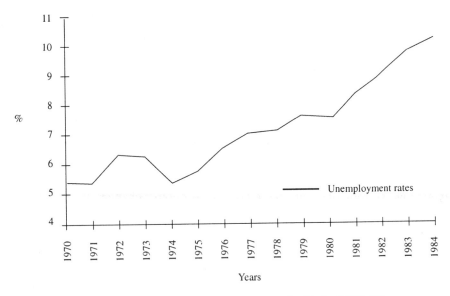

Graph 4   Standardised unemployment rates in Italy 1970–84

Source: *OECD Economic Outlook*, No. 38, December 1985.

without giving any sign of slowing down. Italian real GDP succeeded in recovering only slightly from 1975 slump of -3.6 per cent with the devaluation of the lira in 1976. However, at the beginning of the 1980s it was again registering negative levels.

Italian industrial and banking sector tended to single out as a fundamental cause of the country's industrial sector crisis, the unsustainable labour costs, and thus to identify in the elimination of the wage indexation system, so strenuously defended by the trade unions and the left political parties, the only viable solution to the Italian economic crisis.

With respect to this argument, it is true that the real income per industrial worker tended to increase between 1976 and 1985 (+ 12.8 per cent). However, it is also true that the real labour cost per unit of product in industry was decreasing (-10 per cent from 1976 to 1985). Indeed, the impact of this decrease on industrial profits is clearly demonstrated by the performance of the profits/costs ratio which increased from 19.7 per cent in 1976 to 24.6 per cent in 1985. Furthermore, comparing Italian real wages with those of its main European partners in the mid-to-late 1970s, wage pressures do not appear to deviate excessively.

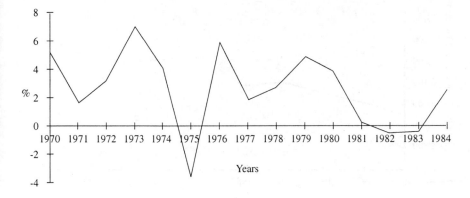

Graph 5   Growth of real GDP at market prices in Italy 1970–84

Source: *OECD Economic Outlook*, No. 38, December 1985.

Table 5   Costs and profits analysis in Italian industry 1976–85

Years	Real income per worker	Labour cost per unit of product	Profits/costs ratio
1976	2,951.0	698.0	19.7
1977	3,009.8	701.4	19.1
1978	3,054.5	694.9	21.1
1979	3,099.4	668.7	23.4
1980	3,087.1	641.2	24.3
1981	3,216.8	667.5	20.3
1982	3,211.9	669.9	21.4
1983	3,189.1	663.3	21.4
1984	3,229.1	628.4	24.0
1985	3,329.1	627.7	24.6

Source: Banca d'Italia, 1986.

It seems at least economically inappropriate to put all the blame of Italian industry difficulties on the labour wages protection system and on the social sectors defending it. Some responsibilities may also be attributed to the economic strategy chosen by the private sector, particularly big business, to cope with the consequences of the recession and which was aimed more at the maintenance of the profitability levels than at the increase of national investment.[63]

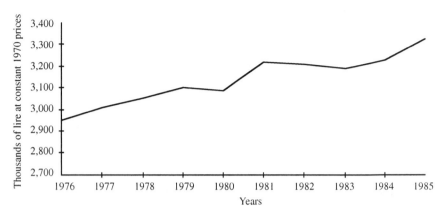

Graph 6   Real income per industrial worker in Italy 1976–85

Source: Banca d'Italia, 1986, tav. aB 14.

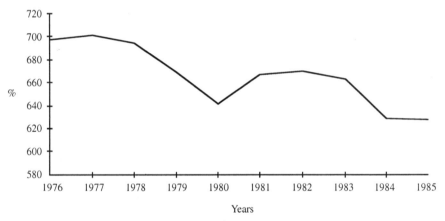

Graph 7   Italian real labour cost per unit of product in industry 1976–85

Source: Banca d'Italia, 1986, tav. aB 14.

Turning to the purposes of this contribution, it should be recalled that the prolonged recessive phase, by weakening the pressures on the labour market, limited substantially the workers' bargaining power, and encouraged the entrepreneurial and the financial sector to try to break those rules or institutions which limited their autonomy.

However, the decrease of the union bargaining power was not homogeneous. Certain strata of workers enjoyed greater protection under

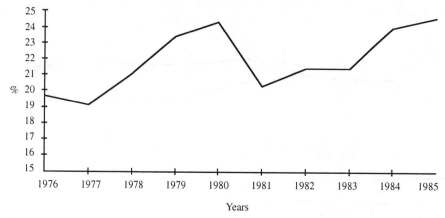

Years

Note

The profits/costs is given by the gross management yield over inputs + labour costs

Graph 8   Profits/costs ratio in Italian industry 1976–85

Source: Banca d'Italia, 1986, tav. aB 16.

Table 6   Real wages

Year	Italy	France	West Germany	Great Britain
1973	102.4	101.5	100.7	100.7
1974	102.8	104.6	103.7	107.9
1975	106.7	106.8	102.2	112.6
1976	105.4	104.4	98.5	107.3
1977	106.5	105.3	98.9	103.4
1978	104.9	104.4	98.5	102.2

Source: OECD, 1979–80.

existing laws or by their crucial position in the productive process.[64] Thus, while the recession generally undermined the power basis bases of the union movement, it particularly reduced its capacity to represent the aggregate interests of the workers, that is, to act as a pre-mediator among a set of different interests. This is the role which enables a union movement to maintain a common position during negotiations.

Furthermore, structural interventions in industry, technological innovation, the growing importance of services, the spread of small companies and of the

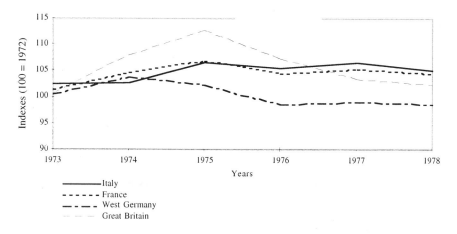

Graph 9   Real wages in Italy 1973–78

Source: OECD, 1979, 1980.

Table 7   Private investment performance in Italy 1960–78

Year	Average growth of business investment
1960–73	4.6
1973–78	-1.2

Source: *OECD Economic Outlook*, No. 26, December 1979, p. 19.

'invisible' or even 'black' economy, are all phenomena which can be regarded as answers to the need, brought about by the recession, to increase industrial productivity and competitiveness. However, they all had the common effect to further fragment the social basis of the unions.

Thus, the context in which the 1984/85 failure matured was one characterised by a growing weakness on the side of the unions. Their power was undermined, on the one hand, by a deep representation crisis and an increasing difficulty to aggregate different interests, and, on the other hand, by a reduced capacity to obtain favourable measures in exchange for their consensus to stricter economic policies.

Corresponding to the decline of the union movement's capacity to influence socioeconomic development is the opposite phenomenon of the rise of private company power, an international phenomenon which has been connected by scholars[65] to the negative phase of the business cycle from the mid-1970s onwards. This undermined previous social achievements in many European countries. There was also the spread of transnational corporations which, being usually less affected by national regulations, called for deregulation in the domestic corporate sector and exported, mainly through the American channel, the Japanese conception of the 'firm as a community' giving rise to the development of a 'corporate identity'.

In this context, both the banking and industrial capital interpreted the pegging of the exchange rates in the ERM as a political device to hasten this decline of trade union power through the imposition from 'outside' of strict anti-inflationary monetary policies (the so-called 'external constraint') whose implementation structurally contrasted with the interests of the labour organisations.

Conclusions

In conclusion, the three main actors not only of the debate over the issue of joining the ERM, but, more generally, of the struggle over the control of political power in the late 1970s appear to be the state, the trade unions and the private capital, particularly the big industry. In the context of the power struggle between these actors going on in that particular historical moment it seems clear that the shift of the power struggle from the domestic to the European level was the only way for the Italian banking and industrial capital to obtain the implementation of a particular set of macroeconomic policies. In turn, similar policies, once committed to, would produce a political and economic strengthening of the banking and industrial capital with respect to both the state and, mainly, the trade unions. It is true that the workers' organisations were experiencing, exactly at that time, a major representative and bargaining crisis. However, they were still strong enough to represent a serious obstacle to the implementation of strict anti-inflationary policies. Indeed, had the industrial and the banking capital sought a direct confrontation with the trade unions and their political counterparts, the most likely result would have been what they were determined to avoid: a strengthening of working class militancy.

Therefore, the issue of the ERM was the battlefield where the struggle for political power among domestic actors took place, in a context in which political power was still exercised at the domestic level. In turn, the nature itself of the agreement on the exchange rate constraints, given the kind of macroeconomic policies it implied and its inherent reduction of state autonomy in monetary policy decision-making, further accentuated those tendencies already present in Italian sociopolitical development from the mid-1970s onwards.

Thus, in the course of the 1980s the true interests of the economic, social and political groups which represented the bases of the ERM consensus, were plainly revealed. In turn, their achievement constituted the political guarantee that their commitment to the ERM was credible.

The question to answer at this point in relation to the crisis of the ERM in 1992 is: it is possible to hypothesise a change in the preferences of the leading sectors of Italian society and economy which threatened the credibility of Italian commitment to the ERM and justify speculative pressures?

Before answering to this question it is worth analysing the political, economic and political economy dimensions of the British position towards the ERM of the EMS.

Notes

1   See Pandolfi's speech to the Chamber of Deputies on 10 October 1978, Italian Chamber of Deputies, (1978)c, 'Atti Parlamentari', VII Legislatura, *Discussioni*, seduta del 13 Dicembre 1978.

2   The official declarations on the issue of the EMS given by Italian government representatives were the following: the speeches by the Ministers Forlani and Pandolfi before a joint meeting of the Finance and Treasury and Foreign Affairs Commissions of the Chamber of Deputies on 20 July 1978, the speech of Minister Pandolfi to the Chamber of Deputies on October the 10th, the declarations by Minister Pandolfi reported in the following sections, the speech by the Governor of the Bank of Italy on 15 October and the one to the Finance and Treasury Commission of the Senate on 26 October , a speech by the Foreign Trade Minister to the XXI Italian Forex Club Congress on 14–15 October and one on 6 November as well as various interventions by the agriculture minister.

Regarding the position of the Foreign Trade Minister, Rinaldo Ossola, while listing the 'minimal requirements' necessary to accept the ERM, claimed from the beginning that the most important condition for Italy to sustain stable exchange rates was the implementation of domestic economic policies aimed at the reduction of labour costs and public deficit (see Ossola, 1978).

3   See Pandolfi's intervention to the Arel Group Meeting on 9 September 1978 in Andreatta et al., 1978.

4   See Pandolfi Declarations to the Chamber of Deputies on 10 October 1978, Italian Chamber of Deputies, (1978a), 'Atti Parlamentari', VII Legislatura, *Discussioni*, seduta del 10 Ottobre 1978. Italics of the writer.

5   Another thorough document establishing those 'minimal requirements' necessary (*'Irrinunciabili'*) for Italy to enter the ERM is given by the speech of the Governor of the Bank of Italy to the Treasury and Finance Commission of 26 October 1978. See Baffi, 1978b.

6   In the form in which it appeared in the interim report of the Monetary Committee of 7 September 1978, it consisted of two propositions:

- *la grille de parites, etablie sur la base des contrevaleurs en ECU des differentes monnaies, serait employee pour fixer les cours limites d' intervention en termes nominaux;*
- *la formule panier ECU serait utilisee pour determiner le degre de divergence des monnaies participantes de facon a en tirer certaines consequences pour les regles d'intervention et/ou d'autres politiques.*

7   Pending the institution of the European Monetary Fund, Italy stressed the need to reform the whole set of credit facilities requiring, for the very short term, an increase of the lending period from 30 to 90 days, and, for the short and medium term, the enhancement of the credit quota up to 25 bn ECU whose greater part had to be allocated to the short term facilities. See Baffi, 1978b, p. 17.

8   It is interesting to note here that in a speech to the XXI Congress of the Italian Forex Club in Ischia on 14–15 October, the Governor of the Bank of Italy underlined how appropriate technical-operational characteristics of the exchange rate agreement were conditions necessary but not sufficient to ensure Italian entry in the System and how the domestic political dimension of Italian commitment to the ERM was, in fact, prevailing over the economic one. See Baffi, 1978a, p. 764.

9   The allocation provided for was 14 bn ECU to the short term and 11 bn ECU to the medium term.

10 The very short-term credit settlement was set in 45 days instead of the 90 days required by the Italian government.

11 As far as monetary and economic affairs were concerned, three official committees were particularly important: the Committee of the Central Bank Governors, the Monetary Committee and the Economic Policy Committee. Together, they dominated the field of financial and economic affairs, reporting directly to ECOFIN. The Committee of Central Bank Governors did not usually meet within the European Community at all, but at the Headquarters of the Bank for International Settlements at Basle. Its identity as a Community body was, in a certain sense, blurred: the Commission was not represented on it as of right, while noncommunity Bank Governors could be and were co-opted, it elected its chairman on its own way and at a time of its choosing and, as Ludlow points out, some, if not all of its members tended to think of it as no more than a useful appendage to the Group of Ten whose meetings usually preceded its own. The Monetary Committee, which like Committee of Central Bank Governors had been established in 1964, was much more of a Community institution, composed of Senior Representatives from each of the nine finance ministries, the deputy Governors of the central banks or their equivalents or nominees, and two representatives of the Commission. However, its Chairmanship did not, as on other Community Committees, change every six months in conjunction with the change in the presidency of the Council of Ministers, but was elected and stayed in office for periods of two years or more.

The Economic Policy Committee (EPC) was a much more shadowy and elusive body, which had taken over the functions of three previous committees, the Short-term Economic Policy Committee, the Medium-term Policy Committee and the Budgetary Policy Committee, in 1974. Its membership tended to fluctuate according to the subject under discussion.

12 On this respect the Italian Communist Party agreed with British demand for a reform of the CAP from a policy of price support to a true policy of structural interventions while the European Council meeting in Brussels on 4–5 December made it explicit that the introduction of the EMS had not to introduce any change in the CAP as it was before 1 January 1979.

13 On 11 March 1978, was established the fourth Andreotti government, a Christian Democrat government with the external support of the Italian Communist Party (PCI), the Italian Socialist Party (PSI), the Italian Social Democratic Party (PSDI) and the Italian Republican Party (PRI). On 31 January 1979, the fourth government Andreotti collapsed after the withdrawal of the PCI from the majority.

Given the failure to establish a fifth Andreotti government constituted of the DC, PSDI and PRI, anticipated political elections were held on the 3 June 1979 with the following results: DC – 38.3 per cent; PCI – 30.4 per cent. In the 1976 elections the results had been the following: DC – 38.7 per cent; PCI – 34.3 per cent, which was its highest historical result.

On the 10 June are held the European Parliament elections: DC – 36.5 per cent; PCI – 29.6 per cent.

14 The '*piano* Pandolfi' was an open document submitted on 31 August 1978 by the Treasury Minister, Pandolfi, to the examination of political parties and trade unions.

15 Italian Foreign Minister, Forlani, himself explicitly recognised that the delay was linked to the 'evolution of the Italian political moment. EMS and the crisis of the government are by now the most important elements of a very confused situation'.

16 At the end of the debate in the Chamber of Deputies, on 13 December 1978, five resolutions were presented over the issue of Italy and the EMS. The first resolution, stating the need for Italy to join immediately the ERM, was proposed by the liberal group and, after being accepted by the government, was withdrawn by the same group which decided to vote in favour of the Galloni's resolution. The latter was constituted by three sections: the first part stating a general commitment to the process of European integration, the second one soliciting immediate Italian entry in the ERM and the last section defining the lines of action for the implementation of the agreement on the ERM. Two other resolutions, one by the Radical Party, the other by the MSI, supporting Italian early participation to the new European Monetary arrangements, were not recognised by the government. Finally, an extreme left group led by Magri and Mrs Castellina proposed a resolution rejecting completely the ability for Italy to join the EMS. See Italian Chamber of Deputies, 1978c, p. 25022.

17 Christian Democratic support to an early Italian entry in the EMS was based by Andreatta, a Christian Democrat senator and economist, on the ground that the costs in terms of the growth of inflation of competitive devaluations of the lira vis-à-vis the other European currencies were no longer sustainable by the Italian economy. Andreatta himself was the protagonist of the DC pressure on Andreotti for the immediate Italian entry in the EMS after the strategic Italian delay. On the 7 December 1978 Andreatta claimed, in his speech to the Italian Senate, that, the Italian delegation having succeeded in obtaining the acceptance of 90 per cent of its requirements to join, there was no reason for the government to delay its immediate entry in the system. During the morning of the same day there had been a private meeting of some DC senators and deputies with the Treasury Minister, Pandolfi, to adopt a common position on the EMS while some members of the DC Executive Committee, Rende, Segni and others, solicited an immediate meeting of the executive to reaffirm DC

support to the EMS. In the evening, finally, Andreotti met with the whole DC delegation led by Zaccagnini which further uttered the DC political will to join immediately the ERM. The only Christian Democratic politician to underline the contradictory behaviour of Andreotti's government was Senator Lombardini.

18 The European Monetary Union represented for the Italian Liberal Party a vital objective both politically and economically and had been supported by it from the beginning.

19 The Political Bureau of the right wing party 'Costituente di destra-democrazia nazionale' had approved on 6 December 1978, in the immediate aftermath of the Brussels Council, a document criticising the Andreotti's government delay in the acceptance of the ERM. This was regarded as, on one hand, a betrayal of the European ideals of Alcide De Gaspari and Gaetano Martino, leaders of the process of European integration during the late 1950s, and, on the other hand, an unacceptable concession to the Italian Communist Party.

20 See Servello's declarations during the debate at the Chamber of Deputies of 12 December 1978, Italian Chamber of Deputies (1978b). See also Valensise's declarations to the Chamber of Deputies on 13 December 1978, Italian Chamber of Deputies (1978c).

21 The Italian Republican Party had immediately greeted with great enthusiasm the project proposed at the Bremen Council and had supported it throughout the whole process of international negotiations. Indeed, the PRI had even threatened to withdraw from the majority supporting the government if Italy had not entered the ERM from the beginning. See La Malfa, G., 1978a, 1978b and 1979; La Malfa, U., 1978a, 1978b and 1978c; La Malfa and Biasini, 1978.

22 See the declarations of Pannella to the Chamber of Deputies on 13 December 1978, Italian Chamber of Deputies, (1978c).

23 In his speech to the Chamber of Deputies, Napolitano, economic speaker for the Communist Party, reiterated the PCI's favourable position to a regime of stability for the European exchange rates given the acceptance of those 'minimal requirements' so many times stressed also by the Italian government. However, in the lack of any explicit commitment by the other European partners to the adoption of symmetrical intervention obligations in the monetary field, and to the transfer of real resources to the weakest economy, as well as, to the reform of some community policies, in the economic field, the only decision to take was to vote against early Italian entry in the system. See the declarations of Napolitano to the Chamber of Deputies on 13 December 1978, Italian Chamber of Deputies.

24 The initial position of the 'new' Italian Socialist Party of Bettino Craxi was in line with the official one of the Italian government as expressed by Minister Pandolfi in his speech of the 10 October and broadly accepted by the whole governmental majority, including the Italian Communist Party (see Cicchitto, 1978a).

However, as the negotiations proceeded and the divergences within the majority increased, the PSI tended to assume a more positive attitude towards the results obtained by the Italian delegations in the discussions over the EMS than the one assumed by the PCI (see Cicchitto, 1978b).

On the eve of the Brussels meeting the gap between the position of the PCI and that of the other constituents of the governmental majority, particularly the DC and the PRI, appeared unbridgeable, to the extent that Luciano Barca, PCI speaker on economic policy, overtly criticised the configuration of the EMS scheme (see Barca, 1978).

In this context the PSI, whose divergences with the Communist Party were not limited to the issue of the EMS (see Garimberti, 1978), assumed the role of mediator within the governmental majority proposing even a gradual approach to Italian entry in the ERM.

In the late proposal of the PSI, presented after the Brussels summit, Italy had to join the basket currency, to accept the constraints imposed by the enlargement of the European Monetary Fund and, eventually, to enter the wider fluctuation bands, from the very beginning of the establishment of the new monetary arrangements, but, before entering the Exchange Rate Mechanism, it was necessary to implement deflationary domestic politics (see Lopez, 1978; Cicchitto, 1978c).

Finally, however, Andreotti's announcement of the immediate Italian entry in the ERM, provoked the resentment of the Socialist Party and its eventual decision not to vote in the Chamber of Deputies on the resolution over Italian entry in the ERM even if its speaker, Cicchitto, openly recognised the need for Italy to join the system (see Cicchito's declarations to the Chamber of Deputies on 13 December 1978, Italian Chamber of Deputies.

25 See the declarations of Magri to the Chamber of Deputies on 13 December 1978, Italian Chamber of Deputies.

26 First of all Italy was characterised by the lowest income pro capita within the European Community apart from Ireland, and by the widest gap in regional development with the highest unemployment rate and the weakest industrial structures. Consequently, it had to realise a growth, and, mainly, investment rate much higher than that of the other European countries.

    Moreover, to avoid relying on protective measures, given Italian import propensity, its export growth rate would have had to be higher than that of the other nations in order to purchase the goods necessary for its homogeneous economic growth. See Spaventa, 1978c.

27 According to Spaventa (1978c) the issue of Italian entry in the EMS was not only political, but so political to induce Italian government to completely overcome an objective assessment of the economic costs deriving to the country from the particular characteristics of the new monetary arrangements.

28 On the other hand, Italian trade unions rejected this plan on the basis that it was exclusively aimed at the reduction of labour costs and of the public debt through cuts in social expenses. See Garavini, 1978; see also Bordini, 1978a.

29 The document was called: 'Piano di risanamento monetario da parte del Presidente della Confindustria Guido Carli'.

30 Pegging a currency to a fixed exchange rate regime implies the loss of national monetary policy and exchange rate policy autonomy, which, in turn, means losing the opportunity to decide the rate of economic growth, at least in the short run, through the setting of nominal interest rates, and to cope with balance of payments disequilibria, both through the decision on nominal exchange rate level and on nominal interest rates. See economic literature on Optimum Currency Areas.

31 Many representatives of the Italian industrial sector gave for granted Italian entry in the ERM before the Brussels Summit. See Savona, 1978; Marcello, 1978.

32 For further details, see Chiti Battelli, 1978.

33 For further details on the position of the INTERSIND towards the issue of the wage setting and costs, see the speech of the INTERSIND President, Dr Ettore Massacessi at the Annual INTERSIND Assembly. See Associazione Sindacale INTERSIND, 1979.

34 Associazione Sindacale Aziende Pubbliche, which was constituted by the public companies of the ENI group.

35 It is extremely difficult to identify in practice the borderline between 'politics' and 'economy' as far as the power struggle of organised economic interests is concerned. One might, with Gramsci, define 'politics' as the 'active' pursuance of economic interests by organised socioeconomic groups. See Gramsci, 1975, p. 29.

36 See exchange rates data in IMF, 1988, pp. 20/34.

37 For a similar interpretation see also Epstein and Schor, 1987.

38 For a detailed account of the measures taken from 1975 onwards, see Addis, 1987.

39 See later in this book for an analysis of the relation between the Bank of England and the City.

40 After leaving the Bank of Italy, Carli became President of Confindustria.

41 This statement is based on the analysis of the position of the Bank of Italy towards the issue of capital accumulation carried out by Balducci and Marconi. See Balducci and Marconi, 1981, p. 79.

   Moreover, in the final remarks to the General Assembly of the Bank of Italy in 1980, Ciampi underlined the Bank of Italy's tendency to support public investments in the course of 1950. See Bank of Italy, 1980.

42 For a more detailed analysis of the policies of the Bank of Italy under Carli, see Nardozzi, 1981.

43 The number of members of the CGIL and CISL grew by 20 per cent between 1969 and 1970.

44 The Italian Communist Party reached its historical electoral peak in 1976 with 34.3 per cent of the votes.

45 Both these measures were taken in 1975.

46 The first two measures strengthening market mechanisms were taken in February–March 1975. In February compulsory reserves quotas were set for all credit institutions at 15 per cent of the deposits increase from the previous year. In March, and this is the measure recalled in the text above, there was the reform of the Treasury Bills monthly auctions allowing also ordinary banks to participate. It is worth noting that in this period Carli was still Governor of the Bank of Italy since Baffi succeeded him only in August 1975.

47 As an example, in the first semester of 1979, Treasury securities were sold worth about 16.600 bn lire, half of which were taken from the Bank of Italy portfolio. See Bank of Italy, 1980, p. 381.

48 Indeed, even if Italian law did not oblige the Bank of Italy to buy all unsold Treasury Bills, it was always interpreted as a commitment by the Central Bank to do it.

49 Payments made by the public sector to productive units in order to lower selling prices or to permit an adequate remuneration of the factors of production (Monti and Siracusano, 1979, p. 224).

50 Grants for the financing of investment, restructuring and conversion (Monti and Siracusano, 1979).

51 New capital contributions, net of repayments, granted by the state to increase the own funds of the recipients (Monti and Siracusano, 1979).

52 For a more detailed analysis of this problem see Arcelli and Valiani, 1979; see also Monti and Siracusano, 1979.

53 Both the banks and the Special Credit Institutions are included in the credit system. It is worth noting here the existence of the phenomenon of double-intermediation consisting in the lending of family savings by the Banks to the Special Credit Institutions which, in turn, lent them to the private corporate sector. It has been calculated that between 1972 and 1981 Banks supplied about 70 per cent of the Special Credit Institutions funds. See Cotula, 1984, p. 224.

54 It is important to note that in the same year, 1975, the Bank of Italy committed itself to buy all unsold Treasury Bills.

55 Art. 39 of the Italian constitution indicates the requisites for a collective agreement to achieve the force of law, but this article has never been implemented.

56 Italian CGIL-CISL UIL Federation was established in 1972 and lasted until 1984 when, during the heated debate over the 'Scala Mobile', it was dismantled.

57 For a detailed account of the changes in the UIL after Craxi's secretary, see Merkel, 1987.

58 For a detailed analysis of this period see Lange, 1986, p. 30.

59 For a thorough analysis of the Italian trade union organisation literature until the early 1980s see Giugni, 1981, p. 324; for a more theoretical review of the relationship between industrial relations and political science see Gourevitch, Lange and Martin, 1981, p. 401.

60 For a thorough analysis of the Italian trade union representation crisis see Regini, 1981, ch. VII.

61 For a thorough analysis of the impact of Italian mid-1970s economic crisis on the union strategy and bargaining power see Vannicelli, 1984, p. 404.

62 For an account of Italian economic policy developments from 1945 onwards see Salvati, 1984.

63 Being an analysis of this strategy out of the purposes of this dissertation, reference will be made to the exhaustive contribution to its knowledge represented by Vannicelli's study (1984, p. 421).

64 In the analysis carried out by Vannicelli, it is possible to identify four distinct groups of workers: a) the 'core' of the workforce consisting of industrial workers usually active in the union movement who were affected by the economic crisis to a lesser extent; b) an expanding group of precarious workers who were pushed by the recession into a condition of permanent, state subsidised unemployment; c) women and young people with little hope to find employment: d) a group of 'unofficially' employed people recruited by the 'invisible' or even 'black' economy (Vannicelli, 1984, p. 404).

65 For a thorough examination of the changing role of the firm in the European context during the last 20 years see Crouch, 1995–96.

2 The UK and the Making of the EMS: A Low Temperature Political Debate

The Disingenuous Conditions of the British Government to Enter the ERM

Contrary to the case of the Italian government, the weakness of the British government in proposing its monetary and economic terms to enter the ERM[1] does not present inconsistencies with its behaviour in the domestic debate. Indeed, more than once in the diplomatic talks leading to the establishment of the European Monetary System, British political and economic commentators lamented the virtual absence of domestic public debate both at the political and at the socioeconomic level. Yet, the conditions required by the British government to enter the new European monetary arrangements were clear even before the Bremen meeting in which the Franco-German scheme was made public, and underwent only slight changes with the evolution of the negotiations.

Already on 30 June, the Chancellor of the Exchequer, Denis Healey,[2] indicated major reservations to his fellow finance ministers about the pegging of sterling to the other European currencies. He proposed as necessary conditions to adopt a similar step, the retaining of the right of a country to devalue or revalue national currencies if balance of payments or inflation trends were out of step with those of its partners. The British Chancellor also wanted to make sure that countries in persistent balance of payments surplus, such as Germany, accepted the obligation to expand their economies faster to avoid the burden of the adjustments of the balance of payments falling solely upon deficit countries. Finally the British government required to link currency alignment with changes in the financial arrangements of the Community, mainly budgetary arrangements, and in the Common Agricultural Policy (CAP).

Even after the proposal was made public, the Treasury remained sceptical to the point of contempt (see Zis, 1990) of most of the detailed content of the Franco-German scheme for currencies presented at the Bremen summit. Only two characteristics of the scheme seemed to be formulated to deal with the points made in discussions on the setting up of the new monetary system. These were that the system should not harm the dollar and that it might indeed be a good idea to set up some form of European Monetary Fund. Moreover, quite apart from all the technical points, the commitment to greater convergence of economic policies was thought unacceptably weak since, as drafted by the Franco-German statement, this merely said that policies 'conducive to greater stability' had to be pursued by 'deficit and surplus countries alike'. On the contrary, Healey insisted that Britain would consider a radical reform of the costly Common Agricultural Policy of the EEC as a major condition of participation in any European Monetary System based on the Franco-German proposals put to the Bremen summit. He argued that changes in the Common Agricultural Policy and a fairer sharing of the defence burden in Europe could provide that transfer of resources required to make symmetrical the commitments to exchange rate stability (see Aitken, 1978a).[3]

Callaghan's success in persuading his European colleagues to institute further studies of the details of any new monetary system, including the question of the transfer of the resources and the need for a convergence in the economies of the member countries of the Community, was welcomed by the Treasury. Despite this, however, it was already clear that there was real hesitation about the appropriate British response to the Franco-German initiative at Bremen. Many ministers and officials were highly sceptical about the Bremen scheme to the extent that 'gossips' began to circulate that the Treasury was about to prepare a British counter proposal based on a two-tier system, in which the candidate countries would work to a different set of rules in order to make some allowance for their higher rates of inflation during a transitional period

British Treasury position did not undergo any substantial change even when talks about the new European Monetary System had become concrete plans. On the contrary, Denis Healey stated at a meeting of Commonwealth finance ministers held in Montreal at the end of September, that Britain might not be joining the proposed European Monetary System since the British economy was strong enough to stand on its own without the need for European support. In the opinion of the Chancellor of the Exchequer, entering the European Monetary System under the proposed terms could even be harmful to Britain. In a paper submitted to senior cabinet ministers he claimed that fixed exchange rates could lead to lower output and employment and might make it harder to cut inflation. He also said that acceptance of the scheme might tend to keep the pound's value artificially high, worsening Britain's trade position. Moreover, the Chancellor implicitly conceded that the scenarios which the paper contained were the only ones which he had chosen to include in a key document he provided to the small group of ministers involved in discussions over the EMS. The paper set out four possibilities which could follow from a British decision to join a system of fixed exchange rates in early 1979, and all of them were quite unattractive. The paper continued stating the eight conditions[4] for British entry in the ERM. Among them there were: durability and effectiveness of the system, inclusion of all members of the Community, higher growth and employment, symmetrical obligations, realignments provisions, preservation of the dollar or any other major international currency value, backing of the arrangements by adequate funds, wider reform of the way the community transferred resources from one country to another. However, by the time the paper was presented by the Chancellor of the Exchequer, namely the beginning of November 1978, none of these conditions had the smallest chance of being taken into serious consideration by Britain's European partners.[5]

The contribution given to the debate on the establishment of the EMS by the Governor of the Bank of England, Gordon Richardson, was negligible. Moreover, it was always in line with the opinions expressed by the Treasury, as clearly appears from the analysis of both contemporary press and the quarterly Bulletins published by the Bank of England itself. Indeed, apart from almost ironic wishes to Jenkins' efforts to reopen the debate on European Monetary Union (see Bank of England, 1978a, p. 65), the only intervention of the Governor which was directly related to the issue of the ERM simply stated that it was not appropriate for him to express an independent opinion. In or out of such a scheme, the Bank of England remained committed to follow policies of prudence in both the fiscal and the monetary field aimed at the progressive reduction of inflation since they were the only guarantee of stability of both the domestic and external value of sterling (see Bank of England, 1978b, p. 534).

Of course the Treasury was not the only ministry of the British government interested in the problem of the new European Monetary System, though undeniably the one most directly concerned by the issue and the most likely to exert real influence on the decision of the Prime Minister. Hence, it is interesting to analyse the positions taken by other ministers of the Callaghan government.

By October 1978 the Cabinet and its key advisers were split about the merits of the scheme and the divisions did not merely cut across traditional pro and anti common market lines. Thus, Eric Varley, the Industry Secretary, and Edmund Dell,[6] the Trade Secretary, were understood to be sceptical about the proposals because of their possible impact on industry and exports while Roy Hattersley, the Prices Secretary, was keeping his options open. The strongest opponents were apparently the expected group of anti-marketeers composed of Peter Shore, the Environment Secretary, Tony Benn, the Energy Secretary, and John Silkin, the Agriculture Minister. However it was the silent moles like Dell and Hattersley, committed Europeans yet weighty sceptics about the Schmidt-Giscard plan for the following stage of European Unity, who made superfluous traditional anti-marketeers' denunciations. On the other hand, support generally for British participation had come from Harold Lever, the Chancellor of the Duchy of Lancaster and a long time advocate of stable exchange rates, Shirley Williams, the Education Secretary, and Roy Mason, the Defence Secretary.

By November 1978, a substantial majority of the Cabinet opposed British membership of the proposed European Monetary System. This opposition emerged on 2 November, after a long discussion at 10 Downing Street during which a number of noted pro-European Ministers expressed their hostility to the proposals. However, no position was either invited or taken by the Cabinet as a whole and the decision on British membership of the European Monetary System was postponed to the end of the month.

A Low Temperature Political Debate on the EMS Issue

The position of the Cabinet on the ERM mirrored the debate on the issue that was going on, or, paradoxically, 'not' going on, both within the two major political parties and between them. This, in turn, reflected the debate which was going on, or 'not' going on, within British civil soc' ty.

The opposition to the EMS of the governing party was fairly well-known. At the 1978 Blackpool conference of the National Executive Committee (NEC) the Emergency Resolution No. 5, expressing 'deep concern' at the proposals of the EMS, was put forward by the anti-community majority. It was 'baulked by sleight of hand'. On the basis of the evidence, it can also be safely assumed that over half of Callaghan's rank and file MPs in the Commons were hostile to any deal with Helmut Schmidt and Giscard d'Estaing.[7] Moreover, at the end of October 1978 a group of anti-market Labour MPs wrote to all constituency parties reminding them of the Labour Party's established opposition to economic and monetary union. The statement issued by the group acknowledged that they expected the overwhelming majority to express opposition to the proposals of the EMS, on the grounds that 'they constitute a threat to unemployment and living standards and to our continued freedom to decide our own economic policies'.

However, the anti-market MPs of the Labour Party were not the only ones to express concerns over the new European Monetary scheme. At a meeting of the TUC-Labour Party Liaison Committee three documents were presented which strongly opposed Britain's entry into the European Monetary System. One, of course, was from a group of anti-market MPs headed by Brian Gould and warned that the EMS would subject Britain to a permanent deflationary regime under European supervision and would transform Britain into a 'pensioner state'. The second one was from the Labour Policy Forming National Executive and declared total opposition to British participation in the scheme. Finally the third, from the TUC, required to consult the trade unions when the final EMS proposals became known. However, the Economic Committee of the TUC had already warned that the proposals known at that stage could endanger Britain's economic recovery.

Further evidence of the governing party's opposition to the European Monetary System came on 9 November with two new initiatives in Westminster to kill the project before it got off the ground. More than one-third of the Parliamentary Labour Party signed a motion rejecting the idea of Britain's joining the system and calling on the government to retain control of the country's economic policy. They claimed that the feeling against the system within the Party was far greater than that indicated by the number of signatures which, in all, were 114. Furthermore, Labour MPs were being sent a paper produced by Geoffrey Bish, head of the Party's Research Department, for the party's influential Home Policy Committee headed by Tony Benn, condemning the system almost out of hand by saying that the EMS would carry great economic dangers for Britain.

The last demonstration of the Labour Party's opposition to any hypotheses of entry in the system came after the publication of the government's Green Paper, on 27 November, when the Labour Party's two Senior Policy Drafting Committees totally rejected the government's formula keeping Britain's option open over the European Monetary System. At a joint meeting with the Chancellor, the Home Policy and the International Committees of the National Executive Committee even called on the government to use its veto to stop the proposed system being set up at all, regardless of whether Britain was a member. The meeting, chaired by Tony Benn, Energy Secretary, passed a three part resolution which called for a free vote on the question of the proposed monetary system and on the publication of the Treasury's confidential working papers on the system. It is interesting to note that the resolution was passed despite the Chancellor's efforts to persuade the National Executive Committee that there was no question of Britain's joining the system if it meant, as it did, according to the reports already published both by the Chancellor of the Exchequer and by the Commons Expenditure Committee, reduced growth or increased unemployment. Indeed, it was exactly the widespread feeling that the government's policy of keeping its options open on the EMS issue was fairly, disingenuous, that restrained the political debate within the governing party from taking off.

Only slightly more lively was the debate within the Conservative Party which, by the time the proposal of a new European Monetary System was put forward, was still in opposition. Reservations about the Franco-German scheme were already expressed by leading Tory figures, such as Geoffrey Howe, Shadow Chancellor of the Exchequer, in the immediate aftermath of the Bremen meeting.

On the other hand, in a speech in London for the Conservative Group for Europe on 12 July, the former Conservative Prime Minister, Edward Heath, who took Britain into the EEC, sharply criticised Callaghan for standing 'limply on the touch line'. Heath also implicitly took to task those members of Mrs Thatcher's Shadow Cabinet who had given only cautious support to the currency scheme. However, this initial conflict was soon overcome to the extent that only a few days afterwards, Heath publicly supported Thatcher's line over the Bremen proposal.

How far the Shadow Cabinet was from Heath's position, was illustrated in a speech by John Nott, opposition spokesman on trade, whose talents were known to be admired by Mrs Thatcher.[8] In his speech he advocated 'constructive interest but considerable caution' over the Bremen scheme, defended the Treasury and defined the European Monetary System as 'an entanglement', 'a currency straight jacket'. Since Britain was the European country with the most advanced international monetary system, and huge multinational interests represented, for example, by BP, he argued that it was not possible to contemplate entering a system which would need huge Central Bank settlements after each speculation against a fixed parity. Such a situation would pose a massive constraint at that country's most sensitive point, namely its currency, and the monetary impact would not necessarily be on the side of restraint. On the contrary, for the weaker economies, settlements could greatly inflate the monetary base. Thus, the approach suggested by the Shadow Cabinet was not that of a rigid currency arrangement, with the transfer of resources between nations made by means of government transfers and subsidies, but rather that of a move to greater convertibility for sterling, to bring it closer to the Deutschmark, and of a removal of all those supply constraints that were considered responsible for the British economy's poor performances in previous years.[9]

The position of the Shadow Cabinet was further clarified in a later article, again by Nott (1978), in the pages of *The Times*, where the theoretical background of the Conservative thought on European monetary integration clearly emerged. This background was based on Hayek's proposal of European currencies' competition eventually leading to the emergence of the strongest one through the free exercise of personal choice and not through the decision of politicians (see Hayek, 1976, pp. 21–2 and 1976; see also Hayek, 1979). This position was reiterated by the Conservatives over and over again throughout the whole process of European monetary integration until it was eventually embodied in the two Treasury documents of 1989–90 proposing alternative ways to EMU (see HM Treasury, 1990b; see also HM Treasury, 1990a).

Apart from these interventions by Nott, Conservative leaders had little more, if anything, to say in public about the EMS proposals. By the end of October 1978, Margaret Thatcher was even put under strong pressure from some senior and influential Conservatives to oppose in public British membership of the European Monetary System. In an attack on the Franco-German proposals, John Biffen,[10] former Tory industry spokesman, speaking to a Youth Conservative Meeting in London, warned that they would conflict with some of the basic policies of the following Tory government. Biffen's views on economic affairs were believed to be largely shared by the Tory leaders. Biffen said that the proposed EMS would require Britain to return to a system of politically fixed exchange rates which would cause serious problems to any Tory government that wished to give monetary policy a key role in its economic strategy. Moreover, he identified a manifest inconsistency between Tory support of a liberal economic domestic trade and monetary policy in the domestic political debate, and the denial of these very tenets by the actions of the European Community. The latter, if supported by the Conservative Party, would be much more likely to bring a loss of credibility at home than a gain of respect in Brussels.

On the other hand, a timid indication of some support in the Conservative Party for the European Monetary System was provided in a Commons motion tabled by Julian Critchley, MP for Aldershot, and signed by 27 other Tory backbenchers, a very small number when compared to the 114 Labour MPs who signed the anti-EMS motion.

Even more timid signs of a very general agreement in principle to an area of stable exchange rates within the European Community were expressed on a few occasions by other representatives of the Conservative Party.

However, it is clear that the official line of the Thatcher Shadow Cabinet was at least suspicious towards the overall project of European Monetary Union proposed by the European Community and, particularly, towards the idea of a new European Monetary System. Its establishment was undoubtedly subordinated to, if not considered inconsistent with, the complete liberalisation of exchange rate controls and the tightening of domestic expenditure disciplines which represented the main objectives of the forthcoming Conservative government.

In conclusion, even if from opposite perspectives and for opposite considerations, the overall assessment of the Franco-German exchange rate initiative by the two major British political parties was a negative one. This consideration may help explain why the political debate both within the two major British parties and between them, never reached a high temperature.

The Attitudes of the British Socioeconomic Sectors with Reference to Frieden's Model

Perhaps more striking than the stalemate in the political debate is the almost complete silence of the social and economic actors. Indeed, according to the model proposed by Frieden, socioeconomic sectors should be mostly concerned with the two interrelated issues of the exchange rate regime and level. With the aim of tracing back the reasons of a similar lack of interest in the ERM issue, this section provide an analysis of the actual positions adopted by the industrial sector, the financial sector, organised Labour and their main representatives.

1   *The City of London and the EMS: A Stalling Debate*

Within the financial sector it is appropriate to separate the opinions expressed by the personnel directly operating in the foreign currency markets, for example, the brokers, and the position adopted by the banking sector, particularly the representatives of the big four British banks, even if the first reactions to the Bremen scheme were immediately sceptical on both sides.

Indeed, both exchange rate analysts in banks and in brokers' offices were frankly apprehensive at what could happen to the exchange rate at the moment the pound had entered the proposed arrangement. They were keen to point out the practical details which had to be worked out before sterling could join the snake even as a second tier currency, freer to float than the existing members. In particular, they expressed doubts about a British Labour government's ability, or indeed, any British government's ability, to enforce quickly the discipline necessary to keep sterling steady against the mark, and about the problems stemming from a steadily depreciating pound inside the EMS. Thus, the first concern of the City was the maintenance of a strong exchange rate for sterling. This was considered inconsistent with entry in the ERM even if in the other European countries and, indeed, in Britain itself,[11] economists tended to associate the pegging of the currency of an highly inflated economy in a fixed exchange rate system more with an over-appreciation than with a depreciation.[12] Even the massive size of the intervention fund to which the nine had proposed to subscribe to back the monetary union did not entirely reassure the sceptics. It is true that a potentially important aspect of Britain's entry in the European Monetary System could be the adoption of measures relaxing British exchange controls, measures long wanted by the Bank of England and the City but strongly opposed by the left and the TUC. However, the City still preferred, to entering the EMS, the adoption by the British government of tight monetary policies specifying targets for domestic credit expansion.

Leading bankers in Britain also added their doubts to the chorus of opinions which was developing against the formation of the European Monetary System (EMS). Lord Armstrong, chairman of the Midland Bank and former head of the Civil Service, said the scheme was worthless and would have been of no advantage to Britain: 'I do not think that this particular scheme at this particular time is worth a row of beans' (see Brummer, 1978a).

In taking an anti-EMS line, Lord Armstrong, who in those years was regarded as a highly important City voice, argued that British trade with Europe, although increasing, was not overwhelming in relation to trade with the rest of the world. So he saw no advantage in hitching sterling to a European currency bloc.

Further evidence of the negative position of the City, and, in particular, of brokers, towards joining the EMS may be found in the memoranda submitted to the all parties Commons Expenditure Committee in preparation for the inquiry by its general subcommittee into the proposals (see Riddel, 1978e). The views of a wide range of economists and interested parties had been sought by the subcommittee headed by Michael English, the Labour MP for Nottingham West. Those asked for memoranda included the TUC, the CBI, the Fabian Society, the National Institute of Economic and Social Research, the London Business School, and stockbrokers L. Messel and W. Greenwell. None of the memoranda were formally published, but the views of several of the organisations were made public separately and most of them, though not all, were critical of the scheme as it stood. In particular, brokers L. Messel told the subcommittee that participation in the scheme would imply the abandonment of Britain's monetary sovereignty and of its own independently chosen monetary targets. This would be a retrograde step, as the evolution of monetary policy in the brokers' view, had been towards responsible financial targets focused on domestic economic objectives. The position of stockbrokers Sheppards and Chase was on the same lines. They argued in their new gilt market survey, that the growth of money supply by the end of 1978 was still faster than would have been permissible in a successful European Monetary System. The brokers said that if the system had been intended to stabilise successfully European currencies, it would primarily require not exchange intervention, but harmonisation of monetary policy. On the contrary, the nine EEC members were far from taking such a step.

On the other hand, neither the British Bankers' Association nor the London clearing banks presented any evidence to the Commons expenditures committee until very late in the day, since the City's major banking groups decided that they could not express a common view on the proposed European Monetary System. In particular Sir Jeremy Morse, Chairman of Lloyds, the London insurance market, and former leading official of the International Monetary Fund, contrary to the position adopted by the chairman of Midland Bank, had a substantially positive view towards Britain's entry in the proposed new European Monetary System. This position was later agreed by other representatives of the banking sector as, in finally taking evidence from the chairmen of three clearing banks, Sir Jeremy Morse of Lloyds, Robin Leigh Pemberton of National Westminster and Antony Tuke of Barclays, the Commons Expenditure Committee heard, for a change, some favourable comments on the proposed European Monetary System. There was no doubt in Sir Jeremy's mind, nor in those of his co-chairmen, that if the system got off the ground at all, Britain should be in it because it would exercise an additional discipline against inflationary policies and it could in due course offer the benefits to trade of a common currency, the ECU, that might permit higher growth in Europe. Whether a 'snake' or a basket was chosen as the numeraire of the system was an important technical question but not the fundamental one since, in his opinion, although the basket might be preferable, the snake could also work. A similar view was taken by Tuke, who argued that a 1 January entry date was not sacrosanct, but that the balance of advantages was in favour of going along with the rest of Europe in the hope that an improvement in the economy would result from being a member of the club. According to Pemberton, in the end, the UK might not join the ERM in the initial phase, but this, in itself, was no solution to any problem since it was undeniably in British interests, as far as possible, to be within the main power centres of the EEC. Thus the British government should aim to join the new monetary system within a reasonable period of time.

These claims were manifestly in contrast both with the opinions expressed in various occasions by the brokers, and with the strong position against British entry in the EMS adopted only few days before by another important representative of the banking sector, the chairman of the fourth clearer, Lord Armstrong of Midland Bank, who had described the proposal as not worth a 'row of beans'. However, this conflict should not be overestimated. It is true that it demonstrated the existence of growing concern on the side of certain sectors of the City at the possibility of losing their central financial role in the world markets, particularly in relation to the management of the ECU. It is also true that it clearly stated City's preference for the implementation of strict monetary policies. However, it was expressed at a time when senior ministers had already concluded that a scheme that fulfilled British preconditions was unlikely to emerge from the ongoing EEC talks. Indeed, it does not seem an irrational strategy to stress the advantages and the positive features of an undesired policy decision which, in any case, is not going to be taken. Moreover, in the case that the British government, any British government, still had some hesitation in implementing those strict monetary policies to which the City of London attached so much importance, underlying the possibility of an alternative European solution could succeed in exerting some pressure for an unambiguous macroeconomic policy shift to monetarist practices.

2 The Scarce Enthusiasm of Industrial Capital

Even less present than the City in the debate over the entry into the European Monetary System, was another sector, the industrial capital, which, on the contrary, one would expect to be primarily concerned with the issue of the exchange rate regime, particularly when adopting Frieden's model of analysis. The first public declarations on the subject by the Confederation of British

Industry (CBI) are to be found only in the second half of October 1978, when many steps had already been taken by the European Countries on their way to the establishment of the European Monetary System. These declarations were few in number and clearly showed that CBI members were afraid 'of being boxed in' an exchange system without sufficient guarantees.

A report of the CBI working party headed by Deryk Vander Weyer, vice-chairman of Barclays Bank, took a broadly similar line to that publicly stated by the Prime Minister, subordinating CBI agreement to entry to the fulfilment of fairly stringent conditions. In particular, the report emphasised the need for freedom to alter parities within the scheme and said that the burden of adjusting domestic economies had to be distributed among member countries to prevent the system from inherently restricting of economic growth. There also had to be adequate credit facilities to support the scheme and arrangements for a better balance between contributions to, and benefits from the EEC related to the strengths of the different national economies. Finally, the CBI also argued that it was necessary for the UK to enter with sterling set at competitive initial rates against other currencies. A similar substantially negative attitude of the CBI towards Britain's entry in the EMS was also manifest in the memorandum it submitted to the Commons Expenditure Committee. This favoured UK entry, but subject to a list of safeguards about the operation of the scheme which were highly unlikely to be agreed by the rest of the EEC.

Of some importance in understanding these declarations of the CBI on the issue of British entry in the EMS and also in assessing them in the light of Frieden's exchange-rate preferences model, is a study about business views on exchange-rate policy which was prompted by the CBI in the late autumn of 1977 and published exactly in the immediate aftermath of the Bremen summit (see Confederation of British Industry (CBI), 1978). The major focus of this study was precisely on the advantages and disadvantages perceived by UK industry and commerce of various exchange rate policy options over the following three to four years. It was carried out by interviewing a selection of about two dozen companies and organisations and by producing a report based on these discussions. The firms involved in the study were selected by CBI staff to ensure a spread of companies, not only in terms of size but also by type of activities and by volume of exports. In particular, the total direct exports from the UK of the 23 companies interviewed amounted in 1976 to around £2.5bn and their total UK employment to around 750,000. The authors sought to differentiate the questions asked between, on the one hand, the impact of the average level of the exchange rate over a period of the next three to four years, and, on the other hand, fluctuations in the rate around an average level.

These are exactly the two sets of preferences considered in Frieden's model.

The answers to these inquiries are of the utmost importance in assessing, at the empirical level, the attitude of the British industrial sector towards the issue of joining a system of quasi-fixed exchange rate which was also perceived to produce an appreciation of exchange rates,[13] and, at the theoretical level, the appropriateness of Frieden's hypotheses on the exchange-rate preferences of economic sectors. Generally, at that time British companies considered the level of the exchange rate to be more important than fluctuations in the rate itself. In particular, with respect to the level of the exchange rate, the authors found that the firms fell into two main groups: those which considered a depreciation to be beneficial and those which were largely indifferent to the level of the exchange rate. Only three companies considered a depreciation to be harmful. About half the companies/organisations interviewed between Autumn 1977 and July 1978 believed that a depreciation of sterling, by something like 10 per cent, would be beneficial to them, although the extent of the perceived gain varied widely. About a third of the companies interviewed thought that a depreciation would benefit them *significantly*. The remaining firms, apart from the three mentioned above, considered that they had little to gain from a depreciation, but also thought that they had little to lose: they were just indifferent to the level of the exchange rate. Many of the companies not unduly concerned about the level of the exchange rate had a significant proportion of their costs, as well as their receipts, fixed in terms of *foreign currency*. In some cases it was because of large overseas operations, where it was felt that profits in terms of foreign currency were not significantly affected by changes in the sterling exchange rate. In other cases it was because the company earned most of its foreign exchange by incurring expenditure abroad (e.g. firms engaged in shipping, or undertaking construction contracts abroad) or, while manufacturing in the UK, required large inputs of imported material or fuel. In all these cases, changes in the sterling exchange rate would have almost as great an impact on costs as on receipts, and so they were felt to make little difference on the performance of the company. The situation was very different for UK manufacturing companies exporting a significant fraction of their output, whose costs were made up to a large extent of wages and materials or components manufactured within the UK. It was these companies who felt vulnerable to an appreciation of the exchange rate, and who could benefit most from a depreciation. A further distinguishing feature was between those companies which sold a homogeneous product where the 'law of one price' applied, those which sold in imperfect markets and were concerned about price competition, and those which possessed a strongly differentiated product and so were to some extent protected from price competition. The first two groups were relatively more concerned at the prospect of an appreciating, or insufficiently depreciating, exchange rate than the last one (see CBI, 1978, p. 14). It must be noted that the UK manufacturing sector was already heavily committed in exporting. In 1977 the value of manufactured export, including the exports of previously imported products, came to approximately £27bn, and accounted for 63 per cent of total exports of goods and services.

With respect to the other dimension of Frieden's model, namely the preferences of the economic sectors over the relative rigidity of the exchange rate regime, one third of the companies analysed by the CBI expressed an explicit preference for a 'free float regime'. Moreover, the firms which preferred less in the way of fluctuations, were mostly concerned with individual exchange rates, particularly sterling against the US dollar, hence the great importance given by the CBI to the relations between the EMS and the US dollar. In general, fluctuations, even quite large ones, seemed to British companies as reported by the CBI survey, a necessary part of life unless and until a new 'international' monetary regime was agreed. More explicitly, the authors of the analysis were 'glad to report that for the most part, firms were prepared to regard fluctuations in rates as an 'acceptable risk'. A risk that, by the way, all companies were aware could be countered by using forward exchange markets, and, indeed, all but five companies made some use of such facilities where appropriate (ibid., p. 23). The authors also emphasised that, while their analysis indicated how business people considered a change in the exchange rate to affect their particular companies, for the most part the exchange rate was seen as only one of many factors with which they had to be concerned. In most cases, other factors, including fluctuations in commodity prices, the rate of domestic inflation and especially the volume of demand, both in world generally and in the particular market in which the firm operated, were considered to be 'of much greater importance'.

The analysis described above may be considered as a genuine survey on the true attitudes of the industrial sector towards the issue of the appropriate exchange rate level and of the preferred exchange rate regime, or simply as a statement of the CBI position towards the ERM. However, it clearly explains why the industrial sector in general and the CBI in particular reserved such a cold answer to the establishment of the EMS.

Actually, the only British economic group at that time to speak openly in favour of the European Monetary System was the Association of British Chambers of Commerce. In a policy document published on 23 November, the Chambers said that their unanimous view was that wholehearted participation in the system was essential for the prosperity of British business and the development of the British economy. Since the paramount requirements for British businessmen were a stable environment at home and an expanding market overseas, if Britain opted out of the proposed European Monetary System, exporters would be put at a competitive disadvantage and there could be 'catastrophic' consequences for the City of London. The report added that the EMS offered some immediate chance of imposing much needed discipline on British governments to resist short term political palliatives at the expense of long-term economic stability. It also stated that the EMS would provide a method of restraining British governments from financial irresponsibility and inflationary policies which undermined the productive capacity of British business. The paper concluded by advocating a single currency for Europe.

3   The Widespread Scepticism of the TUC

The position of the CBI was not so far from the one adopted by the TUC at a very late stage of the discussions over the establishment of the EMS.

In October, the General Council of the TUC considered the establishment of the proposed European Monetary System and recognised that it was desirable to create a zone of greater monetary stability in Europe since the experience of floating exchange rates had not been completely successful or favourable for growth. However the General Council was also aware that there were many disadvantages in pursuing currency stability at any cost. Earlier attempts to establish fixed exchange rate systems in Europe had failed because they had placed excessive strains on those European countries with weaker currencies. There were clear dangers in creating an exchange rate regime which was dominated by the Deutschmark but which did not possess a suitable adjustment mechanism and did not produce a transfer of resources at a Community level to narrow the differences in the GDP per head among member states.

As mentioned above, always in October the TUC/Labour Party Liaison Committee discussed the plans for a European Monetary System. The Committee agreed with the government the conditions for the UK to join the new fixed rate system in Europe. These conditions were the following. First, that the system had to favour economic growth in the world economy. Second, that there had to be a symmetry of obligation for both strong and weak currencies. Third, that the scheme had to be durable. Fourth, that the scheme had to be flexible to allow for adjustments. Fifth, that the scheme had not to damage the US dollar and the international monetary system. Sixth, that there had to be a progressive shift of resources from the strong countries to the weaker countries, which would imply a reconsideration of the EEC budget and of the Common Agricultural Policy (see Trade Union Congress, 1980, p. 297).

Consistently, a paper from the TUC, approved at the end of October 1978 by its economic Committee, did not put forward objections in principle to the EMS. Instead it dwelled at length on the importance of getting the right terms for the UK. In particular, it said that the allocation of resources within the EEC was of the utmost importance and that the Prime Minister should not accept terms that further disadvantaged the Community's poorer regions. Finally the TUC stressed that the system had to leave the government room to attack domestic problems, to introduce employment subsidies, to intervene in industry, and to alter the distribution of income between its own regions.

In November it was reported to the Executive Committee that contacts had taken place between the ETUC (European Trade Union Confederation) Secretariat and the Commission officials concerning the proposed European Monetary System. In the opinion of the Unions, though some details of the scheme had not been settled and there remained considerable differences between member states about the obligations imposed to the governments by the EMS, it was already clear that the agreement would have little direct effect on the CAP, and that no extra funds would be available to the Community. This contrasted with the view of the General Council that the system had to provide for a shift of resources from the stronger to the weaker countries, entailing reform of the Community budget and of the CAP, that it had to be flexible and durable with symmetrical obligations falling on both strong and weak countries, and that it had to promote growth in world economy. The Executive Committee agreed, however, to express support in principle to the achievement of greater monetary stability and a better balance between agriculture and industry, in order to avoid making it more difficult to overcome unemployment and other economic problems. On the other hand, an EMS had not to impose inflation or deflation on particular countries and there had to be clear obligations on both surplus and deficit countries, with a rapid movement towards economic convergence (see ibid., p. 217).

Again in November, a vice-president of the commission addressed the ESC of the TUC (Economic and Social Committee of the Trade Union Congress) on the European Monetary System. He expressed the hope that governments would set up automatic intervention arrangements, supported by arrangements to give early warning of pressures on currencies of members, and that the EMS would be backed by large financial resources to deter speculation against currencies. He also argued that the EMS could not be sustainable without convergence of member states' economic policies and performance. A representative of the General Council, speaking on behalf of the working representatives, said that trade unionists would support proposals leading to the restoration of confidence and of order in the world monetary situation, but that their views on the EMS could only be fully formed when details of the system were fully known. The ESC adopted an opinion, with a number of working representatives abstaining, approving the establishment of a monetary system aimed at achieving monetary stability and order in the Community and at world level, and stating that the system had to be sufficiently flexible to enable realistic exchange rates to be maintained (see ibid., p. 223).

More critical was the position adopted by the TUC in the memorandum presented to the Common's Expenditure Committee. The latter underlined that linking sterling to the other EEC currencies would imply severely deflationary policies in the UK, damaging the prospects for both output and employment.

This assessment was shared with the Fabian Society, an independent Labour Party research organisation, which was also asked to present a memorandum before the all parties Commons Committee. According to the Fabian Society, the effect on the foreign exchange markets of the new European Monetary regime, was likely to be to replace a system where quite small changes in parities occurred frequently with one in which larger parity changes occurred slightly less often, but after great disturbances in the exchange markets. Moreover, the Fabians argued that if the scheme succeeded in creating a fixed exchange rate in which the pound value was kept artificially high, it could prove costly in terms of lost employment, output and investment. However, the possibility to change currency parities could still play a vital part in maintaining the competitiveness of industry in the face of Britain's inflation rate. In conclusion, in the opinion of the Fabian Society, Britain should not join the proposed European Monetary System as this would lead to greater rather than less turmoil on the currency markets and could also result in slower growth, higher unemployment and lower investment in the UK (see Fabian Comments on British Participation in the Proposed European Monetary System; see also Atkinson, 1978).

The report on British membership in the proposed European Monetary System by the House of Commons Expenditure Committee was finally released on 22 November. This included a memorandum on the possible results of British participation by Terry Ward, adviser to the general subcommittee from the Department of Applied Economics at Cambridge. According to the latter,

British entry into the proposed European Monetary System meant lower output and employment over the following three years than under the regime of floating exchange rates. In his memorandum Ward concluded that, though different economic models actually in use could give somewhat different results, it was extremely unlikely that any of them could show the system to have a beneficial effect on output and employment assuming any plausible rate of inflation.[14] However, the memorandum was only an appendix to the report which reached no clear-cut conclusions but sought to be 'a guide to the evidence which identifies the main issues and points of dispute'. The report mentioned certain problems peculiar to the UK, in particular the remaining reserve currency functions of sterling and its use to finance a part of world trade, the impact of its low rate of productivity growth, the existence of stricter exchange controls than in the rest of the EEC and its special relations with Ireland. The Committee concluded that:

> ... in the end, the question of whether the EMS should join an EMS is a political one. It would be a step, though perhaps not a big one, towards greater European Unity ... it may well fail and this could be a good reason for a pro-European being against it. It will probably succeed only if it leads to greater economic convergence ... which many fear for quite opposite reasons.
>
> If it does lead to such convergence that will only be achieved if somebody in the EEC (presumably the Council of Finance Ministers) determines what the common economic objectives of the EEC are and what each member state should do in order to achieve them. Achieving this mutual agreement will not be easy (see Riddel, 1978h).

The Consistent Behaviour of the British Government

Given these discouraging signs coming from the political and socioeconomic actors, and given the fact that general elections were due to take place within a few months, Callaghan had no other chance left than to avoid commitments. Only this strategy could guarantee to the British government some room of manoeuvre and some bargaining power at the European level. This is exactly what happened throughout the whole period of the negotiations over the new European Monetary System.

Already in delivering his report on the Bremen summit to the House of Commons, Callaghan made it plain that Britain would want to see more details of the Franco-German scheme before making any commitment. The Prime Minister told the MPs that the government had taken the view, throughout its discussions with the European leaders, that monetary arrangements were not enough by themselves to ensure a zone of monetary stability. He also insisted that any new system had to take full account of the economic as well as the monetary interests of each member of the European Community.

It was precisely the willingness to join, so impressive in the case of the Italian government in a context of much deeper social and political conflicts, which was seen to be missing in Britain and thus the Cabinet continued to defer decision on entry in the EMS without being able to obtain anything at the European level. Instead, by the beginning of November, Britain, Italy and Ireland definitively failed to convince their EEC partners that any substantial new transfer of resources was a necessary condition of the proposed new European Monetary System. Indeed, a majority of the members of the EPC (Economic Policy Committee), took the view that no extensive additional transfers were necessary to underpin the stability and viability of EMS, insofar as, with realistic exchange rates, the system would not have required any additional adjustment requirements. From the bland prose of the committee's report it was clear that Britain had signally failed to get general acceptance for its central argument that existing EEC mechanisms, and in particular the community budget, were perverse in their redistribution effect.

Despite these failures and the related fact that it was clear to anyone that Britain would not join the system from the beginning, the government maintained a noncommittal position until the very last moment. Even its *Green Paper on European Monetary System* (see HM Treasury, 1978), published on 24 November, a few days before the meeting of Brussels in which a final decision on the issue was expected to be taken, said the government was not yet in a position to decide whether or not it would be in Britain's best interest to join the system. The Green Paper related the proposal to the international monetary environment, and described the kind of system which the government would like to see developed so that it could include and retain all the members of the European Community. In the report, the government made it clear that it would participate fully and constructively only to a European Monetary System which could embrace and retain all members of the Community and which would in fact contribute to the objective of greater monetary stability. It had stated repeatedly, before and after the Bremen meeting, that a new system would not be durable and effective unless it was soundly based on appropriate economic policies. There was to be no currency intervention, however large the resources used for it, and no country, however powerful, could in the long run hold the exchange rates if the fundamentals were wrong. The government insisted that the system should embody the following characteristics:

- it should be durable and effective. If it did not prove to be durable, the stability of the European economy would be damaged with consequent damage to the political and economic development of the Community as well;
- it should be truly European and it should be capable of containing all members of the Community, allowing for the divergences in their economic situation and for the time that was bound to be needed to achieve major progress towards convergence;
- it should provide a base for improved economic growth and higher employment in the Community, rather than create further constraints on growth and employment;
- for this reason, the system should impose obligations on its stronger members symmetrical with those falling on its weaker members;
- the system should be supported by adequate funds for intervention on the currency markets;
- there should be provision for realignments of exchange rates within the system when underlying economic circumstances made this advisable;
- the system should reinforce efforts to improve currency stability worldwide and should not be detrimental to other currencies, including the dollar, or to the standing and effectiveness of the IMF;
- the system should be accompanied by clear progress in making the operations of Community policies as a whole assist in promoting convergence of economic performance of member states. In particular there should be net transfers of resources on the right scale to the less prosperous members (see ibid., p. 3).[15]

None of these conditions appeared to be new in the British debate over the establishment of the ERM. However, commenting on each of them in the following sections of the Green Paper, the government made it implicitly clear that the exchange rates arrangements made so far within the EEC were not likely to fulfil its requirements. In the conclusive remarks of the Green Paper, the country's British government claimed that it could not yet reach a decision on whether it would be in the best interests of the UK to join the exchange rate regime of the EMS as it finally emerged from the negotiations. However, the government's basic objectives would remain unchanged whatever decision was taken: it would vigorously pursue the policies which were necessary for improving growth and reducing unemployment. Moreover, the foundation for these policies had to be traced in an improvement of the industrial performance and in the victory of the battle against inflation. These were considered the only measures able to provide a long-lasting basis for stability of exchange rates.

Summing up, even if the government in its Green Paper never explicitly rejected British entry in the ERM, this was not necessary since it was implied in almost every line of the paper itself. Thus it was no surprise when Callaghan confirmed at the Brussels Meeting of 4–5 December 1978 and at the House of Commons on 6 December 1978, that the UK would not participate to the Exchange Rate Mechanism even if it would join in the development of a European Monetary Fund by depositing one-fifth of Britain's gold and dollar reserves in Brussels.

A case has been made in the previous sections that the explanation of this British government's decision is rooted in the lack of socioeconomic consensus on the UK's participation to the ERM, which, in turn, was mirrored by the lack of political debate both within and between the main political parties. As for the reasons why the British socioeconomic groups did not support the new European monetary arrangements, a deeper analysis of the structure of British capitalism and of the power relations between its components is necessary. To this end, attention is turned in the next paragraph of this chapter.

An Alternative Explanation: The City of London's Postwar Revival and the Implementation of Monetarist Macroeconomic Policies in the 1980s

From the evidence collected on the Italian and British internal debate over the ERM issue it is possible to infer that Frieden's model is not exhaustive of the complex political issues arising at the domestic level from the international economic phenomena nor does it succeed in predicting the actual positions adopted by the domestic economic interest groups. It is true that Frieden proposes economically plausible hypotheses on the interests of social actors in relation to exchange rate issues. These hypotheses, in the absence of any kind of power struggle in the political arena among different social and economic actors, would prove effective in explaining and even predicting interest groups' positions towards the issue of exchange rate level and regime. However, when inserted into the historical reality of the internal debate taking place in a particular country and in a particular historical moment, these hypotheses do not prove to be adequate. To understand the actual terms of the debate it is then necessary to insert it into its historical context and to analyse its historical development in the light of the insights coming from the analysis of the society, of its economic and social structure and of the development of power relations among its economic and social constituents.

In the case of the United Kingdom, the historical context in which the issue of the ERM is to be inserted is that of the division of capital between the City and the Industry. By 1979 this division had resulted in the predominance, or better hegemony, of the financial fraction of capital over the productive one, with all that it implied in terms of commitment to the pursuance of *laissez-faire* and strict monetary policies. Since the dominant fraction in UK did not need to shift the power struggle to the European level to pursue those macroeconomic policies necessary to maintain its economic and political power, UK entry in the ERM was not a live issue in the political debate of the late 1970s. This is demonstrated by the lack of interest in the issue of the ERM shown by almost all sectors of British economy and British political system during the diplomatic talks leading to the establishment of the new European monetary arrangements.

The explanations to this behaviour of the British social actors, in turn, is to be found, as in the case of Italy, in the structure of British capitalism and in the kind of power relations and conflicts its different social and economic actors were experiencing at that time.

1   The Theoretical Debate over the Development of British Capitalism and the Definition of the City of London

The term mostly used by the scholars to define the development of British capitalism and, consequently, to describe the present characteristics of its economic, political, and social organisation is that of 'exceptionalism'. In spite of the agreement among the majority of the authors over the recognition of the peculiar, 'exceptional' nature of British capitalism, however, the hypotheses proposed to explain this phenomenon, as well as the very definition of British exceptionalism, differ in a variety of ways.

In the most widely accepted explanation, exceptionalism coincides with British traditionalism, and this persistence of aristocratic, pre-industrial elements in British polity is seen to have only a symbolic and legitimatory meaning. From this perspective, there is no doubt that Britain has become a truly capitalist, bourgeois, society, but it is one to which the aristocratic and traditional elements have successfully adapted themselves (see Stanworth and Giddens, 1974, p. 100).

However, there is also another fairly well established, but less widely accepted, interpretation of these developments, namely, a Gramscian interpretation rooted in Anderson's seminal work on the subject (see Anderson,

1964). According to this interpretation, traditionalism has remained the dominant force in modern British ideology. Moreover, traditionalism not only has a symbolic or legitimatory significance, but also a materially inhibitive impact on the economic performance of British capitalism itself, since it is based on the hegemony of those fractions of British capitalism which recognise it as their ideological referent. For Anderson, the 'exceptionalism' of British society is owed to the dual nature of British capitalism, that is, the separateness of the financial fraction of capital and the industrial one, and the dominance of the former over the latter. This is reflected in the persistence of aristocratic, pre-industrial forms in the organisation of the civil and political society, as the British financial and banking elite is recognised as the carrier of pre-modern, aristocratic cultural and social values. On the other hand, British capitalist structure is characterised also by the existence of a hegemonic position of the capitalist bloc as a whole as opposed to the non-hegemonic though self-conscious bloc of the working class. Here the concept of 'hegemony' is defined in Gramscian terms as the 'dominance of one social bloc over another, not simply by means of force or wealth, but by a total social authority whose ultimate sanction and expression is a profound cultural supremacy'. In England, this peculiar morphology of the dominant class has resulted in different effective forms of hegemony. These range from social relations, to ideology, from the style of leadership, to the rejection of industrial bourgeoisie utilitarian and liberal ideological contributions.

Thus, according to this interpretation, the present equilibrium in England remains a capitalist one, but within the capitalist class itself one economic and, consequently, social component is hegemonic. This component is the banking sector or better the City of London. The City is not only a dominant economic and social actor, but together with its political referents, that is, the Treasury and the Bank of England, it is considered responsible for the British economic decline from the second half of the nineteenth century onwards. The crisis of British industry is in fact explained as the logical outcome of a long subordination of the needs of productive capital to the economic interests and preferences of the City of London.

At this stage it is important to clarify two points. Firstly, the conceptualisation of the City, and, consequently, the explanation of Britain's pattern of economic development; and secondly the analysis of the economy (City)-state relations.

The most important problem concerns the theoretical definition of the City and, consequently, the specification of the precise nature of its relationships with domestic industry. For many authors interested in the subject (see Aaronvitch, 1961; Overbeek, 1980), the City is simply the centre of British finance capital, that is, in the Marxist definition, the fusion of banking capital with large scale productive capital. A number of objections are raised by other scholars against this conceptualisation of the City (see Ingham, 1984; Strange, 1971), and an alternative definition has been proposed, which puts much more emphasis on a clear identification of the City's economic activities.

At a preliminary stage, it is appropriate to distinguish between the different economic activities of commerce, banking, and finance. The term 'commerce' may be taken to refer to the practice of buying and selling, or the promotion of the exchange of commodities, including money and securities. 'Banking' is defined as the acceptance of deposits and the extension of loans at a rate of interest. 'Finance', in its broader meaning, consists in the provision of money capital for other activities such as production, consumption, trade, state expenditure etc. Whereas, clearly, many of the City's activities are 'financial' in the loosest sense that is, they make money capital available for different uses by means of the markets, they also comprise many commercial practices. Thus, the role of the City's houses as middlemen and brokers in the provision of finance overseas, and domestically for that matter, are best viewed as commercial practices, giving rise to services income. Indeed, net overseas earnings of the City's financial institutions are mainly, if not exclusively, represented by services income, and banking, finance and business services account for 19.2 per cent of total UK GDP (see British Invisibles, 1996a).

Moreover, one of the most distinctive and enduring features of the City's financial role is recognised in the almost complete absence of any direct involvement by its institutions in the means by which surplus value is created. Rather, the City's organisations have acted almost exclusively as intermediaries between investors and borrowers, and have been traditionally characterised by a marked organisational separation from any form of productive enterprise. This has not simply been a matter of an overseas orientation of British 'finance capital' and thus the explanation of British exceptionalism cannot be found only in its imperialist policies. In fact, the City's profits have not been primarily in the form of interest, but rather in the form of brokerage fees or commissions, that is, commercial profit from the trading in various forms of investment capital. Further, as brokers or intermediaries in overseas stocks and bonds, as well as domestic ones, the City firms have not necessarily been interested in the successful long-term performance of the particular share issues in which they dealt. Rather, the reverse is true. One of the most frequent criticisms to the British capitalist model is exactly that of 'short-termism', that is the essentially speculative nature of the activities of the British banking sector,

Table 8   Net overseas earnings of UK financial institutions

£million	1984 Total	1994 Total	1994 Services income	1994 Investment income
Banks	3,723	8,443	7,173	1,270
Securities dealers	198	2,202	1,078	1,124
Commodity traders, bullion dealers and export houses	499	576	576	–
Money market brokers	49	130	130	–
Baltic Exchange	270	262	262	–
Lloyd's Register of Shipping	27	48	48	–
Finance leasing	72	40	40	–
Fund managers	–	450	450	–
Insurance institutions	2,497	3,925	940	2,985

Source: British Invisibles, 1996a. (For more details see British Invisibles, 1996b.)

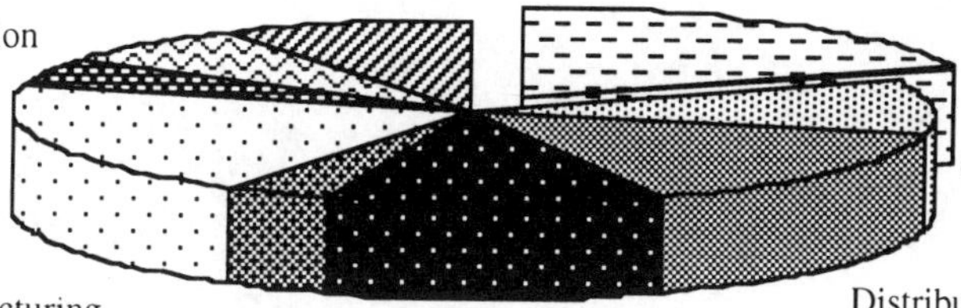

Graph 10 Sectoral share of UK GDP 1994

Source: British Invisibles, 1996a.

particularly in relation to the buying and selling of corporate shares. Further, it is precisely the prevalent short-term attitude of British banks to the financing of productive activity that has been often blamed for the present crisis of British industry.

Thus, the City should not be simply defined as the locus of British finance capital, or in terms of the designation of its constituent companies such as

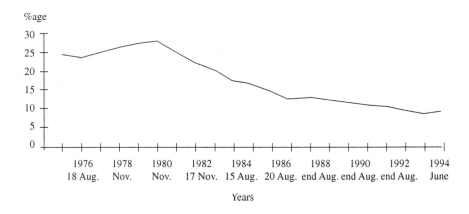

**Graph 11 Bank lending to manufacturing industry in the UK 1975–95
(% of bank lending to industry over total banking lending)**

Source: *Bank of England Quarterly Bulletins*, 1975–79.

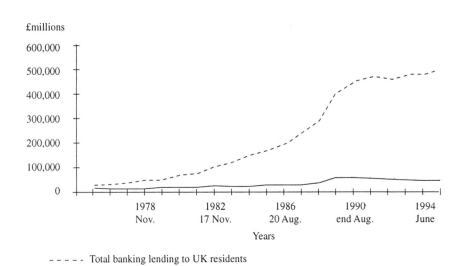

Graph 12 Total bank lending to manufacturing in the UK 1975–95

Source: *Bank of England Quarterly Bulletins*, 1975–95.

banks. It should instead be conceptualised as the institutional structure of short-term, or exchanges, in commodities, securities, money and services. Consequently, its operators, merchant bankers, securities dealers, bill brokers, etc., are understood as intermediaries promoting exchanges predominantly within financial and commercial systems, and in this sense they are wholesalers.

This definition permits one, on one hand, to link the seemingly discrete activities of merchant banking, foreign exchange dealing, bill broking, securities dealing etc., and, on the other, to account for the City's uniqueness in the world. Indeed, then, the City's revival brought about by the expansion of the various short-term money markets such as the Eurocurrency Market, and other new parallel markets, cannot be readily explained by a theory of finance capital. Moreover, a more careful identification of the City's activities, as the one carried out by Susan Strange,[16] is not only essential for an understanding of its economic relationship with domestic industry, but also of the City-state links. These links have been the basis for the political reproduction of the City's conditions of existence and the related defeat of the various industrial strategies that have threatened them.

This leads to a second point related to the conceptualisation of the City of London, namely, the City's continued dominance throughout the twentieth century despite its own economic difficulties and the consequent growth of industrial opposition. Britain's economic power and, with it, sterling pre-eminence have declined. However, not only has the City survived, but also it prospers as much as it ever did in the late nineteenth and early twentieth centuries.

According to some authors, the implementation or maintenance of policies supported by the City, carried out by the state agencies (not necessarily media) of the Treasury and the Bank of England, is owed to the dominance of these institutions within the state system. Their power was not instrumentally related to their penetration by a fraction of bank capital, but was based upon their political role as the real possessors and managers of the state's finances and was the product of a quite autonomous political struggle within the state during the nineteenth century. Moreover, the general coincidence of interests between the City, the Bank and the Treasury in relation to the currency and free trade has not simply been the result of the City's hegemony. During the twentieth century, the Treasury and Bank have also favoured the policies that the City has advocated because of their favourable impact on their own independent practices and institutional power. To support this view, it is worth relying on empirical evidence, which shows how the historical evolution of the City of

London, of the Bank of England and of the Treasury was clearly interconnected.

Thus, more than contrasting an 'instrumental' interpretation of the relation between state agencies and the economy with an 'independent' one, it could be more appropriate to speak about the sociopolitical dialectic relations between the City and its political referents as historically determined. Similarly, the corollary of the City's persisting hegemony, that is industrial weakness, must also be explained with reference to the specific institutional, mediation and political expression of industrial interests.

Summing up, the main element of British 'exceptionalism' is given not so much by the persistence of a traditional, pre-modern polity, as, of course is the case in Britain, but by the fact that this polity is economically, politically and socially dominated by the City and its social and political allies. Moreover, the City is characterised or, better, defined, not as the core of the 'finance capital', but as the locus of merchant or commercial practices, ranging from insurance to brokerage activities. These activities, while on one side limiting to a great extent the expansion of British productive activities, on the other guarantee the prosperity of the City itself as separated from the performance of British economy as a whole. Finally, the explanation of British exceptionalism is not only linked to the establishment, defence and exploitation of the Empire, but is also influenced by the internal dynamics of British social and political development, and, in particular, by the interactions and dialect relations between the City, the Treasury and the Bank of England.

2   *The City's Postwar Revival*

The context in which to insert Britain's decision not to enter the ERM, is thus that of British 'exceptionalism'. Britain is the only industrialised country hosting a centre with such a large share of the world commercial, banking and financial activities. To the extent that this centre, the City, is unique, also Britain is unique.

The consequences of this enduring economic prosperity for the development of the dominant classes, the state system and the economy of Britain, can scarcely be overestimated. It is true that after the second world war the City lived a moment of crisis, as the weakness of sterling in the world depression and the entrenchment of world economy in protective and nationalist policies undermined both its domestic and international power.[17] However, from 1945 onwards, and particularly during the 1960s, a combination of circumstances led to a return to the City's economic prosperity and political power. From the outset it must be noted that the City's basic practices remained essentially the same and the changes have by no means eliminated the financial separation of the City and industry. Further, they have been actively pursued by the intervention of British authorities, primarily, the Bank of England and the Treasury.

The City's postwar revival has been largely based upon, on the one hand, the growth of new 'parallel' markets, namely, Eurocurrency parallel money markets, sterling parallel markets and Eurobond parallel markets. Moreover, also the revival of some old markets, as the foreign exchange and London bullion markets, the international section of the London Stock Exchange, Insurance and Baltic Exchange has played an important role. The context is that of the decline of the international role of sterling both as a reserve currency (used primarily by states as an asset in their official reserve) and as a vehicle or transactions currency (used for settlement of international commercial or financial transactions).[18]

The definition of the City as the entrepôt of merchant and commercial practices more than as the locus of 'finance capital', and the one of the City as composed by a series of quite different international financial market places, help understand how it has been possible for the City to prosper in spite of on the one hand, the decline in British industrial performances, and on the other, the decline in sterling's international role.

The parallel money markets are those in which money is lent and borrowed between banks, companies and other organisations without the control of monetary authorities, that is governments and their central banks. It is already a measure of the City's autonomy that such a development could take place. It is generally agreed that the survival (and later revival) of the City as an international financial centre, after the disruptions of the second world war and the chronic weakness of sterling as an international reserve currency, was brought about by the development of the Eurocurrency markets. Eurocurrencies were simply expatriate currencies, that is currency balances held outside the issuing country in foreign banks or in overseas branches of the issuing country's banks and lent out by the banks as short-term credit instruments to any buyer approved by another bank dealing in the market. In essence, these national currencies act, de facto, as universal world money: mobile, anonymous, versatile, and wholesale in the sense that they can only be dealt through the banks. Most important, for them to become 'Euro', or operative outside their country of origin, there needs to be a financial centre which is free to act as *intermediary* in the market for such currencies: the City.

The first, and the most important of Euro-currencies were the Eurodollars which emerged from the imposition in the US of the so-called 'Regulation

Q'. This is a piece of legislation passed in the 1930s as a safety precaution against the repetition of the 1928–29 speculative dealing on the margins. 'The regulation Q' prevented US banks from paying interest on money deposited for less than 30 days, and allowed only very low interests on other short-term deposits from one to three months. As there was a great need in Europe and in other world countries for short-term credit in the after war period and, especially in London, a high price in the market for it, a market for Eurodollars appeared soon after the main currencies became convertible in the late 1950s.

The reasons why Eurodollars markets developed mainly in Britain and in the City have been traced by Susan Strange (1971) in the fact that only British authorities built in a direct market link between the Eurodollars and the local substitutes. This happened by, first, keeping the UK bank rate above the comparable rate offered by other European countries; secondly, by allowing domestic regular consumers of credit to overbid the Treasury for foreign funds and short-term finance; and, finally, by providing an officially supported system by which insurance against exchange rate changes was available at a relatively cheap rate. Thus, the British authorities, by arranging that the difference between the rate at which Eurodollars could be borrowed and the higher rate at which they could be re-lent to local authorities was wide enough to cover the costs of covering sterling forward, drew large amounts of Eurodollars to the City. This, however, clearly implied a peculiar dependency of these activities from the vagaries of an international market over which British authorities had no control and which responded to many external factors among which US trade and monetary policies were particularly important.

Another market nearly comparable to the Eurodollar parallel market, was the dollar Certificate of Deposit market.

On the side of foreign securities, the 1962 Bank of England decision to allow the issue in London of foreign securities denominated in foreign currencies, usually dollars, permitted the growth of the so-called 'Eurobonds' markets. Extremely important in assessing City–industry relations, is the fact that Eurobonds were not meant to be bought by British investors since, although British residents were not actually forbidden to buy them, they could only do so by using investment dollars. For these dollars they had to pay a premium over the normal sterling dollar exchange rate, at first of 10 to 20 per cent, increased by 1968–69 to 40 or 50 per cent. New Eurobond issues rose from $134 million in 1963 to $3,368 million in 1968, and London had the lion's share of the secondary market (see Strange, 1971).

Credit restrictions imposed in the 1960s to reduce the balance of payments deficit and preserve the value of sterling, occurring at a time when both government and private expenditure were increasing, resulted in the growth of sterling parallel markets. They were operated by sterling money brokers in much the same way as the discount houses. The crucial difference is that the loans on the market were unsecured, and the Bank of England did not act as lender of last resort to the brokers as it did to the discount houses in the 'classic' market by extending rediscount facilities.

Among the traditional markets operating in the City of London, the ones which contributed to a greater extent to the revival of the City after the second world war were the Foreign Exchange and London bullion markets.

The London foreign exchange market is closely related to the Eurocurrency markets. It is the institutional arrangement whereby banks, in the main financial centres exchange their respective currencies on behalf of themselves and of their clients. It is wholesale and is based on the banks' reliance on an intermediary for their transactions, namely, the money brokers of the Foreign Exchange and Currency Brokers' Association (FECBA). Apart from speculative trading in currencies, the market is involved in three basic financial activities. First, the banks may act for themselves by buying in one financial centre and selling in another in order to take advantage of different interest rates, the so-called 'arbitrage' practices. Secondly, payments and investments between individuals, companies, etc., are made through the banks and the brokers. Finally, it is the market through which central banks attempt to regulate the exchange rate of their domestic currencies by either buying or selling. After the disruptions of the second world war and the postwar currency restrictions had almost led to the London Foreign Exchange closure in 1939–51, by the late 1970s London had managed to take the largest share of the overall world market for international currency transactions. The daily turnover in foreign currency exchange in London was of $50bn, while in New York it was $40bn, in Frankfurt $10bn and in Tokyo $2bn (see Ingham, 1984). The Conservative government's liberalisation of the financial system during the 1950s and, in particular, full convertibility of sterling held by nonresidents, restored the London market and put it in a position to take advantage of the expansion of transactions brought about by the international monetary instability of the 1970s.

The international monetary disorder also expanded the volume and velocity of transaction on the London bullion market which, with Zurich, handles the largest part of the world's supply in gold.

Another fast-growing section of the London marketplace was the secondary market in existing issues, as distinct from new issues, of foreign enterprises, established in the London Stock Exchange. This allowed, and allows, dealings in a much longer list of companies than any other stock exchange in the world, thanks also to a unique rule which allowed London brokers to deal, on behalf of their clients, in any stock quoted in any other exchange in the world.

Moreover, the City is also considered the home of insurance business which, after increase in losses and drop in profits in the immediate second world war aftermath, registered in the later 1960s an increase in earnings and in profits which was achieved in spite of the declining use of sterling (see Strange, 1971).

Finally, another unique City institution changed its outlook and operation modalities during the 1960s: the Baltic Exchange for the hire of ships and aircrafts. It contributed increasingly to British invisible exports thanks to its growing involvement in aviation, notably the charter business for air-tourists, in the air-freight market in the second-hand aircraft market. As with the prosperity of the City as a whole, also the prosperity of the Baltic Exchange relied critically on the assumption that not only Britain but most other countries adopted free-trade and *laissez-faire* policies (ibid.).

In conclusion, by the 1970s, after a very short period of crisis connected to the change in the international role of sterling and to the development of new financial markets, the City, thanks also to its institutional nexus with the Bank of England and the Treasury, had fully succeeded in re-establishing its leading role in world financial markets and its dominant position in the domestic economic environment.

3   *The City's Dominant Position and the Implementation of Monetarist Practices in the Course of the 1980s*

Turning to the development of the power relations between the City (commercial and wholesale banking capital) and the industry (productive capital and labour), there is widespread agreement among the scholars that the most protracted and open struggle between them in the twentieth century occurred during the 1960s (see Ingham, 1984; see also Overbeek, 1990; Longstreth, 1979).[19] This is precisely the period in which the City was redefining its role both in the world economy and in the domestic economic and political system. However, despite the formation of the CBI in 1965 and the political support of the Labour government, which led to the establishment of the Department of Economic Affairs (responsible for the implementation and management of the National Plan for growth and employment) industry's bid for hegemony failed. According to the literature (see Ingham, 1984), this happened because of the continued structural integrity of the institutional linkage of the City, the Bank of England and the Treasury.

For many authors (see Strange, 1971; Overbeek, 1990), 1967 is the year in which the City succeeded in overcoming its antagonism with the British productive sector. Moreover, the possibility of open struggle between the two sectors decreased with the increase in the number of multinationals, always more interested in their overseas operations and, thus, less concerned than small business with the contraction in domestic industrial base. 1967 is also the year in which the Labour government agreed, with the International Monetary Fund, on a target for controlling one definition of the money supply, called 'domestic credit expansion' as part of the strings attached to the loan provided by the IMF to support sterling.[20] Thus 1967 marks the end of orthodox Keynesianism, which had considered the money supply to be unimportant for a macroeconomic policy designed to stabilise the economy near to full employment. From 1967 onwards Keynesianism gave way piece by piece to monetarism until, by the end of the 1970s, the government subordinated all its policies to one macroeconomic policy alone: control of the money supply. This much is also clear from both Labour and Tory declarations on the eve of the establishment of the ERM.

In turn, monetarist policies represented the City's preferred set of macroeconomic policies, as public declarations by brokers and banks' officials in the debate over the making of the EMS clearly demonstrate. Exchange rate analysts, operating both in banks and in brokers' agencies, expressed their preference for the adoption by the British government 'of tight monetary policies specifying targets for domestic credit expansion and allowing slightly greater latitude in money supply which would reflect, in addition, any gains or losses in the reserves' (City Comment, 'Euro Snake may cure rather than kill', *Daily Telegraph*, 12 October 1978). These policies were considered alternative to entering the ERM early in 1979. More explicitly, brokers L. Messel told the subcommittee of the Commons Expenditure Committee that participation in the ERM would involve the abandonment of Britain's monetary sovereignty and of its own independently chosen monetary targets. This would be a step backwards, as the evolution of monetary policy had been towards responsible financial targets focused on domestic economic objectives. The position of Stockbrokers Sheppards and Chase was similar. They argued in their 1978 gilt market survey that, if the aim was to stabilise successfully European currencies, the primary step required was not exchange intervention, but harmonisation of monetary policy.

These arguments against British entry in the ERM differed to a very large extent from the ones put forward by the other British economic sectors, particularly the CBI and the trade unions, and coincided almost perfectly with the forthcoming Tory government's programme. In order to understand how monetarist policies implemented in the course of the 1980s responded to the needs already perceived by the City in the 1970s, it is appropriate to identify the three basic elements of Thatcher's monetarism. First, the promotion of *laissez-faire*, that is, unhindered competition throughout the economy. Second, deflationary fiscal policies based on high taxes and restriction of government spending. Third, control of the money supply.

As clearly underlined above, *laissez-faire* was the policy of the City. It was both the cause and the result of the way City markets operated after the developments they underwent during the 1960s and its implementation represented the means through which the City's financial markets, particularly the new parallel ones, could continue to prosper in world economy.

Deflationary fiscal policy was the result of an actively articulated City view. Cutting the deficit was part of the monetarist aim of encouraging *laissez-faire* in the general sense that a reduction in state spending would have the visible monetary effect of 'rolling back the state'. In particular, reduction of the deficit was seen as essential for rolling back the state in a specific area: the City and its financial markets (see Coakley and Harris, 1983). High deficits, in fact, had to be financed and if this were achieved by bank lending, it would jeopardise the aim of controlling the money supply. However if it were accomplished by government bonds and other borrowing in a way that did not increase the money supply it would, it was argued, deprive the private sector of finance producing a 'crowding out' effect which, eventually, would push up interest rates and drive the private borrowers out of the financial markets.[21]

The validity of the 'crowding out rationale' for cutting the state's deficit is tenuous, but crowding out provides a justification for monetarism's deflationary fiscal policy which related it to the aim of *laissez-faire*, the aim of increasing the weight of the private sector in the forces of supply and demand within the City's financial markets. Moreover, from this *laissez-faire* perspective both the refusal to enter the EMS and the third element of Mrs Thatcher's monetarism, that is, control of the money supply, had to follow for, if there had to be *laissez-faire* in the financial markets, there could be no fixed target for the exchange rate. Indeed, in a world of capital mobility there is a sort of a trade-off between the stability of exchange rates and the ability to implement autonomous monetary policies, which means setting interest rates and the amount of the monetary aggregates. So, given the predominance of the monetarist paradigm in the British establishment at that time, the only way to control the rise of prices was to adopt strict monetary policies which made it impossible to target the exchange rate and, thus, to join the ERM.

However, the implementation of these policies by the Thatcher government produced some unanticipated consequences. Two of the crucial markets from which state intervention was withdrawn by Mrs Thatcher's government were financial markets at the heart of the City: the foreign exchange markets and the credit markets. This *laissez-faire* practice in the financial markets meant two things. First, banks and other private agents had no controls imposed over what they could or could not buy or sell on those markets. Most significantly, the removal of all remaining exchange controls in 1979 meant that they could buy foreign assets without restriction. Second, the government would not throw its weight on the opposite side of the balance, to offset private sector movements in order to try to preserve the exchange rate or interest rates at a particular, announced level. Thus, the *laissez-faire* aspect of Thatcher's monetarism entailed an element of self-defeat. It actually nullified any attempt to control the money supply and to set interest rates.

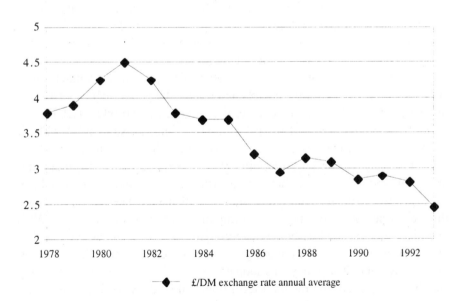

£/DM exchange rate annual average

Graph 13 British £/DM exchange rate annual average 1978–92

Source: *Bank of England Quarterly Bulletins*, 1978–93.

Further, freedom in the financial markets is not the only aspect of *laissez-faire*. The other, the 'rolling back of the state', is the one which produces the most visible effects on the redistribution side and which directly affects employers and workers in the 'real economy' allowing the full force of competition in industry and commerce to operate unimpeded. Mrs Thatcher's government stood out against any kind of public contribution to those firms that suffered from competition, and attempted to ensure that even nationalised industries bowed to the force of competition. Those which were profitable or potentially so were sold to private ownership, while those that suffered from chronic losses were forced to react to them in the manner of private firms, by closures, rationalisations and redundancies linked to productivity improvements. At the same time, the *laissez-faire* policies of monetarist theory undermined trade unions' 'monopoly' power in the labour markets. Wages were to be determined by the demand and supply for labour, without any income policy 'artificially' holding them down and with measures taken to weaken trade unions' ability to push them up artificially. Of course there were contradictions in Conservatives' efforts to promote freedom in financial markets, industry and commerce and the labour markets, nevertheless, *laissez-faire* was the order of the day under Mrs Thatcher's monetarism, and even if competition was not given free rein, its impact was considerable.

Bankruptcy and redundancies in the 'real economy' were increased not only by a monetarist government opening the door to competition, but also by the pursuit of a deflationary fiscal policy. The government's intention to cut its spending, increase its receipts and reduce the public sector borrowing requirement (PSBR) as a percentage of gross domestic product (GDP) was spelled out in the targets of the medium term financial strategy (MTFS) it adopted in 1980. Such a fiscal policy was bound to have a deflationary effect upon the whole economy, reducing the market for firms' products and increasing redundancies. In fact, the government did not manage to hold back state spending to the planned extent since several unanticipated factors affected the outcome, the most notable being the economic crisis itself. With unemployment pushed far beyond anything the government had predicted, it forced an increase in total outgoings on social security, unemployment and related payments. The policy was adopted largely in order to control the money supply, and, indeed, the medium-term financial strategy published its fiscal targets as one element in its targets for the money supply. At the same time, as already explained above, cutting the deficit was part of the monetarist aim of encouraging *laissez-faire*.

The most prominent part of the Conservatives' monetarist strategy was control of the money supply, a brake on the rate at which the amount of money in the hands of British people and enterprises could grow. Here it is pertinent to underline some 'areas of uncertainty', or better, as properly defined by Susan Strange (1986), 'areas of significant ignorance' which appear to be extremely relevant when analysing the City's and Mrs Thatcher's monetarist practice of controlling the money supply. First of all, on two or three extremely important components of international financial flows, namely trade credit from non-banks, very short term credit and financial transfers carried out across frontier within large corporations, there is absolutely no reliable information available. Further, with respect to the Eurodollar market, many scholars (see ibid., p. 125; see also Cecco, 1982) tend to believe that nobody actually knows how much it has added and it is adding to any national money supply.

A second area of uncertainty when referring to the classical monetarist equation $MV = PQ$,[22] and thus, again, to the money supply, is whether it is still appropriate to keep the velocity of money (V) constant (see Strange, 1986) whereas the widespread use of computers networks, private as well as public, by the banks, immensely speeded the transactions velocity of money (that is how quickly money changes hands), as well as affected the more important income velocity (that is how quickly credit is used for purchases).

All this is likely to put any government's policy on the money supply side in the realm of uncertainty, and uncertainty was what undermined the British government's control of the money supply. At first the idea was to restrict 'sterling M3', which included such items as notes and coins, but, predominantly, sterling current (cheque) accounts, deposit accounts and other deposit at banks.[23] By 1982, however, the government had come to consider a broader money supply (or 'liquidity measure'), which also included deposits at building societies as part of the total that had to be restrained.[24] Roughly speaking, control of the money supply meant controlling the domestic stock of spendable resources available to the private sector. The logic of the policy was based on the monetarist's argument which stressed the importance of reducing the rate of inflation of prices and wages and the belief that price increases are caused directly by increases in the money supply. Cutting inflation, rather than cutting unemployment was to be the aim, and holding back the money supply was to be the instrument.

The medium-term financial strategy, which set targets for the state spending and revenue, also set targets for the rate of growth of the money supply, defined, then, as sterling M3 with the aim to decrease the growth range of the money supply by one percentage point per year. In the event, the outcome was that

Table 9   MFTS, 1980 and the outcome

	PSBR		LM3	
	Target	**Actual**	**Target**	**Actual**
1980–81	3.8	5.4	7–11	17.7
1981–82	3.0	3.3	6–10	14.1
1982–83	2.3	3.2	5–9	10.9
1983–84	1.5	3.2	4–8	8.6

Note .

PSBR is given as a per cent of GNP. Targets are those announced in 1980 for the following four years.

Source: Dornbush and Layard, 1987, p. 13.

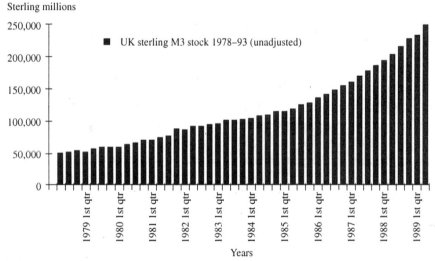

Notes

1   From the fourth quarter of 1981 onwards figures are based on a new broader definition of the monetary sector.
2   The definition of LM3 was changed by March 1984 to exclude deposits of the UK public sector.

Graph 14 British £ M3 stock 1978–89

Source: *Bank of England Quarterly Bulletins*, 1978–89.

the money supply (M3) could not be tightly controlled, even if inflation fell dramatically.

Within the three elements of monetarist strategy, control of the money supply has an ambiguous status and ambiguous unanticipated consequences on the interests of the City. On the one hand it had been associated to *laissez-faire* but on the other hand it is likely to contradict this policy and, indeed, the greatest difficulty of Thatcher's monetarism has been the reconciliation of *laissez-faire*, actively supported by the City, with the control of money supply, which was considered by the Conservative government the only way to reduce inflation. Control of the money supply required the government either to impose direct controls on the banks', and, possibly, other deposit institutions', operations, or to bring its weight to bear on demand and supply in the markets (for credit and foreign exchange) which, again, influenced the position of the banks. The pursuit of the control over the money supply always, therefore, carries the danger that the first of monetarist's three rules could change from 'the promotion of *laissez-faire*' to '*laissez-faire* for all except banks' (see Coakley and Harris, 1983).

Consequently, even if the City supported monetarism, the support of the banks for control of the money supply was always conditional on its being achieved without direct restrictions on their freedom. It had to be achieved without direct control on the banks and with the government operating as indirectly and unobtrusively as possible in the markets that affected them. This distinction between direct and market controls is crucial for monetarists, for they find government influence through market operations more acceptable and more commensurate with *laissez-faire* principles. One type of direct control that had previously been applied to banks was a ceiling on their lending, another was a series of penalties, 'the corset', on expanding their deposits, more properly defined as 'Supplementary Special Deposits Scheme'.[25] In July 1980 the Committee of London Clearing Banks made clear that, if the money supply could normally be controlled only by such means, they would not be in favour of that element of monetarism:

> The banks do not believe that reliance should be placed on direct lending controls other than in the most exceptional circumstances [for] such measures inhibit competition in financial markets and lead to a panoply of distortions ... (see Coakley and Harris, 1983).

Similarly, they felt that it would be undesirable for the government to impose controls or penalties to restrict the growth of the money supply generated by international financial flows for 'it would be liable to inhibit the operation of international financial transactions for which the UK is a major centre' (ibid.).

The City, and in particular the banks, indicated with actions as well as words, that they were committed to monetarism only as long as control of the money supply did not directly interfere with their freedom to generate profits, as the battle of the banks to eliminate the 'corset' clearly demonstrates. This control, which applied over three periods, 1973–75, 1976–77 and 1978–80, imposed, in effect, a tax on banks whose deposits had grown too rapidly and the banks took three steps to circumvent it. One was to build up a surplus of the relevant deposits in anticipation of the corset being imposed, as they did in 1978. Another, defined by Artis and Lewis (1981) as 'cosmetic disintermediation', consisted in making it easier, at a profit, for depositors with surplus funds officially to bypass the banking system by lending money directly, on 'bills of exchange', to the borrowers to whom the banks would otherwise lend depositors' money. Finally, they switched sterling business from the UK to overseas or offshore centres. In 1979 and 1980 the latter two made nonsense of the government's attempts to control the money supply.

Mrs Thatcher's government, given the banks' dislike of direct controls, attempted to use indirect or market methods of control to achieve its money supply objectives introducing changes that, according to Artis and Lewis (1981), signalled a deliberate effort by the authorities to rethink the basis of monetary controls. The removal of exchange rate controls in October 1979,[26] paved the way to the enactment, the same month, of a New Banking Act. After a review of banking activity undertaken by the Bank of England and the Treasury, in March 1980 a consultation paper was published. From this resulted the abolition of the 'corset', or Supplementary Special Deposits Scheme in June 1980, the announcement of the end of the reserve asset ratio in November 1980, and its interim reduction from 12.5 per cent to 10 per cent in January 1981, new operational techniques for open market operations beginning in November 1980, and experimentation with systems of monetary base control foreshadowed in March 1981.

Summing up, it contained a commitment to market forces in the allocation of credit in a context in which banking and financial activities in sterling could be externally produced in Euromarkets free of domestic regulations, and, in particular, free of exchange control regulation which could impede access to these markets. Moreover it implied a shift from the usual definition of money supply in terms of various bank deposits and notes and coin to what Artis and Lewis have defined a 'supply-side approach to control'. This focused on the 'supply side' counterparts of LM3, namely, the PSBR, sales of the public sector debt, reserve flows and bank lending to private sector. In particular (see Artis and Lewis, 1981):

Increase in LM3 = PSBR - gilt sales + increase in bank lending + net external flows - increase in non deposit liabilities.

The attraction of this approach for the Thatcher government was that the PSBR, gilt sales and net external flows could be identified with fiscal policy, debt management and exchange rate policies, respectively. Now, part of the shortfall between the PSBR and gilt sales to insurance companies, pension funds and other non banks, has to be financed by bank loans to the government (while another is financed by people buying National Savings Certificates). Because banks loans to the government increased the money supply, Mrs Thatcher's government and its City supporters determined to control the money supply almost exclusively by means of this counterpart by systematically reducing the PSBR. Accordingly, where state expenditure cuts have been made, they have been justified on the grounds that a reduction in the PSBR was a prerequisite for the control of the money supply.

Eventually, however, the combined effects of supporting benefits payments during the 1980s economic crisis and of increased military spending, led to an overrun of the PSBR targets contained in the MTFS and to the government increasingly relying on non-bank sources (gilt sales, National Savings). All this, (given the fact that the authorities retained and used discretionary control over short term interest rates) implied an increase in the interest rates. This result, in turn, had perverse effects on net external flows since high interest rates tend to attract overseas funds into bank deposits and reserves in the UK, thereby increasing the money supply.

According to the literature, the City's preferences over the level of high interest rates were equivocal (see Coakley and Harris, 1983). On the one hand some banks, the deposit, or 'High Street' banks, profited considerably from high interest rates because they increased their profit on lending. Moreover, high interest rates in the UK may prove a decisive competitive advantage for the financial markets of the City of London. On the other hand, however, it has been noted that high interest rate levels under Mrs Thatcher's regime were accompanied by volatility. Indeed, in accordance with the promotion of *laissez-faire*, demand and supply in the credit markets were increasingly left to their own devices with less smoothing by the Bank of England. For those banks that did not have a large base of current account deposits a sharp and

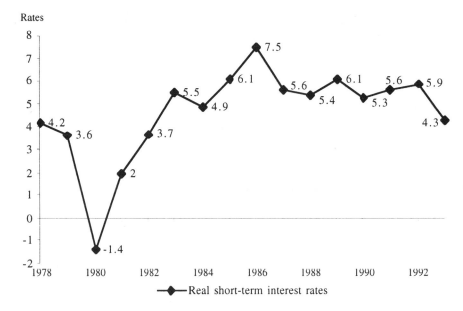

Graph 15 UK real short-term interest rates 1978–93

Source: *OECD Economic Outlook*, June 1955, No. 55.

sudden rise in rates increased their costs. However, given the structure of the British financial system, and particularly the connections between most investment and merchant banks and the big high street banks, it is possible to claim that the City of London would be advantaged by a strong currency-high interest rates policy.

Having clarified how the British government's macroeconomic choices of the late 1970s were related to the interests of British leading socioeconomic sectors, the question to answer at this point is whether there was during the 1980s a shift in the macroeconomic policies preferences of the British interest groups, and, mainly, of the City of London. Indeed, a shift of preferences from targeting the money supply to targeting the exchange rate would justify a change of position of the British government towards the ERM of the EMS. It would explain why, eventually, the British authorities decided to enter the European exchange rate arrangements.

Notes

1 It is interesting to note here that the subcommittee of the all-party Commons Expenditure Committee was told in Brussels that the British government had participated in public discussions of the scheme in Britain far less than any other EEC government had done in their own countries with the result that such discussions as there had been had been restricted to technicalities. See House of Commons, 1980. Moreover, it has already been noted that Callaghan chose a Treasury official, Couzens, to represent him in the secret talks whereas the Treasury opposition to the EMS project was clear from the very beginning of the diplomatic discussions. For a similar interpretation see also Ludlow, 1982, pp. 104/117.

2 It is Healey himself, in his memoirs (1989, p. 439), who points out how the Treasury was 'strongly against the EMS in principle from the beginning' while he was fairly agnostic until he realised how it was likely to work in practice and he turned against it.

3 It is very interesting to note that these conditions, even though they were associated in the last months of 1978 to the establishment of the European Monetary System, still represented the most important political economy goal of the British government three years after the system begun to work while the issue of joining the EMS had completely disappeared from any British government concerns. In fact, in a 'restricted' memorandum of the Secretary of State for Foreign and Commonwealth Affairs to the National Economic Development Council at point 6 it is possible to read: 'The FCO seeks to protect economic interests in the EC. Current aims are: a balanced and equitable Community budget, reform of the Common Agricultural Policy, removal of non-tariff barriers within the Community and fair trading opportunities.' See National Economic Development Council, 1981, points 6 and 22.

4 The same conditions were proposed by Healey in his Green Paper on the EMS at the end of November. See HM Treasury, 1978, p. 3.

5 For a similar interpretation see Zis, 1990, p. 113, and Ludlow, 1982. It is also important to note, regarding this, that among the Labour backbenchers there was a strong opinion that the eight pre-conditions for British entry that the Chancellor of the Exchequer outlined before the general subcommittee of the all-party Commons Expenditure Committee would rule out membership on the target date of 1 January 1979.

6 That Edmund Dell was strongly against the EMS in principle from the beginning is reported by Healey in his memoirs. See Healey, 1989, p. 439.

7 A look at press articles of that period is already enough to prove a similar claim.

8 In Nigel Lawson's memoirs John Nott is reported to have been a regular attender of what was known as 'Margaret's ultra loyalist breakfast group', a weekly economic breakfast meeting with a small number of like-minded conservatives which Margaret Thatcher used to hold in her early government years. See Lawson, 1992, p. 108; see also Emery, 1978.

9 It is important to stress here that, in fact, the first measure taken by the new Tory government was not, of course, to join the ERM but to eliminate exchange rate controls, a measure strongly wanted by the Bank of England and the Treasury and necessary for the City to remain a world class financial centre.

   In his memoirs, Nigel Lawson clearly reports the pressures on the side of Bank of England and Treasury officials to relax and, eventually, eliminate exchange rate controls: '... when we came to office it was very clear that officials, irrespective of their own views, expected us to abolish exchange control ... most of the top people at the Bank of England actively wanted to see it go, with the support of some ... of the official Treasury' (Lawson, 1992, p.

39). He also clearly states the importance that the manoeuvre had for the City: 'Without it the City would have been hard put to remain a world-class financial market' (ibid., p. 41).

10 Another member of 'Margaret's ultra loyalist breakfast group'.

11 A number of economists, including Pepper, Ward, Blackaby, Burns and Budd, submitted papers to the House of Commons Expenditure Committee advising against full and immediate membership on the grounds that this would have implied: the loss of independence in deciding domestic economic policies, the loss of the power to decide the speed of the inflation rate decrease, higher unemployment, higher exchange rate level yielding contractionary pressures, instability due to divergent inflation rates within EEC countries. See Zis, 1990, p. 118 for further details. See also the position adopted by the British Treasury and reported above.

12 In this regard it is interesting to note that only a few years later Walters, Mrs Thatcher's economic advisor, will identify exactly in this mechanism of overvaluation of the currencies of inflationary countries the main flaw of the ERM. See Walters, 1986; see also Walters, 1990.

13 This was exactly what happened in the immediate aftermath of the establishment of the EMS when the currencies of the countries with the lowest inflation rates and the strongest balance of payments, notably Germany and Japan and to some extent even Switzerland, fell, while some of those with the highest inflation rates appreciated. In particular, within the European Monetary System the Deutschmark dropped below its central ECU parity and the lira rose well above it. For further details, see Rose, 1979.

14 Ward had carried out simulations comparing a base run with estimates reflecting an unchanged or an annually adjusted exchange rate.

He assumed a 6 per cent annual rise in world trade, a 4 per cent a year rise in world prices and that the UK earned balance of payments surpluses in each of the years 1979–1981 in order to be able to repay debt at the rate of £1.5bn in 1979 and 1bn in both 1980 and 1981. It was also assumed that a floating rate would have maintained the cost competitiveness of British goods at the same level. On this basis, total output, as measured by GDP, would have been 2.7 per cent lower in 1981 and employment 375,000 lower under fixed exchange rates (EMS) than under a floating regime, even if earnings had only risen by 5 per cent a year.

However, if earnings had increased by 15 per cent a year, there would have been a loss of GDP in 1981 of 8.4 per cent and 1.07m fewer people in employment.

With the exchange rate adjusted each year to restore cost competitiveness to meet 1978 levels, there would still have been a loss of 0.7 per cent to output and 125,000 fewer jobs in 1981 compared with the floating regime on the basis of a 5 per cent rise in earnings.

At a 15 per cent wage inflation, there would have been a 2.2 per cent loss of GDP and 300,000 fewer jobs.

According to Ward the corollary was that fiscal and monetary policy would have needed to be that much tighter under these versions of a monetary system to bring the lower output required to achieve a satisfactory balance of payments.

15 It must be noted that this request was reiterated at a time when the EPC had already decided against any substantial adoption of 'parallel measures'.

16 See Strange, 1971, for further argumentation on the subject.

17 For a thorough account of the interwar developments in British capitalism, see Overbeek, 1990, ch. 3.

18 See Strange, 1971 for further details on the subject.

19 Susan Strange (1971) defines the 1960s as 'a crucial decade of transition in the international use of sterling', in particular, the transition was from the Master Curency role of sterling to the Negotiated Currency role.

20 For a thorough analysis of the credit and monetary controls introduced in the UK during the 1960s and 1970s, see Artis and Lewis, 1981.

21 As pointed out above, this was what had happened in Italy.

22 M = quantity of money, V = velocity of money, P = prices, Q = real income.

23 In the definition of the Bank of England, Sterling M3 comprises notes and coin in circulation with the public, together with all sterling bank deposits (including certificates of deposit) held by UK residents in the private sector. In particular, until March 1984 sterling M3 comprised: Notes and coin in circulation with public + UK private sector sterling sight deposits + UK private sector sterling time deposits + UK public sector sterling deposits; in March 1984 the definition of sterling M3 was changed to exclude the deposits of the UK public sector.

24 Because LM3 appeared to be an unreliable indicator, M1 was added as a monetary target in 1982, as was PSL2, a broad measure of liquid assets including building society shares and Certificates of Deposits (CDs). M1 was replaced by M0, the monetary base, in 1984. This was because M1 included rapid growing shares of interest bearing deposits and M0 had a higher correlation with GNP. In October 1985 the government temporarily abandoned LM3 and made M0 the monetary target. In the 1986 Budget the behaviour of LM3 was validated by specifying a high target range, and a more moderate rate growth was given for M0. See Dornbush and Layard, 1987.

25 For a thorough analysis of the subject see Artis and Lewis, 1981, ch. 6.

26 It is important to note here, that with the establishment of the ERM the use of capital controls to protect domestic monetary policies and the official parity of the exchange rate, in many European countries adhering to the new monetary arrangements, particularly in Italy and in France, not only was recognised and accepted, but even intensified, while in the UK virtually all remaining exchange controls were abolished in October 1979. See Berrel, Pain and Cnossen, 1996.

3 The UK and Entry into the ERM: Domestic Considerations and External Threats

On October 1990 John Major, the successor of Nigel Lawson as Chancellor of the Exchequer in the last Thatcher government, issued the following statement:

> It has become increasingly clear that the government sustained policies of high interest rates and firm budgetary control are now reducing inflationary pressures in the economy. Monetary growth has fallen very sharply to within its target range and the growth of demand has slowed and continues to do so. The rise in oil prices will continue to feed through for some time but the prospect is for a substantial reduction in inflation over the coming year both in absolute terms and in relation to inflation in other European countries. In these circumstances, a reduction in interest rates is now justified; so the Bank of England is announcing that its minimum lending rate on Monday will be 14%, one per cent below the current rate of banks' base rates. A tight monetary policy and a firm exchange rate remain essential to bring inflation down. To reinforce our framework of monetary discipline we have decided that the UK should now join the exchange rate mechanism of the European Monetary System. We have proposed therefore to our European Community partners that, as part of the common procedure, we should join the ERM on Monday morning with a central exchange rate at around DM 2.95, and initially with 6% margins (Major, 1990b).

The announcement of UK decision to join the ERM, though given so little emphasis in the above reported statement, had taken 11-and-a-half years to be pronounced, years in which many had changed their ideas over the ERM issue. Also the positions of British social and economic actors towards UK membership of the Exchange Rate Mechanism had radically changed from those expressed in 1978. Indeed, analysing the declarations of British actors in 1990 there appears to be a substantial consensus in favour of the move.

British industry immediately welcomed with enthusiasm the Chancellor's decision to enter the ERM and to reduce interest rates. The Confederation of British Industry said it was delighted with both moves, which were supposed to help sustain business confidence in a difficult economic climate. It also added that joining the ERM would bring much greater predictability for UK business in quoting for export orders.

Financial markets also reacted enthusiastically to the announcement even if on grounds opposed to those of the industry. Billions of pounds were expected to be attracted into the City's financial markets in the following months as a result of the decision causing sterling to reach quickly the top of its permitted band within the EMS. The combination of high UK interest rates and full entry into the EMS was expected to transform sterling into a 'high yielding Deutschmark', as defined by Steven Bell, chief economist at the UK merchant bank Morgan Grenfell, with the consequent expectation of a strong appreciation of the British currency towards other European ones, particularly the DM. In the stock market, with the FT-SE index about 30 points down before the move, it finished about 70 points up on the day of the announcement. The UK government bond market also rallied, with the longer dated bonds rising by 3 per cent. The main concern of the City markets was that the view of the pound as a high-yielding Deutschmark encouraged speculation in sterling, forcing premature, and ultimately, inflationary, cuts in interest rates to stop the inflows. This justified limits on the prospects for further interest rates cuts. There was also the likelihood that because of the Bank of England's full funding strategy, intervention in the foreign exchange market to depress the pound would bring forward the likely resumption of issue of new Gilts further adding to inflation. Thus it was necessary to ban the adoption of lax monetary or fiscal policies.

The decision to enter the exchange rate mechanism was particularly welcomed in the UK banking industry as a sensible measure which would enhance London's position as a financial centre in Europe. Sir John Quinton, the chairman of Barclays, the largest clearing bank, said: 'Thank goodness. I have been advocating this for five years or more. If we had gone in, then we would not be in our present plight' (see Lascelles, 1990). Christopher Johnson, Chief Economic Adviser of Lloyds Bank, welcomed the ERM in an article published by the Lloyds Bank Economic Bulletin bearing the meaningful title: 'ERM: better late than never', in which he clearly stated: 'It would have been futile to wait for inflation to come down before joining, because ERM membership will help to reduce inflation more effectively than a domestic monetary and fiscal policy' (see Johnson, 1990b). The statement was echoed by most of the City's leading institutions as Lord Alexander of Weedon (1991), chairman of Natwest, pointed out when he claimed: 'One of the benefits which many of us see from our joining the ERM is that it will impose a rigid anti-inflationary discipline.'

The Trade Union Congress also greeted Britain's decision to join the Exchange Rate Mechanism of the European Monetary System, which they had been advocating since 1989. It was considered an historic first step towards full economic and monetary integration within the EC Community even if the TUC sensed that sterling's entry into the exchange rate mechanism of the European Monetary System would have an immediate impact on the tone, and possibly the settlement level, of forthcoming pay negotiations (see Trade Union Congress, 1990d).

Given these changes in the positions of the different economic and social actors, it appears clear that Frieden's model does not help to predict change or to explain why change occurs. The simple reason is that the model is a static one. It does not even contemplate the possibility of a modification in the actors' attitudes and, consequently, it is not able to explain why change occurs. The solution to the problem is to analyse the issue in the broader context of the historically defined power relationships between the different social and economic actors and their repercussion at the political, institutional level.

In the case of the UK, the analysis so far carried out has highlighted the existence of a fracture within British leading socioeconomic capitalist groups between productive capital and financial capital, with a dominance of the latter over the former. The questions which have to be answered now are the following: did the macroeconomic preferences of British groups of interest change during the 1980s? How did they change? Did this change conceal a change in power relationships between the different socioeconomic actors, and in particular, between the City and the industry? What kind of impact did all this have at the political and at the institutional level?

To answer these questions a more detailed study of the evolution of British actors' position towards UK entry in the ERM is required and will be carried out in the next sections.

The CBI: Changing Preferences in the Second Half of the 1980s

The CBI's public conversion to the Exchange Rate mechanism dates back to the beginning of 1985. However, its private lobbying to bring the matter at the political level had already started in December 1984, during the discussion of CBI proposals to the Chancellor for the 1985 Budget.

On 20 February 1985 the CBI's policy-making body voted for the first time by an overwhelming majority to support ERM entry thus reversing the 1983 Council decision that the time was not right for sterling to enter (see House of Commons, Treasury and Civil Service Committee, 1985; see also Arends, 1985). At the heart of the CBI's momentous economic policy shift appeared to be the growing concerns about excessively high interest rates, which, in the words of Sir Terence Beckett, Director General of the CBI, were 'at their highest level since the war'.[1] This was coupled with the need to retain the competitive advantage gained through sterling depreciation which, with or without the government's consensus (and the matter was the subject of heated debates within British political and economic circles[2]) had been going on since 1982[3] and had provoked worrying crises in July 1984 and in the beginning of 1985. Commenting on the CBI's Council decision, Sir James Cleminson, president of the CBI, claimed that the pound had finally reached a suitably competitive level for Britain to participate fully in the EMS. It must be noted that what worried British industry was not the depreciation of the pound, but the decision of the government to avoid, by rising interest rates, the inflationary pressures the depreciation caused. Hence, the CBI, in its traditional annual budget submission strongly recommended British membership of the ERM.

However, Lawson's 1985 Budget not only did not mention the ERM, but also seemed to discard the adoption of a policy of 'benign neglect' towards sterling's depreciation. On the contrary, it committed the Treasury to maintain steadily downward pressures on inflation also by reacting to exchange rate fluctuations with changes in short term interest rates (see Lawson, 1985).

Thus, throughout 1985, the CBI continued to see in British entry the solution to its problem of how to maintain both low exchange rates and low interest rates. Speaking to the House of Commons Select Committee on the Treasury and the Civil Service on November 1985, Kenneth Edwards, the Deputy Director General of the CBI reaffirmed the substantial shift in industry position towards the EMS. Moreover, he clearly stated that the frustration felt by the industrial sector originated not from the volatility of the exchange rate, which, despite its depreciation was still considered overvalued in relation to the DM, but from the decision to raise interest rates to maintain its level (see House of Commons, Treasury and Civil Service Committee, 1985).

By 1986 the government seemed to have abandoned its anti-inflationary pledge contained in the 1985 budget and to have reverted again to an attitude of 'benign neglect' towards sterling depreciation.[4] Between the last working day of 1985 and the same period of 1986 sterling fell from DM3.5 to DM2.85

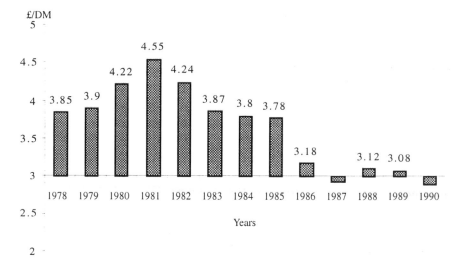

Graph 16 British £/DM exchange rates annual average 1978–90

Source: *Bank of England Quarterly Bulletins*, various issues.

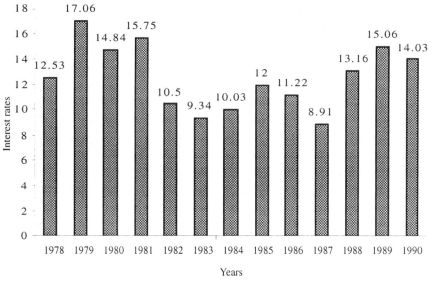

Graph 17 UK short-term interest rates* 1978–90

*   UK 3 months Interbank interest rate, last working day

Source: *Bank of England Quarterly Bulletins*, various issues.

while UK short term interest rates even decreased from 12 per cent at the end of 1985 to 10.9 per cent at the end of 1986 (see Bank of England Quarterly Bulletin, various issues). In these circumstances British industry had no reason to push for entry in the ERM, and indeed in the CBI budget recommendations for 1986 there is not even one word about the ERM issue (see Confederation of British Industry, 1986).

Meanwhile, Nigel Lawson, in his 1986 Budget speech, showed no hesitation in declaring that he would resist any temptation to raise interest rates any further (Lawson, 1986). He even foreshadowed the possibility of decreasing interest rates (ibid.).

It was no wonder that business leaders expressed delight at the Budget. Sir Terence Beckett, Director General of the Confederation of British Industry, underlined that 'the overall shape of the Budget should enable interest rates to be brought down'. Further, an euphoric Institute of Directors welcomed the Budget as one of the 'most innovative and breath taking' and predicted that the Chancellor had regained the confidence of the business world.

The comments of the TUC were much less enthusiastic. The trade unions described the budget 'as a pygmy budget when we are facing giant problems' (Evans, 1986, p. 18).

That the 1986 budget concealed a macroeconomic policy shift in favour of the industrial sector is demonstrated by the fact that the City's independent economists had forecast a negative impact of the budget on growth and inflation. However, Lawson reacted to the City's worries in an even offensive way by saying to the press that: 'Anyone who just feeds data into a model and believes what comes out' declared Lawson 'is an idiot' (see Stephens, 1986).

On the issue of the EMS the Chancellor was much more reluctant to answer the journalists' questions. When asked about the widespread rumour that it was Mrs. Thatcher, and not he, who was still against membership, he limited himself to an aseptic: 'As you know, the government is totally united on everything' (ibid.). Indeed, the official line of the government did not contemplate the possibility for Britain to join the ERM.

The situation was slightly different with regard to the existence, early in 1987, of an exchange rate target vis-à-vis the DM. It is true that the policy of shadowing the DM, and, much less, the existence of a DM/L exchange rate target, was never made official by the Chancellor of the Exchequer. However, it is also true that it was immediately detected by the specialised press and, consequently, by public opinion. Therefore, Thatcher's claim, in her traditional interview with the *Financial Times* on 20 November 1987 (see Owen and Rutherford, 1987; see also Riddell, 1987), that she was completely unaware of the existence of such a policy[5] has not been taken seriously by any commentator (see Stephens, 1996). However, since there was never any announcement of the Treasury's decision to shadow the DM, it is hardly possible to record interest groups or economic actors' reactions towards what was actually a momentous macroeconomic policy shift.

The opportunity to stabilise the pound, after the almost uninterrupted downward trend, was provided by accord of the G5 in Louvre on 22 February 1987 which was designed to keep under control dollar exchange rate, given its unsustainable depreciation against both the DM and the yen. The agreement provided for a more stable framework for setting international exchange rates by establishing a series of loose targets zones for the dollar against the German and the Japanese currencies. It also devised a set of intervention commitments for Central Banks (ibid.). The G5 Paris deal allowed the then Chancellor of the Exchequer Lawson, in his March 1987 Budget speech (Lawson, 1987b), to assume, rather more clearly than usual, that the trade weighted sterling index would not change in the following financial year and allowed financial commentators to speculate on the existence of a £/DM exchange rate target.

Industry reacted enthusiastically to the Budget, arguing that it was responsibly cautious and would help growth without triggering high inflation. This meant for the industry that the budget, by maintaining stable the exchange rate, allowed cuts in interest rates without fuelling inflation.

The City also is reported to have reacted favourably to the Budget. As Michael Hughes, Chief economist of Barclays de Zoote Wedd, put it, 'if you wanted to give an impression of solidity and strength of purposes, than this was it'. Nomura International, the Japanese finance house, said that 'the general shape and tone of the budget is broadly welcome and should provide further strength for equities, gilt edged securities, as well as for the currency' (see Evans, 1987).

The reaction of the Trade Union Congress and of unions generally was much more hostile. 'This was a throwaway Budget, not a give-away Budget', said Norman Willis, TUC General Secretary, 'the TUC wanted the Chancellor to invest in Britain's future. He has chosen instead, the short term easy way out ... the ordinary families of the nation will pay a heavy price for such blatant opportunity' (ibid.).

These reactions were not directly centred on the issue of shadowing the DM for the simple reason that such a move was not even mentioned in the 1987 budget. It is true that the Chancellor's commitment to maintain a stable exchange rate of the pound, 'with the rate against the Deutschmark of particular importance' (see Stephens, 1987b; see also Brittan, 1987b) was eventually expressed openly at the traditional Mansion House speech to the City on 4 November 1987. This commitment was justified on the grounds that 'it gives industry most of what it wants, and provides a firm anchor against inflation'. However, Lawson never explicitly mentioned the existence of a £/DM exchange rate target nor did he set the range of economic policy the Treasury was to adopt to fulfil this commitment which was still inserted in his commitment to the policy of currency stability embodied in the Louvre accord (see Stephens, 1987b).

That industry was particularly interested in exchange rate policy and would welcome an exchange rate target provided that it guaranteed the maintenance of the competitiveness gained with the 1986 devaluation, was not a mystery. The CBI's survey on the impact of monetary policy published in August 1987 (see Confederation of British Industry, 1987a, p. 14) showed that one in 10 of all firms in the early 1980s decided, as a result of the high level of sterling against major currencies in 1980–81, to locate production abroad rather than supply markets from the UK. Almost all were firms with a high concentration of export business. Though the relative strength of the pound proved to be short lived, such investment decisions could not be reversed. Moreover, one in five of all firms replied that the high level of sterling had led them to withdraw from or reduce their commitment to specific export markets. This was true not only for low exporting companies, but also for companies with high rates of exports (seven out of 13 registered export sales exceeding 30 per cent of total sales while one company indicated that its export sales were greater than 60 per cent).

From this survey it seems clear that the high level of sterling during the first term of the Thatcher government had deeply affected British industry. Consistently, business position towards exchange rate policy also changed with regard to the pre-Thatcher period, showing a much greater interest of all industry, or, at least, of all the companies surveyed and, of course, of the CBI, towards exchange rate policy.

However, in 1987 the CBI attached more importance to the maintenance of a low level of sterling and to the pursuance of a low interest rate policy than to stable exchange rates. The first aim had been achieved with the 1986 devaluation of the pound and in 1987 there was a widespread belief in the business community that it could be guaranteed by a policy of exchange rate targeting. Thus, in 1987 the Confederation of British Industry appeared much more interested in asking the Treasury to pursue the second aim. Indeed, John Banham, the CBI's Director General, welcomed the cut of the base rate to 9 per cent on 4 November 1987 as a measure which would reduce costs and improve the ability of British companies to compete overseas. Instead, he did not even mention the ERM issue.

Sterling's exchange rate towards the DM remained around DM 2.95–3.00 until March 1988 (see Stephens, 1996) and during this period the CBI did not campaign in public in favour of ERM entry.

However, when sterling begun to rise again, reaching the level of DM 3.20 at the end of 1988 (see Bank of England Quarterly Bulletin, various issues) the CBI's public reaction to the new policy shift followed almost immediately. In the course of two one-day conferences held by the Confederation of British Industry at Centre Point, London, on Friday 29 April and Thursday 21 July 1988, many CBI officials started pleading again UK membership of the ERM and announcing lobbying both at the European and at the national level.

March 1988 had marked the end of Lawson's attempt to maintain low exchange rates and low interest rates, by shadowing the DM. These were the kind of macroeconomic policies preferred by British industry. Throughout the whole of 1988 both interest rates[6] and exchange rates rose,[7] inflation reached 6 per cent at the end of the year and the current account was heading for a record £15bn annual deficit. As the economic situation worsened, British industry pressures to join the ERM increased and appeared increasingly linked to the new challenges of the 1992 European Single Market.

In *Building on business success: CBI economic priorities for 1989*, published in January 1989 (1989a), the issue of UK membership of the Exchange Rate Mechanism of the EMS was explicitly linked to the competitive challenges arising from the building of the internal market.[8] However, it was later in 1989 that the CBI published its 'manifesto' on the question of European Monetary Integration: *Report European monetary Union: a business perspective* (see Confederation of British Industry, 1989b). This was the outcome of the work of a special working group of the CBI economic and Financial Policy Committee established after the publication in April 1989 of the Delors Committee Report on European Monetary Union. Its terms of reference were to recommend to the CBI Economic and Financial Policy Committee the policy the CBI should adopt towards the Exchange Rate Mechanism of the European Monetary System and greater monetary integration within the European Community, and the response the CBI should give to the Delors Committee Report.

The Report produced by the working group was strongly supported by the CBI National Council and, therefore, is to be considered not only as a statement of the CBI Economic and Financial Policy Committee, but as an 'input from a business perspective (as opposed to a political perspective) into the wider debate of economic and monetary integration within Europe' (ibid., p. 5). The conclusions of the working group, as published in the Report, called for an immediate British entry into the Exchange Rate Mechanism without waiting for the abolition of the exchange controls, the completion of the single market, or the establishment of an appropriate exchange rate. The latter, however, by the time the Report was published had reached precisely the same level of around DM3 per pound which had been so welcomed by the CBI during the 1987–early 1988 attempt to shadow the DM.[9]

Moreover the Report stressed the importance of entering the narrow fluctuation band. This last remark is particularly important in order to understand the internal economic policy aim that the CBI wanted to achieve by joining the ERM. In the second half of the 1980s, thanks also to the arguments made by Walters in his critique to the ERM (see Walters, 1986; see also Walters, 1990), there was a widespread belief in British economic and political circles that full membership of the EMS with inflation rates above the other EC members,[10] associated with high interest rates[11] designed to bring inflation down, would imply upwards pressures on sterling exchange rate. However, in a system of pegged exchange rate as the ERM the British currency was not allowed to exceed a given fluctuation range. Thus, British authorities would be compelled to lower interest rates in order to avoid a realignment, which, incidentally, in the ERM became a matter of intergovernmental decision. Clearly, the narrower the exchange rate bands, the easier it was for interest rates to be lowered. This is why the CBI, in its 1989 policy statement, explicitly supported entry in the (plus or minus 2.25 per cent) fluctuation margins. The possibility that lower interest rates could burst inflation was rejected by the CBI report on the grounds that ERM membership *per se* would mean lower inflation rates, given the credibility it was supposed to add to a government's anti-inflationary commitment.

This economic policy aim was associated with that of fully securing to British industry the benefits stemming from the completion of the 1992 internal market. Moreover, given the developments made by the process of European Monetary Integration, the CBI document of 1989 already revealed the fear of the business community that the UK might lose the opportunity to influence the further development of the EMS by being perceived as a non-participant. The CBI was very critical of a Single European Currency or a permanently fixed exchange rate system as envisaged by the Delors Report. First, a similar arrangement implied the loss of exchange rate flexibility, which in turn, removed the possibility of relying on exchange rate movement to address higher inflation, that is, lower competitiveness. Furthermore, they implied the dismissal of the possibility to alter exchange rates in response to asymmetrical real shocks, like a decline in the world price of oil. If the exchange rate tool was ruled out, the only mechanisms available for adjustment were changes in wages and prices. This meant greater pressures on companies to adjust their costs and prices to ensure competitiveness. Finally, a single currency also implied the implementation of common or, at least, coordinated fiscal and budgetary policies at the European level, a move strongly opposed by the CBI.

The Report concluded that:

> In the short term, the priority for UK business is to become a full member of EMS by joining the ERM. The decision to move further, to European Monetary Union, is largely a political decision (Confederation of British Industry, 1989b, p. 17).

Moreover:

> The transition to a common currency will depend upon success of the regime of fixed exchange rates and must therefore be seen as *an evolutionary process* (ibid.).

As already pointed out, the conclusions of the Report were endorsed by the CBI's National Council and the CBI National Conference (see Confederation of British Industry, 1990b, p. 1). It is thus possible to conclude that in November 1989 that part of the business community represented by the CBI was at least very critical towards the Delors' plan for EMU and favoured a more evolutionary approach.

In the course of 1990 the domestic economic concerns which had urged the CBI to press for UK entry in the ERM seemed to be gradually overwhelmed by the fear of being sidelined in the process of European Monetary Integration and, consequently, of losing the opportunity to reap the full benefits of the Single Market.

The feeling was that events in the European Community were proceeding at a much faster speed than the British business community, and, indeed, the British government, were expecting. Thus CBI position towards the ERM and the EMU (two issues which, by that time, were becoming increasingly difficult, if not impossible, to separate) changed repeatedly.

At the Strasbourg summit in December, the EC member states had reiterated their agreement, reached at the Madrid summit in June, to use the

Delors proposals as a 'useful basis' for further work towards full European economic and monetary union. In particular EC members had agreed that stage one of the move to EMU, as laid down in the Delors report, had to start no later than 1 July 1990. Further, an intergovernmental conference had to be convened to consider the Treaty changes required for the final two stages, including those associated with the establishment of a European system of Central banks.

The implementation of stage one of the Delors' Plan proceeded rapidly. At the beginning of 1990 it was announced that the remaining French and Italian exchange controls were going to be eliminated well in advance of the deadline of 1 July 1990. Furthermore, from 8 January 1990, the Italian government adopted the narrow plus or minus 2.25 per cent exchange rate bands for the lira.

Given these developments, the alternative of an evolutionary approach to European Monetary Union, which had been envisaged by the 1989 CBI document as a possible one, could no longer be considered valid. The proposal of an evolutionary approach to EMU, based on competition between the national European currencies within the European Community in the context of full capital liberalisation, had been disclosed by Nigel Lawson at the meeting of the EC Finance Ministers at Antibes on September 1989. Then it was published by the Treasury in November 1989 as the UK government's official alternative to the Delors' approach to EMU.

On February 1990, the CBI rejected the Treasury's proposals on the following grounds. First, the Treasury maintained that, instead of phasing-in a common currency, the benefits of the improved ERM (with fewer realignments and smaller exchange rates bands) would reduce exchange rate uncertainty and so reduce much of the transaction costs associated with volatile currencies. European markets could then be allowed to adopt whichever currencies they wanted, probably, in time, opting for the currency of the EC members with the soundest economic performance. However, these suggestions provided little guarantee for the CBI that a regime of permanently fixed exchange rates and a credible commonly accepted European currency would actually emerge. Secondly, the Treasury failed to explain how a tenable relationship would be formed between the Central Bank responsible for the chosen European currency and the governments of the other EC members, who would continue to be responsible for their own economic policies. Thirdly, and more important for the CBI at that stage, the exact timing of sterling entry into the ERM remained unclear given the preconditions stated by the Treasury.

However, the CBI was still considering the move towards a commonly accepted European currency as a long term objective, as an extension of exchange rate stability. It attached a number of conditions to any further step towards EMU beyond those already agreed as part of stage one of the Delors' plan. First, a well functioning ERM with sterling in it, was essential before moving on to further stages. Second, EC countries had to enjoy greater stability of exchange rates and greater convergence of inflation rates. Third, the opening up of national markets implied by the 1992 programme and the liberalisation of capital movements had to be further advanced. Finally, the CBI did not accept that binding rules on fiscal policy were implied in the move to monetary union (see Confederation of British Industry, 1990b, p. 2). The CBI concluded that, it was urgent for the UK 'to play its full part in discussions on EMU' to avoid losing the opportunities that the Single European Market would bring for business (ibid., p. 4).

The exact nature of these opportunities for British business generally, and British manufacturers in particular, became clearer with the publication of a report about the linkage between the ERM/EMU issue and the 1992 single market as perceived by industry (CBI/Price Waterhouse, 1990).

The report, based on the responses of 80 manufacturing exporters in the UK, quantified the likely impact on UK manufacturing of future membership of the ERM and outlined the perceived benefits and costs of EMU. The link between ERM membership and the 1992 Single European Market was very clear to manufacturers. According to the Survey results, 59 of the respondents considered that ERM membership would provide at least some benefit to their strategy toward European markets leading up to 1992 with 36 per cent stating that the benefit would be significant. UK membership of the ERM would reinforce attempts by manufacturers to secure market share in the run up to 1992 by increasing total UK manufactured exports by almost 4.5 per cent in the first year of entry and by an average of some 6 per cent for each of the next five years. The issue of stabilising exchange rates was of minor importance. According to the survey results, 88 per cent of the value of exports invoiced in ERM currencies was subject to some form of hedging technique, that is, action taken to limit fluctuations in sterling equivalent value of currency receipts. Regarding the progress to EMU, although UK manufacturers had, at that time, little direct contact with the ECU, the report concluded that its greater use would benefit business. In particular it would make European trade less costly and more straightforward, provided an additional incentive to trading within Europe and increased prospects of lower interest rates. Although ERM entry would provided in itself, some stimulus to use the ECU, the incentives would be enhanced by further progress in achieving EMU. Respondents saw considerable benefits from the use of the ECU as a representative European currency alongside existing fixed European exchange rates and particularly if the ECU were to replace existing currencies.[12]

Thus, in 1990, considerations about the need to gather the full benefits of the 1992 single market appear to weigh at least as domestic economic considerations in the CBI's stance in favour of UK membership of the ERM and of full participation to EMU talks. Certainly, much more than they had done in 1988.

The last development of the CBI position, in view of the intergovernmental conference to be held after 1 July 1990[13] and of the new British proposal for moving beyond stage one of EMU put forward in the Chancellor's speech to the German Industry Forum on 20 June 1990 (see HM Treasury, 1990b), took place in the summer of 1990. In this occasion, the European Monetary Union Working Group was reactivated to consider the implications of these developments on CBI policy on EMU. Its views were strongly endorsed by the CBI Council on 25 July 1990 and were sent to the Chancellor to form the basis of the CBI's input to the intergovernmental policy. Regarding the ERM the CBI stated:

> ... Failure to enter the ERM before the intergovernmental conference would seriously weaken the UK's position in subsequent negotiations on EMU and call into questions its future participation. The CBI is therefore urging immediate UK entry into the ERM within the wider (+/-6%) bands, with a move to narrow (+/-2.25%) bands, once UK inflation begins to show a clear downward trend (Confederation of British Industry, (1990b, p. 2).

This move was necessary in order to 'allow the UK government to indicate to the rest of the EC that it intended to play a full part in discussions on EMU' (ibid.).

It seems clear how, with the renunciation by the CBI to the condition of sterling's entry in the narrower bands of the ERM, the need to play a full role in the establishment of the EMU in view of the 1992 internal market had completely overcome domestic economic policy concern.

A further confirmation that in its stance on the ERM the CBI was driven by concerns over the achievement of the internal market, is that it fully accepted the government's hard ECU approach to the process of monetary integration. According to the CBI, the Chancellor's hard ECU plan was meeting many of the CBI requirements for an evolutionary approach and also had the following advantages. The UK's government proposals recognised the importance of following a path to EMU that was conducive to achieving low inflation and inflation convergence between member countries. In particular the proposals for the new currency were aimed at avoiding inflationary pressures, by preventing its value against existing EC currencies from being reduced and placing additional obligations on EC members to pursue policies to maintain the value of currencies. The proposals set out a realistic basis for developing a widespread use of the ECU as an additional common European currency. The CBI believed that the ultimate transition to a single currency would be smoother if the use of the ECU were encouraged in the process. Although the plan did not guarantee that a single currency would emerge, it provided a useful intermediate step, beyond ERM membership, in an evolutionary process towards EMU.

That the fear of being left out of any further development of European integration in the forthcoming intergovernmental conference, scheduled for December 1990, took precedence over any previously made domestic economic considerations appeared clear also in the first declarations released by the newly elected CBI President (see Corby, 1990a) at the very eve of UK entry in the ERM. 'Whatever the outcome of this December's intergovernmental conference,' he claimed, 'British business must not be sidelined. The worst outcome of all would be where the UK is unable to play its full part in the transition to achieving the single currency' (ibid.).

UK membership in the ERM had acquired, by that time, the broader meaning of sending a strong positive signal to the other European partners of UK commitment to the progress of European monetary integration, particularly in view of the 1992 Single European Market.

Summing up, even if the CBI's conversion to the European exchange rate arrangements dated back to the beginning of 1985 (when it was urged by the need to counteract government's reliance on a high interest rates policy designed to keep down inflation and to react to sterling's devaluation) the shift in Lawson's macroeconomic policy choices from 1986 to March 1988 seemed to meet British Industry preferences and to limit its pressures for UK membership of the ERM. However, with the end of the implementation of macroeconomic policies favourable to the industrial sector, the CBI saw no alternatives to a fully-fledged commitment to British entry in the ERM. Eventually, the domestic policy goals, prominent until the publication of the Delors Report in April 1989, were increasingly overcome by foreign economic policy considerations driven by the growing fear that the UK marginalisation in EMU talks and developments would imply the impossibility to fully reap the benefits of the 1992 internal market programme.

Having outlined the preferences of the industrial capital, and before turning to the financial side, it is worth having a look at the position of the trade unions. The aim is to assess whether there was a coincidence of interests between the industrial employers and employees and whether the preferences of the industrial sector as a whole prevailed over the interests of the City of London.

The TUC: 'Building the Social Dimension of the Internal Market'

For the trade unions 1988 represented the year of a major policy shift in their attitudes towards the European Community. It marked the reversal of their policy of opposition to Britain's membership of the EC[14] and the beginning of a process which would lead the trade unions to endorse UK full entry in the European Monetary System and even to accept further developments in the progress towards European Monetary Union.

The first phase of this process, including the historic visit of the President of the European Commission, Jacques Delors, to the TUC Congress, was to raise awareness of the 1992 issue. However, though the 1988 Congress gave a bold and clear lead on the European Community and 1992, it did not address the issue of UK and the ERM.

The position of the trade unions towards the Internal Market was expressed in the TUC policy statement *Maximising the Benefits, Minimising the Costs: TUC Report on Europe 1992* (see Trade Union Congress, 1988), published in 1988, which followed the extensive discussions on the issue held at the European Trade Union Confederation Congress in Stockholm on May 1988. The General Council and the ETUC had pointed out that the unchecked operation of market forces would increase disparities of income and opportunity between regions and industrial sectors unless it was accompanied by employment creation measures and coordinated policies to encourage balanced social and economic development. The General Council considered that maximum economic advantage from the single market in the long run would be achieved only if social inequalities were reduced. Thus social measures were considered part of the essential quid pro quo in the construction of an economic market. In the conclusions of its 1988 Report, the TUC wanted to ensure that the benefits of the single European Market were shared across all regions. Reform of the EC structural funds had to assist peripheral and less prosperous areas in the south and north of Europe. Finally, a broad European programme of infrastructure investments was considered essential to return to full employment. The TUC and affiliated unions gave urgent priority to the impact of the 1992 programme on Britain's industrial structure. In particular, the TUC was greatly concerned that investment by British companies in people and new products was jeopardised by takeovers based on short-term profit considerations.

Summing up, the TUC's historic acceptance of the European Single Market programme in 1988 was counterbalanced by its concern about 'building the social dimension of the internal market' (Trade Union Congress, 1988, p. 28) and its commitment to making pressures for a 'European Charter of Workers' Rights'.

The approach adopted in *Maximising the Benefits, Minimising the Costs*, the TUC's preliminary Report on Europe, was paralleled by the Labour Party.[15] Unfortunately it rapidly became clear that the government was adopting a narrow and short sighted approach to the Single Market which the TUC had to counter.

By 1989, and particularly after the 15 June European parliamentary election won by the Labour Party, they moved to a new phase of activities on Europe. In the beginning of this second phase, following the call of 1988 Congress, the General Council set up a Committee on European Strategy. An account of the Committee's work, and of the other committees of the General Council is set out in the report *Europe 1992* (see Trade Union Congress, 1989a). The TUC greeted as a big step forward on their way to 'Building the social dimension of the internal market', to which the General Council attached great importance, the publication of both the draft Social Charter in May 1989, (with the support of all governments except the British) and the draft European Company statute.

In the light of these developments, in June the General Council, on the basis of a Report of the Economic Committee, examined the proposals and implications of the Delors Committee Report on Economic and Monetary Union in the European Community. The General Council welcomed the Report as a major landmark in the debate on economic and monetary union and accepted that many of the changes it outlined could work to the benefit of workers in Britain and Europe. However, they did express some reservations about the report. They took the view that full employment was not given sufficient prominence as a macroeconomic objective, and that the achievement of price stability appeared to be the primary concern, the emphasis being on monetary, rather than economic union. Moreover, no reference was made in the report to the importance of economic and political consensus and cooperation in economic policy-making.

The General Council also reiterated the concerns expressed by the ETUC in the Executive Committee's December 1988 Resolution, notably, the inadequate references to collective bargaining and the assumption that there existed a simple and clearly defined relationship between wages and productivity. They were particularly concerned about the Report's assumptions regarding the implications for collective bargaining of convergent inflation rates, particularly since monetary integration in Europe did not necessarily remove cost of leaving differentials in member countries. Finally, concern was expressed about the appropriate role for local, regional and national authorities in economic policy formation and the need for adequate safeguards for full democratic accountability. The control of the European System of Central Banks was considered to be a major issue, given the inherent dangers of establishing an autonomous monetary authority outside the control of member governments. A statement elaborating on these issues was drawn up by the ETUC Economic Committee in June. However, the General Council's main concern remained that progress on monetary union and the evolution of European institutions to regulate the flow of capital should be matched by progress on the social dimension, and that the objectives of a Central European Bank needed to be defined in wider economic and social terms, beyond the management of currencies and exchange rates. More specifically, it was felt that the ramifications for collective bargaining and industrial relations of economic and monetary union needed to be examined in much more detail, while the effects on British industry also required further consideration.

Since the first stage of Economic and Monetary Union required full membership of the Exchange Rate Mechanism (ERM) in July, the General Council considered a further detailed analysis of the arguments for and against Britain's becoming a full member of the EMS, in the light of developments at the Madrid summit held in June. The General Council had previously considered in detail Britain's full entry into the EMS only in October 1978. At that time the TUC's view was that entry into the ERM would mean deflation, which would hit growth and jobs. However, according to the 1989 General Council, since 1978 there had been many changes in both the TUC's policies toward the European Community and Britain's economic position and it was felt that, despite the entrenched position of the UK government, the industrialised world was moving from free exchange rates to a system of flexible control. Thus, the General Council accepted that a return to a system of managed exchange rates would benefit the growth of world trade and increase the scope for international economic cooperation. Moreover, Britain's early entry into the Exchange Rate Mechanism, combined with policies to increase macroeconomic coordination and reduce regional disparities, could actually help avert a possible future recession, caused by speculative pressures on the pound and consequent rises in interest rates. The immediate benefits to Britain would come less from exchange rate stability than from the use of the DM as an anti-inflationary 'anchor' allowing interest rates to be lowered without causing inflationary pressures. The General Council judged that, on balance, there were certainly more long-term advantages to being in the ERM than outside, although there were clearly risks as well as benefits. Entry would need to be accompanied by an equal degree of commitment to economic policy cooperation as well as monetary cooperation between the EC governments, including a strong European regional policy. Finally, the General Council recognised that, although further discussion on Britain's entry into the exchange rate mechanism were essential, they would support early entry at an exchange rate below DM3.00.

TUC discussions of further aspects of European Monetary Union continued throughout the 1989/90 Congress year with a further, detailed consideration of the Europe-wide implications of the Delors Report taking place at an ETUC seminar held in February 1990. The seminar was attended by 70 people from affiliated organisations and from European industry committees and discussed a range of issues around the work of the Delors Committee with a view to guiding the work of the ETUC Executive Committee. In April, the ETUC Executive Committee discussed the outcome of the seminar and agreed a wide-ranging statement which recognised potential advantages of EMU so long as a number of considerations were taken into account. They said that:

> ... the fundamental objectives of EMU should be to promote sustainable development, full employment and social cohesion as well as price stability;
> EC structural funds should be further strengthened to counteract the uneven effect of EMU on particular sectors and regions;
> the social partners should be involved in drawing up policies and follow up procedures;
> the central bank (Eurofed) should be democratically accountable;
> the implications of EMU for collective bargaining on the EC social dimension should be studied;
> all EC countries should fully join the European Monetary System as soon as possible (see Trade Union Congress, 1990c).

Regarding domestic economic policy considerations, the TUC Budget submission of January 1990 (see Trade Union Congress, 1990a) was drawn up with a clear focus on measures which could influence the economy in the year ahead, and which provided a credible alternative to the high interest rates policy. The statement warned that the interest rate weapon was more powerful than in the past because of the high level of debt, but also that its impact was highly uncertain. It was more likely to hit investment before the government's main target of consumer spending and credit. The submission, therefore, called for Britain's early entry into the Exchange Rate Mechanism at a competitive exchange rate to allow an early cut in interest rates together with additional tax incentives for industrial investment.

The 1990 Budget submission was presented to the new Chancellor, John Major, at the January meeting of the NED Council. The Chancellor repeated his belief that the problems of the economy were temporary, and high interest rates were working. He seemed to blame his predecessor for errors in economic policy. There was, however, agreement between the CBI and the TUC submissions on the dangers of recession; the need for entry into the ERM so as to cut interest rates, and extra incentives for industry (see Trade Union Congress, 1990c, pp. 182–3).

The blame on the government's reliance on a high interest rate policy as the main cause of Britain's fundamental economic problems, particularly, inflationary pressures and trade unbalances on manufactured goods. The impact on consumer spending, and, thus, on inflation, of the pursuance of similar policies was mixed. Interest rates might have a devastating impact on some household incomes, but for savers, especially those in higher income brackets, they might actually increase spending power thus vanishing their counter-inflationary purposes and accentuating income distribution inequity. Moreover, since industrial investment was starting to fall, it might be too late for many companies before high interest rates reduced private consumption to levels which would satisfy the chancellor. What had happened in the UK, according to the TUC analysis, was that with the high level of consumer spending, investment, whether financed domestically or by foreigners, had not been able to grow sufficiently to overcome supply constraints causing inflation and trade deficit. The 1988 'give-away' budget and the complete liberalisation of domestic capital markets had both contributed to the increased spending power available to consumers. A new approach in the 1990s had to reflect changed circumstances, above all the influence of European developments.

By August 1990 that meant for the TUC that Britain had to enter the ERM at a competitive exchange rate as soon as possible. By August 1990 it was also clear what the TUC meant by 'competitive exchange rate'. Entry well over DM 3, favoured by those commentators, mainly in the City, who endorsed membership as a counter-inflationary move, was rejected for the disastrous impact it would have on British industry. To those who argued that Britain had to enter at the lowest exchange rate possible, perhaps as low as 2.35 DM, because this would be sustainable in the longer run, the TUC answered that this move could prove inflationary, partly because imports would cost more, but mainly because consumer credit would again start to grow too quickly. Thus, the TUC favoured a middle option, taking Britain in at an exchange rate close to DM2.70 to the pound and within the broad band, which allowed the pound to move up or down by 6 per cent. This would give a maximum range between the lower limit of about DM2.50 and an upper limit of about DM2.90 to the pound and would allow a cut in interest rates, using the much stronger mechanisms available within the ERM to defend the pound against speculative attack. Finally, this would help to stimulate growth and investment and retain industry's competitive position.

This position was not so far from the one that the CBI had adopted by the summer of 1990. The idea that Britain should not be sidelined in the discussions about European Monetary Integration was also a common ground between British social partners.

However, the TUC did not share the CBI's favourable position towards the Chancellor's proposals for the Intergovernmental Conference on EMU to be held on December. On the contrary, the TUC believed the intergovernmental conference on economic and monetary union should focus not on detailed aspects of monetary union, including the debate surrounding the 'hard ECU' or 'basket ECU' in stage II of the Delors Report. Indeed, the first aim had to be the creation of a European industrial relation system. It had to be clear that a central objective of economic union was to secure the highest level of employment through economic cooperation on growth and employment objectives. Further provisions might include a commitment to establish new interventionist funds to deal with economic 'shocks', and agree expanded and strengthened EC regional policy. All new community institutions had to be democratically accountable, and in the case of a Eurofed, ensure liaison between economic and financial advisors.

The majority of these proposals were not only ignored, but even opposed by the CBI, and this was particularly true for everything to do with the development of any budgetary or social policy at the European level.

It is not possible, thus, to conjecture any convergence of positions, or, much less, any kind of alliance, between the two sides of industry, even if both agreed on a negative assessment of the government's high interest rate policy, and both urged early UK entry in the ERM.

This position was certainly a major shift in the TUC policy towards the

European Community and the process of European Monetary Integration. This shift, however, appeared to have been driven not so much by discontent with the Conservative government's economic policies, as was the case with the CBI. The TUC had never supported the government's macroeconomic stances anyway, not even during Lawson's Chancellorship.[16] Instead, this shift was grounded on the growing belief that by shifting the balance of political and economic power from the national to the European level, the TUC's concerns over the parlous and, indeed, worsening situation of the British welfare state,[17] as well as over its growing inability to influence the management of the British economic, political and social life (after the strokes that the Thatcher administration had regularly delivered to its already decreasing power[18]), could find an answer in Delors' bid for a social, if not socialist, European Community.[19] This belief had strengthened between 1988 and 1990 thanks to what the TUC perceived as the many steps forward that the Delors Presidency was taking in 'building the social dimension of the internal market'. These included: the agreement in the Commission to the draft European Company Statute including workers' rights; the adoption, in December 1989, by the Council of Ministers, of the Social Charter by 11 votes to one (the one being the British government) or the adoption by the Commission of the Social Action Programme; and the programme to translate the Charter into practice. Very important in convincing the trade unions to change their stances towards Europe was also the political success of the Labour Party at the European level. The parliamentary European election of 15 June 1989, turned the tables on the Tories in the European Parliament (32 seats to 45 became 45 seats to 32) making the British Labour group the largest national group in the European Parliament, and the Socialist group the largest European group. All this was at the root of the TUC acceptance of the Internal Market programme and of its endorsement of UK early entry in the ERM.

Concluding, since the political power of trade unions in Britain had reached its lowest level for many years in the course of the 1980s, the explanation of the British government's decision to enter the ERM has to be found in the evolution of the relations between the two factions of British capital, the productive and the financial one. Indeed, they still represented the dominant coalition in the political as well as economic organisation of British society. It is thus necessary to analyse the evolution of the City's macroeconomic preferences in the debate about the ERM taking place in the second half of the 1980s, to trace back the origins of the British government's change of attitude towards the EMS.

The City in the Second Half of the 1980s

1 The Chancellor's Abandonment of Monetarist Practices in the Second Half of the 1980s and the City's Reactions

The considerable success of Mrs Thatcher's first administration in bringing inflation down below 5 per cent had been sustained and greeted by the financial sector. However, the policies adopted by the beginning of the second Conservative term, and, particularly, from 1986 onwards, seemed to abandon the rigid monetarist path which had marked their implementation in the early 1980s, and showed greater attention to the necessities of the productive sector. This, of course, raised growing concerns on the credibility of the British government's anti-inflationary stance within the financial community, but these concerns were unanimously voiced, taking the shape of true discontent, only after 1988.

In this section, the economic developments and the conduct of monetary, fiscal, and exchange rate policies since 1984 will be analysed, explaining why the UK government progressively abandoned its monetarist path and why this change was strongly and unanimously denounced by the financial community only from 1988/89 onwards.

The first budget of the new Chancellor of the Exchequer, Nigel Lawson, seemed to confirm the previous term's firm counter-inflationary policy (see Lawson, 1984a, p. 16). In the 1984 Red Book (Financial Statement and Budget Report), the Treasury published its 'illustrative projections' for the path of inflation and growth.

Table 10 1984 middle-term financial strategy projections

	Money GDP	% change GDP	Inflation
1984/85	7.9	3	4.8
1985/86	6.7	2.25	4.4
1986/87	6	2	3.9
1987/88	5.7	2	3.6
1988/89	5.1	2	3

Source: Budd, 1989.

The MTFS showed levels for money GDP (GDP at current market prices) and provided general comments about the assumed path for real growth and inflation. The Treasury stated that policy would respond, as necessary, to changing economic conditions, 'But whatever the response to short term fluctuations, the trend will be maintained, bringing with it continued progress to lower inflation' (see Lawson, 1984b, p. 21).

In the event the path was considerably different. Three per cent inflation was achieved by 1986/87, but only with the help of the fall in oil prices while the rate accelerated after that and exceeded 7 per cent in 1988/89.

Table 11 UK macroeconomic variables real development, 1984–89

	Money GDP	% change GDP	Inflation
1984/85	7	2.25	4.5
1985/86	9.5	3.5	6
1986/87	6	3	3
1987/88	10	4.5	5
1988/89	11	3.5	7.25

Source: Budd, 1989.

Moreover, apart from 1984, when the output was affected by the miners' strike, the growth of the economy exceeded the original assumptions. By 1988/89 GDP was 6 per cent higher than assumed in the 1984 MTFS. It seemed that the government was prepared to risk higher inflation in pursuit of faster economic growth. However, the government had never admitted that its ambitions with regard to inflation had changed, and it was difficult to tell whether it had changed its priorities or had made policy errors failing to understand what was happening.

A further sign of detachment from the previous targets came from the path of growth of monetary aggregates. In the 1984 Red Book, the section on the MTFS provided target ranges for Narrow money (M0) and Broad money (£M3). The figures given for 1984/85 were described as 'targets' while the figures for the later years were described as 'illustrative ranges'. In the event, although the growth of M0 was kept within its 1984 target ranges for most of the following four years (even if it was well outside the original range during 1988/89) broad money was kept within its target range only during 1984/85. Thereafter it exceeded the 'illustrative ranges' of later years with a marked acceleration of the growth of broad money during 1986, the year of sterling's devaluation.

Tracing the government's attitude to monetary policy year by year, the 1985 version of the MTFS presented the same ranges for monetary growth as in 1984 and the Red Book said that equal weight would be given to the performance of broad and narrow money. However, the 1986 Red Book showed that £M3 had grown twice as rapidly as planned. Thus, a more generous target was set for 1986/87 and no ranges were given for later years.

In the autumn of 1986, the government abandoned broad monetary targets altogether and the growth of £M3 during 1986/87 was about 20 per cent compared with the target range of 11–15 per cent (see Lawson, 1986, p. 16). This action was defended in the 1987 Red book by reference to high real interest rates, the end of over-funding,[20] and the growth of competition in financial markets which had led to rapid growth of private sector liquidity and borrowing. It was anticipated that broad money would continue to grow well in excess of the growth rates of money GDP. The Red Book argued that M0 bore a more stable relationship to money GDP, with a steadily increasing velocity of circulation.

This meant the definitive abandonment of the monetarist strategy pursued throughout the first Thatcher government and reiterated in the 1984 budget. However, while targets for £M3 had been abandoned, the Treasury pretended to be maintaining its strategy of controlling money GDP, and hence inflation, by controlling M0 whose range was set between 2 and 6 per cent (see Lawson, 1986, p. 18). The actual growth of M0 during 1987/88 was within the target range, at about 5 per cent. In the 1988 budget, the target for the growth of M0 in 1988/89 was set at 1–5 per cent as anticipated in the 1987 MTFS.

Summing up, the last five years of the 1980s saw a switch of emphasis away from broad money towards narrow money as the main indicator of monetary conditions. Targets for £M3 were exceeded, even after the limits had been raised, and then abandoned in the autumn of 1986. However, the growth of M0 was kept within its target ranges until 1988. Finally, the growth of PSBR, the third pillar of the first Thatcher government's monetarist strategy, could not be blamed for adding to money creation since, though in 1984/85 the PBSR was larger than planned, because of the miners' strike, in the following years it was far smaller than envisaged in the 1984 MTFS (see Budd, 1989b).

Regarding exchange rate policy, the new Chancellor of the Exchequer, Lawson, seemed to have favoured the depreciation of sterling going on from 1982 until the beginning of 1988. Indeed, this trend was not sufficiently counteracted by an adequate policy of interest rate increases, particularly in

Table 12 UK public sector borrowing, 1984–90

	£ bn		% of GDP	
	1984 MTFS	Actual	1984 MTFS	Actual
1984/85	7	10.1	2.75	3.1
1985/86	7	5.8	2	1.6
1986/87	7	3.4	2	0.9
1987/88	7	-3.5	1.75	-0.75
1989/90	7	-14.3	1.75	-3

Source: Budd, 1989.

the period between the 1986 and the 1988 budget. This added to the suspicion that the government was giving priority to supporting growth of GDP instead of pursuing anti-inflationary policies. The policy of shadowing the DM was interpreted by both the financial community and the productive sector, more as a means to maintain British industry competitiveness than as an anti-inflationary tool.[21]

Despite these major shifts in the conduct of macroeconomic policy by the Conservative government, there did not appear to be an overt, strong opposition to the Chancellor's decisions until the beginning of 1988.

Obviously, the City of London had applauded the first Lawson Budget of 1984 which, in the words of the opposition leader, Neil Kinnock, '... does much more for the City of London than it does for the country of Britain' (see Owen, 1984, p. 18).

City brokers were generally enthusiastic about the budget and according to brokers Simon and Coates Lawson had revealed some magic talents (see Pauley, 1984). In the meantime, the stock market got carried away in a wave of euphoria (see Stephens, 1984). The good news for the City operators and markets were fairly clear: a public sector borrowing requirement of £7.25bn in 1984–85, and the City was fairly confident that the government could hit it, and Lawson's determination to stick to his targets for lower inflation (ibid.).

The mood of the City had undoubtedly changed by the following year's budget. Many critics in the City voiced concerns about the Chancellor's anti-inflationary credibility and suspected that Lawson was covertly relaxing his policies. At the turn of the year the City had feared that the Treasury would lower interest rates, allow sterling to depreciate further and countenance a large borrowing overshoot not worrying too much about the effects on inflation (see Wilkinson, 1985). However, Lawson's highly publicised tightening of policy in mid January (with a 4.5 percentage point rise in interest rates), his 1985 budget commitment to firm anti-inflationary policies, and particularly, his pledge to resist any sharp fall in sterling's value by keeping interest rates at whatever level was necessary to maintain downward pressure on inflation,[22] succeeded in reassuring the City for the time being. Even the very large overshoot, by about £3bn, of his £7.3bn borrowing target for the financial year 1984–85, was generally accepted as the result of the miner's strike (see Wilkinson, 1985; see also Budd, 1989b).

That the City of London was still attaching a great importance to the monetarist practices of targeting the money supply, which were still considered alternative to exchange rate targeting or joining the ERM, is clear from reading the memoranda submitted by some City representatives to the Treasury and Civil Service Subcommittee inquiry on the EMS in mid-1985. Asked about their opinion on British full membership of the EMS, Dr. Brendan Brown of Phillips and Drew answered on 13 May 1985: 'I do not favour British full membership of the EMS. My views have not changed on this' (see House of Commons, Treasury and Civil Service Committee, 1985, p. 48). Moreover, he supported his rejection of the ERM by underlining how this had to be considered alternative to any autonomous monetary policy. Similarly, in pointing out that: 'The UK is quite clearly the least appropriate member of the EMS' (ibid., p. 54), Tim Congdom, for Messel & Co., claimed that:

> The main benefits of the EMS for its existing membership seem to have been twofold: Fluctuations in real exchange rates may have been lower than would otherwise have been the case. ... The need to watch their exchange rate with the DM may have caused macroeconomic policy in France, Italy and some of the smaller countries to be more responsible. ... The first of these benefits is not easy to quantify; the second is of no relevance to the UK at present since it has its own domestically-imposed financial guidelines (that is, the money supply and the PSBR targets in the medium term financial strategy) (ibid., p. 55).

In the light of these positions it appears clear why the City greeted with relief Lawson's 1985 budget. It is much more difficult to explain why the 1986 budget did not provoke major concerns in the City of London. After all, it marked the abandonment of the policy to target broad money for counter-inflationary purposes and confirmed the Chancellor's decision to stick to his policy of benign neglect of sterling's depreciation by resisting any temptation to raise interest rates,[23] and, even disclosing the possibility to decrease them.

Even if some City economists voiced concerns about the over-optimistic forecasts for growth and inflation included in the Chancellor's budget (see

Stephens, 1986), the City is even reported to have reacted warmly to the 1986 budget (see Stephens and Cassel, 1986). This appears to be even more puzzling if it is taken into consideration that from 1988/89 onwards, the 1986 budget was widely blamed in the City as the starting point of those loose monetary and exchange rate policies. These policies had caused British inflation to upsurge and the British government's credibility to diminish to the extent that entering the ERM was increasingly considered the only possible anti-inflationary move (see Budd, 1989b and 1989a; Johnson, 1990b; Lord Alexander of Weedon, 1991; Johnson, 1990a; *The Banker*, June 1989).

Also the 1987 Budget, with its implicit commitment to a policy of exchange rate targeting and its complete abandonment of £M3 targets, was cautiously welcomed by the British banking and financial sectors as a solid and Conservative one.[24] 'There was no call for anything other than the masterly inactivity which the Chancellor offered', said economists at Goldman Sachs, the US securities house (see Bush, 1987) and Christopher Johnson, the economic adviser to the Lloyds Bank, greeted it as being 'short and simple enough' without any comment about the major exchange rate and monetary policy changes it contained (see Taylor, 1987).

That this mild reaction to expansionary budgets was a deliberate political choice of the City of London appears clear from the fact that two years later their retrospect judgement of the 1986–87 economic policy decisions was to be reversed completely. Moreover, already in 1987 many independent economists were voicing their concerns about the inflationary consequences of the Budget. Independent economists at Alexander, Laing & Cruickshank, for example, considered the Budget not prudent at all and, actually, 'one of the most feckless and over expansionary budgets for some considerable time' (see Bush, 1987). They argued that the tax cuts coupled with the higher spending announced in the autumn represented a sizeable stimulus to the economy which was in serious danger of overheating. They warned against further deterioration in the current account, higher inflation and pressure on sterling, but nevertheless conceded that Lawson could have taken far greater risks (ibid.).

The question to answer at this point is why the City of London did not react strongly and, indeed, appeared even to support Lawson's gradual shift from the counter-inflationary stances of the previous Thatcher government, to the measures favouring British industrial sector's bid for lower interest and exchange rates. Is it possible to hypothesise a shift in the balance of power between the productive and the financial capital to explain the change in British macroeconomic policies?

The answer to both questions is to be found in the major changes the City market structures and institutions were undergoing precisely in the period between 1986 and 1988 and which, without doubt, absorbed many of the City operators energies and interests.[25]

2   The 1986–87 City Revolution

The first official piece of regulation relating to the organisation of the City was produced only in 1976 and was urged by the EC member states as pressure on the British government to start harmonising the organisation of its financial and banking system with the organic legislation of the other European countries.[26] Thus, the August 1976 White Paper attributed to the Bank of England the formal faculty of authorising the activity of deposit-taking institutions and divided them into two major groups: *recognised banks* and *licensed deposit-taking institutions*. While for the second group some strict licensing and controlling requirements were provided, the first group of institutions, including the whole traditional banking system, clearing banks, merchant banks and discount houses, was still characterised by the privileging of informal prudential supervision criteria.[27]

The publication of the White Paper gave to the City of London the legitimisation to participate, and deeply influence, the content of the forthcoming first EEC directive on the coordination of laws, regulations and administrative provisions relating to the banking activity. This required a prior authorisation system for credit institutions to be set up by December 1979. It was Robin Hutton, a City merchant banker, who succeeded in convincing the other member states in Brussels to abandon the project of adopting a communitarian banking law. He also succeeded in including in the EC banking directive the City's definition of 'supervision': it had to be limited to prudential regulation and not influence banking management through the implementation of norms (see Cianferotti, 1993). Thus, despite British membership of the European Community, what had been recognised by Lord O'Brien, then Governor of the Bank of England, in 1973 as the major competitive advantage of the City of London over the other financial centres, notably, its '... freedom from vexations of banking legislation equalled in few countries in the world' (O'Brien, 1973, p. 123), could, to a very large extent, be maintained.

In fact, the first Banking Act, receiving the Royal Assent on 4 April 1979, although attributing to the Bank of England various powers, usually formal ones relating to the releasing of licenses and recognition, did not provide for the explicit imposition of any duties or responsibilities with regard to supervision especially of the recognised banks (see Ryder, 1979, Introduction). Again, as in the 1976 White Paper, it privileged the centrality of the system of informal supervision with wide discretionary powers on the side of the Bank of England to decide which institutions could obtain the recognition as banks (see Bank of England, 1982, p. 34). It was a system which privileged once again the importance of the 'personal factor' as the decisive variable in defining Bank supervision and confirmed the traditional division between the *gentlemen* and *the others*. Thus, it is no surprise that in 1983, four years after the issue of the Banking Act, the *Economist* (1983, p. 69) could claim: 'London's Banks, theoretically governed by the 1979 Banking Act, in practice know no masters but the Bank of England and their own clubs.'

The unrestrained deregulation of the financial markets undertaken in the course of the first Thatcher government, however, increased not just individual salaries, but also the risks connected to the banking and financial practices of the City of London. The situation became worrying when one of the prominent City bullion dealers,[28] Johnson Matthey, became involved in the financial collapse of one of its smaller parent companies, the recognised bank Johnson Matthey Bankers (JMB), on 1 October 1984.[29] As the then Governor of the Bank of England put it,

> We felt it was vital to prevent any contagious spread to other members of a central and traditional London market, any failure within which could have quickly sent serious shock waves through the UK banking system (see Leigh Pemberton, 1984, p. 473).

Since this statement was clearly reflecting the concerns of the most important City representatives, in the event it was decided to solve the problem within the City itself: 'The rescue operation was a characteristic of the City of London' (ibid.). Thus, the Bank of England, with the consensus of the City's major bankers, decided to buy the JMB at the symbolic price of £1 and in a few months the Central Bank was able to establish, with the decisive but reluctant participation of the major City Banks, a Guarantee Fund of £150m.

Even if, eventually, it had no major consequences, the JMB crisis did point out how the lack of prudential supervision by the Bank of England could have worrying spill-overs also on the City institutions' activity and returned to the government's agenda the reform of the 1979 Banking Act:[30]

> The Johnson Matthey affair doubtless has lessons for the Bank of England too, illustrating as it does the challenge for devising a supervisory regime which achieves regulation without strangulation. I can assure you that we shall be

working on these lessons very seriously (Leigh Pemberton, 1984, p. 473).

Thus, on 17 December 1984, Nigel Lawson, the Chancellor of the Exchequer, who in his memoirs claims to have been very critical towards the Bank of England rescue of the JMB (Lawson, 1992, p. 404), made a statement to Parliament announcing the set up of a Committee to look into the UK system of Bank supervision and make recommendations. This Committee, however, was to be chaired by the Governor of the Bank of England, Leigh Pemberton, and composed, among others, leading representatives of the City, such as the distinguished commercial banker Deryk Vander Weyer, a former Deputy Chairman of Barclays Bank and an outstanding commercial banker of his generation (ibid., p. 405). The Report of the Leigh Pemberton Committee, published in June 1985, proposed the unification of the supervision procedures of the licensed institutions and the recognised banks and a more detailed filling up of the *returns* provided for by the authorised institutes. However, it considered the possibility of an explicit request by the Bank of England for information on the management of the single banks only in cases of need (See *Report of the Committee set up to consider the System of Banking Supervision*, 1985). Overall, the Report seemed to suffer from the impossibility to solve the inconsistency between two goals. On the one hand, the need to avoid worrying situations of instability as the one experienced with the JMB crisis by providing a system of consolidated supervision. On the other hand, the need to maintain the momentum of the City's financial boom triggered by the unrestrained liberalisation of financial and banking activities.

The City of London was, indeed, enjoying, by the mid-1980s, a moment of great prosperity, sustained by the government's implementation of high interest rate policies (see Johnson, 1989d). Financial and business services, overlapping if not identical with the overseas earnings of the City of London, increased from 1.9 per cent of GDP in 1980 to 2.8 per cent in 1986 and 1987 while the invisibles[31] balance rose from 0.7 per cent of GDP in 1980 to 2.9 per cent in 1986 when it peaked as in the mid 1970s (see Johnson, 1990a).

However, as indicated by the *Financial Times* (19 December 1985, p. 18), 'rising levels of profits have made it possible to escape the consequences of imprudent or fraudulent behaviour. History shows that this is the kind of climate in which standards of business practices can easily deteriorate.' Thus, the Leigh Pemberton Committee Report became in December 1985 a White Paper which allowed for the traditional involvement in the discussion of all the parties concerned, before the presentation to the House of Commons of a specific draft law.

The bargaining between the City, the government and the opposition party about the reform of the 1979 banking act went on from the beginning of 1986 until the end of 1987. The major issues at stake were two. The first was regulation of relationships between the supervisors, the auditors and the management of banks. The solution of this problem, in the event, was left to the discretionary judgement of the Bank of England. The second issue was the establishment of an external Board of Banking Supervision to assist the Governor in the exercise of his supervisory powers. Eventually, its configuration was that of an *advisory* and not of an *executive* body as demanded by the opposition.

It is true that the Banking Act 1987, in force from 1 October 1987, increased the supervisory powers of the government and of the Bank of England, according to the necessities of the new deregulated financial markets. However, it ultimately confirmed the traditional flexibility of the British supervisory regulation privileging the discretionary powers of the Bank of England in its implementation. Indeed, the Banking Act 1987 maintained the fundamental provisions of the 1979 Act. It required the issue of an authorisation to exercise the banking activity which was subjected to the acceptance of deposits in the United Kingdom and which could be withdrawn if one of the minimum criteria (see Bank of England, 1988, Sch. 3) provided by the law was not fulfilled. A major change was the elimination of the distinction between the recognised and licensed institutions. This, however had proved useless to cope with major financial crises, which usually tended to involve both categories of credit institutions. Generally, the Bill did not purport to regulate every aspect of prudential supervision, and the mechanics of continuing supervision were deliberately left to the implementation of the Bank of England without recourse to detailed statutory provisions (see Lewis, 1987, p. 51). Indeed, it was up to the Bank of England to decide if the owners and the managers of an authorised institution were 'fit and proper persons' (see Bank of England, 1988, Sch. 3, para. 1), or if the management of the Institution was carried out 'with integrity and the professional skills appropriate to the nature and the scale of the activities of the institution concerned' (ibid., para. 5), or if banking activity was exercised with a 'general prudent conduct' (ibid., para. 4(9)) with adequate capital (ibid., para. 4(2) and 4(3)) and liquidity (ibid., para. 4(4) and 4(5)). The traditional British legislator tendency to regulate only the conditions of entry and exit from the banking activity, and leave to the discretionary and informal action of the Bank of England the implementation of prudential supervision, far from being reversed, was, instead, substantially confirmed by the new banking legislation (see Cianferotti, 1993, p. 138). Paradoxically, the regulatory wave of 1986–87, seems to have been prompted by the deregulation undertaken in the first Thatcher's administration.[32] This, as shown by the elimination of distinction between licensed and recognised banking institutions and, even more, by the diversification of Building Societies' activities allowed by the 1986 Building Societies Act, by increasing the competitive challenges to the financial operators produced as a major consequence by the need of their de-specialisation.

Another important area in which the process of deregulation produced a similar result regarded the relationships between the banking system and the stock exchange. Also in this case the *re-regulation* (see Gowland, 1990, Introduction) of 1986–87 concealed a phenomenon of liberalisation of the markets and de-specialisation of the operators.

The prelude to the 1986 London Stock Exchange reform, the so-called 'Big Bang', was represented by the 1975 deregulation of the New York Stock Exchange, which brought about a reduction in the transaction costs, and by the 1979 abolition in the UK of any control on foreign currency dealings. This decision, aimed at strengthening London's financial markets, had inevitably to be followed by a reform of the Stock Exchange which took the form of the 1986 Big Bang.

The London Stock Exchange was being increasingly bypassed by big institutional investors. Not only were British investors using foreign securities firms for their purchases of overseas securities, but foreign securities firms operating in other markets were creating markets in British securities. This was associated with a decline in the competitive position of the London Stock Exchange, most especially compared with New York. As the costs for large institutional investors of dealing in New York were lower than in London, the London Stock Exchange was being bypassed. Moreover, technology had the effect of making location as such increasingly less relevant for securities trading (see Cianferotti, 1993).

The 1986 Reform of the LSE interested both the institutional-organisational aspect and the technological one and was based on four main innovations. First, the abolition of fixed minimum commissions. Second, the abolition of the distinction between *brokers*[33] and *jobbers* with the creation of the *market makers*. Third, the opening up of the Stock Exchange to external institutions. Finally, the introduction of new technologies aimed at offering a system of continuous bargaining through video-terminals.

The Big Bang represented a further step in the process of de-specialisation and concentration of financial institutions. In fact, with the creation of a single market operator, the *market maker*, able to exercise all the activities connected to the Stock Exchange practices,[34] the big groups, mainly linked to the Clearing Banks, were able, by acquiring Stock Exchange firms, to offer services grouped into banking (traditional finance and corporate advice), securities (equities and debt), capital markets and investment management (see Skerrit, 1986, p. 83). Even if the clearing banks had already entered the Stock Exchange in the mid-1970s through the acquisition of Merchant Banks,[35] the consequences of the Stock Exchange reform were decisive for them. The merger of commercial and investment banking allowed them to strengthen their position of middlemen, the one historically defining the City's predominance in the world financial markets. Consequently, the reform increased the economic and political power of the City's big institutions also in the domestic context. As a further guarantee of the autonomy of the financial sector in general, and of the City's big institutions in particular, the deregulation of the Stock Exchange was accompanied by the issue of the Financial Services Act (FSA)[36] establishing a new regulatory framework for investment business activities. This piece of legislation regulating the activities of financial intermediaries broadly defined was, in fact, aimed at increasing the range of activities that the banks were able to exercise also by protecting them from the unfair competition of other institutions. Non-banking intermediaries could, indeed, be advantaged by the mere fact that credit institutions were not allowed to issue securities (see Cianferotti, 1993). In addition, the transition from broking of new products to trading them in a mature market had greatly increased the risks of banking activities (see Skerrit, 1986, p. 83).

The system was based on the introduction of the authorisation to perform any investment business activity[37] to be granted directly by the Securities and Investment Board (SIB), a self-regulating body, recognised by the government and, thus, performing public functions.[38] This authorization could also be obtained by belonging to one of the five Self-Regulating Organisations (SROs)[39] authorised by the SIB, or to one of the Recognised Professional Bodies (RPBs) for which investment advice was only a secondary activity. There was also a category of financial intermediaries, among which the Insurance Companies, for which authorisation was automatic. Without authorisation, investment business was considered a crime and the SIB was endowed of criminal prosecution powers as well as civil remedies. Over the authorised societies, the SIB and the SROs could exercise the traditional powers of the self-regulating bodies: appropriate and effective sanctions as well as the suspension and even the withdrawal of the authorisation.

Summing up, also in this case the British Legislator, by issuing a flexible normative framework privileging secondary norms (rule books) and self-regulating practices, did confirm the tendency to granting the widest possible degree of autonomy and discretion to the financial institutions.

In the light of the events reported above it now appears much less puzzling why the City of London, and, in particular, its biggest institutions did not appear, in the period between 1986 and 1987, particularly interested in the conduct of monetary and exchange rate policy by the Chancellor of the Exchequer and might even have seemed favourable to the implementation of macroeconomic policies which undoubtedly met British industry preferences. This did not conceal any shift of domestic political power from the financial to the productive capital, even if, given the momentum and the importance for the City of the political decisions to be taken during this period, it may be well hypothesised a bargaining process between the winning and the subordinate sector of the leading socioeconomic groups, also in view of the general elections that were to be held in 1987. On the contrary, the Stock Exchange Big Bang represents the last stage of a process which had already started in the mid-1970s: the definitive submission of the productive capital to the financial one. Better, it reveals the almost complete absorption of the productive sector by the financial one, with all that it implied in terms of the prevailing of short-term considerations over long term ones in the management of the British productive sector. From the mid-1980s revolution onwards, short-termism had, indeed, become a structural characteristic of the British capitalist system.

3   *City's Concerns and Political Responses at the End of the 1980s*

As the reform of the British financial and banking system ceased to be the main concern of the City of London, and as the pursuance, in the preceding two years, of loose macroeconomic policies began to produce their effects in terms of higher inflation, what had previously been only veiled concerns, became overt criticisms of the Chancellor's decisions and open demands for policy changes.

The most evident sign of this change in the attitudes of the financial community was the publication in the Bank's Quarterly Bulletin of an editorial (see Bank of England Quarterly Bulletin, 1988, pp. 3–9) containing a clear warning that the economy was at risk of overheating[40] and asking for a reaffirmation of the priority of the government's anti-inflationary stances over any exchange rate considerations. The Bank of England was explicitly asking for the implementation of strict counter-inflationary policies. These, given the evident failure to control the growth of monetary aggregates, meant rising interest rates and restraining the growth of the domestic demand through the implementation of restrictive fiscal policies.

However, the Chancellor of the Exchequer did not seem to have understood the importance that the financial community was attaching to the implementation of similar policies. Contrary to what the Bank of England had been asking for, the Lawson March 1988 Budget was centred on tax cuts and an already announced £2.5bn increase in public spending in 1988–89 (see Stephens, 1988).

The City immediately expressed its concerns over the size of his tax give-away and raised fears that £4bn of tax cuts might exacerbate Britain's trade account problems. Ian Harwood, Chief UK economist with Warburg Securities said the Chancellor had chosen a relatively tight monetary stance compared with his fiscal stance and he had been optimistic with his £4bn current account deficit forecasts. Bill Martin, chief UK economist at Phillips and Drew described the £4bn give-away as 'slightly chancy' and warned it could increase overheating. Kevin Boakes, Chief UK economist at Greenwell Montagu reported 'slight disappointment' at the extent of tax cuts since he feared it

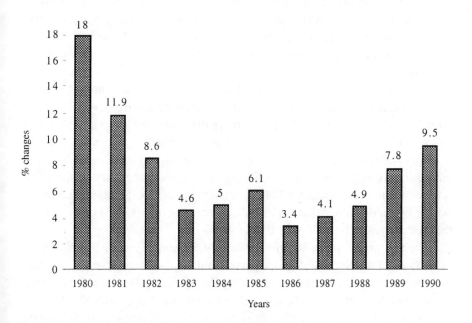

Graph 18 UK consumer prices 1980–90

Source: OECD, 1994.

would do little to slow the pace of growth in consumer spending which was increasing upward pressure on inflation. In general, market reaction to the Budget was not positive with prices on long-dated British government securities more than a point lower by the close of trading and share prices decreasing on the following day, with the FT-SE 100 Share Index closing 14.2 down at 1,825.7.

The other issue at stake was the Chancellor's decision to counteract upwards pressures on sterling's exchange rates by decreasing interest rates. By the end of the first week of April, sterling was at its highest for two years, reaching DM3.15. In response, Lawson cut interest rates to 8 per cent, the lowest level for a decade, a move that Bank officials, in the light of the overheating in the economy fuelled by Lawson's budget tax cuts, made no secret to welcome with much less cheer than they might sometimes be obliged to sound.

By mid-1988 the Chancellor found himself in dire relations with the Bank of England, while the markets and the City had shown no sympathy for his latest macroeconomic decisions. As a matter of fact, his decision to cut rates further to 7.5 per cent on 17 May was the last of its kind to be made by Nigel Lawson, and had to be reversed only two weeks later. By early August he had pushed up interest rates in half-point stages to 11 per cent, the highest level for two years, and by the end of November they had reached the level of 13 per cent.

Lawson's chances of influencing British economic policy-making, as well as his political fortunes, seemed to have faded away. However, the most worrying thing was the lack of any alternative strategy to cope with a fast raising inflation which, at the end of the year, reached 6 per cent.

Was narrow money a reliable guide to the growth of demand? Should targets for broad money be reinstated? Should the government adopt an explicit policy for the exchange rate? Was the credibility of UK counter-inflationary policies so undermined that the British government required to borrow it from the Bundesbank by joining the ERM?

The solution to these questions was, at the beginning of 1989, still a very controversial matter within the City itself, but what must be noted here is that the uncertainties regarded the means, not the goal, which was, as it had been at the beginning of the Thatcher era, to maintain the high value of sterling.

The conviction that the Middle Term Financial Strategy as such could no longer be considered a credible path towards lower inflation was widespread by that time in the City. An editorial in *The Banker* of June 1989 underlined how the Treasury, by increasingly succumbing to the temptation to 'fine tune' aggregate demand, had seriously reduced the anti-inflationary power of the MTFS. In fact, the novelty of the MTFS lay not in the use of monetary and fiscal policy to fight inflation but in the government's public commitment to an internally consistent set of medium-term, anti-inflation targets designed to affect inflationary expectations. Its success depended on whether the private sector believed the government had the will and technical capacity to achieve its targets and the extent to which it was convinced that hitting the targets would have the desired effect on inflation. However, with monetary targets publicly discredited, the MTFS had become largely ineffectual as a device for influencing expectations. The editorial concluded by proposing as an alternative to the anti-inflationary credibility of MTFS joining the European Monetary System.

The economic commentator of the Barclays Bank Review had reached opposite conclusions on the same issue (see Budd, 1989b). If it was accepted that the immediate cause of British problems at the end of the 1980s was an excessive growth in demand, then it was obvious that steps to reduce demand should have been taken earlier. The question, according to him, was whether the government ignored obvious warning signs. There had been at least two occasions on which the government's own chosen indicators signalled a potential problem. The first was in 1986 when £M3 broke out of a range that had already been raised from earlier versions of the MTFS. Rather than take measures to tighten policy, the government suspended and then abandoned targets for £M3. It concentrated instead on M0, which stayed within its range during 1986/7 and 1987/8. The second occasion on which it ignored its own warning signs was in 1988 when it allowed M0 to exceed its target range and it did so, because it concentrated instead on preventing sterling from rising above DM3 responding to the oft repeated calls from industry for exchange rate stability. Thus, the policy of shadowing exchange rate was explicitly indicated in this article as a major cause of renewed inflationary pressures in the UK and the government's policies were recognised as favouring the industrial sector. The argument went on suggesting that the government had to take the growth of the broad money supply into account in assessing monetary conditions, but without defining a specific set of numbers. Indeed, and this was implicit in the article, the mistake of the government had been not that of targeting broad monetary aggregates, but of publicising its goals undermining its credibility each time it failed to achieve them. As far as exchange rate policy was concerned, the experience of early 1988 showed that the attempt to manage the exchange rate within narrow limits could conflict with the aim to control the growth of the money supply. The government could not independently choose a monetary target and an exchange rate target. If the government was successful in bringing inflation under control, it was possible that one side effect of its policies would be a stable exchange rate. It was also true that the rise in the exchange rate since early 1988 had helped to bring inflation down, but it did not follow that the conduct of policy would be improved by attempting to stabilise the exchange rate at its current level by joining the exchange rate mechanism of the EMS.

In the event, the debate in the City about the reinstatement of broad money targets or full membership of the EMS was really part of the long lived debate about rules vs. discretion. If it was not possible to trust the government in the management of the economy, it might be better to impose rules, even if borrowed from abroad, than to allow it such a discretion (see Budd, 1989b).

In retrospect, and on this point there seemed to be a widespread agreement within the City's commentators in early 1988–89 (see Budd, 1989b and 1989a; Johnson, 1990b and 1990a; Lord Alexander of Weedon, 1991; *The Banker*, June 1989), the years from 1986 to 1988 had not been good ones for those in the City who believed that the authorities should be allowed to use their discretion. However, this argument did not necessarily lead to choosing the European Community rules, had it not been for a fear that, by that time, was gaining momentum in the British financial circles: the City's fear to lose its dominant financial position in Europe as a consequence of the process of European integration.

In 1989, the competition with other European financial centres, particularly Germany, did not appear to represent a concrete threat to the London financial sector as it would do later on. However, there were already signs that the question of the impact of the Single Market on the competitiveness of the British financial sector was acquiring importance. Balance of payments problems were starting to interest not only the manufacturing sector, but also the overseas earnings of the City of London. The financial and business services saw their traditional surplus fall from 2.8 per cent in 1986–87, to 2 per cent in 1989, and the invisibles balance fell from 2.9 per cent in 1986 to 1.1 per cent in 1989 (see Johnson, 1990a). Concerns were voiced that this path could worsen with the completion of the 1992 programme.

Since a major reason for London's strength in finance was the low level of regulation in its markets, a major fear of financial operators was that one effect of the harmonisation of regulation within Europe in view of 1992 would be to take this advantage away from London (see Foley, 1989). Indeed, if harmonisation resulted in a deliberalisation of London's markets to bring them more into line with the rest of Europe, the outcome was likely to be a loss of business not only to European centres but also to other financial centres outside Europe. The competition with New York and, particularly, Tokyo did not allow for such distractions. The UK had been the leading financial power for the century before the first world war, and the USA for the quarter century after the second world war, but by the end of the 1980s the City feared that Japan was increasingly emerging as a financial leader (see Johnson, 1989a).

Although sterling's international use had risen rapidly after a period of eclipse, it had only half the yen's share of the bond market and one-third of its share of cross-border bank loans. Moreover, the US dollar still accounted for over half of all international bank loans, and 45 per cent of international bonds while the Swiss franc had second place, with 15 per cent of the market. But it was in terms of banks that Japan had seized a decisive lead in world finance from 1986 onwards. Japanese banks had, in 1989, 38 per cent of the international market, with claims of over $0.5trn. However, the UK's invisible earnings were at $150bn more than her visible exports; some way behind the USA, but well ahead of Japan. It was in fact as an international financial centre that London could still claim world financial leadership, with banking assets of $1.1trn, or just over a fifth of the market compared with $1 trn for Tokyo and half that amount for New York. Still, Tokyo was clearly challenging London, and had almost caught up in terms of the foreign exchange market, with a daily turn over of $87bn, compared with $90bn for London; but both were well ahead of New York with $59bn. When it came to domestic equity markets, Tokyo was the undisputed world leader, after the rise of the yen and the recovery from the October 1987 crash, with a valuation of $3.8trn, compared with $2.5trn for New York and $740bn for London. However London still led the world in foreign equities, with about 550 listed on the International Stock Exchange, compared with 110 on Tokyo and 80 on New York.

Summing up, to cope with the growing competition in the international financial markets, the City of London needed a more integrated EC, so as to gain the same economic advantages that the USA and Japan receive from their large internal markets. More clearly:

> The London financial market will be overtaken in all respects by the Tokyo market if it does not become the nub of a bigger European financial market, with a unified stock exchange offering Japanese investors the depth they now find in the USA.

However, as explicitly stated in the quotation above, the City of London needed also to take the lead of the process of European integration in order to avoid decisions, as the passing of a European law regulating financial markets, that could produce negative consequences on its European leadership. But this, of course would required 'the UK to join the exchange rate mechanism of the EMS' (see Johnson, 1989a).

Thus, the City's anti-inflationary arguments for joining the ERM, still put forward by some of its representatives (see Young, 1989), were increasingly coupled by its growing concern to lose the opportunity to influence the process of European integration by remaining outside the European Monetary System. On the contrary, the City needed to control this process in order to cope with the mounting competitive pressures from the other world financial markets. The latter consideration, of course, became increasingly important with the agreement among central bankers within the Delors Committee on further steps towards European Monetary Union and its endorsement by the majority of the EC heads of state and government, in mid-April 1989.[41]

The Treasury's memorandum to the Prime Minister for the Madrid Summit of June 1989 discussed many of the issues concerning the City of London. In this memorandum, the Chancellor of the Exchequer, perhaps in an attempt to regain the credibility and, thus, the influence lost,[42] admitted that monetary policy had been too lax in the period when sterling had been shadowing the DM and gave much emphasis to the role the ERM might play in avoiding any repeat of an upsurge in inflation. Further, the document put forward a scheme to delay if not derail any timetable for economic and monetary union (EMU). According to this scheme, Britain would play an active part in the relatively innocuous stage one of the process and, in doing so, it might detach that phase from the more threatening stages two and three. The principal danger for Britain was Delors's insistence that agreement to embark on the process would be a commitment to complete it: the goal of British diplomacy in Madrid had to be to break that link. However, the Chancellor's document also warned about the risks of isolation in Europe, the choice being between engagement in the debate and banishment to the sidelines. A threat to veto EMU would be a futile gesture since the other eleven governments could always establish new arrangements outside the Treaty of Rome to create a single currency. Moreover, accepting banishment to the sidelines would involve a heavy political and economic price. If Britain became a 'semidetached' member of the Community it would lose influence in Washington as well as in Brussels, Japanese investment in Britain would be threatened, and so would be the prosperity of the City of London. The document concluded that a pledge that sterling would join the ERM by July 1992, the date set for the completion of the Single Market, was conceding very little in exchange for the possibility of entering the debate over the making of EMU.[43] Lawson suggested that Thatcher attach two conditions to the ERM pledge. First, all member states must dismantle their remaining capital controls well before July 1992. Second, sterling should be admitted to the mechanism with the wide, 6 per cent, margins of fluctuations. Lawson is reported to have pushed for ERM membership on many other occasions,[44] without succeeding in moving Mrs Thatcher from her steady opposition. This time, however, it was different, and, no doubt, it was different because this time Lawson's stance reflected completely British financial actors' concerns and change of attitudes towards the ERM and the process of European Integration.

Mrs Thatcher's statement to the European Council on the morning of 26 June unveiled the change in the British government's position towards the ERM issue. She underlined Britain's commitment to implement from mid-1990s onwards the measures outlined in the first stage of the Delors report, strengthening economic and monetary policy coordination within existing institutions. The Prime Minister declared herself to be 'fully behind most of the proposals in that stage, particularly those liberalising financial and capital markets'. Britain was also ready to reformulate its long standing opposition to sterling's entry in the ERM: 'I can reaffirm today the United Kingdom's intention to join the ERM, but the British Government must be free to decide the timing' (see Stephens, 1989a).[45]

Although she stated that the timing would be linked to progress in bringing inflation down and, in Europe, to the successful abolition of exchange controls and progress towards the completion of the single market, the timing of UK membership was largely a matter of domestic politics (see Stephens, 1996). This much was clearly understood also by contemporary commentators.

That Mrs Thatcher, in pronouncing her Madrid statement, had not bowed to the pressures of her senior ministers, particularly Howe and Lawson, as insinuated by the press, but had responded to the change of attitudes towards the issue in the financial circles, was clear just a few days after the European summit when she decided to remove Geoffrey Howe from the Foreign Office in July 1989.

Nigel Lawson's resignation three months later also carried an air of painful inevitability, the last of his mistakes having been that of failing to identify a credible alternative path to stages two and three of European Monetary Union. As the Delors plan became the basis for further discussions over EMU, the City's concerns over its role in the European market increased as well as its demands to the British government to take the lead in the process by devising an acceptable alternative to the Delors proposal.

Thus, at an informal meeting in Antibes on 10 September 1989, Nigel Lawson floated his idea of 'freely competing currencies' as an alternative to stages two and three of the Delors plan for a single community currency and European central banking system (see HM Treasury, 1989). Lawson claimed that free competition among community currencies,[46] and the possibility to substitute one for another in transaction and savings, was the 'logical extension' of that greater monetary cooperation agreed by EC leaders under stage one of the Delors report.

However, not only were the reactions to Lawson's plan among the European community partners distinctly unfavourable. It also failed to gain domestic consensus. In particular, the City's objections to the proposals were centred on the following points. First, a currency could be legal tender only if it was acceptable to the payee as well as to the payer, but, in the case of freely competing national European currencies, most people would continue to accept only their own national currency, on the principle of matching assets and liabilities. Second, competition between banks across frontiers, a major aim of the 1992 programme, would be distorted, because people would choose a bank on the grounds of its currency of borrowing or lending, rather than its low interest spread and efficient performance in any currency. Third, and extremely important for the City, if the competition were really free, the DM would soon win it, and drive other currencies out of the market.[47] Indeed, the UK chancellor's notion that 'good' currencies should drive out the 'bad' in a kind of monetary Darwinism could not be considered acceptable by anyone within the European Community, except, perhaps, by Germany. In particular, it was not acceptable for the British financial sector, since the good currency was clearly represented by the DM and the proposal eventually envisaged a sort of economic and political dominance of the 'winning' country over the others (see Goodhart, 1989).[48] Finally, from the City's point of view, if, as it should, the competition allowed currencies to go up and down against each other, it would be incompatible with the whole idea of monetary union, and, so, unacceptable to the other European partners supporting EMU. Thus, even if the proposal had been conceived only with the intent to delay the discussion and implementation of the of the Delors plan, its more likely outcome was to irritate those ERM countries which shared Britain's reservation about the Delors plan's ultimate goals of common currency and a European Central Bank, as well as those, such as France and Italy, which wanted to move quickly to an intergovernmental conference paving the way to economic and monetary union (see Johnson, 1989c, p. 249).

In conclusion, the reaction of the City to the Chancellor's ideas was a negative one, while its preferred strategy was an unglamorous one: to slow the monetary union bandwagon by pointing out the very great economic and political difficulties involved in the planned institutional changes that the Delors programme envisaged to bring about union (ibid.). Here Britain's weight and the Bank of England's[49] expertise in monetary affairs would provide a much more welcome support than the Treasury's market-based alternatives to Delors.

With his resignation on 27 October 1989 Lawson put an end to what had been an impossible situation both for him personally, and for the government, whose macroeconomic policies seemed constantly undermined by the ever more explicit struggle between him and the Prime Minister. As Lawson put it in his resignation letter, officially urged by the impossibility of finding a common ground with Thatcher's personal economic advisor, Alan Walters: 'The successful conduct of economic policy is possible only if there is, and is seen to be, full agreement between the Prime Minister and the Chancellor of the Exchequer.'

The markets did not seem to react negatively to Lawson's departure, which, in fact, was almost universally considered as a 'dignified and necessary exit' (see Brittan, 1989). After a first moment of uncertainty, City observers were keen to point out that any adverse impact would not be long lasting if the drawn-out disputes over full membership of the European Monetary System and interest rate policy were resolved.

The new Chancellor of the Exchequer, John Major, a political Chancellor 'closely attuned to the mood at Westminster as well as in the dealing rooms in the City ' (Stephens, 1996, p. 145), immediately reassured the financial markets in his first substantial statement on economic policy made to his Huntingdon, Cambridgeshire, constituency on 27 October. He confirmed that he favoured a firm exchange rate for the pound and that the defeat of inflation remained the government's highest priority. As sterling continued its downwards trend, the Chancellor strengthened his commitment to pursue a strong pound policy by reacting to exchange rate falls through higher interest rates[50] and with a tight fiscal and monetary policy to combat inflation.[51]

There is little doubt that this met completely the City's macroeconomic preferences as they had been expressed by some of its representatives since the beginning of Major's Chancellorship. According to Peter Leslie, the Deputy Chairman of Barclays Bank, the City of London's survival as the number one financial centre of Europe depended crucially on the UK being a full member of the EC. Lord Roll, president of SG Warburg group, commenting on the Chancellor's declarations in the Commons on the 30 November, said that, while the technicalities of economic and monetary union seemed far removed from the problems which banks normally had to worry about, the prospect of a stable exchange rate environment would have a profound effect on domestic and cross-border financial transactions. If this could be combined with steady growth and low inflation, there would be a new and powerful challenge to creative financial services.

John Major's first and only Budget in March 1990 also proclaimed, in the first sentence of its MTFS, that its central objective remained 'the defeat of inflation' and linked this aim to exchange rate policy adding that 'action to maintain the soundness of the currency remains a prime duty of the government' (see Major, 1990a). In the examination of policy carried out in his Budget speech (ibid.), Major rejected the reintroduction of credit control as a means to control inflation on the grounds that: '… it is extremely unlikely that credit controls would work in the modern world in anything other than short term' and that, indeed: '… governments of all persuasions throughout the western world are abolishing credit controls and are relying on interest rates to control money and thus, inflation'. He also addressed the requests coming from some City sectors favouring the reintroduction of a target for broad money claiming that the unpredictability and uncertainty of its behaviour made it an unreliable point of reference for an anti-inflationary stance. Thus, the only anti-inflationary policy choice remaining was to commit the government to pursue a stable exchange rate policy by pursuing a high interest rates policy in the short term and, eventually, entering the ERM.

As sterling's exchange rate continued to depreciate[52] and as Thatcher failed at the Strasbourg Summit of December 1989 to prevent the other 11 governments from calling an intergovernmental conference, also the City started to regard entry in the ERM as the only solution to British inflationary problems[53] as well as the only opportunity that Britain had to retain even the smallest chance to influence the process of European Monetary integration.[54]

As far as the need to guarantee British voice in the European monetary integration process was concerned, and given the dismissal of Lawson's previous ideas for an alternative path to European Monetary Union, by early 1990 the search was for a much needed more convincing British proposal to put forward at the intergovernmental conference.[55] In the event, Major completely endorsed the City's suggestions for an 'hard Ecu' alternative to stages two and three of EMU. The initial 'hard ECU' scheme was put forward by Richards, Director of Public Finance at HSBC Samuel Montagu, who sent it to the Second Permanent Secretary to the Treasury, Wicks, on 22 November 1989, receiving his strong encouragement. On 4 January 1990, Richards produced the proposal called 'The next stage to an evolutionary approach to EMU' which was sent to the Treasury and to Sir Michael Butler, Director at the Hambros Bank, and chair of the European Committee of the British Invisible Exports Council. During the following six months, Sir Michael Butler, in his role of chair of the European Committee of the British Invisibles Exports Council, worked with Paul Richards to develop a more convincing project within the City, Treasury and Bank of England's framework.

The central idea of the City's thesis[56] was that there was a pragmatic alternative to the 'Big Bang' proposed by Delors. In the Delors plan national currencies and central banks were to be replaced by a supranational 'Eurofed' issuing a single currency. In the 'hard Ecu' plan, instead, governments should concentrate on developing the existing European Currency Unit. The ECU already had a significant role in official transactions between central banks and was the unit they used for lending and borrowing within the EMS. Though outside the ERM, Britain already held 20 per cent of its foreign exchange rate reserves in ECU in the European Monetary cooperation fund. More broadly, the City of London was developing a private capital market in ECU.[57] Thus, the proposal was to develop the ECU as a common currency and, crucially, to allow a new European Monetary Fund (EMF), possibly, to be located in London, to put ECU notes into circulation. This 'hard ECU' would be so defined as to ensure that it could never be devalued against any of the community's twelve national currencies. Central banks would be obliged to redeem their own currencies for ECU on demand (the so-called re-purchase requirement) and, eventually, the EMF could develop into an embryonic central bank and the ECU into a single currency.

These principles formed the basis of the British government's alternative path to EMU presented by the Chancellor of the Exchequer for the first time in a speech to the German Industry Forum on 20 June 1990.[58]

However, to push this plan through the European member states, the British government needed more than ever, to enter the ERM but there were still too many political problems to be solved before taking a similar step. First, Thatcher's leadership had been too much committed to its stance towards the ERM to survive any decision to enter it. Then there was the problem of solving the leadership crisis within the Conservative Party that the long-lasting struggle between the Prime Minister and her previous Chancellor, and the traumatic way in which it had been solved, had further fuelled. All this, in turn, was deeply connected to the need to avoid calling for a general election in a moment in which the Labour Party seemed to gain a growing consensus after its European election victory in June 1989.

The solution of these interrelated problems will mark the British government's decision on the timing of UK entry in the ERM.

Notes

1   At the beginning of 1985 sterling faced a major exchange rate crisis. By the end of the first week of January, sterling was headed towards $1.15 and on Thursday 10 January it fell at $1.13. Lawson reacted raising interest rates by 1 per cent to 11.5 per cent in mid January and up to 14 per cent at the end of the month. See *Financial Times*, 1–30 January 1985. At the end of the year UK three months' interbank interest rates had raised to 12 per cent from 10 per cent at the end of 1984. See Bank of England Quarterly Bulletin, various issues, table 18.

2   For more details about it see Stephens, 1996.

3   Sterling's annual average exchange rate towards the DM reached its peak in 1981 when it was DM4.55 to £1 while 1982 annual average was DM4.24 and it continued to decrease in the following years.

4   For further details on the matter see Stephens, 1996.

5   'At the moment', she said, 'everyone is geared to the DM, save us. The DM at the moment is slightly deflationary. That means that the whole of Europe is geared to a slightly deflationary policy. Now, we have not been so geared and we have had a greater degree of freedom in relation to both the dollar and the DM and I just think that I am grateful for that.' See Owen and Rutherford, 1987.

6   At the end of 1988 UK three months' interbank rates were at 13.16 per cent from 8.91 per cent at the end of 1987. See Bank of England Quarterly Bulletin, various issues.

7   At the end of 1988 £/DM exchange rate had raised from DM3.20 instead of DM2.97 at the end of 1987. See Bank of England Quarterly Bulletin, various issues

8   In 'Building on Business Success' the CBI argued that: 'A more stable exchange rate provides a climate in which companies are encouraged to invest. With the prospect of the single European market in goods and services by 1992, exchange rate instability adds an extra dimension to planning problems.' See Confederation of British Industry, 1989a.

9   The annual average of the £/DM exchange rate in 1989 was, exactly DM3.08. See Bank of England Quarterly Bulletins, various issues, table 18.

10 UK retail price index in August 1989 was the highest within the EC reaching quota of 7.3 per cent. See Confederation of British Industry, 1989b, p. 13

11 At the end of 1989 UK three months' interbank rate was at 15 per cent. See Bank of England Quarterly Bulletins, various issues.

12 For the survey conclusions see Williams, 1990.

13 The Council of Ministers meeting in Dublin on 25 and 26 June had decided to convene two intergovernmental conferences in Rome in December. The first was to discuss means of strengthening democratic institutions and revision of the Treaties to promote qualified majority voting. The second had to prepare for European Economic and Monetary Union (EMU).

14 The TUC became firmly anti-European during the early 1980s. Indeed, the 1981 Congress passed a resolution calling on a future Labour government to withdraw from Europe without a referendum. This policy was re-endorsed at the 1983 Congress. See Marsh, 1992.

15 See further this chapter.

16 See above for TUC position towards Lawson's budgetary policy in the years 1985–86–87–88.

17 For an example of the TUC concerns over the situation of the welfare state and of British public services, see Bickerstaffe, 1989, in Trade Union Congress, 1989b, pp. 423–4.

18 The Thatcher government's strategy to reduce to its minimal historical record trade union power was a regular, step by step process at the end of which the legal balance between unions and employers had significantly changed. There have been five major pieces of trade union legislation passed since 1979. These five acts – the 1980 Employment Act, the 1982 Employment Act, the 1984 Trade Union Act, the 1988 Employment Act and the 1990 Employment Act – have significantly changed the legal position of unions. The blanket immunity enjoyed by unions, as distinct from unionists, was removed by the Employment Act 1982; the definition of a legitimate trade dispute has been successively narrowed so as to reduce the immunities enjoyed by unionists; the legal basis of the closed shop was initially restricted by the 1980 and 1982 Employment Acts and subsequently removed in the Employment Acts of 1988 and 1990; under the Trade Union Act 1984 unions are required to hold secret ballots for the election of officers. This legislation also requires unions to conduct political fund ballots. The Employment Act 1988 gives individual unionists a series of rights vis-à-vis their unions. It also prevents unions from disciplining members who refuse to go on strike or cross picket lines while the 1990 act makes unions responsible for their members' unofficial action unless the unions repudiate the strike, or make it official after a ballot. For a further detailed analysis of the impact of Mrs Thatcher's industrial policies on the power of the TUC see Marsh, 1992.

   In her memoires, Mrs Thatcher claims: 'Unlike some of my colleagues, I never ceased to believe that, other things being equal, the level of unemployment was related to the power of Trade Unions. ... So both Norman Tebbit, my new Secretary of State for Employment, and I were impatient to go ahead with further reforms in Trade Union law. (Eventually) we had made substantial progress in reducing the overbearing power of Trade Unions.' See Thatcher, 1993.

19 Haggar, of the TUC, declared in the RAI programme Europa + Europa of 17 July 1996, that the trade unions were convinced to change their position on Europe by Jacques Delors and his projects. For a similar interpretation of the TUC policy shift in 1988 see also Marsh, 1992.

20 Over-funding was the practice by which the government sought to reduce private bank deposits, and hence £M3, by selling greater amounts of public debt than required merely to finance its own deficits.

21 See above this chapter.

22 In the words of Lawson: 'There can be no doubt about the government's commitment to maintain monetary conditions that will continue to bring down inflation. Short term interest rates will be held at the level needed to achieve this.' See Lawson, 1985.

23 In his words: 'I thought it right to resist the pressure, which for a time was very strong indeed, to raise interest rates still further.' See Lawson, 1986.

24 See also above this chapter.

25 On the enormous importance of the City revolution to enhance the City's international competitive position as well as its leading domestic role, see also Moran, 1991, p. 69.

26 'The 1979 Banking act, the first attempt at statutory banking supervision in Britain, was prompted by ... the EEC eager to harmonise the ground rules throughout the community in the interest of fair competition.' See *The Economist*, 1983.

27   For further detail see Cianferotti, 1993, p. 94.

28   The City Bullion Market, or London Gold Market, is the exclusive club of only five banks, Johnson Matthey, Mocatta & Goldsmith, Sharps-Pixley, Rothschild and Samuel Montagu (a subsidiary of the Midland Bank), whose representatives meet every day of the week but Saturday and Sunday, at 10.30 am and 3.30 pm in the Rothschild's Centre Point, to fix the price of gold.

29   For further details on the subject see Lawson, 1992, p. 403.

30   On the importance of scandals for the City revolution see also Moran, 1991, p. 79.

31   The invisibles account comprises services, interest, profits and dividends (IPD) passing between the UK and other countries, and unrequired transfers to and from the government and the private sector. In 1990 Services were 28 per cent of total invisible credits, equally divided between financial and business on the one hand, and transport and travel on the other; IPD were 67 per cent and transfers 5 per cent.

32   For more consideration on the deregulation/re-regulation paradox of the Thatcher governments, see Gowland, 1990, Introduction.

33   The brokers were those Stock Exchange agents who operated in the interest and with the capital of their client. The jobbers operated with their capital and created the market for each kind of asset. The separation of function of broker and jobber, so distinctive a feature of the London Market, dated only from 1908. Minimum commissions were introduced about 18 months later to defend 'single capacity' by preventing the newly purified jobbers from directing business through complacent brokers to their erstwhile clients and counterparts on privileged terms. One rule could not survive without the other. See Hollis, 1986, p. 18.

34   Namely, assistance in the issue and valuation of securities, distribution and sale, and sales management in the secondary market.

35   See above this chapter.

36   The Financial Services Act was passed by Parliament on October 1986.

37   The Act seeks to regulate all types of investment business. Schedule 1 to the Act covers five categories of business in relation to investments: a) dealing in investments; b) arranging deals in investments; c) managing investments; d) advising on investments; e) operating collective investment schemes, such as unit trusts.

'Investment' is widely defined in Schedule 1 to the Act, and includes: a) securities; b) options; c) futures; d) long-term insurance contracts; e) contracts for differences.

Examples of these investments are:

a)   securities: stocks and shares, bonds, debentures, certificates of deposit, government and local authorities bonds and units in unit trusts. The statutory definition of 'securities' is so wide that it was considered appropriate to make an express exemption for cheques and other bills of exchange, bank drafts, letters of credit and bank notes;

b)   options: options to buy or sell an investment, sterling and foreign currency, gold silver and platinum or an option to buy or sell any such option;

c)   futures: contracts for the sale of commodities and land where the price is agreed at the contract date and the subject matter of the contract is to be delivered at a future date. Contracts made for commercial purposes, not investment, are excluded;

d)   long-term insurance contracts: long term insurance business, as defined by the Insurance Companies Acts, but not personal health and injury insurance or term assurance (that is life insurance which terminates on the expiry of 10 years or earlier death);

e)   contracts for differences: these are contracts under which a profit, or loss, arises by reason of currency exchange rates or price fluctuations in property of any kind, for instance, currency and interest rate swaps and index linked National Savings Certificates. See Laidlaw and Roberts, 1990, pp. 97–107.

38 The SIB personnel was to be chosen among the City operators and nominated jointly by the Trade Ministry and by the Bank of England.

39 The SROs are: the Trading Securities Association, TSA, born by the agreement between the Stock Exchange, SE, regulating the activity of securities and bonds operators, and the International Securities Regulatory Organisation, ISRO, representing the brokers acting in the international financial markets, and, particularly, in the Euromarket; the Association of Futures Brokers and Dealers, AFBD, controlling futures and options markets; the Financial Intermediaries, Managers and Brokers Regulatory Association, FIMBRA, representing a wide number of little, independent brokers acting, mainly, in the common funds and life-insurance sector; The Investment Management Regulatory Organisation, IMRO, grouping the operators managing the portfolios of institutional investors as Banks, Common Funds, Pension Funds and Insurance Companies; the Life Insurance and Unit Trust Regulatory Organisation, LAUTRO, constituted by insurance societies and investment funds. See Laidlaw and Roberts, 1990, pp. 97–107.

40 For a similar interpretation, see Stephens, 1996, p. 96.

41 The question of European Monetary Union, had been re-proposed as a major issue during the 1988 Hanover European summit, when the EC leaders agreed upon the establishment of a committee to study steps towards economic union.

   However, British diplomatic success in creating a committee dominated by conservative central bankers, held to be temperamentally disinclined to embrace monetary union with enthusiasm, had contributed to the underestimation in the British economic and political circles of the real ability of further steps towards EMU. See Norman, 1989a.

42 An attempt which was already evident in Lawson's 1989 Budget announcing tight fiscal policies and the government's determination to control inflation. See Lawson, 1989, p. 12.

43 See Stephens, 1996 for the text of the Memorandum.

44 For a thorough and primary source on the issue, see Lawson, 1992.

45 All British commentators agreed that Thatcher's statement unveiled a substantial change of position of the British government towards the issue of sterling's entry in the ERM. See *Financial Times*, 27 June 1989.

46 Lawson's proposal was based on Hayek's early ideas on competition in currencies as expressed in Hayek, 1976a, 1976b and 1979. See also Talani, 1993, chs 4 and 6.

47 These points are clearly expressed by Christopher Johnson, Chief Economic Adviser at Lloyds Bank. See Johnson, 1989c, p. 249.

48 For further criticisms on the idea of currency competition see Currie, 1989; Woodford, 1990. For a more general assessment of the theories of currencies competition, see De Cecco, 1992; see also Talani, 1993, ch. 4.

49 The evolution of the position of the Governor of the Bank of England towards the ERM/EMU issue can be traced by looking at the following interventions: Bank of England Quarterly Bulletin, 1989a and 1989b; Leigh-Pemberton, 1989; Bank of England Quarterly Bulletin, 1990a, 1990b, 1990c, 1990d and 1990e; Bank of England Quarterly Bulletin, 1991.

50 On 30 November 1989 the government attempted to clarify its exchange rate policy saying in the Commons that the Exchange rate was one of the monetary indicators taken into account when setting interest rates. 'That has been and remains our policy', he said. He did

not mention specifically that the government wanted a strong pound but Norman Lamont, Chief Secretary to the Treasury, told MPs during Treasury questions that the government continued to favour a 'firm exchange rate'. Treasury officials later described sterling's depreciation in previous weeks as 'unwelcome'. See 'Exchange rate policy outlined', *Financial Times*, 1 December 1989.

51 On 4 December 1989 the new Chancellor reiterated his commitment to a firm exchange rate for the pound with a tight fiscal and monetary policy to combat inflation in the House of Commons Treasury and Civil Service Committee. Throughout the session, Major repeated that interest rates would have been fixed in the light of the exchange rate. See Norman, 1989b.

52 By late December 1989 sterling had slumped by 17 per cent from DM3.28 of the beginning of the year, to DM2.72.

53 In fact, financial markets reacted with almost uniform disappointment to the Budget which came under fire for failing to support sterling or tackle inflation. Disappointment in the markets was keenest over the lack of an explicit commitment to join the exchange rate mechanism of the European Monetary System. See 'Disappointments for the markets', *Financial Times*, 21 March 1990.

54 For a similar interpretation see also Stephens, 1996.

55 Despite its pressures to enter the ERM, in fact, the City was extremely critical towards Delors plan for EMU.

Gilles Keating, Director of Research at Credit Suisse First Boston, argued against central EC controls on the ground that markets were a much better way of achieving fiscal coordination. As European Monetary Union developed, price stability was best assured by competition among central bank monetary policies because they assured the private sector's anti-inflationary voice was heard. M. Keating also believed that monetary union could be achieved almost entirely without European Federal institutions.

56 Indeed, in the course of an interview with the author, Richards claimed that the principles enshrined in the hard ECU proposal were agreed upon by the vast majority of the British financial community and by the British officials.

57 For an account of the situation of the City's ECU markets see Edmonds and Shea, 1991.

58 The main elements of the Chancellor's ideas were the set up of a European Monetary Fund (EMF) whose functions could have been:
   –   manage the exchange rate mechanism of the EMS;
   –   coordinate exchange rate intervention with external currencies such as the dollar and the yen;
   –   help manage medium term balance of payments lending, to the extent that the community was involved in this;
   –   manage and promote the ECU by issuing ECU bank notes for general circulation in the Community. Acting as a currency board, the EMF would have initially only issued notes that were fully backed by its own holdings of various EC currencies. At this stage the ECU would have been still defined as a basket of Community currencies.

On the last of these functions, the Chancellor's preferred option was to go further and extend the EMF's powers to enable it to issue and manage a hard ECU, a new international currency which would initially have had the same value as the ECU, and, at realignments, would have never devalued against other community currencies. The EMF would have also controlled the supply of hard ECUs to ensure it stayed within narrow margins against the other community currencies. It would have also set interest rates on hard ECUs. See HM Treasury, 1990.

The proposal was explained to Britain's European partners by the Governor of the Bank of England at a meeting with the European Currency Inter-Group of the European Parliament and the European Parliamentarians and Industrialists Council in Strasbourg on 11 July 1990. See Bank of England Quarterly Bulletin, 1990b.

Finally, the British proposals were clarified at the eve of the intergovernmental conference in the Treasury's document: 'The UK proposals for a European Monetary Fund and hard ECU: making progress towards economic and monetary union in Europe.' See ibid.

PART II
THE DEATH OF CONSENSUS

4   Italy and the Departure from the ERM: Purely Economic Interests vs Political Economy Strategies

The analysis of the attitudes, preferences and power relations of Italian economic interest groups in the process of European monetary integration has led to the conclusion that a major role is to be attributed to the Italian industrial sector's interests, particularly those of big industry. These interests, given the characteristics of Italian capitalism, are intimately connected to those of the banking sector.

The attitude of big Italian enterprise towards the whole process of European integration, and, to a greater extent, the process of European monetary integration, in the last 20 years, may be summarised in the claim: 'Let's bring all problems to Brussels since it will be much easier to solve them there than in Rome' (see Talani, 1997a).

In the shift of the political debate and power struggle from Rome to Brussels, the most powerful Italian entrepreneurs, and Agnelli above all, have immediately recognised the chance to overcome many of the obstacles which made it difficult to implement at the domestic level set of particularly tough macroeconomic policies. In short: 'Brussels could compel Rome to do what it was impossible to obtain at the national level' (ibid.).

In particular, Brussels represented, for Italian big industry, the opportunity to exert the most effective pressure for the acceptance and implementation of those national economic policies most opposed by the Italian trade unions. This had been the case with the Italian entry in the ERM, and this continued to be the case throughout the whole of the 1980s.

However, the issue of exchange rates has always been a very delicate one for the Italian industrial sector. This is due to the intimate linkage between the level of exchange rate and the performance of exports, a linkage that, even if it could be ignored or set aside in periods of sustained internal demand, caused many problems in periods of recession. To the extent that exports represented a substantial part of industrial activity, whenever the commitment to fixed or quasi-fixed exchange rates collided with the need to improve economic performance, Italian industry started insisting on the need to devalue.

Thus, the attitude of Italian industry towards the process of European Monetary integration has always been geared to the attempt to balance two inconsistent strategies. On the one hand, the strategy to shift the power struggle from the national to the supranational level with the aim of overcoming internal opposition to the implementation of a desired set of policies. On the other hand,.the strategy to keep exchange rates in line with the desired performance of exports with the aim of sustaining industrial business and profits. In periods in which the power struggle with the trade unions was particularly tough, as at the end of the 1970s, or in periods of sustained growth, as in the second half of the 1980s, the first consideration prevailed over the second. However, in periods of recession the contradiction was bound to explode, and it did explode at the beginning of the 1990s (see Fossa, 1996; see also Villari, 1992).

In the next section the impact of the early 1990s recession on the Italian industrial sector will be analysed with the aim to dig out the considerations that led Italian industry, particularly big industry, to shift its preferences from fixed to floating exchange rates.

The Impact of the Early 1990s Recession on the Italian Industrial Sector: A Confindustria View

The analyses published by Confindustria[1] showed that in 1992 the Italian economy was at the apex of a new recessive phase. The fall in the production rates had been accompanied (apparent demand remaining constant[2]) by a further worsening of the real current account balance. It is this simultaneous fall of supply, internal demand and current account balance which must be considered one of the peculiar features of the early 1990s economic slow-down.

Another important aspect is that the profitability of Italian companies had been falling at a much higher rate in the early 1990s than in the previous recession of the early 1980s, although the fall in production rates had been much less marked than that characterising the earlier period. Finally, there was a sharp worsening of companies' financial status combined with their growing dependence on bank lending.

In the following sections, each of these aspects of the early 1990s recessive

Table 13 Growth and productivity indicators in Italy between 1986 and 1992 (% changes)

Years	GDP	Investments	Overall productivity	Product per unit of labour	Product per unit of capital
1986	2.9	2.2	2.1	2.3	1.1
1987	3.1	5.0	1.6	3.1	1.2
1988	4.1	6.9	2.0	3.3	1.8
1989	2.9	4.3	1.3	2.9	0.6
1990	2.2	3.2	-1.1	0.0	-0.5
1991	1.3	0.9	-0.5	0.1	-1.4
1992	0.9	-0.9	0.1	0.9	-1.2

Source: CSC.

Table 14 GDP, demand, exports and inflation in Italy 1990–92 (% changes)

	1990	1991	1992
GDP	2.2	1.3	0.9
Internal demand	2.4	1.9	1.0
Net exports	-0.3	-1.0	-0.1
Inflation	6.1	6.3	5.4

Source: CSC.

phase will be analysed with the aim to trace back the macroeconomic preferences of the Italian industrial sector on the eve of the 1992 currency turmoil.

1   The Fall in GDP, Export and Internal Demand

In Confindustria's analyses, one of the peculiar aspects of the early 1990s recession was given by the simultaneous fall of production, internal demand and net exports. With respect to production indexes, the comparison with the early 1980s recession was considered particularly meaningful. As clearly shown by figures, the recessive period of the early 1990s was less tough in the early 1980s. Moreover, in the latest recessive period there was a clear mismatch in the timing of the business cycle's turns in the different European countries.

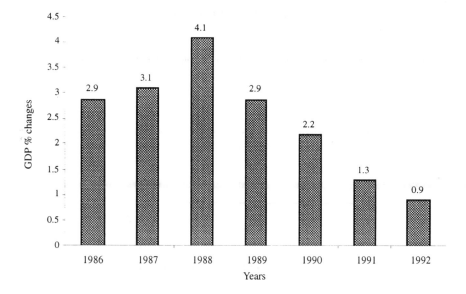

Graph 19 GDP % changes in Italy 1986–92

Source: CSC.

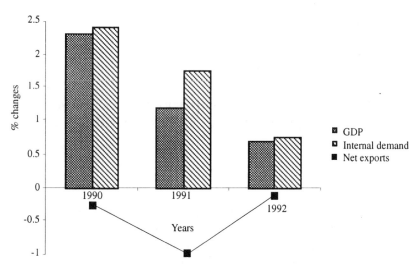

Graph 20 GDP, internal demand and net exports % changes in Italy 1990–92

Source: OCSE, Fmi, national bulletins.

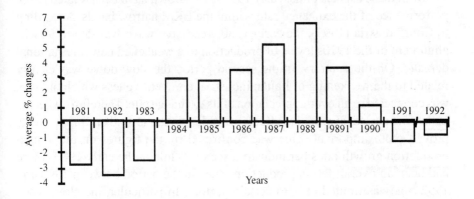

**Graph 21 Italian manufacturing industry average % production
changes 1981–92**

Source: CSC.

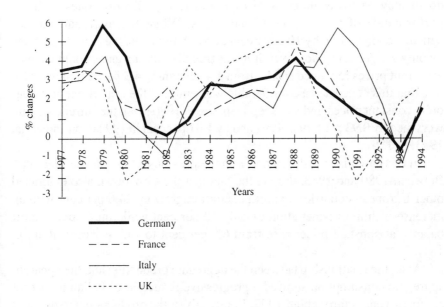

**Graph 22 Italy, UK, France, Germany real GDP % changes from
previous period 1978–94**

Source: OECD, 1994.

Both these aspects of the early 1990s slow-down have been related to the performance of the exchange rate within the ERM narrow bands. According to Confindustria (1993), the early 1980s recessive wave was due to a swift alignment of the 1970s levels of production to a weakened new international demand. On the contrary, in the second period the slow-down was clearly related to the weakening of Italian industrial competitiveness which, in turn, was connected to an over-appreciation of its exchange rate. Therefore, whereas in the first period quantitative effects prevailed, in the second one price effects proved more important. This was confirmed by the figures on the annual production growth rates per industrial sector. While in the early 1980s there had been an overall fall in production rates, in the period between 1990 and 1992 this was limited only to certain sectors. In particular, the slow-down interested those sectors which characterise the Italian export specialisation model and which, on the contrary, were not affected by the recession of the early 1980s.[3]

Given this strong relation between the production slow-down and the performance of Italian exports, the characteristics of the early 1990s slow-down may be better understood by comparing production rates with the performance of the balance of payments. While the aggregate import penetration increased by 10.9 per cent at constant prices, the export one grew by only 7.2 per cent. Moreover, if it was true that the current account balance at current prices remained stable, from 4.4 per cent to 4.3 per cent, it was also true that this concealed a considerable worsening of the import-export trade-off at constant prices. Indeed, keeping prices at 1980 level, the current account worsened by 0.93 per cent in 1991 and by 1.91 per cent in 1992 (Confindustria, 1993, p. 130).

In this case also the difference with the previous recession was clear-cut. Between 1980 and 1983, despite the fact that the slow-down also embraced other European countries, export penetration grew by 24.6 per cent with an increase of import penetration of only 10 per cent while the import-export balance at constant prices rose from 6.8 per cent to 14.7 per cent (ibid., p. 131).

Also, the relationship between the aggregate production and the apparent aggregate consumption showed a progressive reduction of Italian industrial competitiveness throughout 1992. In fact, given the production, the demand for imports was bigger than that for exports. The fact that internal demand exceeded internal production for nine years consecutively demonstrated the existence of a competitiveness problem. This, according to Confindustria, had eventually acquired a structural dimension since Italian industry had lost competitiveness to foreign competitors not only in growth periods, but also in recessive ones. Indeed, the constant appreciation of the real exchange rate in the last years of Italian participation in the EMS, argued Confindustria (1992, ch. 4), had resulted in the erosion of the competitiveness margins which Italian companies had gained by means of the structural interventions of the late 1970s, early 1980s. It was true that Italian entry in the EMS in 1979 initially reduced the production costs (ibid.) of Italian companies. However, subsequently, the commitment to fixed exchange rates had eroded the initial gains and had prevented, if not blocked altogether, the achievement of a strong competitive position in the export-oriented sectors.

Furthermore, the progressive deterioration of the current account, and particularly the increase of imports, did not seem to be related to any limit on the supply side. In this respect too, the comparison with the early 1980s offered some interesting insights. In fact, while in that period, the collapse of demand in the industrial sector had led to a reduction of the productive capacity, in the following recessive phase it was possible to notice an increase in the productive capacity and, at the same time, its growing underutilisation (Confindustria, 1993, p. 133).

2 The Decline of Company Profitability

The distinguishing aspect of the early 1990s recession was, however, the worsening of profitability in the industrial sector. Affected in international competition, by the over-appreciation of the exchange rate, and at the same time by exceptionally high interest rates, Italian companies had experienced a progressive erosion of the profitability margins gained in the years of strong production growth, and had to sustain the growing pressure of financial charges.

In this context, the role played by the fall in competitiveness levels might be better understood by analysing the dynamics of production costs.

Despite a decrease in the growth rate of the overall input costs (variable costs), from 1989 onwards output prices were lower than costs, since the decrease of competitiveness led companies to lower prices sacrificing profit margins. The positive effect of the exchange rate appreciation on the side of costs was, thus, completely overcome by the negative effect on prices. As a result, between 1988 and 1992 profitability margins decreased by 11.2 per cent, while between 1980 and 1983 there had been a fall of only 3 per cent.

The differences between this recession and the previous one also appeared clearly in a sector analysis. Making 100 the level of profitability margins in

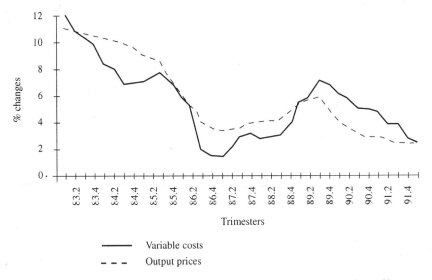

**Graph 23 Italian industrial transformation: costs and prices %
changes 1983–92**

Source: ISTAT.

the year preceding the production slow-downs (respectively, 1980 and 1988), the index reached a substantially lower level during the second recession. Indeed, while in 1980/83 the decrease of manufacturing company profitability was almost insignificant (-1.7 per cent) in the period between 1988 and 1992 it acquired worrying dimensions (-12.6 per cent on average).

The importance of these factors for the definition of the industrial sector exchange rate preferences on the eve of the crisis cannot be underestimated. After all, Confindustria did not conceal in its reports the existence of a clear relation between the position of Italian currency within the ERM and the poor performance of industrial profitability.

3   The Change of Companies' Financial Status

Another important indication of the depth of industrial crisis at the beginning of the 1990s is given by the analysis of its financial situation.

In the course of the 1980s, thanks to the overall improvement of the external economic conditions and of the business cycle, Italian companies, particularly big ones, had succeeded in substantially reducing their financial needs and in limiting their debts with the banking system.

Confindustria figures relative to the percentage financial composition of 1790 industrial and service companies[4] showed the changes occurring in their financial structure in the second half of the 1980s. In particular, it was held that the strong increase in the self-financed component, growing from 49.5 per cent of 1983–85 to 70.4 per cent of 1986–88, had allowed the increase of technical investment and the simultaneous reduction of financial debts.[5]

Table 15 % composition of company finances in Italy, 1983–91

	1983–85	1986–88	1989–91	1991
Technical investments[1]	57.8	64.8	56.8	63.4
Financial investments	13.7	25.2	33.1	32.3
Liquidity[2]	11.8	4.2	1.9	0.4
Currency[3]	16.7	5.8	8.2	3.9
Overall investments	100	100	100	100
Self-financing	49.5	70.4	48.5	46.6
Capital and reserves	23.0	6.6	10.9	8.1
Granted aids	6.7	5.6	4.6	5.4
Financial liabilities	15.1	12.2	29.6	31.1
Other liabilities	6.8	5.2	6.4	8.8
Overall resources	100	100	100	100

Notes

1   Without cumulative financial charges.
2   Cash, banks and fixed-interest securities.
3   Store, commercial credits and other asset changes without commercial and other short-term liabilities.

Source: Mediobanca in CSC Reports.

However, the 1990s production slow-down as well as the consequent worsening of companies' profitability from 1989 onwards, produced a decrease of the gross operative margins[6] which, in turn, determined the reduction of the self-financing opportunities and of the support by private shareholders. As a result, the overall indebtedness index, given by the level of indebtedness for each lira of capital and reserves, deteriorated.

According to Confindustria figures, the level of this index for private companies, which had reached its minimum of 1.9 per cent in 1986, was 2.6 per cent in 1991. The figures of the 'Centrale dei Bilanci', relating to 15,000 Italian private companies and used in Confindustria report, also showed an overall worsening of the industrial financial situation from 1989 to 1990. In 1990 the turnover growth rate for the industrial transformation companies at current prices decreased to 4.64 per cent, almost 7 per cent less than in 1989 and more than 9 per cent less than in 1988. Moreover, the enlargement of the divergence between self-financing and investments increased the weight of bank credit over value added. The situation was further worsened by the increase of short-term credit in relation to medium- and long-term credit.

Table 16 The financial situation of Italian industrial transformation companies 1982–90

	1982	1984	1986	1988	1989	1990
Turnover*	–	16.69	7.16	13.95	11.38	4.64
Investments/value added	–	15.37	15.98	17.99	18.46	19.31
Self-financing/ fixed investments	–	167.66	191.25	166.3	136.64	128.27
Financial liabilities/ value added	75.60	80.03	71.91	72.97	82.28	91.72
Short-term financial liabilities/ overall financial liabilities	50.73	52.66	51.57	53.66	54.27	55.96
Financial charges/ gross operative margins	51.91	44.93	32.57	26.40	31.60	39.95

* Turnover at current prices (1982 = 100). Annual per cent change.

Source: Centrale dei Bilanci.

A more accurate assessment of the change in companies' financial situation might be effected by differentiating between financial stocks and flows (Banca d'Italia, *Conti finanziari sulle attivita' e passivita' finanziarie dell' economia*, various issues). In the first semester of 1992 the flow of corporate external financing increased by 68,000 billion lire, about 15.6 per cent more, while at the end of 1991 it had increased by 10.5 per cent and at the end of 1990 by 17 per cent. Moreover, in the same period, short-term bank credits grew by 40.1 per cent leading debts with bank to reach 65 per cent of the overall corporate external financing.

Regarding the level of interest rates, the figures of Confindustria showed that the small and medium companies were charged the highest interest rates. Comparing the early 1980s recessive wave with that of the early 1990s, Confindustria pointed out that in the latter the divergence between the interest rates applied to the biggest and to the smallest credits was growing again. It is also worth noting that the reduction of nominal interest rates during the 1990s slow-down concealed an opposite trend of the real interest rates due to the simultaneous decrease of the level of prices.

Conflicts and Common Interests among the Italian Socioeconomic Groups

1   Setting the Problems: The Industrial Sector and the Level of Real Exchange Rates

From the above analysis it is possible to draw some interesting consequences which can be useful in identifying the change in economic sector preferences during the early 1990s economic slow-down and its relationship with the European exchange rate arrangements. First, the fall in production rates, although less remarkable than that of the early 1980s, was related to the performance of the balance of account. Indeed, on the one hand, the decrease in production levels interested to a wider extent the manufacturing sectors which characterise the Italian export specialisation model. On the other hand, an overall worsening of the real balance of the current account accompanied the slump, despite the fact the early 1990s crisis was not concomitant in all European countries.

Confindustria, in its 1992 and 1993 economic reports, has linked both these phenomena to a worsening of Italian industrial competitiveness which, in turn, was connected to an over-appreciation of the exchange rate in the ERM. Whether this explanation sounds plausible or not, it is meaningful that Confindustria expressed this opinion on the eve, and in the immediate aftermath, of Italian departure from the ERM.

Apart from Confindustria, the rest of the industrial community had not concealed in the course of 1992 the linkage between the exchange rate policy and the poor performance of Italian exports. Contemporary commentators even noted how dangerous for the stability of the lira were the repeated references to devaluation

Ennio Presutti, President of Assolombarda,[7] pointed out during the annual convention of the association in June 1992, how the severe decrease of the industrial production of Milan, -2.4 per cent in 1991, was due to the 'exchange rate straight-jacket'.

The President of the Association of the Small Enterprise, Giorgio Grati, explicitly stated that small enterprise was suffering from the loss of competitiveness due to the overvaluation of the real exchange rate.

For big industry it was Giorgio Falck, the major entrepreneur of steel industry in Italy, who demonstrated the contradictions of the Italian government and of Confindustria on the issue of the exchange rate and called for an immediate devaluation of the lira. In an article published by the *Corriere della Sera* on 20 July 1992, he defined as 'foolish' the whole attitude of the government towards the exchange rate issue. He pointed out how the increase in interest rates, as well as the loss of the foreign reserves by the Bank of Italy to defend an unsustainable exchange rate, more than neutralised fiscal measures aimed at cutting public deficit. On the contrary, an early and not too 'dramatised' devaluation of the lira would allow the whole industrial sector to regain the competitiveness lost.

He was echoed by Danilo Carabelli, President of the Federlombarda, Ettore Fortuna, leader of Mineracqua and Carlo Alberto Corneliani, of Federtessile, all members of Confindustria ('Totosvalutazione tra le imprese', *Mercati Finanziari*, 23 July 1992), as well as by other important entrepreneurs including Giordano Zucchi, owner of Zucchi Bassetti, and Angelo Pavia, owner of Liabel.

On the other hand, the silence of FIAT should not be found too surprising. Of course, the crisis also hit hard the core of Italian big industry, the car industry, to the extent that in 1991 it experienced a further reduction of 0.7 per cent in the export of cars and the doubling of the external deficit, from -1,829bn lire in 1990 to -3,988 in 1991.[8] In particular, FIAT Group, which, alone, accounted for 3.5 per cent of national GNP, saw an unprecedented reduction in car production, declining by 300,000 units both in 1991 and in 1992. A number of plants were closed, including the Autobianchi factory in Desio, the Lancia factory in Chivasso and the Innocenti plant in Lambrate. Operative margins also collapsed, from 4,670bn lire in 1989 to 662bn lire in 1991 and the substantial worsening of the overall net financial position of the group reached the level of -270bn lire with a decrease of 840bn lire from the previous year. However, contrary to small and medium industry, FIAT could count on the providential support of the government to survive the crisis. Indeed, the government punctually intervened. It provided non-refundable funds for about 3,000bn lire, granting financial help to Algeria to allow the agreement on the establishment of an Algerian FIAT plant in Tiaret, as well as paying for the entire costs of the 'Cassa Integrazione' and of the 'Prepensionamenti' of more than 10,000 surplus workers.

Summing up, that the overvaluation of the Italian exchange rate and the difficulties experienced by Italian economy at the beginning of the 1990s were deeply connected to the performance of the lira in the ERM was by no means a mystery. In an interview with the author, Giuliano Amato, Italian Prime Minister from 25 June 1992 explicitly claimed:

> As early as June 1992 the whole of Europe knew that Italian real exchange rates were overvalued and that the stability was maintained only through excessively high interest rates. It was a situation similar to when the blow of the *Scirocco* announces the storm: everyone was expecting a devaluation of the lira (see Talani, 1997b).

Moreover, the figures of the Bank of Italy show clearly that Italian real exchange rates started to appreciate sharply in 1988[9] maintaining very high levels in the two years preceding the crisis and peaking exactly on the eve of the devaluation, on the third trimester of 1992 (+9.5 per cent vis-à-vis 1987) (see Graph 24).

Many contemporary economists also noted the consequences of a similar trend on Italy's competitive position. Prof. Paolo Savona had explained the effects of the overvaluation of the lira on the Italian economy, calling for a depreciation of the exchange rates, as early as in January 1991 ('Dovevate svalutare prima!', *La Stampa*, 4 July 1992). In an article in June 1991, Micossi, then director of the 'Centro studi Confindustria, had pointed out how in 1990 the lira had appreciated in real terms by 5.3 per cent vis-à-vis industrial countries and 2.4 per cent vis-à-vis the EC (see De Nardis and Micossi, 1991).

Later on, when the difficulties of the lira inside the ERM became evident, other economists warned about the impact of the overvaluation of the lira on the performance of the industrial sector and supported the option of an early devaluation of the currency. In August 1992, Siro Lombardini, President of the Italian Society of Economists, claimed that an early devaluation of the lira would be the only solution to the exchange rate crisis. The lira was 'clearly overvalued' and recognising it would be a coherent act that the markets would certainly appreciate. According to Victor Uckmar, Prof. of Finance at Genova and of Fiscal Law at the Bocconi University, the competitive position of Italy needed a devaluation since 1990 (Uckmar: riallineare. Confindustria: no', *Il Secolo XIX*, 26 August 1992).

Given all this, the behaviour of the markets, which from June 1992

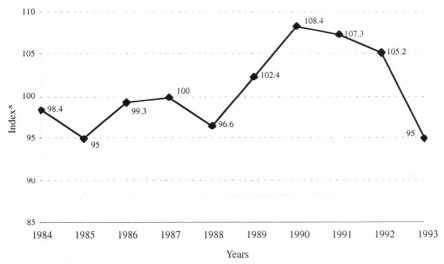

* Increase = real appreciation, decrease = real depreciation.

Graph 24 Italy real effective exchange rates 1984–93

Source: Bank of Italy.

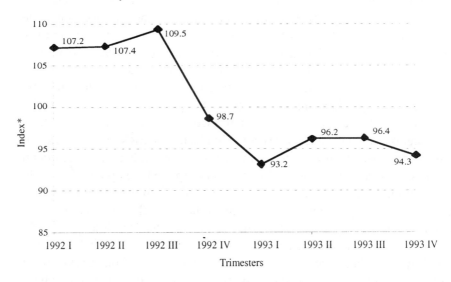

* Increase = real appreciation, decrease = real depreciation.

Graph 25 Italy real effective exchange rates 1992 I–1993 IV

Source: Bank of Italy.

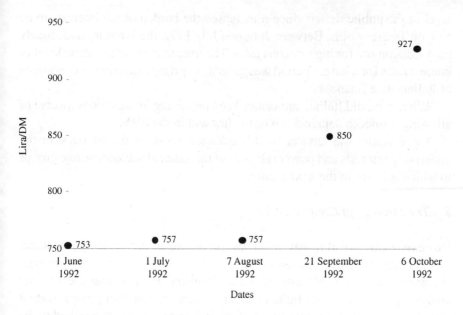

Graph 26 Italian £/DM nominal exchange rates, selected dates

Source: Barucci, 1995.

onwards[10] had been undermining the position of the lira within the ERM bands cannot be considered completely irrational.

The true mystery, as correctly pointed out by Spaventa, is, instead, why the Italian government did not decide to devalue the lira inside the ERM before the situation collapsed and the lira was compelled to leave the ERM altogether.

Indeed, an early devaluation of the lira was an option to which even Schlesinger, then President of the Bundesbank, seemed fairly open, to the extent that on 18 June 1992, immediately after a speculative attack on the lira and making clear reference to the Italian government, he claimed: 'The EMS is not a fixed exchange rate system. It has become like that because some governments refuse to devalue' ('Bankitalia in trincea per difendere la lira', *La stampa*, 19 June 1992).

The decision to devalue would certainly reduce the pressure of the markets, allowing the Bundesbank to decrease interest rates and the Italian central bank to maintain interest rates at a level more appropriate to the conditions of the economy in that period.

Moreover, the high level of interest rates had a significant impact on the level of the public deficit since it increased the burden of the interests to be paid on Treasury bills. Between June and July 1992, the Treasury had already paid 1,880bn lire for high interest rates. The maintenance of the same level of interest rates for a longer period was judged very dangerous for the conditions of Italian state finances.

Why, then, did Italian authorities keep on raising interest rates instead of allowing a smooth depreciation of the lira within the ERM?

Once again, the answer to this question must be traced back in the underlying interests and power relations of the national socioeconomic groups to which we turn in the next section.

2   The Strategy of Confindustria

However paradoxical it may seem, the behaviour of the Italian government on the issue of the devaluation of the lira was by no means inconsistent with the preferences and interests of Italian industry. Even if many economic analyses produced by the Italian industrial sector during that period made it clear to what extent the difficulties of the Italian economy were linked to the performance of the lira, the official position of Confindustria was resolutely against any hypothesis of devaluation. Indeed, already before the results of the Danish referendum on Maastricht, the hypothesis of a devaluation of the lira had been circulating within the industrial circles. For example, at a gathering in Varese Italian entrepreneurs explicitly required the newly elected President of Confindustria, Abete,[11] to ask the government for the devaluation of the lira ('Abete: per la competitivita' non serve svalutare la lira', *Mercati Finanziari,* 2 June 1992; 'Abete: svalutare la lira sarebbe una vera follia', *Il messaggero,* June 1992). Abete rejected this request categorically on the grounds that: 'The devaluation of the lira it is not at all the solution of the problem and Confindustria is not favourable to it. We must instead solve with coherence the problem of labour costs and of inflation' (*Mercati Finanziari,* op. cit.).

Similar declarations were reiterated more and more frequently in the course of the summer of 1992. On 18 June 1992, after the speculative attacks brought increased market interest rates[12] to 14.81 per cent, Luigi Abete restated his position saying:

A devaluation of the lira is not in the interests of anyone, apart from the foreign market operators who speculate on the exchange rates. The real economy and the productive world do not want it. ... We think that those who believe that the speculative attacks and the rise of market interest rates may trigger an increase in the Official Discount Rate and a devaluation of the lira are wrong ('Confindustria: il cambio non si tocca', *La Repubblica*, 19 June 1992).

Again, on 3 July, in the middle of a new, violent wave of speculation, Abete, echoed by Cipolletta ('E' un problema della SME. Parla Innocenzo Cipolletta, direttore generale della Confindustria', *Il Giornale,* 4 July 1992; 'Calma Europa', *Il Secolo XIX*, 4 July 1992), General Director of Confindustria, claimed:

> The devaluation of the lira is not a useful shortcut and the international investors must understand that, if they believe in the devaluation of the lira, they are completely wrong. ... To restore industrial competitiveness it is necessary to implement an austere wage policy ('La Confindustria tiene botta: non si svaluta', *Il Messaggero*, 4 July 1992; see also 'Non si riallinea, ma riducete i tassi', *La stampa*, 4 July 1992).

Even when the contradictions inside Confindustria exploded and the issue had to be tackled by the assembly of the association, Abete repeated:

> Our position against the devaluation is not based on ideological or moral considerations but on the general interests of enterprises. We have discussed on the advantages and disadvantages of devaluation and then summed them up. We drew the conclusions of our discussions and hence our *political* position against the devaluation ('Svalutazione, solo danni. Dall'industria un coro di no', *La Stampa*, 21 July 1992).

Given the dire economic conditions of the Italian industrial sector, given the costs of the dogged defence of the lira in terms of higher interest rates and of loss of foreign reserve, given also the many contradictions internal to Confindustria, how can we explain the obstinacy with which the President of Confindustria reiterated its official *political* position against the devaluation?

The solution to this question has been clearly offered by Monti in an article of June 1992. While recognising that the difficulties of the lira in the exchange markets had clear economic justifications, Prof. Monti categorically ruled out any hypothesis of devaluation of the lira. This could not happen 'before a deep financial recovery and *a deep change in the relations between the state and the labour market* was put forward, approved and implemented' (author's italics). Further, he explicitly claimed that a devaluation before the approval and implementation of such a programme would make 'less cogent the pressure necessary to overcome the opposition to the definition and realisation of similar measures'. Therefore, it was necessary to delay the moment of the realignment which, however, 'after the complete realisation of those measures' would be absolutely necessary to 'allow the recovery of the economy' (see Monti, 1992).

In an interview with the author Giuliano Amato, Italian Prime Minister during the summer of 1992 disclosed that this was exactly the strategy of the Italian government.[13] In that occasion he claimed that: 'We [Amato and Ciampi[14]] were not interested in a devaluation of the lira in July 1992 since we wanted the agreement on labour costs and a devaluation would have been an obstacle to it' (see Talani, 1997b).

The reason was because:

> The situation of currency crisis was certainly understood by the social partners in Italy, including the trade unions. The atmosphere was already heavy in June 1992. The social partners understood that there was a problem of international financial credibility which made it urgent for everyone to reach agreement, also considering the fact that, if the boat were to be shipwrecked, no one wanted to be blamed (ibid.).[15]

On the other hand, it is not particularly difficult to demonstrate that this was also the strategy of the industrial sector generally and of Confindustria in particular during the summer of 1992.

Indeed, right from the start of the currency turmoil, Abete had been very keen to associate his declarations on the stability of the lira with some claims on the need to solve, as soon as possible, the problem of labour costs. The list of all the speeches by representatives of Confindustria or of the industrial community in general on the need to solve the problem of currency stability by reaching immediately an agreement on labour costs is endless.[16] However it is worth reporting the words of Micossi, Director of the Confindustria Study Center: 'We [Confindustria] have been the first to propose an appropriate wage policy as the instrument to remain stable within the narrow ERM bands' ('Il calvario non e' finito', *La Repubblica*, 30 August 1992).

Sometimes these declarations even acquired the form of a true 'ultimatum'. This is the case of the declarations of the representatives of the 'Centro Studi Confindustria (CSC)' at the presentation of its annual Report on the Business Cycle 1992 (Rapporto sulla Congiuntura). In 1991, Stefano Micossi noticed the level of industrial workers' remuneration increased by 9.1 per cent and labour costs grew by 8.4 per cent. With fixed exchange rates and with the Bank of Italy committed to the defence of the lira, the CSC considered this pattern of costs and wages unsustainable for Italian industry. If the government did not take the lead in substantially reversing this pattern, it was anticipated that there would be an inevitable and terrible financial crisis (see Micossi, 1992). This was also the opinion of Giorgio Bodo, head office of FIAT studies centre, who, on the occasion of the presentation of the report claimed:

> In this situation, the actual real exchange rate is really too heavy. If the government does not take serious decisions to control inflation and the deficit, devaluation will be the only possible solution ('Monito degli industriali al governo: misure drastiche o la svalutazione', *La Repubblica*, 26 June 1992).

The position of Confindustria on labour costs was completely endorsed by the Confapi to the extent that they adopted as their own position the document on the subject presented by Abete to the government and to the trade unions. Indeed, 'the progressive loss of competitiveness due to the impetuous increase of labour costs' ('I costi strangolano le piccole imprese', *Il Sole 24 ore,* 28 June 1992; see also 'Il peso della crisi e' tutto sulle aziende', *Il Resto del Carlino*, 8 July 1992) was considered by Alessandro Cociro, newly nominated President of Confapi, as one of the most pressing problems of small enterprise.

There were even some entrepreneurs who made public the strategy of the industrial sector by explicitly calling for devaluation after the solution of the problem of costs. Bruna Soresina, General Director of Federmeccanica, claimed, on the eve of the agreement on the July Protocol, that a devaluation was necessary to better the conditions of Italian companies but only 'after having achieved the objectives of the reduction of inflation and strengthening of the system' ('Fra gli industriali cresce la voglia di svalutazione', *Il Giorno*, 31 July 1992).

In the light of the insights coming from these declarations, it becomes clear that the industrial world was not opposed to a devaluation of the lira for 'ideological or moral reasons' ('Svalutazione, solo danni. Dall'industria un coro di no', *La Stampa*, 21 July 1992), but only for *political* ones. Namely, they needed to defer the moment of a devaluation, whose necessity was evident to anyone, entrepreneurs and financial markets alike, in order to gain bargaining power in the 'battle of wages' with the trade unions. Indeed, devaluation was considered by the industrial sector a necessary condition but not sufficient to solve its problems: the other important objective was the block of 'wage bargaining' and the definitive elimination of the 'Scala Mobile'.

After all, a devaluation of the lira could be obtained without demanding it explicitly or even by pretending to be opposed to a similar solution in public occasions. Instead, the climate of tension and of tragedy that the continuous attacks on the lira created in the Italian political debate was necessary for the industrial elite to pose the question of wages as crucial in order to avoid a terrible financial crisis.

It is thus possible to explain why Confindustria and industry generally had always been opposed, in their official declarations, to the devaluation of the lira. By doing so it was possible to create a situation of crisis and tangible tension in which to present the intervention on wages as the only plausible solution but whose only outcome could be a substantial devaluation of the lira within or outside the ERM.

3 Confindustria, the Trade Unions and the Battle of Wages

The tendency of Confindustria to approach the problem of labour costs through the mechanisms by which they are determined, starting from indexation, was, indeed, a long dated one (see also ch. 1), and represented the core of the industrial and wage policy of Pininfarina's presidency (see Unnia, 1993, p. 185).

After a long controversy between the CGIL, CISL, UIL, Confindustria and the government, the latter had, with the law no. 191, 13 July 1990, prorogated the mechanism of the Scala Mobile for the whole year 1991. However, from January 1992, the mechanism was again under the bargaining autonomy of the social partners (see CNEL, 1990, p. 30). At the expiration of the deadline, the government confirmed, with the 'Protocollo' of December 1991, its firm decision not to allow any other prorogation by law of the Scala Mobile. It, indeed, stated that by 1 June 1992 all the problems relating to a new general system of bargaining and to the structure of retribution had to be tackled.

The negotiations did not in fact start until June 1992 since, while the trade unions had shown many times their willingness to settle the issue as soon as possible, Confindustria seemed reluctant to face a period of harsh confrontation with its social partners to reach a difficult agreement. Moreover, the Italian entrepreneurial class tended to interpret the Protocol of December 1991 as the definitive death declaration of the 'Scala Mobile' and wanted to enforce this interpretation by not paying the 'scatto di contingenza' due for May 1992. This was what eventually happened.

The situation in which the dialogue on the issue of retribution was reopened was, thus, particularly heated. The battle was doomed to be extremely hard unless there was some external factor pressing the trade unions, or, better, the CGIL, to accept the agreement as the only possible alternative to the abyss. This external factor was represented by the speculative attacks on the lira.

This does not mean that the speculative attacks were provoked by the Italian economic elite,[17] but simply that the Italian employer class as a whole acted within the limits of the possible.

The negotiations were opened again on 2 June 1992, after the Governor of the Bank of Italy, Carlo Azeglio Ciampi, in his speech to the annual assembly of the Central Bank had explicitly claimed:

> If the dynamics of nominal wages both in the public and in the private sector is not made consistent with the stability of the exchange rate, the decrease of inflation will become slower, competitiveness will deteriorate, both internal and external market shares will be lost, income will fall and employment and investment rates collapse (Ciampi, 1992a, p. 16).

Confindustria immediately put up for discussion a 'global plan' aimed at revolutionising the Italian industrial relations system. The employers' association made the following requests. First, it asked for the implementation of the art 39 of the Italian Constitution.[18] Second, the definition of two levels of 'concertation' (*Concertazione*), the first inter-confederal, to define the wage policy contents, the second territorial, to define the issues of interest to all sectors. Third, the activation of two levels of wage bargaining, one per category (*per categoria*) every six years on the normative issues, and one per industry (*settoriale*) every two years to negotiate wage agreements. The agreements at plant-level (*aziendale*) were accepted only as an alternative to the industry-level ones.

Abete, President of Confindustria since May 1992, proposed the elimination of every kind of indexation and allowed for the application of a mechanism of the 'Scala Mobile' only in case of contract vacancy (*vacatio contrattuale*) or lack of implementation of the national agreements ('Ad Abete il primo round sul salario', *Il Mattino*, 3 June 1992).

As already underlined, Confindustria's proposals were also immediately endorsed by the ASAP, Intersind and Confapi, the other employer representatives admitted to the negotiations.

On the contrary, by the beginning of the negotiations the trade unions had not been able to define a common position. Far from it, CGIL, CISL, UIL arrived at the meeting of 2 June 1992, with three documents each differing from the others on very substantial issues.

The CISL started from the assumption that it was possible to give up any form of indexation mechanism in exchange for the maintenance of all bargaining levels. Sergio D'Antoni, secretary of the CISL, had been repeating all the time that his federation was ready to renounce any kind of wage indexation if Confindustria accepted making 'integrative bargaining' (*contrattazione integrativa*) compulsory. The only requirement was to guarantee a gross minimum wage of 900,000 lire completely indexed to the inflation rate in case of contract vacancy.

The CGIL, the biggest Italian trade union, started from the opposite assumption that some form of wage indexation had to be retained. According to its secretary, Bruno Trentin, the new 'Scala Mobile' had to be equal for everyone and had to be paid every six months. The amounts had to be established in advance on the basis of programmed inflation rate. However, an annual mechanism of realignment with the effective inflation rate based on the ISTAT index had to be guaranteed.

Finally, for the UIL any kind of automatic index had to disappear, while it was up to the law to establish that wages, as well as prices, had to be linked to the programmed inflation rate stated annually by the Parliament. However, no mechanism for 'catching up' with effective inflation was provided in its document ('La trattativa parte in salita', *Il Giornale*, 2 June 1992; 'CGIL, CISL e UIL in ordine sparso. C'e' intesa solo sui salari del '92', *Il sole 24 ore*, 2 June 1992).

Trade unions' divisions on the approach to the problem of labour costs and of the 'Scala Mobile' were also reflected in the different assessments the various federations gave of the Confindustria document. A substantial part of the CGIL rejected a negotiation on those bases, while the socialist component of the CGIL, headed by Ottaviano del Turco, the CISL and the UIL looked on it with some favour. However, the trade unions excluded from the outset the possibility to sign separate agreements ('CGIL, CISL e UIL divise sul piano Confindustria. Trentin: inaccettabile', *Avvenire*, 3 June 1992).

Eventually, the issue risked to provoke a definitive fracture within the Italian Trade Union Confederation, since the achievement of an agreement, particularly on the question of the 'Scala Mobile', seemed impossible throughout the whole course of the negotiations ('Sulla scala mobile e' guerra. Bordate contro Trentin', *Il Manifesto*, 5 June 1992; 'Scala Mobile: torna l'incubo S. Valentino', *Il Manifesto*, 6 June 1992)

On 18 June 1992, just before a new round of discussions with the government, the three federations succeeded in finding an agreement but only on principle, which left aside the core of the problems to be tackled ('Sul costo del lavoro intesa sindacale per gli aumenti '92–'93', *Il Giornale*, 18 June 1992; 'Uniti ma non sulla contingenza', *l'Unita'*, 19 June 1992; 'Costo del lavoro: altra fumata nera', *La Stampa*, 20 June 1992), namely the issue of wage mechanisms and of the structure of bargaining.

The negotiations with the government and the employers, as well as the discussions within the Confederation and the CGIL itself, went on until the end of July in an atmosphere of growing political and economic disarray, with the position of the lira within the ERM continuously under attack. Only on 31 July 1992, the trade unions announced that were able to propose a common document. This showed a substantial shift in the position of the CGIL towards the demands of Confindustria. The CGIL-CISL-UIL abandoned the idea of an indexation mechanism to realign wages with inflation, apart from the case of contract vacancy (*vacatio contrattuale*), and opted for a defence of the wage purchasing power completely relying on bargaining. On annual contract renewals the trade unions would ask for wage increases based on programmed inflation and, in case of substantial difference between the latter and effective inflation, they would require an increase of minimum wage levels. According to the proposal of the trade unions, national contracts should last three years, while Confindustria wanted only two years. Finally, the document provided for two levels of bargaining both for normative issues and for wage ones, while Confindustria accepted only one level of wage bargaining ('Salari, per i sindacati scala mobile archiviata', *Avanti*, 30 July 1992).

However, also this proposal of the trade unions was rejected by Confindustria and by the government. Indeed, the Protocol eventually signed on 31 July 1992, represented a major victory for the employers, and a major defeat for that part of the CGIL which had been opposed to it from the very beginning of the negotiations. The trade unions had agreed to the almost complete elimination of the 'Scala Mobile' and had accepted the block of wage bargaining at plant level for the whole of 1993 in exchange of a forfeit sum of £ 20,000 per month for all workers. The more complex question of the structure of wage bargaining, not tackled by the Protocol, was left to future negotiations.

Immediately after the signing of the Protocol and immediately before resigning as secretary of the CGIL, Bruno Trentin explained that his decision had been determined by 'the worries for the extremely difficult economic and financial situation of the country'.

The strategy of Confindustria and of the government had been completely successful, and the 'ultimatum' between the devaluation and the agreement on wages had been perfectly credible. Indeed, the acceptance of the trade unions of the Protocol on labour costs was based on the assumption of exchange rate stability. In the event of devaluation the basis itself of the trade unions' consensus ('Abete: svalutare la lira sarebbe una vera follia', *Il Messaggero*, 2 July 1992), which was the need to pursue an anti-inflationary wage policy, collapsed in the light of its possible inflationary impact, which would find the trade unions without any tool to defend wage purchasing power. Needless to say that this was what punctually happened in the wake of Italian departure from the ERM.

In September the battle was open again for the implementation of the Protocol and for the beginning of the negotiations on the second part of the reform, the one relating to the structure of bargaining. This bargaining process, according to the July agreement, should be over by mid-September. However, this time the entrepreneurs did not seem particularly keen to reopen the issue.[19] They had obtained an important victory on the side of labour costs. Now it was necessary to think about the other important issue, competitiveness, whose achievement the devaluation of the lira would certainly facilitate.

Indeed, by September the position of Confindustria towards the devaluation had clearly changed. After a meeting with President Abete and with the director Cipolletta, Paolo Passanti of the Centro studi Confindustria anticipated:

> The party in favour of the devaluation is getting stronger also within Confindustria. I cannot exclude that in the next days our [official] position on the cost of money and on devaluation will change ('Cresce il partito della svalutazione', *Avvenire*, 6 September 1992).

Moreover, a survey of the '*Espresso*' which had interviewed one third of Confindustria assembly (53 members over 155) showed that 44 per cent was favourable to the devaluation of the lira.

Outside Confindustria, the other employers' associations were more explicit. Cociro, President of the Confapi, explained: 'Given the fact that a realignment of the currencies is already scheduled before 1997, ... it would be better to have it now' (see 'Speriamo in un rialzo di breve durata', *Corriere della sera*, 5 September 1992).

At this point, the government was also ready to devalue and asked its European counterparts for a similar decision to be taken. In the words of the then Italian Prime Minister:

> In a secret meeting in Paris on August 23–25,[20] 1992, pressed by the Italian requests, the German authorities declared themselves in favour of a revaluation of the DM. However, this time France opposed categorically any such solution before the referendum of September 20 (see Talani, 1997).

The markets did not need more signals and the speculative attacks of 13 September 1992 compelled everyone to accept a devaluation which, by that point, only needed to be formalised.

This was the outcome of the struggle between the trade unions and the employers' associations. To complete the picture of the power relations between Italian interest groups at the eve of the departure of the lira from the ERM it is necessary to consider the position and preferences of the other important component of Italian capitalism, the banking sector. This, together with industrial capital, had provided the basis of consensus on which the ERM founded its credibility.

4 The Banking Sector and the Apparent Battle of Interest Rates

As could easily be imagined, the reactions of the banking community to the decision by the Italian authorities to offset the difficulties of the lira by raising interest rates were not very negative, at least at the outset.

The banking community had already defended the choice to keep high interest rates in a period in which the lira was still overvalued and the ERM was still not under strain. At that time, mid-1991, the need to support the exchange rate inside the ERM was only one of the considerations leading Italian bankers to justify a policy of high interest rates. The other ones were of a more structural nature such as the need to finance public expenditure through the allocation of Treasury bills, to contrast inflationary pressures, to sustain the gathering of savings, to attract foreign capital as well as to compensate the banking system for the increased risk of lending to industry (see Bianchi, 1991a; see also Arcucci, 1991; Bianchi, 1991b).

As the effects of the recession started to worsen and the industrial community begun to complain about the excessively high cost of credit,[21] the official position of the banking community changed. The increase in the cost of credit was increasingly justified as the only way to defend the lira inside the ERM (see Petrini, 1992; see also 'Le banche sempre piu' esose. Caro denaro, via ai rialzi', *Il Mondo*, 26 June 1992; Esposito, 1992). However, the broadening of the spread between the prime rate[22] and the rates on bank deposits[23] (which grew by more than 3 per cent in the course of 1992, from 6 per cent to more than 9 per cent (see 'Banca ladrona?', *Panorama*, 20 September 1992)) clearly demonstrates the capacity of the banking system to take advantage of the difficulties of the lira.

It is in this context that the declarations of the representatives of the banking community in favour of the maintenance of the lira within the narrow bands of the ERM must be understood. Indeed, at the annual convention of the Italian Banking Association in Rome on 24 June 1992, the ABI president claimed:

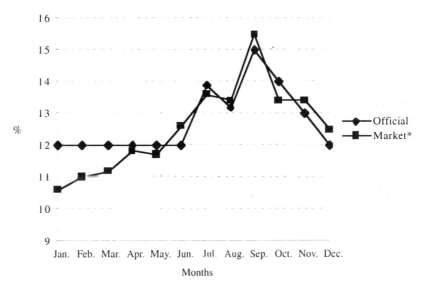

* Average data

Graph 27 1992: Italian official and market nominal interest rates

Source: Bank of Italy.

> ... The banking system deserves to be considered efficient as a transmission
> mechanism of the monetary policy. In this context, the contribution of the banking
> system to the stability of the exchange rate has proved relevant. The system has
> ...favoured the flow of foreign capital as well as promoted multi-currency
> corporate finance. A similar situation is based on the willingness ... to participate
> to the narrow ERM bands and on an appropriate differential between internal
> and external interest rates (Bianchi, 1992b, p. 9).

However, that this position was not particularly rigid and that there was
much room for change appeared more clearly from the declarations of other
representatives of the banking sector. For example, just after the ABI
convention, Antonio Pedone, President of the Crediop and assistant of the
newly elected Prime Minister, Giuliano Amato, addressed the problem of
devaluation from a different perspective. He claimed that even if it was too
early to speak about a devaluation of the lira, this would prove inevitable in
the future unless the government adopted economic policies 'credible for the
market' ('Svalutare la lira sarebbe inutile e controproducente', *Avanti*, 25 June
1992). Indeed, excessively high interest rates could not be sustained by the

banking sector for too long a period, given their repercussions on the performance of the industrial sector ('Tassi, i rimorsi dei banchieri', *La stampa*, 9 July 1992). This performance, in turn, was extremely important for the bankers, as the level of indebtedness of the industry with the banks had reached worrying dimensions.

As we have seen in Confindustria's analyses, the substantial fall of profitability margins (-12.6 on average in the manufacturing sector) suffered by Italian industry from 1989 onwards made Italian companies much more dependent on credit issued by the banking system.

Also the annual Mediobanca report, published in July 1992, on the aggregate data of the most important Italian companies, 1,790 in total, showed clearly how from 1989 to 1991, their financial situation had substantially worsened while their level of indebtedness with the banking system had been increasing constantly ('E' crisi per l'industria e la crescita si arresta' *Il sole 24 ore*, 1 August 1992).

To what extent this trend worried the banking community, was pointed out by Tancredi Bianchi during the ABI annual assembly of June 1992. In this occasion, the president of the ABI lamented how the rate of cash lending to clients had grown excessively in previous years in response to the worsening of the companies' financial situation. As a consequence, the banking system could suffer in the future of a true liquidity risk. Moreover, the difficult economic situation of the industrial sector, added specific problems of solvency of the clients which were already visible in part in the situation of the so-called bank overdues ('sofferenze') (see ABI, 1992, p. 12), which, however, normally reacted with a two/three year delay.[24]

Given this situation it becomes clear why excessively high interest rates could not be considered in the interests of the banking community, or, as claimed by the President of the ABI:

> I hope the increase of interest rates is just a temporary measure since every operation has some benefits ... and some costs. ... By now benefits overcome costs, but in the long run costs would prevail over benefits.

This would be even more the case in the future, since the decision of the Bank of Italy to strengthen and extend the relations between the banking and the industrial sector by finally adopting the second EU banking directive, further contributed to tie the interests of the two communities. This decision had been unveiled for the first time by the Governor of the Bank of Italy in the course of his 1992 annual speech and had the clear aim to help Italian big industry sustain their difficult financial situation.

Table 17 Indebtedness for each lira of net owned resources (lire) in Italy 1988–91

	1988	1989	1990	1991
1,790 companies				
Total debts	2.9	2.9	3.0	3.3
Debts with banks	0.9	0.9	1.0	1.0
Public enterprises				
Total debts	4.5	4.3	4.0	4.5
Debts with banks	1.5	1.3	1.1	1.2
Private enterprises				
Total debts	2.2	2.2	2.4	2.6
Debts with banks	0.7	0.8	0.9	0.9
Medium enterprises				
Total debts	2.2	2.9	3.2	3.2
Debts with banks	0.8	1.2	1.3	1.3
Industrial companies				
Total debts	2.8	2.7	2.9	3.1
Debts with banks	0.8	0.8	0.9	0.9
Services companies				
Total debts	3.6	3.9	3.5	4.2
Debts with banks	1.5	1.5	1.3	1.5

Source: Mediobanca.

Table 18 Degree of risk of lending in Italy 1988–91

	New bank overdues/ pre-existing lending	New bank overdues/ pre-existing bank overdues
1988	1.7	17.9
1989	1.6	20.1
1990	1.6	25
1991	2.4	41.8

Source: Bank of Italy.

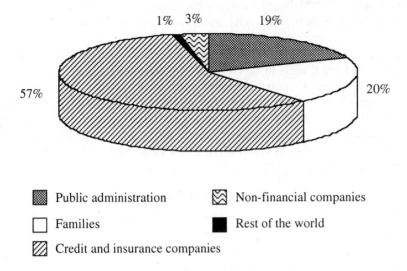

Graph 28 Lending % distribution in Italy 1991

Source: ABI.

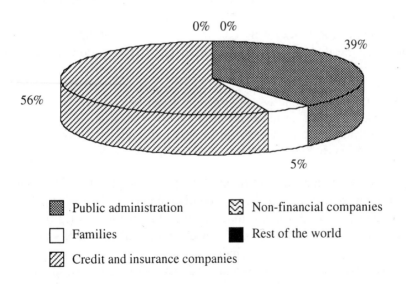

Graph 29 'Sofferenze bancarie' % composition in Italy 1991

Source: ABI.

Ciampi explained the project to the banking community during his speech at the annual assembly of the ABI. In this occasion he declared:

> It is essential that the bank/enterprise relationships develop in a different direction from that traditionally limited to the lending operations, usually carried out by a number of credit institutions contextually, towards forms of global financial assistantship. ... The decision to allow the banks to purchase capital quotas of non-financial enterprises must be interpreted as a step towards that aim. The related substantial and procedural aspects, which are now being defined by the Bank of Italy, will be inserted in the implementation rules of the second banking directive (see Ciampi, 1992b).

With the d.lgs. 14 December 1992, N. 481 and of the 'Testo Unico delle leggi bancarie e creditizie, 27 August 1993', the second banking directive was finally introduced into the Italian legal system. It allowed the banks to intervene directly in the restructuring of Italian big industry by a total amount of 26.000bn lire in 1993 and of 60.000bn lire in 1994 (see ABI, 1994, p. 18).

Thus, the struggle between the banking and the industrial community on the interest rate issue, which, indeed, seemed to characterise the period leading to the departure of the lira from the ERM, must not be overestimated and indeed the interests of the two sectors may be considered to overlap significantly.[25]

Also on the question of wages the interests of the banking sector tended to coincide with that of the industrial. In an early intervention on the issue Tancredi Bianchi declared:

> Actually, the economic systems cannot be balanced and keep growing if the remuneration of the factors of production is not in line with their productivity. Wage dynamics exceeding the differentials of work productivity provoke inflation ... (see Bianchi, 1992a).

In conclusion, in the case of Italian departure from the ERM, just as in its entry, it is not possible to hypothesise a conflict of interests between the Italian banking and industrial sectors. Indeed, given the characteristics of Italian capital structure, the shift in the preferences of the banking sector was led by the shift in the preferences of the industrial one.

As we have seen, the worries and the demands of the industrial sector in the middle of the early 1990s recessive phase were focusing on three main areas. First the overvaluation of exchange rates; second, excessively high interest rates, and finally the need to keep down production costs through the block of wage increases. Indeed, devaluation was a necessary but not sufficient step for the industry, while the banking sector agreed to a similar solution provided that it would not imply excessive costs in terms of lower real interest rates. Both of them, therefore, had a clear-cut interest in the successful (from their point of view) conclusion of the negotiations with the trade unions on the block on wage bargaining and on the definitive elimination of the 'Scala Mobile'.

On the other hand, the trade unions, given also the extent of their internal divisions, were not in a condition to resist the pressures that the government was exerting on them by continuously underlying the negative effects of the labour costs issue on the Italian economic and financial situation.

The result was that all the priorities of the industrial sector were satisfied. The historical agreement on the abolition of the 'Scala Mobile' was, after a decade of conflicts, finally signed by the Confederations of Trade Unions, the lira was free to fluctuate on currency markets and to reach a competitive exchange rate level, while interest rates could start to decrease.

What all this was to mean for the position of Italy in the future European Monetary Union will be the subject of further analysis in the following sections. However, before moving to that issue, the attention must be focused on the change in British socioeconomic attitudes towards the ERM. The aim is to assess to what extent the origins of the British and Italian departures from the system may be compared and to what extent they have different implications for the future.

Notes

1   Reference is made here, mainly to the Annual Reports of Confindustria published in May 1992 and 1993.
2   The apparent demand is defined as the sum between the production and the imports minus the exports.
3   For the textiles it was -2.22 per cent in 1991/1992 while in 1980/83 it was + 2.32; clothes, -1.57 in 1991/92, +2.92 in 1980/83, leather and shoes, -2.25 in 1991/92, + 1.57 in 1980/83, vehicles, - 6.54 in 1991/92, +2.44 in 1980/83. Source: CSC, 1992. See Table 15.
4   Mediobanca's sample. See Confindustria, 1992.
5   Those are measured both in terms of the relation between financial charges and financial debts, and of the relation between financial charges and turnover.
6   Gross operative margins = gross profits over production.
7   The Assolombarda, the association of the entrepreneurs of Milan, counted 4,467 associated enterprises in 1992 with more than 263,000 employers and a substantial weight in the small and medium industry.

8   Data of Institute for Foreign Trade (ICE). See 'La voragine nei conti con l'estero', *La Repubblica Affari e Finanza*, 26 June 1992.

9   For a similar interpretation see Micossi and Padoan, 1994.

10   In June 1992 the £/DM exchange rate passed from 753/753.5 lire per DM of the month to 757 lire per DM of the end and market short-term interest rates reached 14.50 per cent at the end of the month, starting from 12.50 per cent. See Barucci, 1995, p. 23.

11   Abete was the successor to Pininfarina at the presidency of Confindustria in May 1992.

12   Reference is made here to the interest rates paid by the Bank of Italy on the *spot to forward* (*pronti contro termine*) operations.

13   For a similar interpretation see also Barucci, 1995, p. 37.

14   On the other hand, Barucci, then Treasury minister, insisted that the position of the lira in the currency market was unattainable and it was necessary to devalue. See Talani, 1997b; see also Barucci, 1995, p. 38.

15   Amato had already unveiled this strategy to his Barucci and Ciampi on July 17 1992, as clearly reported in Barucci, 1995, p. 39.

16   To have an idea of it, it is sufficient to have a look at Italian newspapers from the beginning of June 1992 until the end of July 1992.

17   Even if parliamentary questions were presented, in July 1992, by Vincenzo Visco, PDS, and Alfredo Biondi, PLI, on the ability that some Italian actors might have speculated against the lira. Also the secretary of the CISL, D'antoni, denounced a speculation against the lira by an Italian subject for a total amount of 1200bn lire. See 'Ente italiano specula sulla nostra moneta', *La Repubblica*, 9 July 1992; 'Visco: italiani gli speculatori sulla lira', *Mercati Finanziari*, 9 July 1992; 'Un lungo braccio di ferro cominciato prima dell'estate', *Il Giornale*, 14 September 1992.

18   The one requiring the representativity of interest groups to allow their involvement in collective bargaining practices.

19   For a similar interpretation, see Mascini in CNEL, 1993, p. 156; see also Talani, 1997b.

20   Actually, Prof. Amato did not remember exactly the date of the meeting, which did, instead, take place on 26 August 1992, in Paris, as reported by Barucci. See Barucci, 1995, p. 50.

21   See above this chapter.

22   The prime rate is the interest rate the banks charge for credit to the best clients.

23   Interest rates paid by the banks for the deposits.

24   Indeed, for the short term lending by 1993 the so called 'partite anomale' (anomalous items), composed by bank overdues, 'crediti incagliati' (stalled debts) and lending whose deadline has expired at least six months, increased by 48.2 per cent from 53.098bn lire at the end of 1992 to 78.714bn lire at the end of 1993, while for middle and long term lending, they passed from 19.000bn in 1992 to 32.000bn in 1993. The bank overdues alone increased by 54.9 per cent in 1992 and by 24.5 per cent in 1993. See ABI, 1994, p. 18; ABI, 1993, p. 14.

25   Again, the reasons why this happened must be traced back in the structure and development of Italian capitalism.

5   The UK and the Departure from the ERM: Betting against EMU

Previous analysis has clarified that the British government's decision to enter the ERM did not conceal any shift of power from the leading socioeconomic capitalist group to a coalition of the two sides of the productive sector. Further, neither did it imply the strengthening of the industrial constituent of capital in relation to the financial one. In fact, in the course of the second half of the 1980s the latter had undergone a major structural change, the so-called 'City revolution' that, far from decreasing, substantially increased its pre-eminence in the British economic and political context.

Thus, the interests underlying the decision to join the ERM have to be traced in the change of macroeconomic policy preferences of the dominant socioeconomic group, namely the financial community and the City. These interests were constituted by, on the one hand, the need to continue pursuing an anti-inflationary policy in the face of clear signs of overheating of the economy and, on the other hand, the need to influence the negotiations leading to the definition of the EMU process. As regards the first dimension, the decision to join the ERM did not bring about the abandonment of monetarist practices and aims. It merely represented a final stage in the move from domestic monetarism, in which many of its policy-making practitioners no longer believed, to the international version of that doctrine, the pragmatic monetarism of the Bundesbank. This move was still extremely controversial (see, for example, Marsh, 1991), both within the City and within the Conservative Party, but it was made necessary by the exceptional commitment of the other European countries to the realisation of EMU. A confirmation of this interpretation comes from the justification of the decision to enter the ERM given by the Governor of the Bank of England following the withdrawal of sterling from the ERM:

... the monetary case for joining was, still in my judgement, not only a very

199

reasonable course but also a desirable one in the light of our knowledge of the time. And the broader political case for being involved in the European debate rather than watching from the sidelines, was a powerful factor in its favour (see Leigh-Pemberton, 1992).

However, the balance in favour of the 'external' version of monetarism through the commitment to the ERM was very unstable. It was doomed to be overthrown soon after the failure of the British government to secure the interests of the dominant socioeconomic group in the negotiations going on in the IGC.

In the following sections it will thus be necessary first to verify what those interests were and how the British government pursued them. Then, an analysis will be carried out of the way in which changing City's preferences undermined the credibility of the British commitment to a fixed parity for the pound, eventually leading to the departure from the ERM. Finally, the position of the British industrial sector, on both the employees' and the employers' sides, will be analysed with the aim of verifying to what extent it had an impact on the fate of the pound in the ERM.

The main hypotheses underlying these sections are, following the conclusions of the argument so far, that the preferences of the financial community, and, in particular of the City, should be decisive, the preferences of the industrial capital not so relevant, and those of the employees not relevant at all.

The City and the British Government's Attitudes Towards the IGC and the Maastricht Agreement

One of the main issues debated with some concern in the British financial circles at the eve of the intergovernmental conference on European economic and monetary union was represented by the structure and powers of the future European central bank which at that time was still called 'Eurofed' (see *The Banker*, 1991a). In general, the British financial community was sceptical of the idea itself of a politically independent central bank with a single monetary policy for all EMU members (see *The Banker*, 1991b). However, when Karl Otto Pohl, the Bundesbank's governor, presented a detailed proposal for a European central bank at the intergovernmental gatherings of December 1990 (ibid.), the debate focused on technical details.

In particular, concerns were voiced about the vital role of central banks as 'lenders of last resort'. This could be intended in two ways. One was the old

UK sense of the specific handling of money-market flows as a tool of monetary policy, where different countries have different ways of reaching the same objective. The second was in the sense of a central bank having an acknowledged responsibility for the general health of the banking system under its supervision. A compromise phrasing had been reached in the European central bankers' proposals, leaving it open for individual governments to agree on the Eurofed's structure. However, this left open many questions. First, there was the problem of the number and types of supervisory functions to be attributed to the Eurofed. Second, the extent to which it would and could be responsible for deciding whether and how to bail out troubled banks in each country. Third, the nature and sources of the funds used to organise rescue operations all over Europe. Finally, the degree of political power the national central banks had to transfer to the Eurofed to allow it to exercise a supervisory role (see *The Banker*, 1991a). The destination of the Eurobanks' earnings appeared also to be among the issues still to be settled given the fact that running a central bank was, no doubt, a highly profitable business.[1]

Another sensitive point was represented by the role of national fiscal policies and the extent to which they could be restricted by membership of the EMU. Disapproval of the monetary financing of the budget was not in serious dispute, but major concerns were expressed over the degree of interference that the Eurofed could have on the conduct of fiscal policy by the national governments (see *The Banker*, 1991b).

Institutional reform was another critical area. The proposals to extend qualified majority voting to prepare for the 1992 Single Market and also for EMU were substantially rejected on the grounds that they posed threats to democratic accountability.

Equally contentious was the problem of defining all the preconditions to the third and final stage to EMU. Indeed, in the absence of broadly similar inflation and interest rates, levels of productivity, unemployment and so forth, monetary union became a straitjacket on output and employment in weaker countries and a pressure for large budgetary transfers which could not be sustained in the long run.

Underlying all this there was the broader debate over the definition of the transition phase to EMU, or stage two. Here the two alternative proposals were given on the one hand by the British government's evolutionary approach, and, on the other, by the Delors plan for a transition of only three years. According to the British financial sector, the latter concealed the fear that the ERM could not be sustained short of a full monetary union and a single currency (see Minford, 1991).

Finally, concerns were voiced on the possibility that the EMU would become a mere two-tier system in which the ECU bloc was only formally different from a substantial Deutschemark bloc (see *The Banker*, 1991c; see also *The Banker*, 1991b).

The British government's draft Treaty provisions presented at the beginning of the intergovernmental conference on EMU as an alternative to the Delors plan, addressed many of the issues concerning the British financial sector (see *The Economist*, 1991a).[2] First of all, the alternative British proposal ignored phase three and offered a model for phase two based on its plan for a 'hard ECU'. This was a thirteenth parallel currency in competition with national ones which might only eventually, through market forces, succeed in becoming a single European currency.

Moreover, in the British approach the independent European central bank would be substituted by a European Monetary Fund controlled by the European central bankers[3] whose only task was to manage and issue 'hard ECUs' in exchange for national currencies. The EMF would not influence national monetary policy directly and much less national fiscal or budgetary policy. It could only force a national central bank whose money became weak to buy its own currency back from the fund with hard ECUs or other currencies.

Finally, the anti-inflationary aim, the only characteristic of EMU that appealed to the British financial sector, was reached through the definition of the hard ECU as a currency that could never be devalued against any other European currency (see HMSO, *The British Proposal for a Hard ECU and a European Monetary Fund*; see also *The Economist*, 1991a).

The reactions of the European partners to the British proposals were very cold from the beginning (see *The Economist*, 1991a). No other country appreciated the core of the British plan, that is, that the hard ECU had to be a real currency issued by a new institution, in parallel to the other national currencies. In particular, Germany's Finance Minister, Theo Waigel, reacted very negatively to any idea of such a parallel currency. He argued that the British definition of the transition phase would split monetary authority between national central banks and the European Fund, and this, in turn, would create uncertainty and inflation with the money supply within Europe much harder to control. Only the French and Spanish said that they liked bits of the British plan, for instance encouraging the use of the ECU during phase two and making the ECU hard. However, they would leave the hard ECU as a basket currency for use as a unit of account, and not, until by fiat it displaced the national currencies, as real money.

Things went even worse as the negotiations within the intergovernmental conference went on. Therefore, as early as March 1991 John Major hinted that Britain would not block the changes in the Rome Treaty needed to set up EMU, provided that the other countries permitted Britain to join in its own time. Thus, in the draft Treaty drawn up by Luxembourg an opt-out clause for the UK was, for the first time, formalised. The Luxembourg draft Treaty provided for countries to delay participation in the final stage of monetary union, which was expected to begin after 1997, when a single currency would be established and control over monetary policy would pass to a European central bank. British officials discarded the Luxembourg proposals as unsatisfactory because the text emphasised exemption for economic reasons rather than political reasons and did not offer the UK an adequate guarantee.[4] However, it was clear at this point that the British attempt to influence substantially the process leading to EMU had failed completely and that the British would find themselves for the rest of the IGC confined to a rearguard battle over the wording of the opt-out clause (see Buchan, 1991). This issue, however, certainly deserved some attention in view of the forthcoming general election. Indeed, a proper opt-out clause gave the government 'a chance to keep the ball in the long grass until after the elections' (see Oakley, 1991). Euro-decisions postponed were, in the British Conservative Party, splits postponed and Neil Kinnock's total silence on the matter suggested that Labour was equally ready to have it fudged until after the electoral round.

As a matter of fact, the Luxembourg draft Treaty marked the formal abandonment of any alternative hypotheses to the Delors plan and the achievement of an agreement between France and Germany over the most debated issue of the powers and structure of the ECB in the transition phase to EMU.

On the one hand, the French, backed by the European Commission, wanted the bank set up in 1994, at the start of the 'transitional' phase two, on the grounds that having a bank in place and a strict timetable, would spur governments to get their economies ready for monetary union. On the other hand, the Germans wanted the new bank set up just before the final phase, otherwise it could rival the authority of the Bundesbank within the European Monetary System. They also opposed setting a date for the start of the final phase until there was a marked convergence of national budget deficits, inflation and interest rates. Luxembourg proposed an insubstantial phase two starting in 1994. The committee of central bank governors would call itself a council and try to coordinate national monetary policies while the new central bank, to be set up in 1996, would be busier, promoting the ECU, collecting statistics, linking up payments systems and preparing to run monetary policy.

By the end of 1996 the Commission and the bank were to report to ECOFIN on progress towards economic convergence and, ultimately, a summit would decide if the Community was ready to set a date for the final phase. If all went well, the ECU could replace national currencies in 1998.

Though neither Theo Waigel, the German minister, nor Pierre Beregovoy, his French counterpart much fancied this compromise, they showed some signs of softening. Waigel restrained from insisting that no date should be set for a single currency until lots of hard-to-meet indicators of convergence had been met. The French hinted that the year in which the new bank appeared did not matter greatly, so long as the final phase was not postponed.

The Luxembourg draft was less contentious about the new central bank, since there was already broad agreement. In phase three it would resemble the Bundesbank, its ruling council would include between five and seven full-time directors, and each country's central bank governor. Neither the Bank nor Council members would take instructions from governments or other EC bodies. However, the Bank's president had to report annually to the European Parliament and to ECOFIN and was liable to questioning from both. The ECOFIN remained responsible for setting the exchange rate policy the Bank had to follow.

With the Luxembourg document the bases of EMU had been set and, though some discussions still had to be held on the issue of the convergence criteria, it was already clear what the substance of the new treaty was. However, it was clear that not one of the British government's conditions had been accepted.

Many of the details left in the dark by the Luxembourg draft were later sorted out in the Dutch draft Treaty presented by Wim Kok, the Dutch Finance Minister in the finance ministers' meeting in Brussels on 9 September. The Dutch document definitively solved the problem of the timing of the establishment of the ECB. It provided for the establishment of a European Monetary Institute in 1994, at the start of phase two, which was to have more powers than the Committee of central bank governors, but would not be the fully-fledged central bank that the French and the Italians wanted. The new institute would take on and coordinate tasks like fostering the use of the ECU and linking up payments systems, but national central banks would remain in charge of monetary policy. The draft foresaw the European Commission and the EMI's reporting, before the end of 1996 on the member states' progress towards economic convergence, progress that was to be assessed according to a series of stiff conditions.

A high degree of price stability, apparent from a level of inflation close to that achieved by the member states with the best performances on prices.

A sustainable government financial position, which was apparent from budget deficits that were not deemed to be excessive.

Currency within normal (2.25 per cent) fluctuation margins of the European monetary system's ERM for at least two years without devaluation against any other member state currency.

A close approximation of comparable interest rates relative to those member states with the best performance in terms of price stability.

These conditions caused a furore because they implied that some European countries would not be able to join the union at the same time as the fiscally sound, low inflation EC northern states and implicitly yielded the acceptance of a 'two-speed' process. These indications of a 'two speed Europe' were supported by a suggestion in the Dutch paper that as few as six EC countries could start the union from 1996 with the others joining later.

The British authorities greeted with unexpected enthusiasm the Dutch proposals on economic convergence. Perhaps this was because

> ... for those who are sceptical about Britain's joining the final stage of EMU it is tempting to think that it will be easier to refuse to do so if only a limited number of our partners participate in it from the outset. The cynics might favour policies leading to a two-speed Europe, because such policies will be so divisive that the whole EMU project will fall apart (see Brittan, 1991).

On the other hand, the UK Treasury did not like the setting in the plan of 1 January 1994 as the starting date for stage two. It also had reservations about stage three being initiated by as few as six nations, and feared that the EMI could undermine national control over monetary policy in a stage when union had yet not started.

The Dutch proposals allowed a broad consensus to emerge on a number of issues. It was agreed that the decision to move to EMU had to be a collective one, taken by all 12 members, and that at least eight countries, not the Dutch six, had to be ready for it. It was also agreed, with Italy dissenting, that countries wanting to join the currency agreement would have to meet strict convergence criteria, that phase two had to start in 1994 and that most countries wanted it to have a monetary institute, not a central bank. Finally, it was stated that no country would be allowed to stop others moving forward, or to be coerced to join phase three against its will, or to be arbitrarily excluded from currency union.

The basis of the consensus was then broadened in an informal meeting at Apeeldoorn, in Holland, on September 21st-22nd where the EC financial ministers reached informal agreements on the most contentious issue of the transition to 'stage three' and a single currency. Phase two would start in 1994 with the creation of the European Monetary Institute (EMI) which would coordinate, but not control, national monetary policies. Before the end of 1996 the Institute and the European Commission would report on the Community's readiness for phase three, taking note of how much progress had been made towards economic convergence. The Community would be ready for the final phase if seven or eight countries, the number was yet to be agreed, could pass the convergence tests put forward in the Dutch plan. The ECOFIN would recommend whether and when phase three should start. The European Council would decide these issues by unanimous vote, while the ECOFIN would then, by majority voting, settle the questions such as which country should join the currency union, the rates at which their currency should be fixed, and what special arrangements should be made for those lagging behind. The EMI would turn into Europe's central bank as soon as the date for the final phase had been set and those countries left out of the final phase would be associated with the bank, but without full voting rights.

Norman Lamont, then Chancellor of the Exchequer, refused to commit Britain to joining a single currency. He disliked the idea that only Britain was to have a derogation from phase three, and proposed instead that only those countries which were willing and able should opt in to phase three. The other ministers disagreed on the ground that this would have led to a two-speed EMU.

The British government also rejected the so-called Delors compromise. This suggested that a declaration could be added to the treaty, saying that Britain's participation in a single currency would depend on a future vote of its parliament, a formula eventually adopted in the Maastricht agreement. According to the British government too many issues were still to be solved before reaching a compromise on the opt-out clause. There was no agreement on whether and how the ECU could be hardened during phase two, on how much authority the monetary institute should have, and on how to discipline the governments that borrowed too much. On all this the British ministers seemed to believe that they could strike a deal in time for Maastricht, but events did not confirm their hopes.

These concerns reflected to a very large extent the ones of the financial community on the eve of the Maastricht summit. While the issue of hardening the ECU was not relevant at all at the beginning of the Maastricht gathering, since it had never been on the agenda of the other EC member states, there was still something to do on the issue of the powers and structure of the EMI.

The British financial sector clearly preferred to limit the powers of the EMI making it virtually an extension of the committee of central bank governors. However, the protocol attached to the Maastricht documents on the EMI's draft statute made it clear that the committee of governors would be dissolved and that the aims of the EMI were extremely important. These ranged from the realisation of conditions for the move to the third stage of EMU, to the making of the preparations required for the conduct of a single monetary policy in the third stage and for the establishment of the ESCB and the creation of a single currency. They also included the aim of overseeing the developments of the ECU. Alongside these commitments the new technical organisation would also have jobs such as running the EMS.

Once the outcomes of Maastricht summit confirmed the fears that had characterised the British attitude towards the IGC, the City of London reacted by rejecting the whole EMU process. The grounds on which this rejection was based reflected the concerns expressed by the British financial sector at the beginning and during the work of the IGC.[5] A general point was that there was no guarantee that EMU would work in practice, while there were examples of attempted monetary unions that had ended in disasters. Moreover, the idea of an independent ECB was considered 'catastrophic' since, apart from being the 'most powerful financial institution on the planet', it was also endowed with vital political responsibilities. It would have the power to decide the level of taxation and the level of public expenditure, the power to set the level of interest rates and exchange rates, and the power to determine the money supply. It was pointed out how Maastricht was about 'the unparalleled centralisation of monetary policy within a European central bank modelled on the Bundesbank'. However, to start with, it was not clear whether an independent bank was better than a dependent one. Secondly, it was instead very clear that the Bundesbank was not the major factor in Germany's economic success, since Germany's monetary stability did not derive from its un-elected central bank, but from the monetary stability afforded by its economic leadership of Europe. Thirdly, the Bundesbank was not the right model for a ECB, since it was an under-performing model, which, however, had been chosen in Maastricht as a reflection of the German power over other European countries.

The macroeconomic foundations of the EMU project were also considered intrinsically flawed. They were based on three assumptions falsified by the evidence, that is, the idea that fixed exchange rates were better than floating exchange rates, that low unemployment flowed from low inflation and that monetary policy could control inflation.

Concerns were then expressed over the possibility that all the member states would satisfy, and keep satisfying, the convergence criteria. It was also held difficult that member states could remove their social, economic, demographic, and technological differences, whose destabilising effects could only be overcome through the adoption of a major system of intra-Community subsidies or transfers with a perverse and pernicious impact on European unity and stability. Eventually, the only foreseeable and foreseen consequences flowing ineluctably from EMU were 'begging, humiliation, arrogance, contempt, resentment and outrage' which, indeed, are hardly sound principles on which to conduct relations between peoples.

The possibility to opt-out from stage three of the process was welcomed, but a major problem arose from the absence of an opt-out clause for stage two and the EMI. Stage two committed Britain, and the other member states, to 'achieving lasting convergence' (see Treaty on European Union, Art. 109e2), to financing the preparatory works for monetary union, despite the opt-out. Stage two also committed the Treasury and the Bank of England to devoting resources to the preparation of monetary union, always despite the opt-out.

With respect to the EMI, its council, consisting of the full time president and the governors of the national banks of the member states, would be independent (see Treaty on European Union, Art. 8 of the Protocol on the European Monetary Institute) and this was considered inconsistent with the duty of the governor of the Bank of England always and in every occasion to foster British interests. Furthermore, the EMI would have legal personality, a seat, a full time salaried president, its own staff and its own capital. It would monitor the functioning of the EMS, run the very short-term financing mechanism of the ERM and prepare for monetary union and the ECB. However, the EMI would disappear with the establishment of the ECB, and Britain's participation in executive decisions to do with monetary union would cease, unless she opted in. Given the amount of powers attributed to the EMI and given its substantial definition as a Eurofed 'in fieri' the main concern of the British financial sector became: 'Who is going to run the powerful new institution?' (see *The Banker*, 1991d).

It is within this context that the ill-fated campaign of the City to bring both the European Monetary Institute and the European central bank to London should be seen. The realisation that, because of Maastricht, EMU could happen by the end of the decade put a very high premium on hosting both institutions and made everyone in Britain worry about their location. The Labour Party added to its electoral manifesto the claim that a Labour government would use its presidency of the European Community in the second half of 1992 to push the case for Britain to house the new European central bank (see Webster, 1991). The Bank of England's Deputy Governor, Eddie George, in a speech to the foreign exchange conference immediately after the conclusion of the Maastricht summit, signalled the shift towards a more open advocacy of London (see Marshall, 1992). Of course, the City itself was the most interested party in the whole matter, with its analysts and bankers saying that if the institutions went elsewhere it could be a damaging blow to the City's status as an international financial centre. They claimed that if the EMI went elsewhere it would probably take the ECU market with it. However, much more than the ECU market could be lost if the ECB also was set up elsewhere: as one of the world's largest central banks, it would be an influential presence in the markets, through foreign exchange intervention and money market management. Much of the Euro-deposit market would follow the ECB, and so, in time, might part of the foreign exchange market and if all the EC's reserves came under its control, it would be responsible for foreign exchange holdings of $300bn. Consequently, most of the world's large commercial banks, would want a close relationship with it. Japanese and American institutions might hope to site headquarters in the same city as the central bank and certainly, many of the small European institutions would leave. What particularly concerned the City was that EMI and the ECB might go to Frankfurt, London's main European rival, as, in fact, eventually happened.

It was a delicate problem for the Conservatives too, who normally had the interests of the financial community at heart and thus many measures were taken by the Conservative government in favour of the City of London's bid to host the EMI and the ECB. Major awarded London his personal backing at the Downing Street meeting on 13 May 1992. The Corporation of London, the City's governing body which, together with the London Lord Mayor, the Bank of England, and representatives of the big banks, was leading the bid, was given Treasury help, in the form of a £1.5m budget for the campaign, and the support of embassies abroad.

Underlying all this, there was the City's fear of losing both its economic power, that is, its dominance of the European financial markets, and its competitiveness in the international financial markets in favour of a German dominated, Bundesbank shaped, ECB set up in Frankfurt. This was paralleled by the fear of losing its domestic political power by losing the opportunity to decide, or influence the decisions, over the setting of exchange rates, interest rates, monetary supply, and even fiscal policy. However, the dilemma for both the City of London and the British government, the one underlying British insistence for an opt-out clause, was that they could not simply decide to remain outside the process. Indeed, some of the consequences of EMU could be avoided by remaining outside, like the loss of domestic macroeconomic policy power. However, others, like the de facto German political dominance, the loss of the City's European financial primacy or the loss of international competitiveness, were linked to the process itself, and could be avoided only by stopping or destroying it. As the paper published by Ian Milne in cooperation with the so-called 'City of London Concern Over Maastricht' group (COLCOM)[6] put it:

> If Britain opted in to EMU, an end would come to the unique and extraordinary thousand-year success story that is the British political system. If she stayed out, she would suffer from, and pay for, the consequences of the rest of Europe's EMU (Milne, 1993, p. 5).

The only solution to the dilemma was to destroy, or at least delay it by subtracting credibility from the whole EMU project. Since much of the Maastricht route to monetary union hung on the survival of the ERM, one of the ways to reach this aim was to undermine the credibility of the British commitment to the Exchange Rate Mechanism of the European Monetary System. This could be obtained through voicing the British financial community's discontent with the working of the European monetary arrangements. After all, entry in the ERM in October 1990 had signalled both the City's desire to be at Europe's centre and to secure low and stable inflation after the errors and the convulsions of the 1980s. Whereas the second task could be considered successfully complete, in the first area the British government had not been able to influence effectively the future of European monetary integration.

The next section will deal with the position of the City of London in the debate over the position of sterling in the exchange rate mechanism. The aim is to verify whether the consensus of the British financial community to the European exchange rate arrangements faded in the course of 1992, and, if it happened, how the British government and the financial markets reacted to this shift in the City's preferences.

The City and the Crisis of the Pound Within the ERM

1 The City and the Debate over the Position of the Pound in the ERM After Maastricht

The performance of sterling in the Exchange Rate Mechanism of the European Monetary System had by no means been disastrous. Although it had been given the possibility to fluctuate against other ERM currencies within a six per cent margin, for most of its period in the ERM it had moved safely within the 2.25 per cent band accorded to the core EMS countries, without interest rates being forced up. On the contrary, UK nominal interest rates showed a clear downwards trend in the period sterling remained in the ERM while, by the end of the Maastricht summit in December 1991 there were already irrefutable signs of low underlying inflation (see OECD, 1991).

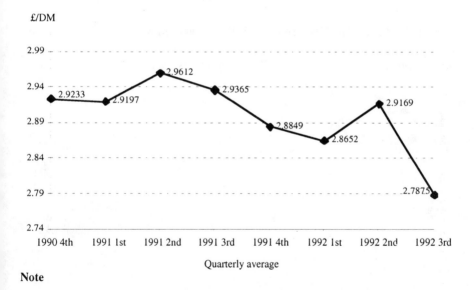

Quarterly average

Note

The fluctuation band for sterling in the ERM was between DM2.7780 and DM3.1320. If we consider a +/- 2.25 per cent fluctuation band, the margins for the £/DM exchange rate were between DM2.8836 and DM3.0163.

Graph 30 British £/DM nominal exchange rates in the ERM

Source: Bank of England Quarterly Bulletin, various issues.

Interest rates

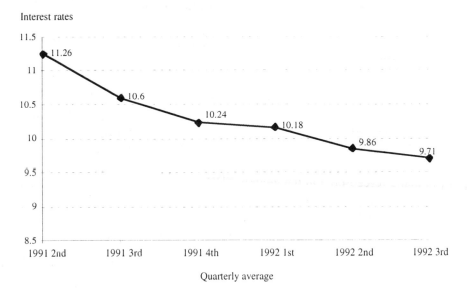

Graph 31 3 months' UK Treasury bill interest rates

Source: *Bank of England Quarterly Bulletins*, various issues.

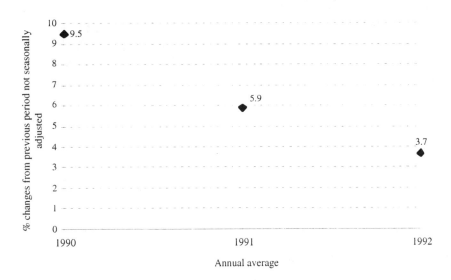

Graph 32 UK consumer prices % changes 1990–92

Source: OECD, 1992.

Despite this, in the immediate aftermath of the IGC on EMU, representatives of the City of London (see Narbrough, 1992), together with Tory leaders (see Ridley, 1992; see also *The Guardian*, 1992a) and Members of Parliament (see Dawnay, 1991), some eminent monetarist economists (see *The Times*, 1992; see also Minford, 1992), and many press commentators (see, for example, Wolf, 1992; *Financial Times*, 1992a)[7] started voicing loudly their discontent with the ERM arrangements. Indeed, at the beginning of January 1992, not only Mrs Thatcher, whose position had never been favourable to entry in the ERM, was said to have advocated in private conversations, supported by a significant number of Tory MPs, an 'un-apologetic realignment, free of overtones of failure' (see *The Guardian*, 1992a). Also City's economists started calling for a devaluation to boost the prospects of economic recovery before the general election, on the grounds that hitching the pound to the German mark had forced interest rates to be at least 3 per cent higher than they should have been (ibid.). Paul Turnbull, chief economist at Smith New Court PLC[8] said it was 'economic self-flagellation', referring to France, Italy and Britain defending their currencies against 'a buoyant DM by maintaining brutally high interest rates'. Brendon Brown, chief international strategist with Mitsubishi Finance International in London, thought a revaluation of the DM 'would make very good economic sense, enabling the high unemployment countries to bring down interest rates and boost their economies'. He was echoed by David Smith, of a brokerage company, according to whom Germany's fiscal imbalance was not just crowding out investment in Germany but in all of Europe (see Ipsen, 1992a). Bill Martin, of the City analysts UBS Phillips and Drew, argued that in order to dispel market expectations that one devaluation might be followed by another, it had to be big enough, well in excess of 10 per cent (see *The Guardian*, 1992b). Sir Douglas Wass, then chairman of Nomura International plc, explicitly confirmed, in an interview with the author, that during the early 1990s there was no way to maintain the level of interest rates as high as keeping the EMS parity would have required (see Talani, 1996).

In the meantime, economists such as Prof. Walters, the former personal adviser to Mrs Thatcher, and Professors Minford and Congdom, kept on claiming that sterling entered Europe's ERM at the wrong exchange rate. Consistently, they called for the pound to float downwards prior to sharp reductions in interest rates to head off an even more serious recession.

The grounds on which devaluation was required were thus very standardised: the need to let interest rates fall in a period of recession, the urgency to devalue the pound to increase industrial sector competitiveness, and the pressing need to solve the growing problem of high unemployment. However, the worries of the City of London for an overvalued exchange rate and too high interest rates sharply clashed with its traditional preference for a 'strong pound' policy. Moreover, this attitude was also inconsistent with its own economic forecasts as well as with the position adopted by the Confederation of British Industry. Indeed, all City forecasts for the UK economy in 1992 foresaw an increase of GDP, on average, from -2.2 to 1.7, as well as a reduction of interest rates (three months' interbank), from 10.5 to 9.2 (see Johnson, 1992). Here the point is either that the City's economists themselves did not believe in their forecasts, or that they believed it possible to get out of recession and lower interest rates also without devaluing the pound, unless they already assumed devaluation in their forecasts.

Table 19   Forecasts for the UK economy 1991–92

City companies	Date	Gross domestic product		Retail price inflation		Interest rates (3 months)	
		1991	1992	1991	1992	1991	1992
BZW[1]	December 1991	-2.3	2.3	4.2	4.2	10.5	10.0
Capel	December 1991	-2.1	2.0	4.1	2.6	10.5	9.0
CSFB[2]	December 1991	-2.0	1.6	4.1	3.5	10.5	7.5
Goldman	December 1991	-2.4	1.7	4.1	3.5	10.5	9.0
Hoare	December 1991	-2.3	2.5	3.8	4.3	10.5	10.8
Lloyds	December 1991	-2.0	1.9	4.0	3.6	10.5	9.5
Lombard	December 1991	-2.4	0.6	4.2	2.9	10.5	8.0
Midland	December 1991	-2.0	1.0	4.2	3.5	10.7	9.0
Morgan	December 1991	-2.4	1.5	4.2	3.8	10.6	9.5
Natwest	December 1991	-2.1	1.9	4.2	4.4	10.5	9.5
Shearson	December 1991	-2.2	1.2	4.1	4.5	10.3	9.5
UBS[3]	December 1991	-2.3	1.3	4.2	4.2	10.5	9.0
Warburgs	December 1991	-2.3	2.0	4.1	3.8	10.5	10.0
City average		-2.2	1.7	4.1	3.8	10.5	9.2

Notes

1   BZW: Barclays De Zoete Wedd.
2   CSFB: Credit Suisse First Boston.
3   UBS: Union Bank of Switzerland.

Source: Johnson, 1992.

Another interesting point to note is that the Confederation of British Industry, far from asking for devaluation, was overtly against it (see this chapter). As Neil Williams, head of economic policy for the CBI put it, 'It is fools gold ... It would lead to higher interest rates, not lower' (see Ipsen, 1992a). The existence of a broad consensus within the British industrial sector on the need to stick to ERM parities for the pound was confirmed also by Douglas McWilliams, economic adviser to the Confederation of British Industry. He claimed that he was pleasantly surprised by the number of industrialists supporting the UK government's anti-devaluation line. Of CBI members he estimated that 'most would go along with a small rise in interest rates rather than a devaluation'. Finally Sir Brian Corby, the CBI President, on 16 January ruled out devaluation as 'unnecessary, unacceptable and counterproductive' (see Marsh, 1992a).

Despite believing that industry was uncompetitive, also the Labour Party became against devaluation. Its benefits would be eroded both by 'catch up' wage claims and by higher interest rates, as the markets demand a premium against the prospect of future devaluation (see *The Guardian*, 1992b; see also *Financial Times*, 1992b). The position taken by the Labour Party, in the run up to the general election due to take place at the latest on 9 July 1992 (see Stephens, 1992a), made a sterling devaluation by the Conservative government much less likely. Moreover, it enhanced the Conservative Party's chances of winning the election. It was by then clear, in fact, that the election campaign would be fought on economic policy grounds.[9] However, it was even clearer to anyone that the Major government's economic policy had been and was still based on, in the lack of any credible alternative (see ch. 3), the decision to link the pound to the DM within the ERM as an anti-inflationary tool, and so was its political credibility. Indeed, the Conservative government (see Owen, 1992), through its Chancellor of the Exchequer, Lamont, answered those expressing concerns about the unsustainable consequences of sterling's entry in the ERM, by rejecting any suggestion that membership of the EMS exchange rate mechanism condemned the UK to slow growth. In an interview to the *Financial Times* on 31 December 1991, the Chancellor defended the government's decision to take sterling into the ERM on October 1990 when inflation in Germany was rising and the German authorities were determined to take action to control it. 'That has obviously made life difficult for us. But we must not forget that it is low inflation that has made Germany into an economic success story. That is why we joined the ERM, to achieve German levels of inflation', he said, and then he addressed directly to those, 'not all of them well intentioned' (Norman, 1991), voicing concerns about ERM membership:

> There is something profoundly depressing about the way that there was so much enthusiasm in business and in the press about joining the ERM and yet, within a year, some of the same people want to deny the disciplines that the ERM entails (ibid.).

As both parties supported British membership of the ERM, even those sectors of the City of London which were truly discontented with this policy preferred to maintain their support for the government so long as there was no alternative proposal by Labour. Then, after the election, the whole issue could be decided by events, or better, by the impersonal and unaccountable international markets. In the meantime, that it to say, pending the general election, the markets remained substantially calm,[10] and calls for the devaluation of sterling subsided until the election was won by the Conservative Party in April 1992.

As soon as the 'honeymoon' of the new government with public opinion and with market ended, the pressures against the UK's commitment to the ERM soared again from the same economic and political sectors that had attacked the ERM at the beginning of 1992. In the leading articles of the *Financial Times*, the *Times*, the *Daily Telegraph* and even the *Guardian*, press commentators started again to suggest that Europe needed a realignment within the ERM to avoid a protracted and unnecessary slump (see *The Guardian*, 1992c). At the same time, Conservative MPs, supported by Baroness Thatcher, renewed demands to cut interest rates despite membership of the ERM. Sir Peter Tapsell, the MP for Lindsay East and long time supporter of Michael Heseltine, even suggested that Britain should withdraw, at least temporarily, from the ERM (see Webster and Leathley, 1992).

Many economists also voiced their concerns about the perverse effect of the UK's commitment to the ERM. In a letter to the Times on 14 July, six monetarists, including Sir Alan Walters, warned that the recession could continue into 1993 and beyond unless Britain left the ERM (see *The Economist*, 1992). Wyne Godley, Professor of Applied Economics at Cambridge University, did not believe there would ever be a recovery fast enough to reduce unemployment if there was not both a devaluation and a reduction in interest rates. Moreover, as long as the ERM was an obstacle to devaluation Britain had to withdraw. According to Patrick Minford, Professor of Economics, Liverpool University: '... Britain needs a cut in interest rates at least of 3%. Britain should suspend its agreement to support sterling within the ERM....' For David Currie, Professor of Economics at the London Business School: '... In the circumstances of the recession, a case can be made for combining devaluation with a large cut in the PSBR. This package was ruled out for electoral reasons, but may now be politically feasible' (see *Financial Times*, 1992c).

What is more relevant to our purposes, however, is that also within the City of London the voices against sterling's position within the European monetary arrangements multiplied. In mid-July 1992, John Shepperd, of SG Warburg Securities, the London investment group, said: 'The longer the recession drags on and the Bundesbank keeps German interest rates high, the stronger the ability of devaluation.' David Brown, of the London office of the Swiss Bank Corporation foresaw: 'This week the markets have caught the devaluation jitters. It is going to be a difficult few months' (see Marsh, 1992a). Others viewed devaluation as a sensible measure to enable UK interest rates to be reduced and end the longest recession for 50 years. Paul Chertkow, head of global currency research, UBS Phillips and Drew claimed:

> The ERM is not working as Britain thought it would. The plan was that low inflation would bring low interest rates and lead to prosperity. But due to the special circumstances of German unification we have high interest rates throughout Europe, which are inappropriate given the weak economies of many countries. With the UK still in recession, most economists would agree that base rates at 10% are too high. Britain should cut interest rates by two percentage points and see what happens. If the pound fell below its ERM limit, and direct intervention failed to move sterling back within its bands, than the UK should either devalue, or leave the system altogether (see *Financial Times*, 1992c).

Roger Bootle, UK Chief Economist at Greenwell Montagu, suggested that though it had been right for sterling to join the ERM at a testing exchange rate to reduce inflation, it would be dangerous to stick with this same policy when the risk facing Britain was not inflation, but slump. The best solution was a DM revaluation but, failing this, if by December the UK economy showed no recovery, German rates showed no sign of coming down, and UK inflation was low and falling, then sterling should devalue (ibid.).

Indeed, such calls, far from enhancing the chances for growth in British economy, created a vicious circle. By pushing the pound lower, they made interest rate cuts even less likely, which in turn hindered recovery, and so prompted further calls for devaluation. Moreover, neither Major nor Lamont could opt out of the ERM. Given the strong opposition to ERM membership within the Tories file and rank, this would represent for them a major political setback, and would certainly create a leadership crisis inside the Conservative Party with the almost obvious result of their departure from government. As

Gavin Davies, Chief UK economist, Goldman Sachs put it:

> A free float for sterling which would succeed in getting base rates markedly lower, would now be such a political set-back for the Chancellor and the PM that it would be contemplated only in the most extreme economic circumstances. These dire circumstances have not arrived yet, and are unlikely to do so. The outlook is for continuing political discontent, but discontent which is not powerful enough to force any of the possible ERM resolutions in the near term. This is likely to leave the financial markets permanently fretting that a sterling devaluation or free float may be just around the corner until there is much firmer evidence of economic recovery (ibid.).

He was echoed by Dennis, Chief Economist at the Industrial Bank of Japan in London (see 1992) who claimed:

> The twin impact of high real interest rates, which are heading for 7% as inflation expectations are falling, and massive personal and corporate debt, which is not being reduced with such low inflation, means that remaining in the ERM could result in irreparable damage to the supply side of the economy. For the UK devaluation, and, therefore, in effect, leaving the ERM, is unlikely to be considered before things get much worse, unless the French referendum is negative, because of the domestic political implications for Major and Lamont on the UK's consequent isolationism on Europe and damage to its anti-inflation credibility. Next year, though, could see the UK economy suffer new problems with growing difficulties over the financial system and this may result in the UK leaving the ERM unilaterally, if the failure of Maastricht has not already destroyed the ERM.

Notwithstanding this, and despite the weakening of the pound within the ERM as well as the reiterated statements by both Major and Lamont rejecting the hypothesis of a realignment, the campaign against the ERM by some sectors of the British financial community gathered pace throughout the whole of summer 1992. On 29 July 1992, Brian Pearse, Midland Bank's Chief Executive, sharply criticised the government's policy towards sterling for its high value in the ERM (see Norman and Blitz, 1992). Further, in an article in the *Daily Telegraph* on 13 August 1992, Tim Congdom, Managing Director of Lombard Street Research Economic Consultations, claimed that Germany could no longer boast of its efficient economic management and, therefore, a better base for a European exchange rate would be a reliable dollar (see Congdom, 1992). At the end of August 1992, asked about the possible consequences of a 'no' vote in the French referendum over Maastricht, a group of City economists gave even a positive assessment of a similar event. Paul Chertkow said: 'a no vote would stop EMU in its tracks. It would almost certainly lead to a big bout of selling of the weak ERM currency such as the pound and the Italian lira, and force a realignment on to the political agenda'. According to Michael O'Hanlon, an international economist at the London office of Kidder Peabody, the US investment bank, a continuation of the ERM after a 'no' vote would almost certainly require a realignment to depress the value of the weaker currencies and allow countries like Britain and Italy to cut interest rates and hasten growth. On the danger that the financial markets could interpret such a move as a straightforward sterling devaluation which might require higher rather than lower interest rates, George Magnus, international bond economist at SG Warburg Securities, the UK investment House, replied that the risks for Britain of a move of this kind would be worth taking. He claimed:

> On balance, a realignment would have beneficial effects for the European economy. If the realignment involved the whole of Europe and was dressed up as being made in the context of the unique circumstances of German unification, then, I think, in the case of Britain, that the markets would be forgiving (see Marsh, 1992b).

Finally, according to Paul Neild, economic Director of the County Natwest brokerage house, 'If the French vote "yes" we would be back to square one with the balance of payments in deficit and the recession getting worse' (see Ipsen, 1992b).

Thus, by summer 1992, it was very clear to all, financial markets included, that the coalition of interests that had supported British entry in the ERM had faded, and that there was instead a growing discontent towards the European monetary arrangements, particularly within the British financial community.

2   The Reactions of the British Government and of the Markets to the Criticisms of the ERM

In the context outlined above, the reiterated statements by both Major and Lamont supporting Britain's commitment to the European Monetary arrangements, could not exert any effective influence on the markets, particularly because they were not followed by facts. Indeed, throughout the summer of 1992, Lamont and Major had repeatedly stated their full commitment to ERM. In an interview in the *Daily Telegraph* on 11 July 1992 the Chancellor of the Exchequer claimed:

> ... For almost two years the government's counter-inflationary strategy has been based on sterling's membership of the ERM. I believe this is the right policy because it will deliver the low inflation we seek. The ERM is not an optional extra, an add-on to be jettisoned at the first hint of trouble (see Lamont, 1992a).

The government's determination to maintain its economic strategy was underlined by John Major the day after as he gave unequivocal backing to the Chancellor's refusal to consider a devaluation of sterling (see Stephens, 1992b). Statements of this kind were then repeated all over again by both Conservative leaders until the very day before the departure of sterling from the ERM.[11] Finally, on 14 September, when the lira was devalued inside the ERM, Lamont released a communiqué stating:

> I particularly welcome the intention of the Bundesbank council to cut interest rates in order to reduce strains within the ERM.[12] This demonstrates the benefits of continuing close co-operation amongst Community countries. The UK government has repeatedly made clear that there is no question of any change in the central parity of the pound against the DM, and that we will take whatever action is necessary to secure that. Sterling's central rate therefore remains at DM2.95 (*Financial Times*, 1992d).

Whatever the PM and the Chancellor might say, however, what counted for the markets was not words, but facts, and facts were not in line with the pledge to maintain sterling's parity.

Since when Britain joined the ERM the government had cut the interest rates nine times, by a total of 5 per cent but it had never increased them, not even in cases of emergency, thus undermining much of the credibility of its commitment to the ERM. Indeed, during the two years of membership, Britain was the sole member, apart from Portugal which joined only in 1992, never to have raised its rates.

No wonder, then, that this time the markets reacted heavily to the clear signs of lack of credibility of the British commitment to the ERM.

On 13 July 1992 international investors ignored the strong statement by Major ruling out a devaluation of the pound and the pound fell into its first lowest level against the DM since entry in the system, DM2.8489 (see Stephens and Norman, 1992). On 14 August, sterling again threatened to fall below DM2.81 on the foreign exchanges and finished at the new low of DM2.8150 in London. This intensified pressures on the UK government to bolster the currency's position on the European Monetary System, that is, to raise interest rates or to leave the system altogether. On 20 August, the British currency reached DM2.8070, 3 Pf above its permitted floor against the DM in the ERM, DM2.7780, and again the government decided neither to intervene on the foreign exchange nor to raise interest rates. On 26 August 1992, in the face of a major attack on sterling, the British government avoided increasing interest rates by selling pounds.

There could be only one epilogue to all this and it punctually occurred after the devaluation of the lira on 14 September. On 15 September, intervention by the Bank of England to buy sterling for DM failed to prevent the pound hitting a new low against the German currency. As UK pension funds and other large investors switched money out of pounds into DM the British currency closed against the DM at DM2.7800, 3.25 Pf down on the day and at the lowest level since Britain joined the ERM. The purchase of pounds by the Bank of England was thought to be relatively modest and not announced to the market (see Marsh and Blitz, 1992). Only on 16 September, when intervention by central banks to sustain sterling failed and the pound dropped below the ERM floor, the Chancellor of the Exchequer raised interest rates twice to 15 per cent from 10 per cent. However, by that time it was already too late and, as sterling closed at DM2.75, Lamont announced the decision to suspend sterling within the ERM and to reverse the interest rate rise setting base rates at 12 per cent.

The irresistible, overwhelming, as well as unaccountable and irresponsible market forces had led to an epilogue that was by no-means unexpected, though the official explanation was that the force of the speculative gale was totally sudden and unprecedented (see Dawnay, 1992c; Lamont, 1992b).

Foreign exchange traders were hardly fazed by sterling's suspension from the European ERM (see Corrigan and Tucker, 1992). Dealers estimated that more than £10bn of capital flowed out of the UK as fund managers and corporate treasurers tried to reduce their exposure to sterling. 'No one was really surprised', said Julian Simmonds, head of foreign exchange trading at Citybank. 'Investors are selling pounds on an entirely rational basis', said Paul Chertkow, head of global currency research at UBS Phillips and Drew, 'To safeguard the value of their money, investors are putting their money in DM instead'.

The responsibilities of the government in failing to restrain the erosion of the credibility of the British commitment to the ERM may be identified easily. The government spent far too long before raising interest rates and thus paraded its reluctance to do so and the Bank of England itself was at fault in not doing

222 Betting For and Against EMU

more to push up the very short-term rates covering the French Referendum period. Another tactical mistake was to say too little about the resources available to defend sterling, most of which had, apparently, not been used. The Bank of England's figures show a decrease in official reserves from August 1992 to September 1992 of only $1.8m, about £1m (see *Bank of England Quarterly Bulletin*, various issues).

There were also political mistakes, such as the PM and the Chancellor publicly hoping for lower interest rates when the only thing to say was that they could go up as much as needed.

The political responsibility of the Major government in the departure of sterling from the ERM would be further evidence if it were true, as hinted by the press, that the British government actually refused a general realignment within the ERM offered by the German government well before Black Wednesday. Accepting a realignment, Major had the opportunity to sabotage Maastricht by weakening the ERM, but then he had to explain that all his macroeconomic policies since joining the ERM in 1990 had been ghastly and unnecessary mistakes. However, how greater would be the benefits, were the markets, the impersonal, politically irresponsible markets, to act in his place! The British government could then escape the responsibility of having put into question the process of European integration, and, at the same time, could enjoy the advantages stemming from both a departure from the ERM and of a much less credible EMU.

Summing up, as a consequence of both the change of preferences of the British financial community and of the government's behaviour, the credibility of British commitment to the European exchange rate arrangement had been substantially eroded by the time sterling came under serious strain. Therefore, the markets reacted rationally attacking sterling in the full confidence that the British government's reiterated pledges to the ERM were not backed by a serious commitment to it by the dominant British socioeconomic groups.

In the event the markets were right, since, as a matter of fact, not only was the pound devalued and then withdrawn from the ERM, but also, Major's leadership and the rest of the Cabinet, particularly the Chancellor of the Exchequer, did not face any major threat. Instead, they emerged safe from a dramatic event, devaluation, which was by no means usual nor uncontroversial in the British political environment. Indeed, the previous devaluation had produced major political strains in the governing party, the Labour Party, including the resignation of the Chancellor of the Exchequer, James Callaghan (see Cairncross, 1992). In September 1992, on the contrary, both Lamont and Major were able to present devaluation as inevitable in the face of the unforeseeable, overwhelming market forces and to escape any responsibility for the epilogue of sterling's experience in the ERM. According to Norman Lamont, sterling's devaluation and withdrawal had been triggered by

> ... the sort of extraordinary circumstances that we have been living through. What I did was simply common sense. The decision I made was an unavoidable one. ... I believe the decision that I made was the correct one, since I have not sought a devaluation, I did not seek to leave the ERM, but we were overwhelmed by these wholly exceptional circumstances (see Lamont, 1992b).

Major launched, on 24 September 1992, an unapologetic defence of the government's decision to abandon the European Exchange Rate Mechanism insisting before the House of Commons that 'there was no choice' and then going on to describe the 'exceptional circumstances' which had led to the decision to take the pound out of the system. To those who asked him how, after years of defending the ERM, he had only just discovered the 'fault lines' in the system, Major replied that no-one had anticipated the size and the scale of the speculative attack against the pound.

Indeed, the Tory rank and file seemed convinced by the official explanation of the crisis. Perhaps it was only that they were not so disappointed by its outcomes. However, immediately after the Black Wednesday newspapers reported a broad consensus of Tory MPs in favour of quashing all talks of challenge for the Party's leadership as irresponsible. By the time of the Conservative conference in Brighton on 8 October 1992 (see Norman, 1992b), also the few voices calling for the Chancellor's resignations had faded away.[13]

Major's leadership and cabinet had thus been able to survive the reversal of all its strategy for economic policy. This is something which could hardly be possible had this reversal not been backed by the most powerful British socioeconomic actors.

The Commitment of the Industrial Sector to the European Monetary System in the Run-up to the Crisis

At this point, it will be worth analysing in more detail the position adopted by the industrial sector as a whole, that is, by the employers' and the employees' organisations, in the debate over the place of sterling in the ERM and over the EMU. This is especially interesting given the fact that the industrial sector should be the most affected by the recessive effects of the supposedly overvalued exchange rate and of the supposedly high interest rates necessary to maintain parity within the ERM. Consequently, it should be more interesting than the financial community in dropping the parity or suspending the pound's participation in the system altogether.

1   *The Confederation of British Industry Strengthens its Support for the Process of European Monetary Integration*

The development of the CBI's stance towards the process of European monetary integration has been exhaustively dealt with in a previous section. Here it will be enough to point out how, far from abjuring its support to the ERM, in the course of the intergovernmental conference, the employers organisation even strengthened its commitment to the realisation of the process of European Monetary Union.

As far as the ERM is concerned, declarations pointing out the advantages of the UK's membership of the mechanism were made over and over again by representatives of the CBI throughout the whole period of the IGC (see Confederation of British Industry, 1991d). Further, the goal of 'making a success of ERM membership' (see Confederation of British Industry, 1991e) was inserted in the business agenda (ibid.) for the forthcoming general election as a main priority.

What is more interesting, however, is that with the development of the negotiations over EMU within the IGC, the position of the CBI towards the issue also developed.

The priorities of British business at the beginning of the intergovernmental conference on EMU, as reported in the document *Agenda Europe: Completing the Single Market* (see Confederation of British Industry, 1990), did not differ very much from the ones already stated in its previous publications on the issue. As Sir Brian Corby, CBI President, claimed, in the introduction of the document, the overriding business priority was the successful completion of the Single European Market, on schedule by the end of 1992, fully implemented and enforced. This alone could provide a sure foundation for the community's continued development (ibid., p. 5).

Thus, the CBI strongly supported the goal of achieving closer economic and monetary ties within Europe on the ground that this was a vital ingredient on the road to achieving a genuine internal market (see Banham, 1990).

However, the CBI still believed that EMU had to be achieved by an evolutionary process whose first step for the UK had been the move to take sterling into the wider bands of the Exchange Rate Mechanism. This move would allow the UK to play its full part in achieving EMU, including discussions at the Intergovernmental Conference (see Williams, 1990). As already stated in the previous documents, the CBI supported the UK government's hard ECU plan as providing one feasible way of moving to the second stage of EMU. This would provide a sound basis for moving towards a genuine single European currency, once a greater degree of economic convergence had been achieved and when there was a genuine political commitment to do so.

The Chancellor's hard ECU plan met many of the CBI requirements of an evolutionary approach and had also the advantages of clearly pursuing an anti-inflationary aim and boosting the use of ECU, which was considered by the CBI the smoother way to achieve a single currency. Although the plan did not guarantee that a single currency would emerge, it provided a useful intermediate step, beyond ERM membership, in an evolutionary process to EMU (see Confederation of British Industry, 1990, pp. 13–14).

However, as the intergovernmental conference proceeded and the UK government's plan for an evolutionary approach to EMU failed to receive any backing among the other European member states (see ch. 3), the CBI started abandoning it. Instead the CBI proclaimed itself satisfied with the direction of the discussions on the grounds that the steady progress being made in moving toward further stages of EMU, represented, at that time, by the Luxembourg proposals for 'stage 2',[14] was perfectly in line with its policy.

What seemed to worry the employers to the utmost level was the possibility of a two-speed progress to monetary union and the effects on business of the UK exclusion from the core EMU countries. This scenario would jeopardise British business' ability to gather the full opportunities of the Single Market.

As many of the details left foggy by the Luxembourg draft were sorted out in the Dutch draft treaty, the CBI redefined its position towards the IGC in a memorandum to the National Economic Development Council stating the priorities for Europe's business (see Confederation of British Industry, 1991b). The document explicitly endorsed the decisions of the IGC and expressed the CBI's full and almost unconditioned commitment to a single currency by claiming. The only two requests the CBI made to the UK government were: '... to ensure that a phased approach to EMU is adopted and that any discussion of a two-speed EMU is avoided' (ibid., p. 4).

Economic and Monetary Union became one of the six priorities[15] the CBI identified for the UK presidency of the EC as fundamental steps towards the realisation of the overriding objective to ensure that the Single Market was achieved.

The need to guarantee competition within European countries through the removal of all barriers to trading as well as the world competitiveness of European business, lay at the heart of this new CBI position. In this context, it is easy to understand why British business could not accept any hypothesis of discrimination within a two-tier EMU.

Eventually, the CBI recommendations for the Maastricht IGC on EMU were perfectly in line with the proposals accepted by the European member states. There should be a phased approach towards EMU within the Community whose first stage was represented by the participation of all member states to the ERM, possibly, within the narrow band; this should lead into a transition to fixed exchange rates and then a single currency. The success of each stage should be ensured before moving on. In particular, greater convergence of inflation, at sustained low levels, was needed before exchange rates could be fixed permanently. Measures should be taken to enhance the use of the ECU so that it could gradually assume the role of a single currency. This might require some shift in the composition of the ECU during the move from its role as a basket of currencies. The single currency should be managed by a European central bank committed to sustaining price stability and be independent of short-term political interference. To this end, such a bank should be based more on the Bundesbank model than on the Bank of England. Finally, the move to a fixed exchange rate should be followed as quickly as possible by the adoption of a European single currency. This was necessary not only to reinforce the commitment, but also to permit business to enjoy the full benefits of monetary union (see Eberlie, 1991c).

Consistently, the position of the major employers' organisation following the Maastricht Summit was characterised by full support of the Maastricht decisions on EMU, as well as by the reiterated commitment to the ERM discipline against any hypothesis of devaluation or withdrawal of the pound.

Indeed, the CBI strongly welcomed Maastricht's conclusions and considered the agreement on EMU perfectly in line with the objectives suggested by the CBI to the government and to the European Commission through UNICE. According to the CBI, the EMU agreement accorded with the CBI policy on the issue because it provided the basis for the EC to move towards a single currency on an evolutionary basis. A single currency would have, then, reduced uncertainty and removed the expenses of hedging and transaction costs as well as enforcing the anti-inflationary discipline achieved by the ERM. Moreover, being the basis for moving ahead towards a single currency represented by economic convergence, it was difficult to believe that the UK would fail to move ahead with the rest of the community. On the contrary, the

UK's progress in reducing inflation and interest rates and its emphasis on controlling public expenditure, meant for the CBI that the UK was already much closer to meeting the agreed criteria than most other member states.

As regarded the so-called opt-out clause[16] the CBI tended to minimise its relevance. It claimed that the clause was important since it provided political safeguards for the UK. However, it also underlined how it would not be in the interest of the country to be sidelined in the EMU process, and how the CBI had always been anxious that the UK participated fully in the move to monetary union.

The CBI stated that it would work actively to secure the ratification of the Maastricht agreements and that it looked at the UK presidency of the EC in the second half of 1992 as a chance to give further impetus to securing business needs on EMU. In particular the CBI would strive to ensure that the UK was able to meet each of the economic convergence criteria. This meant, according to the CBI first that the government should remain committed to reducing inflation and interest rates, controlling growth of public expenditure and, also, entering sterling into the narrow ERM band. Second that it should be aware of the potential benefits to business arising from a single European currency. Finally, that the new monetary institutions established to coordinate/control the single currency should operate to the best of business' interests, this meaning that the ultimate single European central bank had to be committed to achieving and maintaining price stability (see Williams, 1992).

Given these premises, it should not be particularly surprising that, as noted above, the Confederation of British Industry, in aftermath of the Maastricht agreement, far from asking for devaluation, as many other economic and social sectors did, was overtly against it.

In the CBI memorandum to the National Economic Development Council, *The Road to Recovery*, of 20 December 1991 the CBI restated its fully fledged commitment to the European exchange rate arrangements claiming that:

> The CBI accepts that the room for manoeuvre in monetary and fiscal policy will be limited in 1992. The UK's commitment as a member of the exchange rate mechanism must be honoured, devaluation is not part of the CBI's economic policy strategy. This commitment should be reinforced when the circumstances allow, by moving to the narrow bands of the ERM (see Confederation of British Industry, 1991c).

This position was then publicly supported by CBI representatives in the debate, taking place at the beginning of 1992, over the role of sterling in the

ERM. According to Neil Williams, head of economic policy for the CBI, devaluation was a 'fool's gold' which would lead to higher, not lower, interest rates (see Ipsen, 1992a) while for Sir Brian Corby, the CBI President, it was 'unnecessary, unacceptable and counterproductive' (see Marsh, 1992a). It was even estimated by Douglas McWilliams, economic adviser to the CBI, that most CBI members would have gone along with a small rise in interest rates rather than devaluation (ibid.). Moreover, while the City of London voiced concerns over the recessive pressures imposed on the British economy by the UK's membership of the ERM, the CBI was keen to point out how participation in the system had yielded positive effects on interest, exchange and inflation rates (see Confederation of British Industry, 1991c, p. 6).

The CBI also pointed out that its members welcomed the medium term stability of the ERM and had adapted remarkably well to it. Manufacturing labour costs increased by only 0.8 per cent between the first quarter of 1991 and the third, manufactured exports rose by 5 per cent in 1991 and by a further 3 per cent in the first half of 1992 (see Confederation of British Industry, 1992) while exports to the EC went up by 8 per cent in 1991 from the previous year (see Confederation of British Industry, 1991d).

Finally, it is true that levels of real interest rates had been higher in the recession of the 1990s than in either those of the mid-1970s and early 1980s. However, the CBI believed that this reflected mainly the better progress made in the 1990s in reducing UK inflation rather than abnormally high nominal interest rates. The CBI also thought that keeping UK inflation on a firm downward trend was the *sine qua non* of further reductions in interest rates (see Williams, 1991b) and that the best anti-inflationary framework was the ERM discipline (see Corby, 1991). Therefore, the CBI did not support any devaluation of sterling within the ERM which could only push up interest rates by adding to the uncertainty surrounding sterling (see Confederation of British Industry, (1991c, p. 7).

After the general election of April 1992, the new President of the CBI strongly reaffirmed the extreme importance of the process of European monetary integration for British business. He underlined the need to support the Maastricht agreement by stating:

> The Treaty is vital for UK business because it commits member states to progress towards economic and monetary union, improving the prospects for currency stability and, ultimately, a single currency (see Angus, 1991).

Thus: 'Nothing should distract our minds from the great benefits of a common market and the desirability of the UK being a leading part of it.'

To those who argued for a realignment within the ERM, or even for leaving the mechanism altogether, the CBI answered that neither of these solutions would guarantee lower interest rates. Indeed, for British rates to be lower than German ones the market had to believe that there was the prospect of a rise in the value of sterling against the DM. The markets would consider devaluation a sign of relaxation in British anti-inflationary stance and would ask for a premium on sterling forcing interest rates up. The only alternative to maintaining parity within the ERM was to let sterling float freely outside it, but this would be extremely risky for the whole commitment to economic and monetary union, which the CBI strongly endorsed, and would set back British ambition to be at the heart of the Community for a long period. Not least, this would also leave Britain without a credible anti-inflationary framework of any kind (see Davies, 1992a).

Yet calls for devaluation and, even, for withdrawal from the ERM increased and left the British employers' organisation with a set of questions well summarised by Sir John Banham, CBI Director General:

> Why should sterling weaken against the German mark when the UK has lower inflation, lower wage increases and a far smaller budget and trade deficit, not to mention far lower unemployment if the new lander are taken into account?
>
> Why should commentators persist in talking about the collapse of UK manufacturing when even the disappointing January trade figures showed export volumes fully 63% higher than their pre-1979 peak, in the days when Britain was supposedly the workshop of the world, but in reality was in steady relative decline?
>
> Why it is such an unwelcome surprise that the UK share of world trade is raising; that export volumes of manufactured goods exceeded those of France in December, for the first time in 15 years; that the real manufacturing profits last year were higher than in any single year in the supposedly golden era of 1979-1986 and were only some 15% below their all time high?
>
> Why did most people not notice that the trade gap for the last quarter of 1991 was revised downwards by two thirds to little more than £200m a month, before taking account of the appreciation in the UK's overseas asset portfolio of £150bn? (see Banham, 1991).

The answers to these questions did not lie in the interests of the British employers. They had been warning against this constant undermining the credibility of British ability to fulfil the requirements of ERM membership by exaggerating the intensity of the recession and thus calling for the need of lower interest rates inconsistent with ERM central rate and bands. These calls came from other British economic and political forces. However, the industrial employers did not seem able to resist the power of these forces, and could only bend to their will trying to get the most advantages from an epilogue of sterling's membership of the ERM which they had not wished for and accepted with some reluctance (see Davies, 1992b; see also Sentance and Walsh, 1992; Confederation of British Industry, 1992, p. 7). Indeed, Howard Davies, CBI Director General, at the announcement of sterling's withdrawal from the ERM, claimed:

> We are disappointed that the government has been blown off course by the currency markets. We think the government should urgently restore some certainties to its financial policies. The absence of clear guidelines will further weaken business confidence and the prospects for economic recovery (*Financial Times*, 1992e).

He was echoed by the CBI President, Sir Michael Angus who said: 'As an industrialist I find it hard to credit what it is happening to our currency. We do not need a devaluation of sterling. Perhaps, a lot of currency speculators do' (ibid.).

Even the cut of 1 per cent in interest rates announced in the immediate aftermath of the crisis failed to gain the CBI's support. Instead, it launched a fierce attack on the government's failure to curb its own spending or to control inflation with Britain outside the ERM. In his attack on the government, the CBI Director General, Sir Howard Davies, confirmed that the abandonment of the ERM should not give way to benign neglect of the exchange rate, since the depreciation of the exchange rate was a potential source of inflationary pressure (see *The Guardian*, 1992c).

If these were the reactions of the employers' side of British industry to sterling's devaluation and departure from the ERM, it would be interesting to have a look at the employees' side. This, though completely cut off from the government's macroeconomic decisions (the last defeat having been the announcement of the abolition of the National Economic and Development Council[17]) and still struggling against pit closures, was, no doubt, the British economic actor most concerned by the consequences of recession.

The TUC and the Struggle Against Exclusion

The position adopted by both the British Trade Union Congress and the ETUC in the negotiations over European Monetary Union reflects the limited bargaining power of the trade unions on macroeconomic issues. Indeed, rather than trying to influence the decisions regarding the timing and institutional characteristics of EMU, the employees' organisations tended to consider the process leading to a European Single Currency as 'inevitable' and to focus on other aspects of European economic integration.

In its debates on the issue, the TUC were keen to distinguish between areas of policy which were likely to happen 'almost regardless of the views of the social partners' (see Trade Union Congress, (1991b) and those which could be influenced at the European level. The trade unions tended to include monetary union in the first group, and to put pressure on the issue of economic union and measures to promote economic and social cohesion. This, in turn, was related to progress on the social dimension and on measures to improve productivity, and hence the collective bargaining agenda, and the role of trade unions as social partners at both the national and EC levels.

Consistently, the TUC required the IGC to take the economic growth and employment objectives seriously also through the establishment of appropriate institutions. It also demanded provisions for the transfer of resources to member states in economic difficulties, as already set out in the draft Treaty before the IGC.

The TUC stressed the importance of fiscal policy under EMU stage III. It pointed out how, within a system of constraints on budget deficits and the level of public debt, structural funds and regional policy became an important adjustment mechanism between the weaker members of the EC but also how they risked recreating the national tensions of the Common Agricultural Policy.

A key element in developing possible policy responses to the issue of pursuing cooperative growth policies, was, then, a clear assessment by the Commission of what affects competitiveness, and how to correct underlying differences in industrial productivity and trade performance. These, according to the TUC, ultimately depended not on real wages, but on non-price factors, such as quality and research and development (R&D), training and investment. The pursuance of similar policies at the European level could represent an important, and perhaps fundamental, corrective mechanism for differences in economic performance between member states. It also was the only plausible way, according to the TUC, for companies to deal with the competitive pressures coming from EMU.

Overall, the approach was to ensure that companies became 'resource developers', rather than 'asset strippers'. In this context legislation following the social charter was essential to deal with the thousands of small companies whose attitude was the total opposite of this (see Trade Union Congress, 1991b).

The priorities of the TUC in the course of the intergovernmental Conference, were thus represented by the social dimension, the Social Action Programme, Treaty revision, social dialogue and the industrial dimension and trade union links.[18]

With respect to EMU, the General Council of the TUC continued to monitor issues discussed in the intergovernmental conference on European economic and monetary union and made input to the ETUC statement on EMU adopted at the ETUC congress in May. This statement confirmed the trade union concern that the aims of EMU should be to promote sustainable economic growth and full employment, as well as to reduce inflation. Moreover it suggested that regional policies should be strengthened, and a common set of social standards be developed, and that weaker economies should be enabled to move to EMU at their own pace.

In discussion with the European Parliamentary Labour Party (EPLP) it was noted that there should be a linkage between EMU and institutional change, including such change affecting social provisions. EPLP members had raised the need to promote economic convergence between EC countries as a condition for EMU so as to ensure that peripheral countries also benefited from it. A narrowing of regional disparities was also required before the introduction of a single currency. The EPLP wanted also to ensure political control over decisions of the central bank, but there was still a range of views as to how that control had to be carried out. On the other hand, the General Council of the TUC recognised that care should be taken not to set aims for economic convergence which were impracticable and which would, in fact, make it impossible to establish EMU (see Trade Union Congress, 1991c).

That the goal of reaching EMU was not put under question appeared clearly in the report produced by the General Council on the Maastricht Treaty and endorsed by the 1992 Congress which called for, on a clear balance of consideration, the ratification of the Treaty itself (see Trade Union Congress, 1992a). Though growth, unemployment, and social and regional cohesion objectives had not been inserted among the EMU convergence criteria, the TUC did not reject the Maastricht provisions on EMU. Even if the Maastricht fiscal criteria, and, particularly the requirement on the deficit might appear over-restrictive, according to the TUC, the EC Commission's report, *One*

Market, One Money, had made it clear that a deficit to fund investment would be far more acceptable. In turn, an investment based deficit would imply a long-term fall in the ratio of public debt to GDP and improve the underlying economic growth potential of the economy, thus also increasing employment opportunities (see Trade Union Congress, 1991d). If interpreted in this way, the fiscal criteria could not be held inconsistent with the TUC objectives. Indeed, the convergence conditions were very similar to policy objectives of the British government in any case, but without EMU there would be no move towards replacing the Bundesbank with an institution responsible to the community as a whole or an enhanced role for ECOFIN.

Of course the TUC would have wished to see different conditions for economic and monetary union, and announced a political battle in the 1990s to ensure that growth and unemployment targets were given proper weight in the move towards EMU. However, they basically accepted the Maastricht way to a single currency since: 'As has consistently been the case in the evolution of the EC, economic union will drive political union' (see Trade Union Congress, 1992b).

Therefore, the opt-out clause negotiated by the British government was judged by the TUC inconsistent with national interests since it seemed inconceivable that Britain would wish to stand aside from the progress towards monetary union. In the long-run the UK, as with the ERM, would find it untenable to remain isolated from those states joined in monetary union, while in the meantime, the opt-out only restrained the UK from influencing further developments of the project (ibid.; see also Trade Union Congress, 1991d). Instead, the General Council took the view that it was realistic to seek a political commitment from the member states of the Community, with a willingness to adopt positive policies 'in the framework of the move towards EMU' (see Trade Union Congress, 1992a).

This was the strategic objective for the trade union movement in the 1990s to be incorporated in the TUC's developing campaign for full employment.

Immediately after the Maastricht summit, the General Council, through the ETUC, started pressing for a cooperative growth strategy to be agreed by the EC member states to provide the context in which EMU could be achieved through minimum negative effects. On 3 July 1992, a joint statement was agreed with the European employers' organisations in which policies for achieving good results on employment and growth within the process of moving towards EMU were mapped out. The statement said that the strategy would be founded on 'the combination of sound macroeconomic policies and supportive structural policies embedded in a cooperative climate provided by the social dialogue at the national and Community level' (ibid.). Though the statement was not as fully developed as would have been the case with a purely trade union statement, it was a first step towards reaching the 'right kind of EMU'.

In this context it is not particularly surprising that the trade unions hardly intervened at all, if ever, in the debate over the role of sterling in the ERM going on in the course of 1992.

A further explanation to this attitude of the TUC may be found in the words of John Edmonds, general secretary of the GMB general union, who, on the anniversary of British entry in the ERM, said: 'The economic situation is so bad that ERM has been a minor problem. The order of the day is survival' (see Marsh, 1991).

Indeed, devaluation or withdrawal from the ERM did not feature among the TUC requests to the British government to enhance UK manufacturing competitiveness and to create jobs in the 1992 TUC Budget submission (see Trade Union Congress, 1992a).

Given the priority task of returning to full employment, the TUC's work in 1992 followed two main strands. One was to build on the TUC Budget submission on measures to reduce unemployment. The second was to develop measures which would improve competitiveness and strengthen the industrial base. However, neither in its reports on the way to increase British industry competitiveness, did the TUC refer to the ERM issue. On the contrary, in a report submitted by the Trade Union Congress to the Trade and Industry Select Committee, the trade unions were keen to point out how competitiveness was not simply a question of prices of goods and services, and thus its enhancement was not necessarily linked to a sterling devaluation. Competitiveness was directly linked to quality, which was considered a universal requirement in many markets rather than simply a factor that gives an edge over competitors, and, increasingly, to innovation in design and product specification. Price competitiveness did of course matter, but this was determined by production costs, such as wages and salary costs, and, mainly, the price and quality of materials and components, the cost of capital and the efficiency with which resources were managed: the level of nominal exchange rates was not even mentioned (see Trade Union Congress, 1992c).

The TUC way to improving competitiveness, as explained in a series of documents circulated to the National Economic and Development Council (see Trade Union Congress, 1992d, 1992e and 1992i) privileged 'social partnership' between employers and trade unions. Thus it focused on those changes in government policy which attracted wide consensus among the social partners, particularly support for investment, training and research and development. In the UK, by contrast, the more short-term attitudes to employment, together with the weakening of employment protection during the 1980s, had encouraged short-term attitudes to investment, market share and product development. Long-term attitudes towards investment had thus to be accompanied by a new approach to the status of employees, who had to become effective stakeholders in the companies they worked for. A further important issue was the way that merger and take-over pressures, boosted by the increasing shares of profits allocated to shareholders rather than to new investment, reinforced short-term attitudes in manufacturing industry and the need for effective regulatory mechanisms, at the EC and at the national level, which took into account wider public interest concerns, including employment and the consumer.

The government's role in this environment was to provide for stable macroeconomic policies and supply side policies to encourage long-term attitudes to employment investment and innovation. In addition, the government had a direct role to play in investing in skills, infrastructures and R&D, in encouraging inward investment and promoting networks of companies to strengthen the supply chain and, finally, in promoting industrial partnership, particularly in the privileged context of the NEDO (see Trade Union Congress, 1992f). This was a request that certainly did not receive a great deal of attention at the governmental level since on 16 June 1992 the Chancellor announced the decision to abolish the NEDC and to close the NEDO by 31 December.

Devaluation, or withdrawal from the ERM, was thus clearly not in the TUC programme to enhance British industry competitiveness, nor was it inserted among the measures identified to increase employment.[19]

Consistently, when devaluation did happen, the trade unions did not consider British industry's problems solved or on the way to being solved. Instead, they were keen to point out how since Black Wednesday and the devaluation of sterling, business and consumer confidence had collapsed, and there were no signs of action to help bring about a recovery in output, investment and employment. What Britain needed above all, were still policies for growth and policies to support industry of the same kind they had been calling for before the sterling crisis.[20]

The TUC believed that currency instability was a direct consequence of the open financial markets of the European Single Market. This was not only a barrier to the effective stabilisation of exchange rates, either informally or by means of the ERM, but it was also a significant element imposing deflationary policies on the entire Community. Thus, there was probably no satisfactory halfway house between the partial instabilities of free-floating and the full stability of monetary union.

Indeed, the issues concerning the ERM and the EMU were not separable, most notably, in relation to the role of central bankers, to speculative movements of capital, of the relationships of exchange rates to employment, and above all in relation to the convergence conditions set out in the Maastricht Treaty (see Trade Union Congress, 1993b). It must be recalled that the TUC was in favour of Britain playing a full part in rapid progress towards monetary union. This had to happen in the context of the development of a coordinated EC strategy for growth and jobs and of the abolition of the artificial separation of monetary and fiscal policy to be replaced by an authoritative role for ECOFIN as the political counterpart of the European central bank, and as a vehicle for fiscal coordination.

Finally, in the whole ERM episode, the TUC lamented the failure by the government to consult the social partners both when Britain joined and when it was necessary to deal with the new circumstances created by sterling's departure. In both cases the government had no idea of how British industry could respond (see Trade Union Congress, 1992h).

Apart from the TUC's complaints, the fact the that the British government did not take into consideration British industry needs and requests appears clearly from the whole analysis of sterling's experience in the ERM. The whole ERM episode had, in fact, been characterised by the preponderance of the financial sector preferences over any other consideration. British entry in the ERM even if called for by the employers' major organisation since 1985, had been endorsed by the British government only when the failure of the monetarist practices of the 1980s had created a vacuum in the British government's anti-inflationary stance that the British financial community could hardly conceive.

On the other hand, the hastening of the process of European monetary integration with the publishing of the Delors' report on EMU had disclosed to the City of London the dismaying likelihood of losing its dominance of European financial markets, as well as its international competitiveness, in favour of a Bundesbank shaped European central bank based in Frankfurt. This had hastened the need to influence or delay somehow a process that clearly clashed with British financial interests.

However, the other European countries' interests, particularly the German and the French ones, were very strong and neither the City of London nor the British government were able to shape European events. Thus the IGC on

EMU did not constitute a major success from the British point of view, and the disillusion with its outcomes within certain British economic and political sectors, as well as the reiterated attacks to the existing European monetary arrangements, revealed to the international financial markets the weakness of British commitment to the ERM. This led to an epilogue of sterling's experience in the ERM that was far from being unwelcome.

What remains to be considered at this point, is how the British financial preferences over the process of European monetary integration have changed since Black Wednesday and how the British government is likely to pursue these interests in the European context.

Therefore, the aim of the final section of this book will be to identify and, to a limited extent, also predict the position of the British and Italian governments in the debate over the move to stage III of EMU.

Notes

1   For example, the Bank of England passed comfortably over £2bn a year to the UK Exchequer. See *The Banker*, 1991a.

  The issue was then settled in July 1991 when the EC central bank governors decided that the returns would have been shared among the 12 central banks on the basis of each country's GDP and population. See *The Banker*, 1991c.

2   It may be not without reason to recall that the British draft Treaty provisions were based on the first proposal of the hard ECU by Paul Richards, of HSBC Samuel Montagu, and Sir Michael Butler, director of Hambros.

3   However here it must be noted that Lamont was open to granting independence to the Fund on insistence of the other member states.

4   The Luxembourg draft said Ecofin could decide by majority vote to allow a member a derogation if 'the necessary conditions for full participation are not fulfilled'. See *The Economist*, 1991b.

5   The grounds on which this rejection was based are summarised in a paper by Ian Milne, an executive director and head of corporate finance at the City merchant banks of Bank of America and Svenska Handelsbanken, published in cooperation with the 'City of London concern over Maastricht' (COLCOM).

  The generalised scepticism of the City of London towards the Maastricht project for EMU has been further confirmed by a series of interviews held by the author with City personnel in November 1996.

  On the other hand, the most committed supporters of EMU in the City were Lloyds, but here it must be noted that the need to gain the other European partners' support for liberalisation of the European insurance market within the 1992 Single Market project could have played a significant role in the definition of Lloyds' position towards the process of European integration altogether.

  Indeed, while on the one hand, the banking business generally already enjoyed a 'Single Market', since its three prerequisites, the second banking directive and the directives on own funds and solvency ratios had been adopted in 1989, and, on the other hand, the liberalisation of investment services, in particular, securities business, could count on the powerful support of Germany and the so-called 'North sea' group as opposed to the so-called 'Club Med', in the insurance business Britain was still alone and the interests at stake were of enormous importance.

In fact, the two directives on the table by the end of the IGC, the third life directive and the third non-life directive, would have opened the market for both life and non-life business enabling companies to market products anywhere in the EC without needing authorizations for each individual market and without needing to have products approved by 12 different regulators.

On the position of the financial community towards the issue see *The Banker*, '1992 update', April 1991; *The Banker*, '1992 Update', October 1991; *The Banker*, '1992 Update', November 1991; *The Banker*, 'Many a slip ...', December 1991. For the position of Lloyds of London towards the European integration process, including EMU, see *Lloyds Bank Bulletin*, 1991, various issues.

6   The City of London Concern over Maastricht (COLCOM) was a group of the City of London established by Sir James Pickthorn, founder of the City's society Pickthorn, and active from 1992 to 1994. The aim of the City of London Concern Over Maastricht was to promote and encourage knowledge of, and debate about, the Treaty on European Union, especially its impact on the business of the City of London. Among its publications are Milne, 1993; Howe, 1993.

7   '... It would be reassuring to be able to forecast with confidence, as an increasing number in the City do, that this is just a burst of pre-election folly, and that an ERM realignment will quickly follow the British and Italian elections' (Harris, 1992; see also Hutton, 1992a; Balls, 1992).

8   Holding Company of one of the biggest market makers and dealers in securities. See *Who is Who* Edition Europe, Business and Industry, 1996, p. 2483.

9   The most heated Commons exchanges between the Labour and the Conservative Party during the electoral campaign were, indeed, over economic matters. See, for example, Stephens, 1992a.

10   '... What is astonishing is how modest the pressure on sterling has been despite the unceasing clamour in *The Times*, Sunday Times, Evening Standard and related organs, for a large interest rate cut at all costs, irrespective of the ERM.' See Brittan, 1992a.

11   On 14 July, the PM reaffirmed commitment to the Exchange Rate Mechanism; on 15 July, the Chancellor stressed it again to the Conservative backbenchers; on 16 August the Chancellor took to the Treasury steps to reaffirm the pledge to ERM; on 28 August EC Finance Ministers ruled out realignments; on 3 September the Chancellor announced a plan to borrow £7.3bn in DM and other currencies, underlying his promise not to devalue and make these borrowings more expensive; on 5 September EC finance ministers and foreign ministers meeting in Bath reaffirmed their 28 August statement not to realign and pledge to intervene to defend parities; on 10 September Major stressed solid opposition to devaluation to the Scottish CBI in Glasgow.

12   On 14 September the Bundesbank reduced Lombard rate by 0.25 per cent to 9.5 per cent and discount rate by 0.5 per cent to 8.25 per cent in the first interest rate cut in five years.

13   Indeed, in the immediate aftermath of the crisis there had been many Tory MPs supporting the Chancellor of the Exchequer.

John Townend, chairman of the influential Tory back-bench finance committee, said he was 'very opposed to sniping the Chancellor', who had inherited membership of the ERM. He also voiced support for Major, describing him as the best PM we have got'.

Lord Ridley, the former Cabinet minister, said he had 'every sympathy' for Lamont, who had 'done his level best'. The mistake was to have joined the ERM in the first place. See Owen, 1992a.

14 The Luxembourg Presidency circulated a paper about stage 2 of EMU on 23 April. Their proposed timetable was: 1 January 1991, stage 2 starts 1 January 1994: Council of Governors created to advise member states on the direction of monetary and exchange rate policies; 1996: creation of the European central bank, assuming effective reduction in monetary fluctuations. See Eberlie, 1991a.

15 The other five were: the Single Market and its completion; competition within the Community and the wider world; a realistic debate on the Social Dimension; getting to grips with the environment; improving the whole process of consultation, implementation, enforcement. See Confederation of British Industry, 1991b, p. 5; see also Eberlie, 1991b.

16 The protocol attached to the agreement stating clearly that the UK was not committed to move to the third stage of EMU without a separate decision by its government and parliament.

17 On 16 June 1992, the Chancellor announced the government's decision to abolish the NEDC and to close the NED Office by 31 December 1992.

18 For further details on the way these aims were pursued by the TUC and the ETUC see Trade Union Congress, 1991c.

19 It is true that in July 1992 the TUC Economic Committee called for a group of experts to explain the consequences of ERM flexibility on job creation, but this move was not followed by any public statement in favour of sterling's devaluation and, much less, of withdrawal from the ERM. See Trade Union Congress, 1992a.

20 On 23 September 1992, the Trade Union Congress released a statement on sterling's crisis calling 'for sustained domestic policies to promote growth and for progress towards economic and monetary union on the basis of a co-operative growth strategy'. See Trade Union Congress, 1993; see also Trade Union Congress, 1992g. In a report on the Maastricht treaty the TUC claimed: 'Confidence in the economic side of the equation was undoubtedly shaken by the events of Black Wednesday (16 September 1992) when the value of the pound fell by about 15%.' See Trade Union Congress, 1993b.

In a statement of 26 October 1992 the ETUC confirmed: '... The monetary turmoil of September 1992, (has) reinforced the ETUC's key demand, namely that EMU has to be pursued in conjunction with a co-operative strategy for growth and employment.' See European Trade Union Confederation, 1992.

PART III
FUTURE CONSENSUS

6 Italy and EMU: A Widespread Socioeconomic Consensus

Previous analysis has clarified how the socioeconomic consensus on which the credibility of the commitment to the ERM was founded disappeared during the early 1990s and how this was related to the economic interests of Italian industrial and banking sectors. The purpose of the following section is to examine whether and how the events of 1992–93 changed the attitude of Italian economic groups towards the establishment of European Monetary Union. The final aim is to identify the bases and motivations of Italian socioeconomic consensus to the final goal of EMU.

Industrial Capital and the Issue of Competitiveness

1 The Impact of Devaluation on Italian Industrial Performance

In the previous chapters it has been pointed out how the withdrawal of support for the ERM by Italian industrial capital was determined by the effect that the overvaluation of the lira had on Italian competitiveness and, consequently, on the performance of Italian economy.

Indeed, the departure of Italy from the European exchange rate arrangements seems to have facilitated the recovery of the Italian business cycle and to have helped Italian industry to regain those profitability margins lost during the early 1990s. Between September 1992 and December 1994 the nominal effective exchange rate of the lira depreciated on average by 27 per cent (32 per cent vis-à-vis the DM) and of a further 14 per cent on average during the first quarter of 1995 (19 per cent towards DM) (see Confindustria, 1995a, p. 9). The level of competitiveness, measured in terms of real effective exchange rate, however defined,[1] showed a related increase. This, according to the definition used, ranged from 25 per cent, for the index based on unit labour cost, to 10.5 per cent for the one based on prices at exports, which, however, is influenced by the increase of import prices (see Confindustria,

243

1995a, p. 63). These different definitions of real exchange rate do not represent alternative measures of competitiveness. On the contrary, when taken together they contribute to the description of the productive structure of a country as compared to that of its trade partners, and, in the case of Italy after the departure from the ERM, show the size of its competitive gains.

However, a more significant indicator of the impact of the devaluation of the lira on the Italian industrial system is, without doubt, represented by the performance of exports. The data show that the increase in manufacturing production in the two years after the crisis was 4.3 per cent on previous year at constant prices in 1994, and it was clearly led by exports. Indeed (see table below), the highest increase of production in 1993/94 was experienced by those industries most export oriented, which were also those to suffer more in terms of production in the period between 1986–92.

Table 20 % production changes and average export orientation* in Italy 1986–94

% average export orientation 1986–94	% annual av. production changes	
	1986–92	1992–94
More than 35%	1.41	1.26
Between 20% and 35%	1.51	0.63
Less than 20%	3.11	0.24

*   Export volume over production volume.

Source: CSC.

Overall export growth in the two years after the devaluation was very marked, more than +25 per cent; this also triggered an increase of average export orientation of Italian industry, from 31.6 per cent in 1992 to 34.2 per cent in 1994 (ibid., p. 22). In terms of market shares of exports, Italy more than recuperated the points lost at the beginning of the 1990s, ranking third in Europe, behind Germany and France in 1994 and reaching the highest level of export share ever achieved in the previous 15 years.

The performance of Italian exports after the devaluation bettered, in terms of shares, in all European markets, and to a lesser extent, in non-European markets as well. From the table below, reporting the development of Italian export share in 11 industrialised countries accounting for 65 per cent of overall

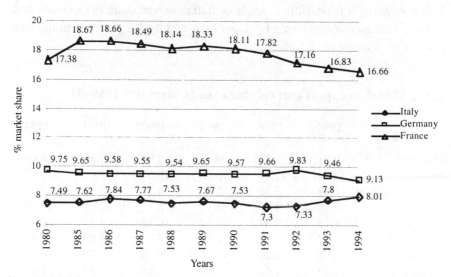

Graph 33 Market shares of the exports of 14 industrialised countries at constant prices

Source: CSC.

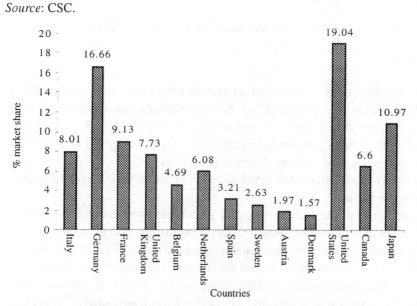

Graph 34 Market shares of the exports of 14 industrial countries in 1994

Source: CSC.

Italian exports, it is possible to see how Italian export share in Germany and France increased respectively by 1 per cent and by 1.1 per cent in the two years after leaving the ERM.

Table 21 Italian export market shares in 11 markets* 1989–94

	1989	1990	1991	1992	1993	1994
Germany	9.21	9.33	9.14	9.00	9.88	9.96
France	12.44	11.87	10.95	10.61	11.09	11.67
United Kingdom	5.97	5.39	5.21	5.36	6.01	5.99
Spain	9.70	9.57	9.12	8.77	10.76	10.54
Portugal	9.46	9.69	10.14	10.15	8.27	10.71
Greece	17.10	15.52	14.02	14.34	13.69	16.47
Holland	4.43	4.20	4.21	4.10	3.70	4.01
Austria	1.77	1.64	1.66	1.66	1.84	1.87
Switzerland	18.0	19.07	17.78	17.35	18.15	17.63
United States	2.73	2.51	2.16	2.17	2.42	2.41
Japan	1.68	1.69	1.45	1.30	1.44	1.66

*   % relation between imports from Italy and total imports in each country.

Source: CSC.

In non-European markets, Italian exports performed well in both the US and Japan in terms of market shares, but this phenomenon was accompanied by another important one, the re-orienting of Italian exports towards the markets of developing countries. Indeed, while the percentage of Italian exports to EU countries passed from 59 per cent in 1991 to 53.3 per cent (-5.7 per cent) in 1994, that directed to developing countries increased by 3.3 per cent in the same period.

Summing up, the Italian industrial sector has been extremely quick to react to the devaluation of 1992/93. This is confirmed also by an analysis of the ISCO published in 1995 (see Calabresi and Carnazza, 1995) which showed that more than 70 per cent of Italian enterprises included in their sample had changed their market position recuperating market shares both internally and domestically and even gaining, in 15 per cent of cases, new shares. Moreover, they consciously modified their commercial strategies (69 per cent), consolidating their stable presence in foreign markets (see Calabresi and Carnazza, 1996).

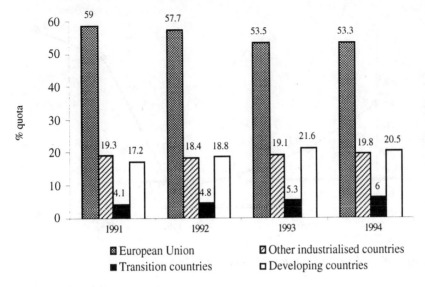

Graph 35 Italian % of exports in different markets

Source: CSC.

On the other hand, the implementation of the 1992 agreement on labour costs led to a negative growth of real wages of industrial workers in 1993 which, even if compensated, to a certain extent, by the increase of import costs, certainly allowed for a marked improvement in company profitability. Indeed, even Confindustria had to admit in its 1995 Report that profitability margins on variable costs (the so-called '*markup sull'estero*') on external market increased on average by 7.4 per cent from 1992 to 1994.

Table 22 Wages and prices annual % changes in Italy 1993–94

	Consumer prices growth rate	Wages Nominal	Real
1993	4.2	3.4	-0.8
1994	3.9	3.9	0.0

Source: CSC.

From the third trimester of 1993 onwards, the improvement of Italian competitiveness, very low labour costs and the containment of prices, allowed

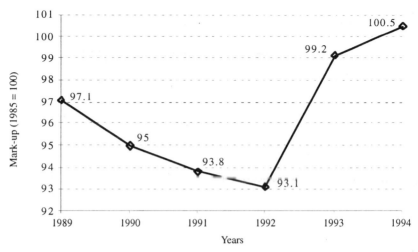

Graph 36 Italian industry mark-up on external market

Source: CSC.

for a substantial bettering of corporate finances. Self-financing of companies persistently increased while bank lending decreased. The dynamics of Italian corporate finances underwent, in the course of the two years following the devaluation, a reversal of the situation of financial flows (flows of assets and liabilities). These passed from a deficit of 52,707bn lire in the first three trimesters of 1992 to a surplus of 285 bn lire in the same period of 1994. The flow of financial assets increased from -795bn in 1992 to +13,746bn lire in 1994, while the flow of liabilities decreased from 51,912bn lire in 1992 to 13,461 in 1994. The improvement in the situation of liabilities was, in turn, due to a substantial reduction of corporate debt with banks, which decreased by 18,200bn lire in 1994, while in 1993 it had increased by 400bn lire.

However, the recovery of Italian corporate finances does not seem to have spilled over onto investment decisions. The ISCO analysis (see Calabresi and Carnazza, 1995) showed that the 1992/1993 devaluation did not have positive effects on the level of industrial investment. Indeed only 20 per cent of the enterprises included in the ISCO sample declared to have changed their investment decisions as a consequence of the devaluation. Of those who had, 15 per cent had decided to postpone their investments, while only 5 per cent anticipated them. This means that the profitability gains coming from the devaluation were not, in the majority of cases, reinvested and did not produce more work opportunities (see Calabresi and Carnazza, 1996, p. 49).

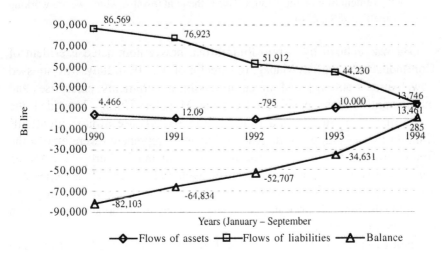

Graph 37 Flows of Italian corporate assets and liabilities 1990–94

Source: CSC.

Summing up, the events of 1992/93 seem to have helped Italian industry to solve those problems pointed out on the eve of the crisis. Indeed, the departure from the ERM had a very positive effect on the industrial sector. How all this is related to the broader question of Italian industry's position towards the issue of European Monetary Union is the subject of the next section of this dissertation.

2 Italian Industry's Position towards EMU: A Paradox?

Italian industry, particularly big industry, not only supported the establishment of a European Monetary Union. Actually, it was one of the major promoters of the process leading to the Maastricht definition of EMU. The Italian Confindustria and Agnelli were among the first founders in October 1987 of the Association for the Monetary Union of Europe (AUME)[2] whose main aim was, to refer to the words of Agnelli, then International Vice-president of the AUME:

> (...) to exert political pressure in favour of the first steps, gradual but sure, being taken towards the goal of further unification. This makes it indispensable to draw up a new Treaty that will lay down commitments and set dates for the

achievement of monetary union. This is the goal towards which we are working (Agnelli, 1989a, p. 4).

He was echoed by Sergio Pininfarina, newly nominated President of Confindustria as well as Managing Director of AUME in Italy, who stressed how 'Aume's action [was] aimed at making governments, enterprises and public opinion more sensitive to European Monetary Union'. He added 'the goals of Confindustria and those of the AUME are almost identical' (Pininfarina, 1989a, p. 7). In general, Italian entrepreneurs were among the first to promote the initiatives for the establishment of a European common currency area. They signed a manifesto in favour of EMU as early as September 1988 (see Scognamiglio, 1989, p. 3), while Agnelli explicitly proposed changing the Single European Act to include a chapter on monetary unification (see Agnelli, 1989b, p. 3).

Not even during the crisis of the Lira in the ERM did Italian industry withdraw its support the Maastricht Treaty whose clauses on EMU it had accepted and approved entirely (see Confindustria, 1992). Moreover, in the course of the heated political debate on the 'ins' and 'outs' which followed the European Council in Madrid of December 1995, Italian industry never lost the opportunity to underline the heavy costs that a non-participation of Italy in EMU would involve.

According to Confindustria's *Program of Public Finances to Remain in Europe*, it was 'essential that Italy does not miss this appointment. The costs of non-participation in the common currency are much more than the sacrifices necessary to satisfy the convergence criteria. ... Participation to EMU will allow us to recover those conditions of monetary stability, low inflation and low interest rates that Italy lost almost three decades ago' (Confindustria, 1996b, p. 50). This position was then reiterated in Confindustria's papers for the 1996 IGC (Confindustria, 1995b). Again in its proposals for the Italian semester of EU presidency, where it was stated that 'an effective Single Market cannot do without, in the medium term, an economic and monetary union, in which it is indispensable for Italy to participate' (Confindustria, 1996a, p. 12).

At this point it is worth asking why Italian industry was so willing to give up Italian autonomy in determining monetary policy and, to a very large extent, also fiscal policy to shift it to the European level with the implementation of the Maastricht clauses on EMU.

From the point of view of Confindustria, the maintenance of independent monetary and fiscal policies is seen more as a problem than as an advantage in that it allows for the persistence of significant interest rate differentials with the other European countries, thus undermining Italian industry's competitive position in Europe. The experience of the ERM, which at the beginning, in a situation of rather heated social relations, had facilitated the adoption of macroeconomic policies in line with Italian industry's primary aim of boosting its competitive position, proved, in the course of the 1980s, to conflict with such an aim. Indeed, the excess of credibility that participation in the European monetary arrangements granted to Italian national monetary and budgetary policies led to an overvaluation of the exchange rate which proved unsustainable for the Italian industrial sector. The latter, consequently, withdrew its consensus to the ERM.

However, the solution to Italian competitiveness cannot be found in a system of floating exchange rates since this leaves to a hard internal confrontation with the social partners, the issue of the implementation of strict monetary and budgetary policies aimed at the achievement of low inflation and interest rates. Furthermore, as an increasingly important aspect in the context of the process of regionalisation of world economy in response to the challenges of global competition, it leaves unsolved the problems of intra-European and extra-European competitiveness.

Thus, neither a system of free-floating exchange rates nor one of quasi-fixed exchange rates would solve Italian industry's competitive problems. Not even a system of nonadjustable fixed exchange rates would be enough, since it would always leave some scope to the implementation of divergent monetary and budgetary policies which would necessarily spill over onto interest rates, creating differentials and, ultimately, exchange rate instability.

Similar considerations are very clear in the minds of Italian industrialists. Indeed, it was exactly on the basis of these considerations that Confindustria and Agnelli, far before the actual crisis in the ERM, had already understood how their interests would be better off in a different European financial and monetary context than the ERM. Moreover, it was exactly on these grounds that they promoted and pushed the Maastricht way to EMU.

The grounds on which Agnelli proposed at the 1989 AUME conference the modification of the Treaty on European Union to insert a section on monetary and financial union, were the following:

The first is that the European Monetary System, the way it is configured today, is insufficient to ensure the proper functioning of the great continental market. It has worked well up to now, but left open the problems of costs and uncertainties coming from exchange rate fluctuations, even if limited ....

The second is that European industry stands in need of a common financial space to accelerate its growth and the process of aggregation and thus attain dimensions adequate for confrontation at the world level .... The third reason is that once we think of a united Europe as an economic power we must also think that this Europe will have to create a currency of its own in order to be able to defend its market against external currency shocks and sustain its commerce with and investments in other countries (Agnelli, 1989b, p. 3).

The President of Confindustria founded his case in favour of EMU on the fact that:

A common currency can accelerate decisively the process leading to a greater coordination of economic and budgetary policies and to full convergence of costs and prices, particularly labour and money ones.

He also warned about the limits of the ERM claiming that:

The strength of the lira during the last months should not lead to the conclusion that the Italian economy has solved its problems and does not need attention any more. Actually this strength ... is the direct effect of our public finances imbalance which compels our financial authorities to maintain high interest rates. This produces a double negative effect on productive activities: on one side it harms exports and, consequently, growth, on the other it leads capital and savings to public bonds instead of productive investments (Pininfarina, 1989b, pp. 10–11).

Similar concerns were expressed also by Scognamiglio who said:

Despite the great successes that have been achieved by the European monetary agreement, the system has now entered a phase of instability. We must therefore go beyond it, because it no longer succeeds in suppressing inflation rate differentials and does not succeed in ensuring full convergence of the economic (that is, fiscal and monetary) policies of member states. ... The EMS, despite the successes of the past, has become a very costly instrument ... and one that is not very efficient because it does not succeed in eliminating national policy differences.

What were the solutions to this failure of the ERM for the Italian industrial sector?

We must either move to a closer form of monetary union than in the past or drop back to ... a system of freely floating exchange rates. ... In the latter case, the process of financial integration, that is, the free circulation of capital will prove impossible. Basically, therefore this means a move towards a fixed exchange-rate system, that is, one with non-adjustable parities, or towards a single European currency. Nevertheless, these two roads are by no means equivalent and, in my opinion, monetary union with a single currency would be far preferably for Italy ....

The reason was:

Because a system of non-adjustable exchange rates without moving in the short-term to monetary unification, would be always possible for the states to allow fiscal policy to diverge (Scognamiglio, 1989, p. 39).

Summing up, what were the advantages of the Maastricht definition of EMU for the Italian industrial sector?

The first, obvious consideration is that the introduction of a single currency for all European countries eliminated *tout court* the problems linked to the over valuation of the lira, and, thus, also, the need of its devaluation. Moreover, the Maastricht definition of EMU solved, once and forever, the problem of Italian monetary policy, that is, the problem of Italian interest rates and prices and of their differentials with the ones of European competitors. Indeed, EMU eliminated national monetary policies altogether and substituted them with a common European monetary policy enforced by a European Central Bank committed to low and stable prices. Lastly, the likelihood of the implementation of lax fiscal policies was well reduced by the implementation of the Maastricht fiscal criteria and by their extension to the post-unification period guaranteed by the Stability Pact (see Talani, 1995).

As can be easily understood, all this has extremely important consequences also in terms of power relations with the other national interest groups, particularly the trade unions. Indeed, it institutionalised the shift of the decision-making process from the national to the European level for a set of politically extremely sensitive macroeconomic policies. Far more importantly, it institutionalised the aims towards which they have to be geared: low interest rates, low prices, low public deficits and debts. These aims, by chance, correspond perfectly to the preferences of the Italian, or better, of the European, entrepreneurs while they might have some uncertain, if not negative, consequences on employment and the labour market.[3]

That these aims met perfectly the preferences of at least the Italian industrial sector appeared clear from the proposals of Confindustria for the 1996 Italian semester of EU presidency. In the name of competitiveness, Italian industrialists asked for a substantial reduction of public expenses for the welfare state which are financed throughout higher taxes and public debt. They also asked for a substantial reduction of labour costs and rigidities, which spill over onto prices thus rendering European products less competitive in the international context. How much easier it would be to achieve these results having rigid limits at the European level on deficit and price growth rates, without having any opportunities for the trade unions to challenge them!

Moreover, the Maastricht treaty guaranteed the definitive achievement of a European Single Market with all that it meant in terms of business opportunities at the European level. Also on this point Confindustria was very clear. In its contribution to the Italian EU presidency it stated:

> The implementation of the Single Market at the normative level may be considered complete. This is not the case for its effective implementation which must be based on a quicker and more complete and homogeneous domestic implementation of European regulations, on the establishment of EMU, on the building of trans-European networks and on the harmonisation of environmental law (Confindustria, 1996a, p. 12).

Finally, the Maastricht way to EMU allowed for the definition of an integrated European trade strategy to react to the challenges of extra European countries, particularly the United States and Japan, but also the quickly developing Asian countries. To achieve this aim, the reliance on a single currency and a single monetary and exchange rate policy would certainly represent a very powerful competitive tool (see Confindustria, 1995b, p. 12).

In conclusion, there was not any paradox between Italian industry's withdrawal of support to the ERM and its promotion of EMU. The strategy had remained the same, to shift policies from the national to the European level, but the instrument of the ERM had proved insufficient and had been substituted by the more advantageous establishment of EMU. Of course, at the basis of this strategy remained the need for promoting the economic interests of the sector. However, the EMU framework allowed for a more stable pursuit of the desired set of macroeconomic policies and aims, since it institutionalised them at the European level and withdrew them from the instability of the day-to-day national political life and confrontation with the social partners.

It is possible to claim that the ERM and the EMU lie on two different 'ontological' plans. This clearly explains why it was perfectly logical for Italian industry to gather the fruits of the collapse of the ERM and, at the same time, call for the establishment of EMU.

To what extent these considerations were shared also by the Italian banking sector will be the subject of the next paragraph.

The Italian Banking Sector and EMU: Dependent and Independent Preferences

The association representing the interests of the Italian banking sector, the Italian Banking Association (ABI) will be taken here as a point of reference to identify the changes of the position of the Italian banking community towards the issue of EMU. In particular, reference will be made here to the position of the ABI in the European Banking Federation (EBF).[4]

While the ABI and the Italian banking community generally, had adopted a favourable attitude towards the making of the ERM in 1978, its interventions in the debate over EMU tended to be inserted in the context of the activity of the European Banking Federation. This was given to the political sensitiveness of the issues relating to the establishment of a common currency area in Europe, both at the international and at the domestic level particularly in the period immediately preceding and following the crisis of the lira.

Of course, the Italian banking community welcomed the Maastricht way to EMU (see ABI, 1991), particularly the fiscal requirements which gave it the occasion to underline, again, the perverse effects of government bond selling on bank intermediation (ibid., p. 6). It also enabled the banks to put the case for the privatisation of public companies (ibid., p. 5) and to advocate the change of corporate/bank relationship from corporate lending to corporate finance (ibid., p. 5). However, the increasingly worsening situation of Italian industrial companies called for some caution towards the process of European monetary integration (see ABI, 1992, p. 3), and official positions were shifted to the European Banking Federation.

Nevertheless, studies on the economic and financial consequences of the establishment of a common currency area in Europe, as well as on the costs of EMU for the banks started to be initiated by the EBF and documents issued on the related technical questions (see EBF, 1993, p. 69; see also EBF, 1995, p. 92). The technical nature of these documents underlies a substantial and explicit acceptance of the process leading to EMU, which was then overtly adopted also by the Italian Banking Association in the aftermath of the departure of the lira from the ERM.

Indeed, in his intervention to the annual assembly of the ABI on 23 June 1993, Tancredi Bianchi, the President of the Association, claimed:

> In them (Italian monetary authorities) we have faith to reach the goal of European monetary integration in reasonable time, hopefully not too far away (Bianchi, 1993, p. 81).

From 1993 onwards and, particularly, after the publication of the Green Book in 1995, the ABI started to be more explicitly in favour of the Maastricht way to EMU and to make explicit its preferences on the subject. According to Tancredi Bianchi, the non-participation of Italy to EMU would be extremely dangerous (*esiziale*). In his words:

> The banking system is aware of the dangers which would derive to the Italian economy if the national productive system as well as the system of financial and credit intermediation had to operate outside one of the three world economic and monetary macro-areas (centred respectively in New York, Tokyo and London). Therefore, the system expresses its belief that all efforts must be made, and all sacrifices must be accepted to enter European Monetary Union and the single currency: the Euro (Bianchi, 1996, p. 18).

That the path to EMU accepted by the banking system was the one decided at Maastricht, was then clarified further by Tancredi Bianchi in his intervention when, reporting the words of the Governor of the Bank of Italy, he claimed that:

> The conditions useful and necessary for EMU are: a decrease of the level of public debt; a strong action aimed at the progressive reduction of the public deficit to reach positive figures; the limitation of inflation and the absorption of unemployment (ibid.).

The unemployment problem was to be solved, according to the banking sector, through the introduction of a more flexible system of industrial relations. This was somehow seen as an inevitable consequence of the process of globalisation, even if changes in the 1993 agreement on the cost of labour were asked to avoid any possible reimbursement of the effective inflation rate (ibid., pp. 22 and 24).

The most important reasons for the banking sector's support to EMU were, however, the need to eliminate or, at least reduce, the public deficit and on the other hand, the achievement of monetary stability.

The impact of public bond trade on the banking system in terms of crowding out, has already been pointed out at length in a previous section. Here it will be enough to underline how many of the considerations on this subject that had induced the banking community to accept the process of

European monetary integration from its outset, were still valid later on. In his 1996 intervention, Tancredi Bianchi stressed how the widespread reliance on public bonds by the Italian savers not only reduced to a very large extent direct banking intermediation, with all that it meant in terms of loss of profits for the banking sector, but also had an impact on the Italian structure of interest rates. In fact, it led to a very limited spread between short-term and long-term interest rates, both active and passive (about 100 points spread for Italian passive interest rates as compared to a spread of 300 in Germany and Japan, of 250 points in France and of 200 in the USA). This phenomenon was due to the banks' need to link the structure of their short-term rates to the high level of interest rates paid by the state on short-term bonds (mainly BOT) and had a very negative impact on the level of banking profits. This negative impact occurred because on the one hand, the high levels of the state's short-term rates made it far less convenient to transform short-term liabilities into long-term assets to gain from the difference between short and long-term interest rates. On the other hand, it made it more expensive overall to gather finances for the banking system, through, for example, the Certificate of Deposit instrument.

Of course this had repercussions for the relations between the banks and industry too. Indeed, high short-term passive rates meant also high short-term active rates, which reduced the incentives for the banks to intervene directly in the finance of the industry (corporate finance). This also restrained industry from recurring to banking lending,[5] particularly in a period of growth, such as the one that the Italian economy experienced after its departure from the ERM (see Part II, ch. 1).

Summing up, the reduction of the public debt was still seen by the banking sector as a necessary measure to promote the overall profitability margins of the banking system, regardless of the business cycle. Further, the solution to the public debt problem proposed by the banking sector, that is, the 'reform' (using a euphemism) of the welfare system, particularly the pension system, opened many business opportunities for the banking sector, like the establishment of pension funds owned and managed by banks and insurance companies (on the model of the City of London) (see Bianchi, 1996, p. 25). Of course, the necessary premise for similar developments was the starting of a 'non-timid' process of privatisation of the banking system which, therefore, was repeatedly called for by the ABI (ibid.).

Another important area of concern for the banking sector as well as another reason to support the Maastricht way to EMU, was the stability issue (see Fazio, 1997, p. 2).

Given the structure of Italian capitalism and the related definition of the activity of the Italian banking system as one of 'credit to industry',[6] the prosperity of the banking sector is very much linked to the prosperity of the industrial sector. Therefore, the interests of these two communities tend to overlap. However, in a context of deeper integration of monetary and financial markets, credit risks, in the form of exchange rate risks, price risks, market risks and position risks, tend to increase (see Bianchi, 1996, p. 26). It is true that the development and spread of new financial instruments has facilitated the recourse to a vast range of hedging practices.[7] However, it is also true that these are not accessible to the whole industrial sector, particularly the small and medium enterprises, given the level of costs and of expertise that they imply. It is, therefore, thought to be a better idea to eliminate completely exchange rate risks and price risks at least within Europe through the establishment of a common currency area managed by a European central bank committed to the maintenance of low and stable inflation rate (see Bianchi, 1996, p. 27).

Further, the process of European monetary integration itself poses many problems of stability, both within the European Community and vis-à-vis nonmember countries, particularly the US and Japan. What particularly concerned the European, and thus also the Italian, banking community, apart from the traditional legal problems connected to the continuity of contracts (see Part IV, ch. 2), was the problem of monetary and exchange rate stability before and after the establishment of EMU as well as during the transition phase.

Summing up, the preferences of the banking sector over the definition of EMU seem to coincide with those of the industrial sector. The reason why this happens does not escape the representatives to the banking sector itself, and is clearly related to the nature of Italian capitalist structure, that is to the structural dependence of banking sector profits on industrial performance.

In conclusion, it is possible to hypothesise the existence of a strong consensus by both the Italian industrial and financial capital on the establishment of the single currency area in Europe based on strict monetary and fiscal policies. The existence of this basis for consensus alone, could be enough to understand the Italian government's unconditional decision to enter EMU from the outset. However, to have a more complete answer to the question why Italy has been so eager to enter EMU immediately it is worth also considering the position of the trade unions, to which we turn in the next section.

EMU and the Progress of the Social Dimension in Europe: Spill-Overs or Side Payments? The Trade Unions in a Power Trap

The strategy of Italian capital, particularly industrial, in the process of European integration *tout court* and much more in the process of European monetary integration has always been geared by the attempt to shift to the European level the decision on a set of politically sensitive macroeconomic policies.

This strategy, far from being abandoned with the failure of the ERM, has been institutionalised throughout the adoption of the Maastricht way to EMU as well as the approval of the Stability Pact, with evident consequences for the trade unions.

Indeed, the path to European Monetary Union, as defined by the Maastricht Treaty and by the following agreement on the stability pact, directly and substantially affects the powers and prerogatives of trade unions in their traditional policy realms. In particular, the statutory ECB goal of a low and stable inflation rate will have undeniable consequences on the limits within which trade unions will be able to conduct wage policies. Moreover, the implementation of monetary policy by the European Central Bank, through the decisions over the level of European interest rates, is undoubtedly deemed to affect investment decisions and, consequently, the level of unemployment. Finally, the rigid limitations on the conduct of national fiscal policy imposed by the Maastricht Treaty for the transition to EMU and by the Stability Pact for its aftermath, are already deeply modifying the terms of the debate over the survival of the welfare state in all its components.

Therefore, the trade unions' position towards further progress on the way to monetary union must be read in terms of reaction to this process of institutionalisation and of the attempt to regain the terrain lost since the beginning of the process of monetary integration.

Indeed, this claim is not only true for Italian trade unions, or, as analysed below, for British ones, but is true for European trade unionism as a whole or, at least, as represented by the ETUC.[8] Consequently, Italian trade unions' interventions in the debate over the establishment of EMU should be seen as both adding and taking stimulus from the broader debate going on within the ETUC.

From the very beginning of the discussions over the Delors Plan for the establishment of a single currency area in Europe, the Italian trade unions did not reject the goal of EMU. However, they tended to insert it into the broader debate of furthering the social and political dimension of European integration. This inclination appears clearly in the proposals of the CGIL-CIS-UIL

for the 1990 Italian semester of Presidency of the Council of Ministers in
which it was claimed:

> At the moment, the tendency which seems to prevail in the European institutions
> is that to attribute to the establishment of European Monetary Union a spill-
> over value with respect to all the other policies which are believed to be induced
> exactly by the implementing of EMU. This propensity, if it leads to considering
> monetary policy as the only integration policy, reproduces at a higher level the
> imbalances, which characterised the whole process of European integration. ...
> Instead it is necessary to guarantee policies of management of the economy
> aimed at ensuring economic and social cohesion, supported by instruments of
> democratic accountability and of social consensus able to integrate and balance
> the mere monetary-economic goal of the integration process (CGIL, 1990, p.
> 55).

The goal of monetary union, by itself, was not questioned. However, it
was underlined that this goal had to be completed with a set of decisions
aimed at giving some substance to the social dimension of European integration
which, on the contrary, had been, up to that point, set aside or treated with
ambiguity. Indeed, declared the Italian trade unions, the steps towards the
achievement of the same status for the economic and the social dimensions of
the European development taken in the summit of Hanover (27/28 June 1988),[9]
of Rodi (2/3 December 1988)[10] or Madrid (26/27 June 1989)[11] had been
somehow frustrated by the contents of the Social Charter[12] and by the delays
in the implementation of the Social Action Programme.

In particular, for the CISL, to achieve a socially integrated Europe it was
necessary to act in different directions. First, in the labour market area, with
some harmonisation of working conditions within Europe to allow for labour
mobility and with the strengthening of vocational training. Second, in the
area of collective wage bargaining, perhaps starting from some kind of
experiment at the transnational level. Third, in the area of the harmonisation
of individual rights, with the implementation of the Social Charter. Finally, in
the area of welfare state with the decision of which model to choose for the
European Community (see *Conquiste Sindacali*, November 1991, p. 11).

Emilio Gabaglio, then Confederal Secretary of the CISL, also insisted on
some conditions that it was necessary to fulfil to give some substance to the
social dimension of Europe. Commenting on the poor performance of the
first meeting of the IGC in Rome on 13 and 14 December in terms of social
debate, he underlined how the building of the economic/monetary dimension
of Europe had to be accompanied at least by the definition of a Community-

level instrument allowing for the consultation, information and participation of the workers inserted in a trans-European productive structure. The second requirement was the definition on the basis of experiments within the EU and agreements with the other European trade unions of a collective bargaining instrument. The third was the strengthening of the role of the social partners at the European level, also through the strengthening of the ETUC (see Gnetti, 1990).

The position of the UIL was rather similar to that of the CISL, apart from the stronger emphasis put on the political dimension of Europe (see Benvenuto, 1990, p. 45) and on the need to pursue the goal of a European Federation, for which the realisation of EMU could represent an important element since: 'The currency could represent the lever of the European Federation. The currency will help as it will help the management of the economy at the European level.'

Thus, the UIL did not reject the goal of monetary union. On the contrary its General Secretary, Giorgio Benvenuto, on the eve of the first gathering of the 1990 IGC wished the 'determination of clear guidelines and deadlines for EMU which will be a strong factor to hasten the path of integration' (ibid.). However, also from the UIL point of view, these developments had to be accompanied by further developments in the social sphere. In the words of Benvenuto:

> It would be extremely serious if, once again, the social issues remained outside the door, excluded from the big issues under discussion. We ask that they fully enter the debate, with the same status of the economic-monetary issues (ibid.).

Even the CGIL, which had been opposed to the process of European monetary integration and to the establishment of the European Monetary System in 1978, had adopted, by the beginning of the 1990s, a much more positive stance towards the issue.

In his speech at the ETUC Luxembourg Congress, Bruno Trentin, General Secretary of the CGIL, completely endorsed the Delors project of European integration founded on the Single Market, the establishment of EMU and the revision of the Treaty of Rome. However, he answered to challenges arising from it by calling for the transformation of the ETUC into an advocate of European integration (Trentin, 1991, p. 74). To achieve this aim it was necessary to act both internally and externally. Internally, by continuing the process of structural reform started with the Luxembourg Congress and by increasing the representativeness of the ETUC. Externally by putting pressure on the national governments at both the national and the European level to enhance the effective role and power of the European workers' organisation. This meant clearly defining the proposal and bargaining powers of the ETUC with respect both to the EU institutions and to the national and multinational companies as well as their national and European interests associations.

In particular, the attention of the CGIL focused on three areas of action. First, the area of organisation through the building of a truly European trade unions confederation able to speak and to act in the name of all European workers overcoming national borders and, thus, also overcoming the need to coordinate different sovereign organisations. Second came the area of rights by elaborating, starting from the Social Charter, the bases of a truly European labour, trade union and social regulation and law. Third there was the area of the role of the social parts through the deepening of the Social Dialogue and the identification of a European level of bargaining (see Lettieri, 1991, p. 75).

Summing up, it is possible to claim that there was a common line of the Italian trade unions towards the developments going on in the monetary realm. This was to counterbalance them by asking for further developments in the European Social policy area and for more power for the social parts at the European level. This was an active position, not a passive belief that EMU would imply further integration in the social dimension by means of spill-overs. Indeed it was substantiated by the strengthening of the ETUC, which with the election of Emilio Gabaglio as General Secretary, became more sensible to the positions of its Italian component and more predisposed to follow this pro-active strategy (see Gnetti, 1991a).

Indeed, exactly in the middle of the 1991 Intergovernmental Conferences, the ETUC was undergoing a major structural transformation. This led, in the course of the Luxembourg Congress of 13–17 May 1991, to the modification of its Statute with the insertion of the category representatives in the executive body and the creation of a narrower directive body composed by the representatives of the national trade unions. It also led to a leadership change, with the election of Emilio Gabaglio, ex Confederal Secretary of the CISL, as General Secretary of the ETUC.[13]

This transformation itself was explicitly related to the need for the European trade unions to react to the marginalisation of the employees' organisations from the latest developments of the process of European integration, particularly in the monetary policy realm. Apart from the fact that this claim was inserted in the preface to the General Resolution of the Luxembourg Congress (see CES, 1991, p. 67), this was also the leitmotif of trade unions leaders' speeches during the Congress.

Limiting the analysis to the interventions of Italian union leaders, according to Bruno Trentin, General Secretary of the CGIL:

> The revision and re-founding of that European workers' treaty represented by the ETUC Statute and Programme must be the reaction to the new European integration phase, opening with the big Single Market, monetary union and Treaty revision. We have in front of us important challenges and also some dangers and a very serious threat, as Jean Le Peyre reminded us: the threat of a true marginalisation of social Europe in the decision-making processes leading, in European and national institutions as well as in big enterprises, to the establishment of European Monetary Union and of European political union itself (Trentin, 1991, p. 74).

Antonio Lettieri, Confederal Secretary of the CGIL, also denounced the marginalisation of the trade unions in the decision-making process of European monetary integration and the need to regain the terrain lost by making pressure on the social and political side of European integration:

> Delors is convinced that once economic Europe has been built, political and social democracy will follow. Unfortunately, this is only a hope, not a reality. There is no automatism between economic development and social dimension. ...Unification has always been our aim, but the one which is going to happen, is managed by the economic forces, by big industry and by the central banks. It is the bankers who decide when the European Central Bank will be established, when the exchange rates will be irrevocably fixed and under which conditions we will have a single currency (Lettieri, 1991, p. 75).

Perhaps more meaningful, given his role of General Secretary of the ETUC, is the fact that this interpretation of EMU was shared by Emilio Gabaglio who defined as extremely 'alarming' the development of the work in the intergovernmental conferences claiming that:

> It seems that the marginalisation of social Europe is going to be confirmed and that the process of European integration will be defined always more by its economic and monetary aims (Gabaglio, 1990).

From these interventions it seems possible to infer that the trade unions entered the debate over the making of EMU only from a very marginal position, or they did not enter it at all, both at the national and at the European level. They perceived the decision-making process on EMU going on in the 1991 IGC as something outside their reach. It was not possible to modify it but it was necessary to react to it by asking for a more powerful position of Social policy and of the social dialogue in the European context in exchange for its acceptance.

Indeed, the ETUC actively called the two IGCs to lay down the concrete bases for the establishment of EMU. However, they also required that the discussions within the IGCs allowed for the achievement of parallel results in all policy areas: the economic, the political and the social ones. They were keen in pointing out that the unification of the markets and of monetary policy had to be realised together with economic and social cohesion. Therefore, further steps were urged towards the definition of a common European economic and budgetary policy, based on the harmonisation of national fiscal systems and of structural policies aimed at reaching territorial equilibrium with the final goal of reducing unemployment and defining a true European social regulation. This regulation had to broaden the scope of the Social Action Programme whose implementation, however, had to be hastened and had to become legally binding for the member states. Finally, the rule of majority voting had to be extended to social issues (see 'Due manifestazioni della CES a Roma', *Lavorosocieta'*, no. 12, December 1990).

Given this starting point, it should not be too surprising that both the ETUC and the Italian trade unions welcomed the decisions taken at Maastricht and tended to consider the signing of the Social Protocol by 11 of the European governments[14] as an important step to balance the developments of monetary union.

Indeed, the Social Protocol represented the final outcome of the incessant bargaining activity of the ETUC. This had been going on from the Luxembourg Congress onwards and had resulted in the reaching of an agreement on 30 October 1991, with the UNICE, the organisation representing European industrials, in which a common position on the role of the social partners in the new Treaty was defined (see Masucci, 1992, p. 46).

According to Ettore Masucci, CGIL official responsible for International Affairs as well as member of the Economic and Social Committee of the European Union, it was indisputable that the Maastricht Treaty marked a turning point in the development of the European social policy. In fact, the Social Protocol opened the doors to the definition by the EU Institutions of a true European social policy and allowed the social partners to play an autonomous role in the European context.

In particular, Masucci welcomed the extension of majority voting to the decisions relating to working conditions and to workers consultation and information, even if he lamented the maintenance of unanimity for the questions regarding social security and protection, dismissals, co-management and migrant workers. Also regrettable was the explicit exclusion from the *acquis communitaire* of everything related to wage policy and trade unions' legislation, in particular the right to strike.

However, what was to be considered a major victory of the ETUC related to the role of the social partners in the European context and to European collective bargaining. According to the Social Protocol, Art. 2.4, a member state might entrust to the social partners, at their joint request, the implementation, through a bargaining process, of EU directives. Moreover in Art. 3 the Commission committed itself to preliminary consultation of the social partners on social issues and to delegate to them, on request, the reaching of the agreement (through a bargaining process).

All this was interpreted by the CGIL (see also Lettieri, 1992 and 1993) as a true horizontal extension of the principle of 'subsidiarity' to include the social partners in the European decision-making process on social issues. Moreover, the Social Protocol also opened the way to reach collective agreements at the European level on the subjects listed in the Treaty, agreements, which, through a decision of the Council of Ministers, could even achieve a European legal status (see Social Protocol, Art. 4). This meant that the door was open to the implementation of a true European bargaining process. A good result, from the trade unions point of view, in exchange for the workers' organisations' consensus on the Maastricht way to EMU with all that this consensus implied in terms of relaxing the national political debate on the measures necessary for the implementation of Maastricht criteria, particularly fiscal ones.

On the basis of these considerations, the Italian trade unions and the ETUC generally were among the social forces promoting the ratification of the Maastricht Treaty in the course of the period of uncertainty of 1992–93. In the words of the ETUC General Secretary:

> We have decided to promote the ratification of it (the Maastricht Treaty) mainly because we believe that the workers would be worse off without Maastricht than with Maastricht: at least, given the establishment of the Single Market, the Treaty gives to the trade unions some more opportunity to try to balance the market from the social point of view (Gabaglio, 1992, p. 33).

Summing up, the provisions of the Social Protocol were considered by the trade unions as such an important achievement that they overshadowed the negative consequences that the Maastricht way to EMU might have on workers' conditions in the short-term and on the power of trade unions itself.

There is, however, at least another way in which the social policy developments agreed in Maastricht might be interpreted. What the employees' organisations tended to consider as a major success could be seen from the other side of the coin, the one of the employers' organisations, as a fair price to pay to gain the social consensus on what was for them a set of extremely beneficial policies. It could be seen as a convenient side-payment.

Concluding, the picture of Italian socioeconomic stance towards the Maastricht Treaty and EMU shows that the Italian government's decision to endorse and actively pursue the policies implied in the Maastricht definition of EMU was based on an extremely broad socioeconomic consensus, even if this consensus was founded on very different considerations.

It has been on the basis of this consensus, indeed, that the Italian government's commitment to the Maastricht criteria has become credible and that Italy has been able to reach the fervently desired goal of a deficit to GDP ratio of 3 per cent. Whether this goal was the only one, or even the most important one, to be pursued by the first left wing government of post war Italian history is a completely different issue.

Notes

1   There is a big debate in economic literature on the best way to define the real effective exchange rate, the measure of competitiveness. See, on the subject, Lipschitz and McDonald, 1991; Turner and Van't dack, 1993.

2   For more information on the history, structure and aims of the Association for European Monetary Union, see http://amue.lf.net

3   According to an analysis of the National Institute of Economic and Social Research published in 1995, meeting the deficit criterion by 1999 could reduce total EU employment by half a million. In particular, over the period from 1995 to 1999 the policy adjustment required to achieve the deficit target would reduce economic growth in Italy by 0.5 per cent per annum. For a thorough assessment of the impact of the Maastricht criteria on the labour market and on employment as well as a complete review of the literature on the subject see Barrel, Morgan, and Pain, 1995. The impact of monetary unification on the capacity for weakest members to react to asymmetric shocks is assessed in Bayoumi and Eichengreen, 1992. For an analysis of the impact of the Maastricht fiscal criteria on the equilibrium level of the real exchange rates see Barrel and Sefton, 1997. On the other hand, some other economists tend to minimize the recessive effects of the Maastricht criteria, see, for example, Viñals and Jimeno, 1996.

4   The European Banking Federation (EBF) is composed of the national banking associations of the EU member states and by the national banking associations of the EFTA countries.

5   In the first semester of 1996 corporate lending decreased of 5,000 bn lire. See Banca d'Italia, 1996.

6 This can take both the form of corporate lending and the more recently inaugurated form of corporate finance.

7 For the impact of financial innovation on hedging practices see Talani, 1997a, 1997e and 1997f.

8 The ETUC was created in 1973 to allow the meeting and confrontation of the various European trade unions and to act as a consultation and pressure body at the European level. With the Congress held in Luxembourg on 13–17 May 1991 its Statute was changed to allow the representatives of the different categories to enter the Executive Committee and a restricted Committee composed by the representatives of the trade unions leaders was created to act as the decision-making body. See Gnetti, 1991b.

9 In the conclusions of the Presidency to the Hanover summit of 27/28 June 1988 it was claimed: 'The European Council underlines the importance of the social aspects in the context of the progresses towards the realisation of the 1992 goal ... the internal market must be conceived in a way to be beneficial for everyone' (CGIL, 1990, p. 56).

10 In the conclusions of the Rodi Summit, 2/3 December 1988, it was claimed that: 'The establishment of the Single Market cannot be considered an aim in itself but it must imply the pursuance of a broader objective, represented by the assurance of the maximum welfare for everyone, in conformity with the social progress tradition characterising European history.' During this summit it was also set the deadline of 1989 for the member states to take the decisions due to 'orient the action of the Member States in the social dimension' (CGIL, 1990, p. 56).

11 In the Madrid Summit, 26/27 June 1989, it was confirmed the need 'to attribute to the social aspects the same importance given to economic ones' (CGIL, 1990, p. 56).

12 At the Strasbourg Summit of 8/9 December 1989, 11 member states adopted the so-called 'Social Charter' and the European Council invited the Council of Minister to deliberate on the proposals of the Programme of Action presented by the European Commission to implement the Social Charter. See Paruolo, 1991.

13 Gabaglio was elected with 28 votes to nine during the Luxembourg Congress of 13–17 May 1991. See Gnetti, 1991a.

14 The twelfth being the British government.

7   The UK and EMU: The City vs the Continent

The outcome of the analysis so far effected is such that the British financial community generally, and the City of London in particular, emerges as the main domestic counterpart of the government as far as foreign economic policy decisions are concerned. The British stance towards the whole process of European monetary integration has, indeed, been deeply influenced by the City of London's preferences in both domestic and international macroeconomic issues. The most logical hypothesis that is possible to infer from these premises is that the future British government's position towards the making of EMU is also likely to be deeply affected by the City's preferences and interests.

It becomes thus necessary to analyse the impact that the establishment of EMU would have on the City's markets and institutions, both in the case of UK's participation and in the case of the British government deciding not to join the common currency area, at least in its initial phase. In the light of the insights coming from this examination, it will then be possible to assess the City of London's overall position towards EMU.

The next section therefore, deals with the impact of EMU on each individual market of the City of London, and, on the institutions acting in them. The aim is to draw conclusions on the advantages and disadvantages for London as a leading financial centre of the establishment of a European single currency area.

The Impact of EMU on the City of London's Markets and Services

1   London Money Markets

London short-term money markets, constitute, together with the Foreign Exchange and with the bullion market, also called the London gold market, the bulk of the prosperous City's wholesale markets (see Shaw, 1981), that is, markets trading in big amounts, of six figures or more. The institutions active in the money markets are the hundreds[1] of banks of the City of London and they operate mainly through deposits, apart from the Certificates of Deposit market.

The traditional London money market is represented by the market in Treasury and commercial bills, that is, promissory notes by the government and commercial firms, guaranteed by the so-called Accepting Houses[2] and discounted by the traditional and closed club of Discount Houses.

These houses act as the *trait d'union* between the Central Bank, which operates in the discount market as lender of last resort, and the commercial banks through securing their short-term balances and investing their resources in bills and other short-term securities. In turn, the Bank of England uses the discount market to influence the liquidity of the banking system. It purchases bills from the houses to increase cash, or sells them to mop up liquidity, while changes in the rates at which these operations are carried out signal the willingness of the Central Bank to modify the banking system interest rate patterns.[3]

In parallel with the traditional sterling money market, a secondary sterling market, consisting of inter-bank, unsecured[4] deposits has developed from the 1960s onwards. Equally unsecured is the local authorities' market, through which short-terms loans are made available to British local authorities and their surpluses are mopped up.[5]

The development of the Certificate of Deposit instrument has allowed for the establishment of a CDs market in the London money markets which include also a Euro-commercial paper market.

However, the most prosperous and important of the short-term London money markets by far, is represented by the London Euro-currency market. The Euro-currency market was established in London as a result of the rigidities in the United States' banking system that allowed international and national interest rate differentials to persist. The most important of these rigidities was the so-called 'Regulation Q', which limited the rate of interest that US banks could pay on deposits. In addition, beginning in 1965 the United States imposed a series of measures designed to restrict capital outflows and to improve the balance of payments position, thus forcing the borrowers to the Euro-dollar market rather than the domestic dollar market.[6] At the same time, however, these restrictions were not crucial for the development of the Euro-currency market in London, since it continued its rapid growth even after the US controls were removed in January 1974. The extremely friendly environment that the British authorities were able to create represented the main reason for the success of London as the host of the Euro-deposits. This was obtained by avoiding subjecting banks acting in the Euro-currency market to official reserve requirements or deposit insurance costs and thus ensuring lower costs and enhancing competitiveness.

London's Euro-currencies market is still thriving by far distancing sterling deposits, which, in the first quarter of 1996 were £688,800 million, as compared to the £1,021,080 million of foreign currency deposits.

Thus, deep, well-developed, money markets, both sterling and foreign currency, are a key feature of the UK financial system, making a major contribution to, and being partly the result of, London's position as a leading financial centre. A market-oriented environment, notably the absence of minimum reserve requirements, is a particular strength of these markets. Whatever the decision of the British government towards joining EMU, however, they were destined to be highly influenced by the establishment of a single currency area within Europe.

Indeed, were the UK to join EMU, the fixing of exchange rates and the implementation of a single monetary policy in Europe will affect directly sterling money markets which, alongside the other national markets participating to the Single Currency, would be substituted by an integrated money market in Euro. In this event, the loss of sterling money markets is

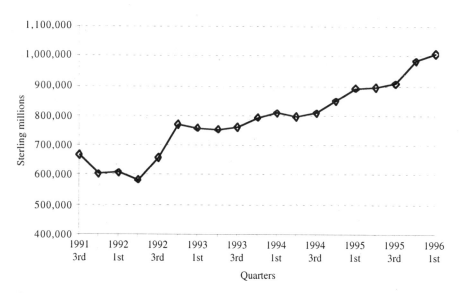

Graph 38 Total other currency deposits in banks in the UK 1991–96

Source: Bank of England Quarterly Bulletin, various issues.

considered within the City of London a competitive threat by itself since, as the City Research Project notes (British Banking Association, 1996, p. 3):

> Foreign Banks have been drawn to London in part to undertake money market activities in an offshore market that was free from reserve requirements and restrictive regulation. But the open nature of the UK banking system has also meant that foreign banks have substantial sterling deposits and loans. Thus the efficiency of the domestic sterling money market is important to London's position as a centre for overseas banks.

Moreover, at the time of the establishment of EMU, some other issues emerged as sensitive ones whose solution in a sense or in the other was likely to exert a great influence on the City's position towards EMU. A very important question related to whether banks would be allowed to access liquidity only through repo-operations[7] with their own Central Bank with some rationing of liquidity within all national Central Banks, or whether remote access would be permitted. Clearly, remote access without rationing of liquidity could allow one national Central Bank to develop as a leading centre for open market operations and there would consequently be a strong likelihood that the market activity in Euros would concentrate in this centre, although national markets would obviously need to remain. The City of London seemed fairly confident that, if open market operations allowed remote access and did not ration liquidity, in the event of the UK's participation, then London would become the natural access to ECB liquidity via the Bank of England and therefore the main centre for money market dealing in Euros (see British Banking Association, Association for Payment Clearing Services, London Investment Banking Association, 1996). However, this optimistic scenario could be put into question by the gathering in another European financial centre, the most likely being Frankfurt, of a 'critical mass of banks' to establish the Euro-money market (ibid.).

Moreover, the City's position as a participant could be very adversely affected, if onerous reserve requirements were imposed by the ECB at zero interest rates or at interest rates lower than market ones. In this respect, it is important to emphasise that London is a leading international, not only European, financial centre, and thus its competitive position towards New York or Tokyo would be greatly undermined by the imposition of similar restrictions. Moreover, onerous reserve requirements could spur the development of offshore Euro-money markets, as the EU banks minimise the amount of deposits subject to punitive charges. These offshore markets, if the

UK were inside the EMU area, would necessarily be set outside the City of London, and, possibly in one of its international rival financial centres. This, of course, made a very strong case *against* Britain's participation in EMU altogether. Indeed, if the UK did not participate in EMU, sterling and other London based-money markets would clearly continue in existence. On the other hand, an ECB regime with requirements set higher than those in the UK, which meant *any* requirement since in the UK there is *none*, could help the competitive position of sterling markets. Alternatively, it could let London become the centre for Euro-Euro deposit trading, as it would become a natural location for excess liquidity seeking to escape the onerous, or even not so onerous, ECB regime. Moreover, the City's position as an *international* money market centre, namely, its dominant position in the already established Euro-currency and Euro-commercial paper markets, would not undergo any threat.

The other major issue concerning London's money markets was the question of terms of access to TARGET[8] for banks in non-participant countries and the outcome of the debate over the provision of intra-day liquidity. The TARGET project provides connections within the EU-wide Real Time Gross Settlement (RTGS) systems, which allow high value payments in Euro to be made in real time across-borders within the EU, rather than just in individual countries in the single currency area. TARGET comprises one RTGS system in each EMU member state and an interlinking mechanism to connect them. Member states not in EMU will be entitled to connect to TARGET, but the terms and conditions for access to intra-day liquidity remained undecided up to the very last moments before the establishment of EMU.

The main point at issue in the EMI debate was whether non-EMU Central Banks should have access to Euro intra-day liquidity on the same terms as Central Banks within the Euro area. In the opinion of both the City of London (see British Banking Association, Association for Payment Clearing Services, London Investment Banking Association, 1996) and the Bank of England (1996) such access had to be available, since intra-day liquidity helps ensure a fully efficient payments system. Moreover, restrictions to access to TARGET could not be justified in terms of the need to avoid monetary policy spill-overs. Indeed, the availability of intra-day liquidity is largely irrelevant for monetary policy, and it is difficult to believe that an occasional spill-over to overnight accommodation would have significant implications for the operation of EMU area monetary policy.[9] The latter could in any case be deterred by the rates of interest charged for overnight borrowing. Accordingly, restrictions on intra-day liquidity could not be justified by monetary policy considerations, and would have to be viewed as discriminatory in the context of the Single Market legislation. However, how effective such measures would be in practice in inhibiting market development, including the establishment of a Euro-Euro market in the UK will depend on the costs and efficiency of TARGET in comparison with the range of alternative ways of making cross-border payments which will continue to be available. In particular, banks use correspondent banking, the ECU clearing and direct access to other payments systems to make cross-border payments. Correspondent banking is the most widely used mechanism and it consists of the banks using as their agents banks in other countries with access to the local payments system. This mechanism would continue to be available in stage 3 but, while it is relatively efficient and cost-effective, it leaves a bank exposed to settlement risk vis-à-vis its correspondents. The ECU clearing, which is a mechanism run by the ECU Banking Association for settling transactions denominated in the basket ECU, was expected to develop into a Euro clearing system, with end-of-the day net credit and debit balances settling across TARGET. As with all such end-of-day net systems, it does not eliminate settlement risk between direct members, or provide intra-day finality of funds. Finally, direct access to other countries' payments' systems (RTGS or others) would also be available to banks with subsidiaries or branches in other countries, and through remote access from a bank in one country to another country's payments' system.[10] Thus, even if the countries participating to EMU sought to restrict nonmembers' access to TARGET, this by no means would result necessarily in a competitive disadvantage for the 'outs'.

In conclusion, among the costs of participation for the London money market it was necessary to include also those relating to the need to adjust to new monetary policy operations directed by the ECB. This would clearly require changes to established UK practices, including the adoption of repo-operations as a monetary policy instrument. More important, it would require the likely abolition of the Discount House system and of the discount market which, under EMU, would not be allowed to rely on the Bank of England's role as lender of last resort.[11]

2   The London Foreign Exchange

The London Foreign Exchange market is the largest in the world. Its daily turnover was $464bn in 1995, an increase of some 60 per cent compared to three years earlier and more than the turnover of New York and Tokyo combined (see British Invisibles, 1996a). Its market share was in steady growth of 30 per cent in 1995.

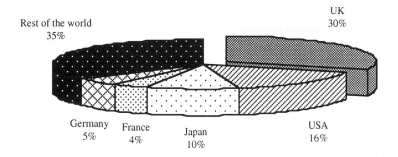

Graph 39 UK share in foreign exchange dealing 1995

Source: British Invisibles, 1996.

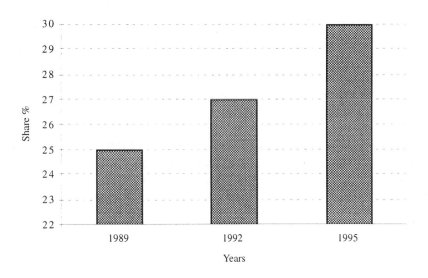

**Graph 40 Development of UK share in foreign exchange dealing,
1989–95**

Source: British Invisibles, 1996.

In 1995 the majority of its activity was linked to the US dollar. Its dominant role in global trade, focused, in particular, on the $/£, $/DM and $/yen trades with the $/DM business predominating in the spot market, while in the forward market trades in the three currencies pairs are of the same magnitude.

Table 23 Relative shares of total turnover in London by currencies traded 1995

	Spot	% Forward	Total
£/US$	3.1	8.3	11.5
US$/DM	11.8	9.7	21.5
US$/yen	5.7	11.3	17.0
US$/Swiss franc	1.7	3.7	5.5
US$/ French franc	0.9	4.5	5.5
US$/Canadian$	0.5	1.9	2.4
US$/Australian$	0.4	1.2	1.6
US$/lira	0.4	2.9	3.4
US$/peseta	0.2	1.8	2.1
US$/other EMS	0.8	5.1	5.9
US$/other	1.2	2.9	4.2
£/DM	2.8	0.4	3.2
£/other	0.4	1.0	1.3
DM/yen	1.9	0.3	2.2
DM/other EMS	4.8	0.9	5.7
ECU denominated	1.1	3.0	4.1
Other cross-currencies	2.3	0.8	3.1

Source: Bank of England Quarterly Bulletin, November 1995.

The market was a wholesale one dominated by banks, accounting for over 70 per cent of trading. Its truly international nature was made clear by the fact that non-UK owned banks were responsible for almost 80 per cent of market turnover, while sterling was involved in less than 20 per cent of all transactions (see British Banking Association, Association for Payment Clearing Services, London Investment Banking Association, 1996, p. 31).

Given its evident global character, if the UK remained outside the EMU area, the competitive threats for London as a centre for foreign exchange trading activity were judged to be fairly low. On the contrary, it was anticipated that the City would still remain a major location for Euro-trading. The loss of revenues consequent on the disappearance of former currencies would clearly be directly proportionate to the number of currencies participating in EMU, as well as dependent on the turnover of Euro-trading. However it would certainly be lower if sterling did not take part in the single currency area, since trading in sterling would not disappear.

On the other hand, if the UK was in the single currency, the disappearance of trades between former national currencies in the EMU area would account for less than 20 per cent of turnover on the London market, a lower proportion than that estimated for the other European Foreign Exchange. Again, this loss could be overcome by trading in Euros (see Levitt, 1996a).

Overall, the London Foreign Exchange would remain neutral to EMU whether sterling entered or not. The only likely implications were legal ones, namely the need for agreement on relevant market conventions and of legal preservation of contract continuity in conversion from previous currencies to Euros.

Lastly, as far as the infrastructure was concerned, the fact that most of the foreign exchange trades were settled on a bilateral basis meant that there would not be the same need for centralised infrastructural preparation that would be required in the money whole markets.

3   The Capital Market

As a premise it is worth clarifying that the capital market is constituted by those markets buying and selling securities. The London capital market, where securities are listed and traded and where market-makers and brokering agencies operate, is the London Stock Exchange. This was called from 1987 onwards, when it linked with the London's Euro-bond houses, the International Stock Exchange, where both primary[12] and secondary[13] markets in securities take place. The Exchange is a Recognised Investment Exchange (RIE) under the terms of the Financial Services Act of 1986.

Since after the Big Bang, firms which opt to be market makers in specified securities agree to display their prices by means of the Stock Exchange Automated Quotation system (SEAQ) and this makes them accessible on screens to other traders. Other smaller firms have not become market makers, and continue acting as mere brokering agencies, buying and selling securities in transactions with market makers on behalf of their clients.[14] Securities, in turn, may be broadly divided into two categories: shares, which may be both equity and preference ones, and bonds.[15]

(i) Bond markets Whereas shares may only be issued by commercial undertakings, bonds, which are mainly fixed interest rate securities, are issued by commercial undertakings and also by governments, local authorities and other public bodies including international organisations. Thus it is possible to identify in London both a commercial bonds market and a government bonds one. The first one is constituted by a national bond market and by the completely international Euro-bond market.

Table 24 Structure of the United Kingdom bond outstanding 1993

Country	Total out- standing[3] US$bn	National Government US$ bn	% of total	Corporate US$ bn	% of total	Foreign[1] US$ bn	% of total	Eurobond[2] US$ bn	% of total
								Traded in the Euro-bond market	
United Kingdom	481.4	281.3	58.4	25.0	5.2	6.1	1.3	169.0	35.1

Notes

1   Bonds issued in the domestic bond market by nonresidents, both companies and governments, that are denominated in the local currency.
2   UK residents' outstanding debt in the form of Euro-bonds.
3   Total British stock in the hands of stockbrokers.

Source: Merril Lynch.

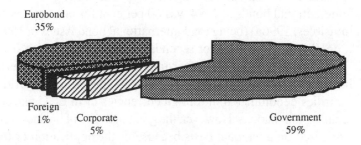

Eurobond 35%

Foreign 1%   Corporate 5%   Government 59%

Graph 41 UK bond-outstanding structure 1993

Source: Merril Lynch.

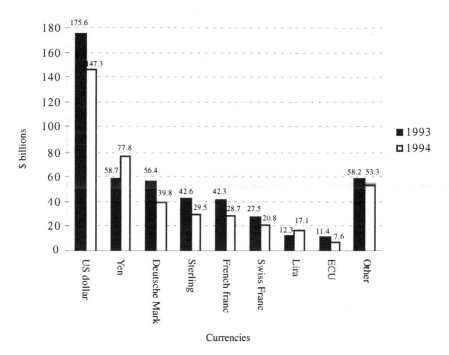

Graph 42 Currency composition of international bond issues 1993–94

Source: *Bank of England Quarterly Bulletin*, August 1995.

The Euro-bond business is centred in London. The turnover[16] of Euro-bond trading in 1993 was £2866bn. The estimated net revenue in 1991 was £327m (see British Banking Association, Association for Payment Clearing Services, London Investment Banking Association, 1996, p. 9). The market share of international bonds in 1994 was 60 per cent for primary market (see British Invisibles, 1996a) (being total international bond issues in 1994 equal to $420.2bn[17]) and 75 per cent for secondary market (see British Invisibles, 1996a). As regards trading in governments' bonds, already before the establishment of EMU a number of governments, including the British one, issued securities denominated in foreign currencies or in ECU placed in the international capital markets. However, the great majority of business remained largely organised on a national basis because of the application of the local presence requirements to national government bond market (see Artis, 1996).

The British government's bond market is called the gilt-edged market and its primary and secondary trading is concentrated in the City of London, although exact details of market share are unavailable (see British Banking Association, Association for Payment Clearing Services, London Investment Banking Association, 1996, p. 7). The transition to a single currency was held to have an immediate impact on the City-based government and corporate debt markets, including the Euro-markets, even if the UK did not participate.

Regarding the corporate bond market, if the UK participated from the outset, UK corporations would have the option, but not the obligation to issue bonds denominated in Euros in the transition phase from 1 January 1999 until 1 January 2002. However, after the latter date, all new issues would have to be in Euros. This raised two major issues. The first one concerned the resolution of legal problems relating to continuity of contracts.[18] The other one related to the possibility, if not need, for companies to re-denominate in Euros existing debt even before start of phase 3, with all that it implies in terms of costs and of the decision over the legal framework in which to effect these operations.

However, corporations could of course continue to issue debt in other non-EMU area currencies, and also via the Euro-bond market. This would allow for the development and establishment of a Euro-Euro bond market, that is, an offshore market in bonds denominated in Euros. The latter, were the UK inside EMU, would obviously be outside London, thus certainly undermining London's share of primary and secondary international bonds trading (see Graphs 43 and 44).

Finally, as pointed out by the Report of the EMU City working group, 'competitive pressures on relationships with both issuers and investors could well increase over time as the markets become more integrated' (British Banking Association, Association for Payment Clearing Services, London Investment Banking Association, 1996, p. 12). If the UK did not participate in EMU, then UK corporations could still issue Euro-denominated debt, either as foreign bonds within an EMU-area state, or as Euro-bonds in the Euro Euro-bond market which, with the UK outside EMU, would certainly be located in London. This meant that, even if the UK did not enter, the London capital markets would need to be able to provide for trading, settling, payments, custody and clearing facilities for the Euro-denominated bond markets. Thus a great deal of preparations had to be carried out if London wanted to maintain its dominant position.

Moreover, some discriminatory action might be taken against the City's markets, either as a trading location or as a base for cross-border activity. In fact, according to the City, even if the Second Banking and the Investment Services Directive prohibited discrimination, in practice they allowed for some loopholes in the Single Market legislation for financial services. A member state might frame rules in a manner which is not overtly discriminatory but in practice obstructs the business of institutions from outside the member state, by, for example, imposing restrictions on institutions lacking a physical presence in the member state concerned. Moreover, the directives allowed restrictions to be imposed where this is necessary for the implementation of domestic monetary policy or for the 'general good'.[19]

For these reasons, the City of London asked the Commission to be more active in identifying and addressing failures to implement EU Directives on the Single Market. It also required any member state contemplating issuing new regulations on the grounds of the 'general good' or monetary policy to communicate them to the Commission and to other member states.

As far as the British government's bond market was concerned, if the UK participated in EMU from the outset, new gilt issues after 1 January 1999 would be denominated in Euros, as would new central government debt issues in all EMU area states. However, as the credit risk posed by each central government issuer would still differ, pricing of all such debt would also show differences. Regardless of EMU, primary market activity would remain national oriented, at least as long as restriction on cross-border primary dealings are not withdrawn, while secondary market activity would remain concentrated in London.

This scenario would be unchanged even if the UK did not enter the EMU, but a potential threat would arise if EMU area states lifted the local presence requirements for the primary market for central government bonds only for each other, and not for non-participants. UK based firms would then miss an opportunity to compete for this business. Some concerns were also expressed over the possibility for the City to maintain its share in non-sterling business, including that of the new Euro-market. Some observers forecasted benefits arising within a unified market where instruments are all denominated in Euros, in terms of increased volumes, lower spreads and the elimination of arbitrage opportunities and niche markets. Some others, however, claimed that the implementation of the Maastricht criteria would reduce the need for central government bond issues and thus constrain growth in the market. The exact impact seemed hard to predict, but the City was keen to point out how the extent to which the EMU-area central government bond market would be unified can be overestimated. Indeed, credit facilities would still exist between member states leading to differences in yields and to the identification of a national central government bond acting as the new Euro market benchmark.

(ii) The market in shares The City's Big Bang day, 27 October 1986, completely

changed the environment in which share trading takes place in the London Stock Exchange allowing for a deep restructuring[20] and re-capitalisation of the market-making firms thanks to the elimination of the single capacity system, replaced the traditional jobbers and brokers. It also allowed for a strong reduction in costs, thanks to the elimination of the fixed commission system.[21]

Within a year from the Big Bang, trade in UK shares had doubled and by September 1987, customer business in domestic British equities was running at over £1.1bn a day, against £0.6bn in 1986, with £0.8bn of further deals taking place among market makers. Moreover, in the first year after the reforms, despite the elimination of the fixed commissions, total commission income, far from falling for competitive pressures, increased to £1.16bn from 0.74 bn in 1985–86, thanks to the big expansion in volumes traded and the greater activity by higher-paying private investors (see Reid, 1988). Under the new electronic system, the market makers insert into the SEAQ screen network the bid-offer prices at which they stand ready to deal. Firm prices are provided for only for the leading companies' shares, the so-called 'alpha'[22] and 'beta'[23] shares. Indicative quotations are given for the smaller 'gammas', even if on request firm prices must be provided for by the minimum two market makers in these shares. Also for the less important 'deltas' firm quotations are given on enquiry. Each share has a screen page from which it is possible to derive the so-called 'touch', the narrowest gap between available buying and selling prices.

Table 25 Funds raised by share offerings in the UK 1989–94 (£ million)

	Ordinary shares (equities)			Preference shares
	Gross issues		Redemptions	Net issues	
	Total	Rights issues			
1989	6,187	2,949	2,636	3,551	1,062
1990	4,402	3,114	908	3,494	728
1991	11,140	9,129	135	11,005	1,137
1992	6,426	3,227	29	6,393	624
1993	16,536	10,891	–	16,534	1,529
1994	14,865	4,926	20	13,739	402

Source: *Financial Statistics*, various issues.

Also the business in international, or foreign, shares,[24] soared after October

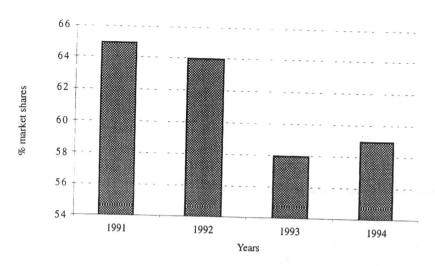

Graph 43 UK share of foreign equities turnover 1991–94

Source: British Invisibles, 1996.

Table 26 Market-share of Foreign equities turnover, 1994

	UK	USA	Japan	France	Germany
Foreign equities turnover	59%	34%	under 1%	under 1%	2%

Source: British Invisibles, 1996b.

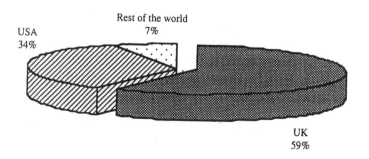

Graph 44 Foreign equities turnover, 1994

Source: British Invisibles, 1996b.

1986, to reach a market share of foreign equities turnover of 65 per cent in 1991. At the end of March 1993 London dealers were quoting firm prices for over 400 European equities and annual turnover had risen to over £150bn (see Artis, 1996).

This exceptional success of the London international equity market,[25] prompted defensive measures in many other European Exchanges. As a result, in recent years London share of foreign equity turnover has been decreasing.

The impact of EMU on the London share markets would be gradual, rather than immediate, but it was likely to pose competitive pressures even if the UK did not join the single currency. If the British government decided to enter, the London market could benefit from the ending of currency restrictions on the investment of institutional investors in the EMU area. At the same time the advent of the single currency might reduce the number of individual stock exchanges in which the investors sought listing, thus intensifying the competition with the City.

It was also clear that the decision to enter would prompt an early demand for Euro equity dealing and listing facilities, at least in the wholesale business. This urged the adoption of the appropriate measures to adapt the settlement and payments systems, and to allow the London Stock Exchange to trade and list, on request, equities denominated in Euros from the beginning of phase 3 (1 January 1999). UK's participation posed also a number of legal questions relating, for example, to the modality and timing of the re-denomination of shares, including the decision over rounding conventions to prevent later litigation.[26]

In the event that the UK did not participate in EMU, equity markets would continue in sterling. However it was possible that issuers from within the EMU area would wish to trade in Euros on the SEAQ International. As a result, the possible business opportunity posed by offering Euro quotations and listing facilities, and related settlement systems, would need to be ready in order to cope with the competitive pressures coming from the consolidation of the other European Exchanges. The City had already begun to see a decline in the UK share of international equity trading and the establishment of the single currency, irrespective of British participation, might heighten the competitive challenge. However, if the preparations were carried out in due time, and the UK markets had adequate access to Euro-liquidity and payments mechanisms, and, generally, if the EMU countries did not adopt discriminatory measures, then the City seemed fairly confident that the UK, even outside EMU, could live with its competitive pressures.

4   *Derivative Markets*

The 'derivative market' is the market in financial futures and traded options which allows investors and financial groups to hedge against the adverse effect of market swings. In the United Kingdom this trading is carried out in the London International Financial Futures Exchange (LIFFE), established in the City of London in 1982.

A financial future is a contract to buy or sell a specified quantity of a given financial asset, like a government bond, on a date ahead at a set price. A traded option, instead, gives the purchaser the right, but not the obligation, to buy (call option) or to sell (put option) a specified amount of a given financial asset at a set price within a specific period of time. For this right, the purchaser pays a premium to the seller of the option (see Artis, 1996, p. 185).

In the LIFFE futures and options contracts on short-term bank deposits and long-term government bonds are traded in a number of currencies. In 1994 the contract on the German government bond future, the 'bund' future was the most traded by far, with 25 per cent of all contracts traded. Attempts by LIFFE to establish futures and options contracts in foreign exchange were unsuccessful. LIFFE is the largest such exchange in Europe with a total volume of business of 148,726,421 contracts in 1994. Always in 1994 it accounted for 17 per cent of market share, in steady growth from previous years.

It must be noted that the City of London has a strong market also in over-the-counter (OTC)[27] derivatives. The Bank for International Settlements inaugural OTC market survey showed that London is the top booking location for contracts, with a 30 per cent market share, at a considerable distance from the other financial centres (see British Banking Association, Association for Payment Clearing Services, London Investment Banking Association, 1996, p. 21).

The considerable UK share of the OTC and exchange traded derivatives markets underlines the contribution of these markets to the City's continuing prosperity. The City estimates 1991 net revenues from OTC interest rate contracts traded in the UK to have been £284m and from exchange traded instruments on LIFFE £363.4m in the same year (ibid.).

If the UK participated in EMU then all exchange listed contracts related to sterling interest rates, along with other EMU area interest rate contracts and the ECU contract, would cease to exist and be replaced by a Euro-rate contract. It was held by the City highly likely that this development would take place from the beginning of phase three. Indeed, the adoption of a common monetary policy within a fixed exchange rate area would lead to the

Table 27 The London International financial futures

Financial instruments	Volume Jan.–Dec. 1994	% of total contracts
3 months Euromark future	29,312,222	19.71
3 months Euromark option	2,943,936	1.98
Bund future	37,335,437	25.10
Bund option	8,574,137	5.77
German BOBL* future	73,043	0.05
3 months ECU future	622,457	0.42
3 months short sterling future	16,603,152	11.16
3 months short sterling option	4,057,878	2.73
Long gilt future	19,048,097	12.81
Long gilt option	2,357,348	1.59
3 months Eurolira future	3,456,437	2.32
BTP future	11,823,741	7.95
BTP option	8,574,137	0.69
FT-SE 100 Index future	4,227,490	2.84
FT-SE 100 Index option	4,786,656	3.22
FT-SE Mid 250 Index future	40,674	0.03
3 months Euroswiss future	1,698,736	1.14
3 months Euroswiss option	19,245	0.01
3 months Eurodollar future	91,738	0.06
3 months Eurodollar option	12,400	0.01
Japanese JGB future	610,925	0.41
Total of financial contracts	148,726,421	100.00
Total of all contracts	148,726,421	100.00

*   Medium Term Notional Bond

Source: British Banking Association, Association for Payment Clearing Services, London Investment Banking Association, 1996.

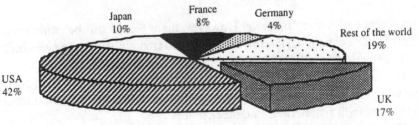

Japan 10%   France 8%   Germany 4%   Rest of the world 19%

USA 42%

UK 17%

Graph 45 Market-share in exchange traded financial derivatives 1994

Source: British Invisibles, 1996b.

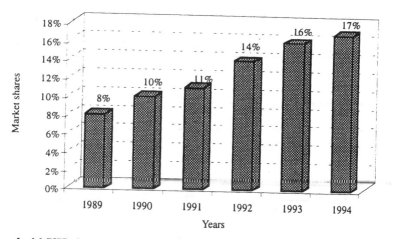

Graph 46 UK share of exchange traded financial derivatives market 1989–94

Source: British Invisibles, 1996b.

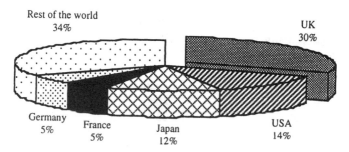

Graph 47 OTC derivatives market shares 1995

Source: British Invisibles, 1996b.

convergence of money markets. However, there would still be some scope for divergence of national interest rates linked to credibility of the irreversibility of the transition for all currencies.

Exchange traded contracts derived from national government bond prices of EMU participants could continue to be traded during the transition phase due to the credit risk between member states.

However, in general, there would be a concentration of business on the Euro-denominated benchmark instruments. As well over 90 per cent of trading volume in interest rate and bond products was, in 1994, composed of assets in currencies which could potentially be replaced by Euro, it would be of critical importance for LIFFE to win high market share of the new markets.

Table 28 Overall EMU impact activity on turnover in financial futures and options – principal Exchanges

Rank	Exchange	1994 turnover (mn contracts)	% Potential EMU impact*
1	Chicago Mercantile Exchange	156.31	10.65
2	LIFFE	148.73	92.27
3	Chicago Board of Trade	139.48	0
4	Marche' a Terme international de France	93.1	91.65
5	Deutsche Terminborse	49.32	41.84

* Percentage of volume of trade in any potential EMU currency interest rate or bond instrument in relation to the total volume of financial contracts

Source: British Banking Association, Association for Payment Clearing Services, London Investment Banking Association, 1996.

If the UK did not take part in EMU, then sterling rate and gilt contracts would continue to be traded. Thus, the proportion of trading volume that would be replaced by Euro-denominated contracts would be around 70 per cent. Therefore, also in the event of non-participation, the City of London had to be able to offer Euro-denominated exchange listed contracts if it wants to retain its dominant position in derivative trading.

Thus, regardless of British participation in EMU, the main competitive issue for the City of London in derivative markets was represented by its capacity to attract the highest percentage of business in Euro-rate futures and options and the Euro-denominated benchmark EMU-area government bond futures and options. Related OTC products would develop in parallel.

To this aim, an important factor was the extent to which LIFFE acts first to grab the new market. If LIFFE was able to win such a head start in Euro contracts and was successful in rolling over open interest in its Euro-mark and Bund contracts into the Euro, then market share could be maintained. However, simultaneous head-to-head competition would split business within exchanges, without any clear concentration in LIFFE. The announcement by LIFFE that existing Euro-mark, short sterling and Euro-lira contracts would settle on Euro-rates after 1999 in the event of German UK and Italian participation in EMU already provided the exchange with a head start over continental rivals. Also an early establishment of appropriate settlement facilities could enhance London's chance of dominating the market.

The extent to which LIFFE's competitive position could be influenced by UK non-participation seemed limited to the City of London since it was hard to see how regulatory or other discriminatory barriers could be erected by participant states to stem the growth of LIFFE outside the EMU area. Also in the OTC markets there was no scope for competitive threats in the event of the UK remaining outside EMU. Legal issues appeared more significant due to a risk of litigation connected to contracts involving the ECU and national currencies subsumed into the Euro during the transition.

5   The Impact of EMU on Some Key City Services

(i) Fund management A very lucrative service strongly developed by the City's Merchant Banks is fund management, which contributes nearer to a half than a third of the banks' profits in aggregate (see Reid, 1988). London is the world's second largest fund management centre after Tokyo (see British Invisibles, 1996) and the UK management industry looks after over £1,500bn of institutional and private client investors. Its success owes much to the surging growth of the United Kingdom pension funds,[28] but also to a favourable regulatory environment and to the pool of highly skilled labour (see British Banking Association, Association for Payment Clearing Services, London Investment Banking Association, 1996).

According to the Institutional Fund Managers' Association, the direct impact of EMU on the industry was likely to be fairly limited. It is true that the extension of currency matching rules to the whole EMU area, requiring up to 80 per cent of assets to be denominated in the currency in which the liabilities arise, would increase the scope of asset diversification in the common currency area, thereby also increasing the opportunities for banks with fund management capabilities (see Levitt, 1996a). However, UK fund managers could benefit from the impact on currency matching rules even in the case of non-participation in EMU. The only downside of non-participation would be that UK fund managers could not gain from the improved transparency of pricing and performance that would be associated with the single currency area.

(ii) Corporate banking Another field merchant banks have made mostly their own is that known as corporate banking. This involves a number of services to the corporate sector. These include advising companies on a range of matters

(among which the conduct of take-over battles is the most important) providing, more generally, professional banking help for 'merger and acquisition' (M & A) activity, handling share offers, devising methods for restructuring or arranging underwriting facilities (see Reid, 1988).

Corporate banking is extremely competitive in the City of London, where companies may find undisputed expertise and professionalism. However, competitive pressures from within the single currency area were expected to increase further with the entry of the UK, since corporations would be likely to rationalise treasury operations and existing banking relationships in the EMU area. Also competitive pressures from outside might increase as a consequence of the imposition within EMU of a relatively onerous regime, for example reserve requirements, on the banking industry.

Against this background, it was essential for British banks to provide efficient payments and related services from the start of 1999. The impact on corporate banking would clearly be less if the UK did not participate in EMU, but to maintain their competitive position British banks ought to be prepared to offer adequate Euro service all the same (see British Banking Association, Association for Payment Clearing Services, London Investment Banking Association, 1996).

(iii) Insurance London is one of the largest insurance markets in the world, with premium income accounting for around 6 per cent of the global total. For international insurance London is the world's largest market, with net premium income of £10.5bn in 1993, while for long-term business the UK industry is the largest in Europe, ranking second for general business.

Since UK insurers are much more involved in the US market than their European counterparts and the most of the London Market business is conducted in dollars, EMU impact on current business was judged to be fairly limited. In the event of British participation, some concerns arose over the possibility for Euro/$ exchange rate to be more volatile than £/$ one. There was also the risk that EMU led to lower exchange rates, reducing the insurance companies' expected returns from premiums on non-profit business.[29]

If the UK entered EMU, insurance companies had to address also costs arising for modifying computer software, particularly in the payments and claims systems. On the other hand, if the UK opted out of EMU, little preparation would be required, namely, the mere conversion of other participants' assets and business into Euros.

As regards insurance funds management activity, the same considerations of general fund management applied.

The City of London and EMU: A Difficult Relationship?

From the analysis above it emerges clearly how the establishment of a single currency area in Europe posed direct competitive threats to the City of London by itself, irrespective of British participation.

In particular, in an EMU area, the elimination of barriers to trade in many relevant City's markets (as, for example, in securities dealing, particularly in the equity market, or in derivative markets) as well as the development of new financial instruments denominated in the common currency, would certainly increase the other European financial centres' chances to grow by grasping the new market opportunities. Thus it would undermine the City of London's until now undisputed financial leadership in Europe.

It is true that British participation would at least eliminate the possibility for the EMU countries to adopt protectionist measures, like conditioned access to TARGET, or the ending of currency restrictions on the investment of institutional investors only in the EMU area. However, it is also true that much more threatening consequences might derive to London as an international financial centre from British entry in EMU.

Indeed, the peculiarity of London as a financial centre is given precisely by its unique international orientation. London is the most international of the leading financial centres and has the largest share of many global markets. The London Stock Exchange has a greater turnover of foreign equities than all other centres combined, £359bn and 59 per cent of global turnover in 1994. It is also estimated that at least 60 per cent of Euro-bonds are issued in London, and an even higher proportion, 75 per cent, of secondary bond trading takes place in London. The London Foreign Exchange market is the largest in the world, with a daily turnover of $464bn which is higher than that of New York and Tokyo combined. At February 1997 there were 565 foreign banks in London, two-thirds of which come from non-EU countries, more than in any other city in the world. Foreign currency deposits in the UK banks account for £1,021,080m, well exceeding sterling ones. London ranks second to the USA in exchange traded financial futures and options, but LIFFE was established only in 1982 and its share of world market has increased from 7 per cent in 1988 to 17 per cent in 1994. It is also the world's largest international insurance market, with net premium income of £10.5bn in 1993, equal to 28 per cent of marine and 38 per cent of aviation risks, as well as the global clearing centre for gold forwards trading and financing. Further, the Baltic Exchange is the world's largest ship-broking market (see British Invisibles, 1996a). Finally, UK financial institutions, predominantly based in the City of

London, earned a net £20.4bn through overseas transactions during 1994 (see British Invisibles, 1996c; see also Bank of England, 1997).

British participation in EMU would certainly undermine this leading international role of the City of London by first of all imposing restrictions on the working of its markets and institutions, and, generally, by submitting the City of London to exogenous controls. Instead, also in the new British regulatory environment controls for the wholesale money markets are only represented by a discretionary supervisory role of the Bank of England while capital markets after the Big Bang are self-regulated through the endogenous organisations of the Securities Investment Board (SIB) and of the SROs.

Moreover, EMU would affect the City's international primacy by eliminating the possibility for London to develop as the main offshore market in Euro or in Euro-denominated assets,[30] an activity which, the UK being inside EMU, would certainly be developed by one of its major world competitors.

Finally, it is also necessary to take into consideration the domestic economic consequences of joining a monetary union. These are usually included in the all-embracing expression of 'loss of sovereignty', but, in the case of the City of London, have the clear-cut meaning of the loss of the ability to influence domestic monetary and exchange rate policies, with all that it implies in terms of loss of domestic political power (see Levitt, 1996b).

Given this analysis of the consequences of EMU on the City's markets and activities, it should not be particularly surprising that, as Paul Richards, Director of Public Finance of HSBC Samuel Montagu, put it, already in November 1996[31] the working assumption within the City of London was that EMU would go ahead without Britain's joining it in the first run.

Also Sir Douglas Wass, Chairman of Nomura International plc, thought, in November 1996, that the British government would not even try to enter EMU from the outset. This was demonstrated by the fact that both British leading parties had committed themselves to run a referendum on the issue (see Talani, 1996f), a referendum which, in the opinion of other authoritative City's voices was very likely to be lost and, thus, it would be an easy way out (see Talani, 1996c and 1996b).

However, as pointed out by Butler, Director of Hambros Bank Ltd. and also EU adviser to the Labour Party, in a lecture at the London School of Economics on 11 November 1996, even if it wanted, the British government, any British government, would certainly not be able to enter in 1999. This happened because first, it was not in the EMS, second, the criteria might not be fulfilled and finally, there was the need for much legislation and regulation to be passed before entering EMU. Therefore, since the government would have other priorities, it would be very difficult to join from the beginning. Moreover, fixing parities and having a single monetary policy abruptly would be, in the opinion of many City representatives, extremely risky, 'a leap in the dark', as Sir Michael Butler told the House of Lords Select Committee on the European Communities (see House of Lords, Select Committee on European Communities, 1996).

According to Malcom Levitt, the first risk of EMU was the threat to the Single Market as a whole. In fact, far from favouring the process of achieving a European Single Market, the progress towards EMU restricted to a limited number of countries could instead run the risk of creating a protectionist area, particularly in the field of financial activities. This would threaten the progress achieved with the passing of the Single Market directives on financial services and insurance. On the other hand, however, in the opinion of the City, if EMU countries relaxed their monetary and fiscal stance after joining either the new European currency will be very weak, or the union will collapse, but, if this happened, European political stability itself will face a serious threat. Moreover, this risk was made more likely by the capacity of financial markets to anticipate it, and thus to pose a risk-premium on exchange rate even within EMU.

There was then also the opposite danger, namely, that the economic policies within the EU will become pro-, rather than counter-cyclical, that is, they will not be able to cope with recessive pressures, and, instead, they would favour them. Regarding this, it was held extremely important that the Stability Pact included a more flexible approach than the one eventually adopted in order to counter cyclical effects, unless EMU led to a genuinely low inflation rate which would almost automatically imply lower interest rates. However, this seemed very unlikely to the City of London, and even if it happened, it had to be perceived by the business community as a permanent effect, and not as a merely temporary event, otherwise it would not favour long-term investment decisions.

Finally, there was the problem of the relationships between those countries with a tradition of fiscal stability, and those with no such tradition as regards the reduction of inflation rates and the reduction of their public deficits and debts, the real threat being that they will not be able to maintain their stances. Regarding this point there seemed to be a genuine concern in the British financial sector over the economic performance of the other member states as they did not want to risk that the degree of economic prosperity reached in the UK might be threatened by EMU. In particular, concerns were expressed over the so-called 'pension issue', that is, the possibility that demographic pressures in the other EMU member states would also jeopardise the UK ability to pay pensions which is much higher than in the other countries thanks to the extraordinary development of the pension fund instrument. Consequently, Mr Richards considered it vital, to avoid serious risks being triggered by EMU, to stress the importance of 'sustainable convergence'. This meant not just meeting the convergence criteria, but creating the conditions to keep them fulfilled also after joining EMU. Sir David Scholey, Chairman of SG Warbourg Group since 1984 and Director of the Bank of England since 1981, 'could see some very unpleasant consequences' (see House of Lords, Select Committee on European Communities, 1996) if member states were generally unable to sustain the convergence criteria, as the pressures which could not be spilled over on exchange rates, would be taken out on the real economy.

Also Sir Michael Butler, if EMU was really going to happen, would prefer it to start with a very small number of countries. It would be even better to use an evolutionary approach, as the one proposed by him and by Richards in the hard Ecu plan, and put off to a later moment the idea of fixing parities and pooling monetary policies, an idea that also met the support of other City operators.

Despite the scepticism still often expressed within the London financial circles towards the EMU project as a whole,[32] as well as towards the Maastricht way to it, from the publication of the European Commission Green Paper on EMU, and, generally, from 1995 onwards, the British financial institutions started thinking that EMU could actually became reality. Consequently, they started considering the issue seriously and establishing working groups to assess its consequences.

The key issue at stake was the impact of European Monetary Union on the City of London with the UK outside. In the opinion of Sir Douglas Wass, 'nobody in the City is concerned about the negative impact of EMU if the UK remains out of it', since the other European cities, such as Frankfurt, Paris or even Amsterdam, do not have the same facilities as London whether it remains out of EMU or not. As, moreover, most of the City's business, and, certainly, the greatest part of Nomura International business, is in foreign currencies, mainly dollars, yen, DM and Ecus, and not in sterling which has lost much of its international role, Britain's refusal to join EMU would not affect the City of London's activity.

According to Sir Peter Middleton, a Deputy Chairman and Director of BZW of Barclays Bank since 1991, as well as a Treasury official, the City 'would not be greatly affected one way or the other'. He considered 'London,

New York and Tokyo as hubs from which a series of spokes go to other financial services which feed into them and actually give them strength rather than take it away' (see House of Lords, Select Committee on European Communities, 1996).

Also the Governor of the Bank of England seemed fairly convinced that 'the attractions of the City as a financial centre depend on a much broader range of issues than the currency we operate in', and that, in the event the UK stayed out, there might be even 'positive benefits' for the City of London (ibid.).

Gavyn Davies, partner in Goldman Sachs since 1988 and principal economic commentator of *The Independent* since 1991, shared the Governor's view and declares himself 'not pessimistic about our ability to become a dominant force in the Euro market in the same way that we have become a dominant force in the dollar market throughout the world'. He thought that the issue of the relationship between sterling and the Euro was not central in determining the outlook for the City, 'what is much more central is getting the regulatory structure of our financial markets right, and getting that structure to continue to induce foreign firms to operate in London as the prime international centre. It is not clear to me that that need may be any more difficult if we are outside the single currency' (ibid.).

On the contrary, according to Malcom Levitt, the real threat for the banking community was a government which decided to enter from the very beginning. This was considered a nightmare for the British banking sector. Indeed, it was undeniable that if EMU effectively started in 1999 the City ought to be ready to offer services in Euro in its wholesale markets and to modify its structures consequently. However, British Banks would incur much higher costs if the UK decided to enter from the beginning, because this would entail changing all the processing, settlement and accounting of retail payments through every medium all over the country. This was a very definitive step, from which it was very difficult, and extremely expensive, to get back if something happened and EMU collapsed or the British government decided to withdraw. Indeed, changing the currency would require changes in every element of a bank's information technology operations, with a total cost to the banking sector of £9.7bn as estimated by the Cap Gemini Sogeti (CGS) Europe's largest computer services company. Thus, although the banks had started to study the impact of EMU on their structures and organisation already in 1995, they were not going to change the retail payments system.

In the opinion of McKenzie also, the risk of financial activities fleeing from London to Frankfurt with the realisation of EMU had been greatly exaggerated. Just looking at the position of London in the exchange markets, international banking or in lending, as well as generally in the dealing markets, it was possible to understand how its leadership was not seriously threatened by the process of EMU. Moreover, London was prominent because it was not influenced by domestic politics, the kind of advantage which was likely to be at risk inside a common currency area. Even if EMU posed some question marks, McKenzie thought that there were clearly going to be many pressures on the City of London from many external sources, and EMU was only one of these. It was therefore not adequate to speak about the impact of EMU on the City of London as a whole, while it was necessary to effect a sector by sector analysis.

Generally, however, there were not going to be major changes in the City with the UK out of EMU. As pointed out at length in the City of London's reports and publications, the main challenge for London if the UK remained out was represented by the risk of protectionist stances of the hard core EMU countries. Regarding this, there was a widespread agreement within the City of London that the British authorities would answer by putting the stress on the Single Market and claiming that also informal discrimination between ins and outs was illegal, as they had already started doing in relation to the debated issue of the conditions of access to TARGET for non-EMU countries (see House of Lords, Select Committee on European Communities, 1996), p. 33: see also Bank of England, 1996; British Banking Association, Association for Payment Clearing Services, London Investment Banking Association, 1996).

However, according to Sir Douglas Wass, in the City of London people did not believe that the core countries would find a way to damage the financial activities of the 'out' countries, also because this would have a negative impact on their own banks. Moreover, apart from the challenges, British refusal to join EMU might well entail some positive consequences, if, for example, the single currency area was subject to reserve requirements since, as the Governor of the Bank of England was keen to point out: 'I do not believe for a moment we would wish to impose (them) if we were on the outside' (see House of Lords, Select Committee on European Communities, 1996, p. 22). The extent to which the Euro was able to capture new markets, in fact, was very much dependent on the regulatory system inside the EMU area and if it was too strict, London would certainly have a competitive advantage with respect to Frankfurt and Paris.

Summing up, it seems that the British government's decision to remain out of EMU in January 1999 put the stress on two major sets of issues. First, whether the EMU area would impose restrictions which would make it particularly advantageous to be out, such as the imposition of non interest bearing minimum reserve requirements with the ECB. Second, how to develop competitive wholesale markets denominated in Euros within the City of London even if the UK did not join, the main underlying assumption being that the impact of EMU on the City's wholesale financial markets would be momentous in any case.

As regards the first set of issues, it was still not certain whether these minimum reserve requirements would be imposed within the EMU area, but it was clear that Germany, and the Bundesbank in particular, believed that this was necessary to control the implementation of monetary policy within the EMU area. If eventually the ECB imposed minimum reserve requirements, this would turn out to be a major advantage for the City of London. Indeed, some people within the City of London tended to believe that, with the imposition of minimum reserve requirements, the City of London would be able to establish a 'Euro-Euro' market, an offshore Euromarket in both currency and bonds. The main flaw of this hypothesis was that, while the US authorities were not concerned about the establishment of a Euro-dollar market in London, the European System of Central Banks would be extremely keen to try to avoid the establishment of a Euro-Euro market outside the EMU area. It remained to be seen, however, whether the ESCB would be able to do it, which, indeed, was a very difficult one to answer.

In the opinion of many within the City, the chances for similar issues to be solved positively for the City of London, would be much enhanced if the UK government took an open position towards EMU, stating that the UK would not join EMU from the beginning, but 'when the time is right'. This is, indeed, the position eventually adopted by the Labour Party at the end of October 1997, when ruling out early British entry in EMU.

Concluding on this first point, in the City of London there are two prevailing opinions. On the one hand, those who believed that staying out was a competitive advantage. On the other hand, those who thought that this competitive advantage would be somehow offset by the other countries by, for example, limiting access to TARGET or not imposing minimum reserve requirements, both limiting the scope or the creation of a Euro-Euro market.

The second set of issues concerning the City related to the preparation for EMU starting from the assumption that, in any case, the City would be more competitive in EMU if it was well prepared. On this point there was a general consensus within the City of London.

According to Sir Michael Butler, 'the City will need to prepare (for the introduction of the Euro), even if we are not going to join if British banks and other financial services companies are not to lose business to their competitors' and in its written evidence, the BBA and APACS argued:

> regardless of whether the United Kingdom is in or out of EMU, City institutions, including banks, will need to be prepared to offer customers a full range of Euro products in the wholesale financial markets. This will necessitate the banking and payments industries having in place the right mechanisms for trading, paying and settling in Euro (see House of Lords, Select Committee on European Communities, 1996, p. 32).

The preparations included first, a great interest and active participation of the City of London in the decisions taken in Brussels over the legal framework for the use of Euro. Second, the establishment of a wholesale payment system in Euros in the City of London. Third, preparation of the computing systems to enable the banks to operate also in Euros in the wholesale markets. Lastly, other changes to the wholesale markets. It was true that these preparations started relatively later in the City of London than in Paris or in Frankfurt. However, it was also true that there were no preparations to EMU going on in the retail business.

Things might actually be different after the establishment of EMU and, according to Sir Michael Butler, if EMU happened, and if it was a success, UK interests, as the interests of any other country, would suffer a lot if it remains outside. Indeed, underlined Sir Michael Butler, if the Euro was created in 1999 all banks would use it and it was an illusion to believe that Britain would have an independent monetary policy. UK interest rates would be European ones plus 1 or 2 per cent as a premium for the risk of not being part of EMU. Moreover, all the world countries, like Japan or Korea, which are now investing in the UK, would be much more tempted to invest in the countries belonging to the European Union. Thus, in his opinion, there was no doubt that in the long run there would be a discrimination in favour of those banks inside the EMU and against Britain if it stayed out and that the City of London would suffer, but this is not likely to happen immediately and not if the government is committed to enter at a later stage.

More generally, Sir Douglas Wass identified three possible scenarios for the development of EMU. The first was the 'optimistic scenario', according to which EMU is a success: the EMU countries find it easy to maintain the Maastricht criteria, the ECB does not implement recessive monetary policies, and the Euro is broadly accepted and traded. In this case, but only in this case, the non member countries would decide to enter. In the second scenario, the first pessimistic scenario, the participating countries cannot sustain the Maastricht criteria without implementing recessive policies leading to low or negative growth and to high unemployment rates, whereas the non-participating enjoy a relatively more prosperous economic situation. In this scenario, the non member countries would not ask to participate but, although there would be some discontent in EMU, nothing would happen. In the last, pessimistic scenario, however, the situation described above, would cause anxieties in the EMU countries, and the system could break down, with even some political consequences, as the victory of extremist parties in the French or German elections, as happened during the 1930s. This would be extremely dangerous and very damaging for the process of European integration as a whole. On the likelihood of these three scenario, it is still difficult to make forecasts, but Sir Douglas considers the first scenario more as a hope than as a true possibility.

In conclusion, as the Thatcher government 'wait and see' attitude towards the Exchange Rate Mechanism of the European Monetary System perfectly matched the British financial sector preferences for a set of monetarist practices inconsistent with the pegging of the exchange rates, also the present British government's 'wait and see' attitude towards the Maastricht way to EMU conceals a balance between the pros and the cons of EMU for the City of London which is still pending on the cons side. That the preferences of the British financial community might change in the course of the process leading to EMU is, of course, a possibility implicit in the approach adopted here.

However, the overall picture coming out from the analysis of the impact of EMU on the City's markets and institutions, as well as from the declarations of some of its authoritative officials, it is possible to infer that at the moment of the making of EMU the City of London still preferred the British government to avoid committing the UK to EMU in any way. Thus, the new Labour government's announcement at the end of October 1997 that the UK would not be joining EMU in 1999, seems perfectly in line with the preferences of the British financial system towards the issue.[33] However, since the success of the City of London has always been linked to its ability to adapt to the changing environment, its markets and institutions will certainly be able to grasp the business opportunities coming from the establishment of a single currency area even remaining outside it.

Of course the City of London is not the only powerful sector within the European Union political and economical area, and of course many other power conflicts within groups of interest of the other EU member states at the domestic, as well as at the European level, will have to be analysed to give a credible answer to the many questions the process of European monetary integration still poses, but this may only be the subject of another research project. As far as this one is concerned, it has reached the point in which it is necessary to stop, and leave the field open to more authoritative interventions.

Notes

1   There are over 540 foreign banks in London, more than in any other city in the world, to which there must be added British banks. See British Invisibles, 1996a.
2   Traditionally, the Acceptance Houses were represented by the restricted club of the merchant banks, but in 1981 the range of banks whose acceptances are 'eligible' was greatly widened including also many foreign groups.
3   With the Thatcher government, the traditional practice to fix a binding key interest rate for the banking system, the old Bank Rate and its successor Minimum Lending Rate, was ended for good, but the informal rates fixed for discount market operations by the Bank of England are equally tying.
4   This means that there is no lender-of-last-resort acting in this market.
5   On the development of these markets see Shaw, 1981.
6   The foreign Direct Investment Regulation prevented US multinationals from financing overseas operations with funds borrowed in the United States while the Voluntary Foreign Credit Restraint Program restricted US bank foreign lending and the Interest Equalisation Tax discouraged foreign borrowers from raising funds in the United States through securities issues.
7   Repo-arrangements consist of institutions selling stock to primary dealers against arrangements to repurchase. These arrangements are active in the London gilt-edged market since 1996.
8   The acronym TARGET stands for Trans European Automated Real-time Gross-settlement Express Transfer, a pan-European system interlinking EU Real Time Gross Settlement (RTGS) systems, that is systems in which payments instructions are transmitted on a transaction by transaction basis within direct members of a system and are settled individually across Central Banks' accounts in real time.
    This eliminates intra-day settlement risk between the direct members of the system, that is, the risk of losses which might otherwise arise through a bank failing during the day and so not being able to honour the payment messages it had previously sent, which is present in alternative net end-of day settlement systems.
    RTGS systems are being developed in all European Union countries as a means of reducing inter-bank settlement risk between members.
    TARGET extends across national borders the risk-reducing benefits of RTGS systems, allowing banks to receive and give intra-day value to cross-border payments. See Bank of England, 1996.
9   By the end of 1997, the terms of non EMU member states participation in TARGET had still not been solved. See Bank of England, 1997, pp. 14–16.
10 By the end of 1997 it was clear that a Euro RTGS system parallel to sterling one will start

to function from 1 January 1999, the so-called CHAPS Euro. This will provide its member banks with a UK facility to make wholesale Euro payments from the beginning of 1999; and they, in turn, will be able to provide a full Euro wholesale payments service to their customers. See Bank of England, 1997, p. 14.

11 For the other changes see British Banking Association, Association for Payment Clearing Services, London Investment Banking Association, 1996.

12 I.e. the new-issue market, that is, the market for the issue and placing of new shares, bonds etc. etc. See Clarke, 1979.

13 A place for the buying and selling of existing stocks, shares, bonds. See Clarke, 1979.

14 For more information on the changes in the City after the Big Bang, see Reid, 1988.

15 An equity, or ordinary share, represents a share in the ownership of a company: the equity shareholders jointly own the company and have the right to vote at general meetings. They are entitled to dividends, but only after all other creditors have been paid, and if the company makes a loss, their shares fall.

Preference shares do not confer voting rights and entitle dividends only up to a fixed maximum, but the claims of preference shareholders take precedence over those of equity shareholders.

Bonds are fixed interest securities which entitle regular payments of interests and to the eventual repayment of the initial sum lent. Their claims have the precedence on both equity and preference shareholders. They may be issued both by private companies and by governments and other public bodies. See Artis, 1996.

16 Figures for turnover may be higher than those for the outstanding debt since bonds, before the deadline, may be traded over and over again.

17 Figures include Euro and foreign issues and publicised placements. Issues which re-package existing bond issues are not included. See Bank of England, 1995.

18 Indeed, within the City of London it was feared that disadvantaged issuers or investors will try to avoid their obligations under bonds to be repaid after the start of the transition which were issued in ECUs or other national currencies subsumed by the Euro. See British Banking Association, Association for Payment Clearing Services, London Investment Banking Association, 1996, p. 14.

However the First Regulation on the introduction of the Euro, now in force in all the member states including the UK, ensures that there will be continuity of contracts. Thus, financial contracts denominated in the national currencies of participating member states will remain unchanged as a result of the introduction of the Euro, except for the change in denomination and hence amount at the conversion rate. Bank of England, 1997, p. 85.

19 These issues are discussed in greater depth in a paper by LIBA, 1996.

20 Indeed, on the eve of the City's Big Bang and in its immediate aftermath a great deal of mergers and take overs went on in the City of London, as the big British Clearing and Merchant banks, as well as interested foreign investment firms, saw the opportunity to enter the renewed London capital market. For a detailed account of the restructuring of the City of London during the City's revolution see Reid, 1988.

21 Nowadays, a substantial proportion of larger deals is now transacted with market-makers 'net', that is without any commission charge, being firms gains represented by the difference between their buying and selling prices. See Artis, 1996.

22 The 'alphas' are the shares of over 130 of the leading companies most widely dealt in; there have to be 10 or more market-makers in 'alphas'.

23 For 'betas' there must be at least four market-makers.

24 Shares of companies from foreign countries, mainly European, listed in London by specialised market-makers.
25 The market-making system for foreign shares is very similar to the one for UK ones, with the participation of both British and international specialised market makers quoting foreign shares on an arm of the Stock Exchange's system, the SEAQ international.
26 For other legal issues see British Banking Association, Association for Payment Clearing Services, London Investment Banking Association, 1996, p. 19.
27 These are all the operations in financial derivatives which are carried out outside the organised Exchange. See Picchi, 1991.
28 For more detail on non-bank financial intermediaries, see Goacher and Curwen, 1987, ch. 8 for Pension Funds.
29 In fact, in these cases premiums are usually kept down by reliance on high investment returns.
30 In its December 1997 report on the Euro, the Bank of England clearly claims: 'The introduction of the Euro represents an opportunity for London rather than a threat. There will be a vigorous Euro-Euro market in London, just as there is a vigorous Euro-DM, Euro-franc, Euro-$ and Euro-yen now' (Bank of England, 1997, p. 12).
31 Which means exactly one year before the new Labour government actually stated that the UK would have not joined EMU on 1 January 1999.
32 Christopher Johnson, former Chief Economic Adviser to Lloyds bank and now UK adviser, Association for the Monetary Union of Europe, claims: 'Meme si la City reste sceptique a' l' egard des merites de l'Euro.' See Johnson, forthcoming.
33 As already pointed out, on 27 October 1998, the Labour Chancellor announced that the UK would exercise its opt-out from stage 3 of EMU and would accordingly not be a participant on 1 January 1999. Summing up the government's position, he said: 'We believe that in principle, British membership of a successful single currency would be beneficial to Britain and to Europe; the key factor is whether the economic benefits of joining for business and industry are clear and unambiguous. If they are, there is no constitutional bar to British membership of EMU; applying the economic tests, it is not in this country's interest to join in the first wave of EMU on 1 January 1999 and, barring some fundamental and unforeseen change in economic circumstances, making a decision this Parliament to join is not realistic; but in order to give ourselves a genuine choice in the future, it is essential that the government and business prepare intensively during this Parliament, so that Britain will be in a position to join a single currency, should we wish to, early in the next Parliament.' See Bank of England, 1997.

Bibliography

Introduction

Interests or Expectations? A Political Economy Analytical Approach to Exchange Rate Commitments

Andrews, D.M (1993), 'The global origins of the Maastricht Treaty on EMU: closing the window of opportunity', in Cafruny, A. and Rosenthal, G.G., *The state of the European Community: the Maastricht debate and beyond*, Longman: Lynne Rienner Publishers.

Andrews, D.M. (1994), 'Capital mobility and state autonomy: toward a structural theory of international monetary relations', *International Studies Quarterly*, No. 38, pp. 193–218.

Artis, M., Gallo, G. and Salmon, M. (1998), *What exchange rate policy should be adopted for the Euro?*, paper presented at the NIESR European Financial Markets Advisory Panel, London: 9 November.

Avesani, R., Gallo, G. and Salmon, M. (1995a), 'On the evolution of credibility and flexible exchange rate target zones', *CEPR Discussion Papers*, No. 1123.

Avesani, R., Gallo, G. and Salmon, M. (1995b), 'On the nature of commitment in flexible target zones and the measurement of credibility: the 1993 ERM crisis', *EUI Working Papers in Economics*, No. 95/6, Florence: EUI.

Bank for International Settlement (BIS) (1990), *Sixtieth Annual Report*, Basle: BIS.

Buchanan, J.M. and Tullock, G. (1962), *The Calculus of Consent*, Ann Arbor: The University of Michigan Press.

Bulmer, S. (1983), 'Domestic politics and European Community policy-making', *Journal of Common Market Studies*, Vol. XXI, No. 4, June, p. 354.

Coakley, J. and Harris, L. (1983), *The City of Capital*, Oxford: Basil Blackwell.

De Grauwe, P. (1996), *International Money*, Oxford: Oxford University Press.

Drazen, A. and Masson, P.R. (1994), *Credibility of policies versus credibility of policy makers,* IMF working paper 94/49, Washington, DC: International Monetary Fund.

Eichengreen, B. and Frieden, J. (1994), *The Political Economy of European Monetary Union*, Westview Press.

Eichengreen, B. and Frieden, J. (1998), *Forging an Integrated Europe*, Ann Arbor: University of Michigan Press.

Flood, R.P. and Marion, N.P. (1996), 'Speculative attacks: fundamentals and self-fulfilling prophecies', *National Bureau of Economic Research,* Working Paper 5789, Cambridge, Massachusetts: NEBR.

Fratianni, M. and Artis, M. (1996), 'The lira and the pound in the 1992 Currency crisis: fundamentals or speculation?', *Open Economies Review,* 7, pp. 573–89.

Frieden, J. (1991), 'Invested interests: the politics of national economic policies in a world of global finance', *International Organization,* No. 45, Autumn.

Frieden, J. (1994), *The Impact of Goods and Capital Market Integration on European Monetary Politics,* preliminary version, August.

Frieden, J. (1998), *The New Political Economy of EMU,* Oxford: Rowman & Littlefield.

Gandolfo, G. (1989), *Corso di Economia Internazionale,* UTET LIBRERIA, ch. 18.

Haas, E.B. (1958), *The Uniting of Europe: political, social and economic forces,* Stanford, California: Stanford University Press.

Hix, S. (1994), 'The study of the European Community: the challenge to comparative politics', *West European Politics* 17(1), pp. 1–30.

HM Treasury (1990), 'Economic and Monetary Union', *Treasury Bulletin,* Summer, London: HMSO.

Krugman, P. (1989), 'The case for stabilising exchange rates', *Oxford Review of Economic Policy,* 5, pp. 61–72.

Ingham, G. (1984), *Capitalism divided? The City and Industry in British Social Development,* London: Macmillan.

Lindberg, H., Svensson, L. and Soderlind, P. (1991), 'Devaluation Expectations: The Swedish Krona 1981–1991', *IIES Seminar Paper* No. 495.

Major, J. (1990b), 'Inflation pressures beginning to ease', *Financial Times Weekend,* 6/7 October.

Martinelli, A. and Chiesi, M. (1989), 'Italy', in Bottomore, T. and Brym, J. (eds), *The Capitalist Class: an International Study,* London: Harvester Wheatsheaf.

Martinelli, A. (1980), 'Organised business and Italian politics', in Lange, P. and Tarrow, S. (eds), *Italian in Transition,* London: Frank Cass.

Masson, P.R. (1994), *The Credibility of the United Kingdom's Commitment to the ERM: intentions versus actions,* IMF Working Papers, WP/94/147, Washington, DC: IMF.

Milner, H. (1992), 'Theories of cooperation', *World Politics,* Vol. 44, pp. 427–95.

Milner, H. (1993), 'The assumption of anarchy in IR theory: a critique' in Baldwin, D.A. (ed.) (1993), *Neo-realism and Neo-liberalism: the contemporary debate,* Columbia University Press.

Moravcsik, A. (1991), 'Negotiating the Single European Act: national interests and conventional statecraft in the European Community', *International Organization,* Vol. 45, No. 1, Winter.

Moravcsik, A. (1993a), 'Preferences and power in the EC: a liberal intergovernmentalist approach', *Journal of Common Market Studies,* Vol. 31, No. 4, December, p. 474.

Moravcsik, A. (1993b), 'Integrating international and domestic theories of international bargaining' in Evans, P.B., Jacobson, H.K. and Putnam, R.D. (eds), *Double-edged Diplomacy: international bargaining and domestic policy,* Berkeley: University of California Press.

OECD (1991), *Economic Outlook*, No. 50, December.

Rosamond, B. (1995), 'Mapping the European condition: the theory of integration and the integration of theory', *European Journal of International Relations*, 1(3), pp. 391–408.

Rose, A. K. and Svensson, E.O. (1994), 'European exchange rate credibility before the fall', *Economic Review*, 38, pp. 1185–216.

Romer, D. (1993), 'Rational Asset-Price Movements without news', *The American Economic Review*, Vol. 83, Issue 5, pp. 112–30.

Sandholtz, W. (1993), 'Choosing Union: monetary politics and Maastricht', *International Organization*, Vol. 47, pp. 1–39.

Strange, S. (1971), *Sterling and British Policy*, Oxford: Oxford University Press.

Strange, S. (1986), *Casino Capitalism*, London: Blackwell.

Strange S. (1998), *Mad Money*, Manchester: Manchester University Press.

Strange, S. (1998), 'What theory? The theory in Mad Money', GSGR Working Paper No. 18/98, December.

Svensson, L. (1990), *The simplest test of target zone credibility*, IMF Working Paper WP/90/106.

Svensson, L. (1991), *Assessing Target Zone Credibility: mean reversion and devaluation expectations in the EMS*, Institute for International Economic Studies, Seminar Paper No. 493.

Underhill, G. and Coleman, W.D. (1998), *Regionalism and Global Economic Integration: Europe, Asia and the Americas,* London: Routledge.

Underhill, G. (1997), *The New World Order in International Finance*, London: Macmillan.

Part I: The Birth of Consensus

1 Italy and Entry into the ERM: Shifting the Domestic Power Struggle to the European Level

Accornero, A. (1994), *La Parabola del sindacato*, Bologna: Il Mulino.

Addis, E. (1987), 'Banca d'Italia e politica monetaria: la riallocazione del potere tra Stato, Mercato e Banca Centrale', *Stato e Mercato*, No. 19, April.

Andreatta, N. et al. (1978), *La lira e lo scudo atti del Convegno dell' AREL del 9 Settembre 1978,* Bologna.

Andreotti, G. (1978), Government Declarations, Debate at the Chamber of Deputies on the EMS of 12 December 1978 in Italian Chamber of Deputies.

Arcelli, M. and Valiani., R. (1979), 'Crowding out: some reflection on economic policy', *Review of Economic Conditions in Italy*, No. 2.

Associazione Bancaria Italiana (1978), *Relazione sull'attivita' svolta negli anni 1976 e 1977 presentata all'assemblea del 21 Giugno 1978*, Rome: ABI.

Associazione Bancaria Italiana (1979), *Relazione sull' attivita' svolta nell'anno 1978-1979 presentata all'assemblea del 5 Luglio 1979*, Rome: ABI.

Associazione Bancaria Italiana (1980), *Relazione sull'attivita' svolta nell'anno 1979-1980 presentata all' assemblea del 4 Luglio 1980*, Rome: ABI.

Associazione Sindacale INTERSIND (1979), *Relazione 1979*, Rome: INTERSIND.

ASAP (1979), 'Elementi del recente dibattito sui problemi dell'economia italiana', *ASAP: notizie sindacali,* No. 169–170, March–April.

Baffi, P. (1978a), 'I cambi: ieri, oggi, domani. Intervento del Governatore della Banca d'Italia al XXI Congresso Nazionale del Forex Club Italiano, Ischia, 14–15 Ottobre 1978', *Bancaria*, August, Vol. XXXIV, No. 8.

Baffi, P. (1978b), 'Il sistema monetario europeo e la partecipazione dell'Italia', *Thema: quaderni di economia e finanza dell' Istituto Bancario San Paolo di Torino*, No. 2.

Balducci, R. and Marconi, M. (1981), 'L'accumulazione del capitale nella visione del governo, della Banca d'Italia e della Confederazione Generale dell'Industria', in Lunghini, G. (1981), *Scelte politiche e teorie economiche in Italia, 1945–1978*, Torino: Einaudi.

Banca d'Italia (1978), *A Blueprint for a European Monetary System after the Ecofin meeting of the 18th September*, 2 October.

Bancaria (1978), 'L'Europa monetaria e la congiuntura italiana', Vol. XXXIV, No. 6, June.

Bank of Italy (1980), *Assemblea Generale Ordinaria dei Partecipanti Anno 1979*, Rome: Banca d'Italia.

Bank of Italy (1981), *Assemblea Generale Ordinaria dei Partecipanti Anno 1980*, Rome: Banca d'Italia.

Bonaccini, A. (1978a), 'Sistema Monetario Europeo: nessun rilancio sul provvisorio', *Rassegna Sindacale: settimanale della CGIL*, Vol. XXIV, No. 41, 2 November.

Bonaccini, A. (1978b), 'Non giova a nessuno l'Europa a due velocita', *Rassegna sindacale: settimanale della CGIL*, Vol. XXIV, No. 49/50, 14 December.

Bordini, M. (1978a), 'Austerita' e piano triennale', *Rassegna Sinadacale: settimanale della CGIL*, Vol. XXIV, No. 32, 7 September.

Bordini, M. (1978b), 'La lira e' divergente cronica', *Rassegna sindacale: settimanale della CGIL*, Vol. XXV, No. 4, 25 January.

Borsa, M. (1979), 'Grande Industria: perche' i colossi hanno favourito l'ingresso nello SME. L'avvocato accetta la sfida', *Euro*, January.

Carli, G. (1978a), 'Guido Carli alla radio tedesca. Le condizioni per pervenire all' armonizzazione monetaria', *Agenzia Giornali Associati*, 11 July.

Carli, G. (1978b), 'Considerazioni generali di Guido Carli su programmi finalizzati, crisi industriale ed esigenze produttive. Per una coerente politica economica e' necessario ridare vitalita' al mercato', *il Sole 24 ore*, 3 August.

Carli, G. (1978c), 'Non conviene una SME che ignori il dollaro', *il Sole 24 ore*, 31 October.

Carli, G. (1978d), 'La questione del dollaro e questa Europa', *Corriere della Sera*, 14 November.

Carli, G. (1978e), 'Intervento di Guido Carli all'IDE. Per un allineamento all'Europa tener d'occhio la realta' interna', *il Sole 24 ore*, 25 November.

Carli, G. (1978f), *Intervento di Guido Carli al ventesimo anniversario dell' UNICE*, Bruxelles, 7 December.

Carli, G. (1978g), *Intervento di Guido Carli al convegno sul commercio estero promosso dall'ICE*, Milan, 12 December.

Carli, G. (1978h), 'Come vivere col serpente', *La Repubblica*, 15 December.

Carli, G. (1979), *Intervento alla conferenza promossa dalla Cassa di risparmio di Foligno: Una politica industriale per lo sviluppo delle piccole e medie unita' produttive*, Foligno, 23 February.

Chiti Battelli, A. (1978), *Liberali e laici di fronte all' Europa*, Lacaita editore.

Confederazione Europea dei Sindacati (1978), 'Dichiarazioni della CES sulla preparazione del Consiglio europeo di Brema del 5–6 luglio '78. Bruxelles, 20 Maggio 1978', *Rassegna Sindacale: settimanale della CGIL,* Vol. XXIV, No. 27, 6 July.

Confindustria (1978a), *Primo rapporto CSC sull'industria italiana*, Rome: SIPI.

Confindustria (1978b), *Relazione di Guido Carli all'assemblea generale della Confindustria*, Rome, 3 May.

Cotula (1984), 'Financial Innovation and monetary control in Italy', *Banca Nazionale del Lavoro Quarterly Review*, Vol. 37, No. 150, September.

Crouch, C. (1995–96), *Lectures given at the European University Institute*, 1995.

De Stefano, D. (1978), 'Intervista sui problemi dell'adesione all'Europa monetaria. Benvenuto mette in guardia il governo: attenti a non toccare la scala mobile', *Corriere della Sera*, 17 December.

Doeringer, P.B. (1981), *Industrial Relations in International Perspective: essays on research and policy*, London: Macmillan Press Ltd.

Eichengreen B. and Frieden J. (1994), *The Political Economy of European Monetary Unification*, Westview Press.

Epstein, G.A. and Schor, B.J. (1987), 'Il Divorzio tra Banca d'Italia e Tesoro: un caso di indipendenza delle Banche Centrali', in Lange, P. and Regini, M. (eds), *Stato e Regolazione Sociale: nuove prospettive sul caso italiano*, Bologna: Il Mulino.

Ezra, D. and Sette, P. (1978), 'Impresa pubblica e cooperazione economica internazionale', *Industria e Sindacato: settimanale dell'associazione sindacale INTERSIND*, Vol. XX, No. 24, 16 June.

Frieden J. (1991), 'Invested interests: the politics of national economic policies in a world of global finance', *International Organization*, No. 45.

Garavini, S. (1978), 'Piano Pandolfi: un documento dai limiti evidenti', *Rassegna Sinadacale: settimanale della CGIL*, Vol. XXIV, No. 32, 7 September.

Giugni, G. (1981), 'The Italian system of industrial relations', in Doeringer, P.B. (ed.), *Industrial Relations in International Perspective: essays on research and policy*, London: Macmillan Press Ltd.

Gourevitch, P., Lange, P. and Martin, A. (1981), 'Industrial relations and politics: some reflections', in Doeringer, P.B. (ed.), *Industrial Relations in International Perspective: essays on research and policy*, London: Macmillan Press Ltd.

Gramsci, A. (1975), *Note sul Machiavelli*, Rome: Istituto Gramsci.

Guatelli, A. (1978), 'Intervista a Bruxelles con il Ministro degli Esteri. Forlani: puo' aprirsi una crisi di governo sulla moneta Europea', *Corriere della Sera*, 8 December.

il Sole 24 ore (1978), 'Come ripristinare la stabilita' monetaria. Un comitato UNICE presieduto da Guido Carli', 27 May.

IMF (1988), *Policy Coordination in the European Monetary System*, IMF Occasional Paper No. 61, IMF, Washington, DC.

Italian Chamber of Deputies (1978a), 'Atti Parlamentari', VII Legislatura, *Discussioni*, seduta del 10 Ottobre.

Italian Chamber of Deputies (1978b), 'Atti Parlamentari', VII Legislatura, *Discussioni*, seduta del 12 Dicembre.

Italian Chamber of Deputies (1978c), 'Atti Parlamentari', VII Legislatura, *Discussioni*, seduta del 13 Dicembre.

Jenkins, R. (1977), 'Europe's present challenge and future opportunity', *The 1st Jean Monnet Lecture*, Florence, 27 October.

La Malfa, G. (1978a), 'Dopo il vertice di Brema: l'America e la sfida dell' Europa', *La Stampa*, 5 August.

La Malfa G. (1978b), 'Difficile Convivenza', *La Stampa*, 16 November.

La Malfa, G. (1979), 'Non mi pento per lo SME', *la Republica*, 2 January.

La Malfa, U. (1978a), 'Un meccanismo che da garanzie', *La Stampa*, 29 November.

La Malfa, U. (1978b), 'Non perdere l'estremo aggancio', *La Voce Repubblicana*, 7 December.

La Malfa, U. (1978c), 'La scelta', *La Voce Repubblicana*, 12 December.

La Malfa, U. and Biasini, O. (1978), 'Circolare inviata dal Presidente e dal Segretario del PRI a tutte le organizzazioni del partito: Il PRI e l'adesione allo SME', *la Voce Repubblicana*, 20 December.

Lange, P., Ross, G. and Vannicelli, M. (1982), *Unions, Change and Crisis: French and Italian union strategy and the political economy*, London: Allen and Unwin.

Lange, P. and Regini, M. (1989), *State, Market and Social Regulation: New Perspectives on Italy*, Cambridge: Cambridge University Press.

Leonardi, R. and Nanetti, R.Y. (1986), *Italian Politics: a Review*, Vol. 1, London and Wolfeboro, New Haven: Frances Pinter Publisher.

Ludlow, P. (1982), *The Making of the European Monetary System*, London: Butterworth Scientific.

308 *Betting For and Against EMU*

Mariano, L. (1978), 'Valuta comunitaria e l'unione monetaria europea', *Banche e Banchieri*, Vol. V, No. 5, May.

Mazzuca, A. (1978), 'Intervista all' On. Giorgio Napolitano, responsabile economico del PCI: La sopravivenza del governo si gioca sul piano triennale', *il Giornale*, 17 December.

Mediobanca (1978), *Bilancio al 30 Giugno 1978*, Milan: Mediobanca.

Merkel, W. (1987), *Prima e dopo Craxi: le trasformazioni del PSI*, Padova: Liviana Editrice.

Modigliani, F. (1978a), 'Operazione Europa: quante cose da cambiare per prendere quel treno', *la Repubblica*, 1 August.

Modigliani, F. (1978b), 'I pro ed i contro per l'Italia', *Corriere della Sera*, 1 December.

Monti, M. (1978a), 'Arduo con la nostra inflazione assumere vincoli di cambio', *Il Sole 24 Ore*, 5 December.

Monti, M. (1978b), 'Proseguire la lotta all' inflazione', *Il Sole 24 Ore*, 6 December.

Monti, M. and Siracusano, B. (1979), 'The public sector financial intermediation: the composition of credit and the allocation of resources', *Review of Economic Conditions in Italy*, No. 2.

Monti, M. and Siracusano, B. (1980), 'In reply to Nardozzi and Onado', *Review of Economic Conditions in Italy*, No. 2.

Napolitano, G. (1978a), 'Come restare in Europa', *Rinascita*, 17 November.

Napolitano, G. (1978b), 'Nell' interesse dell' Italia e dell' Europa', *l'Unita'*, 10 December.

Nardozzi, G. (1980), *I difficili anni 70*, Milan: ETAS Libri.

Nardozzi, G. (1981), 'Accumulazione del capitale e politica monetaria: il punto di vista della Banca d'Italia', in Lunghini, G. (1981), *Scelte politiche e teorie economiche in Italia, 1945-1978*, Torino: Einaudi.

Nardozzi, G. and Onado, M. (1980), 'The relations between banks and enterprises and the public sector as financial intermediary', *Review of Economic Conditions in Italy*, No. 2.

Olivetti, R. (1978) 'L'Italia deve aprire le porte ad aziende e capitali europei', *la Stampa*, 2 December.

Ossola, R. (1978), 'Intervento del Ministro del Commercio con l'estero al XXI Congresso del Forex Club Italiano: l'Italia e lo SME', *Bancaria*, Vol. XXXIV, No. 8.

Palombarini S. (1995), 'Perche' l'Europa non ha ancora una moneta', *MicroMega*, No. 2.

Partito Comunista Italiano (1978), *Quale Europa? I comunisti italiani e le elezioni europee*, Rome, 8–9 November.

Perticone, G. (1978), 'Considerazioni sull'adesione dell'Italia al sistema monetario europeo', *Bancaria*, Vol. XXXIV, No. 8, August.

Petrilli, G. (1978a), 'Per una politica industriale comunitaria', *Industria e Sindacato*, Vol. XX, No. 24, 16 June.

Petrilli, G. (1978b), 'Un passo verso l'Europa: oltre l'adesione', *il Tempo*, 15 December.

Pirani, M. (1978), 'Questa Europa nasce male e sara' troppo tedesca. Intervista a Guido Carli', *la Repubblica*, 29 October.

Regini, M. (1981), *I dilemmi del sindacato*, Bologna: il Mulino.

Rossi, G. (1978), 'Intervista con Giancarlo Pajetta dopo il fallimento dell' accordo di Bruxelles: Europa, e' sincero il PCI? si tentano intrighi e manovre preelettorali, ma Andreotti non e' telecomandato da noi', *la Repubblica*, 8 December.

Salvati, M. (1984), *Economia e politica in Italia dal dopoguerra ad oggi*, Milan: Garzanti.

Sampietro, C. (1979), 'Lo SME: ridare stabilita' all'impresa', *Industria e Sindacato*, Vol. XXI, No. 13, 30 March.

Savona, P. (1978), 'Ad occhi bendati nel valzer dello SME', *Corriere della Sera*, 2 December.

Spaventa L. (1978a), 'Non tornano i conti a chi vuol rivalutare la lira', *La Repubblica*, 19 August.

Spaventa L. (1978b), 'SME: per noi non esiste alcun vantaggio', *Il sole 24 Ore*, 26 October.

Spaventa, L. (1978c), *Il problema dello SME*, Speech at the Chamber of Deputies on 12 December.

Spaventa, L. (1978d), 'Queste ragioni sconsigliano un' ingresso affrettato', *Rinascita*, 15 December.

Spaventa, L. (1978e), 'Qualcuno vuole punire l'Italia', *L'Europeo*, 22 December.

Spaventa, L. (1980), 'Italy joins the EMS: a political history', in *The Political and Diplomatic Origins of the EMS*, Bologna: The Johns Hopkin University, Occasional Paper No. 32.

Spaventa, L. (1984), 'The growth of Public Debt in Italy: Past Experience, Perspectives and Policy Problems', *Banca Nazionale del Lavoro Quarterly Review*, Vol. 37, No. 149.

Vannicelli, M. (1984), *A labor movement in search of a role: the evolution of the strategy of the Italian unions since 1943*, Harvard University, PhD thesis.

2 The UK and the Making of the EMS: A Low Temperature Political Debate

Aaronvitch, S. (1961), *The Ruling Class*, London: Lawrence & Wishart.

Aitken, J. (1978a), 'Chancellor names the price for monetary agreement: Healey demands CAP reform', *The Guardian*, 12 July.

Aitken, J. (1978b), 'Giscard-Schmidt Meeting revises monetary system to tempt Italians: cabinet hardens line against parity, *The Guardian*, 3 November.

Aitken, J. (1978c), 'Chancellor to decide an opening euro-fund account: Callaghan flies patriot's flag over Commons', *The Guardian*, 7 December.

Aitken, J. and Cairncross, F. (1978), 'PM cautious on plan for euro-money', *The Guardian*, 11 July.

Anderson, P. (1964), 'The origins of the present crisis', *The New Left Review*, No. 23, January–February.

Artis, M.J. and Lewis, M.K. (1981), *Monetary Controls in the United Kingdom*, Oxford: Philip Allan.

Bank of England (1978a), 'Speech given by the Governor of the Bank of England to the annual banquet of the Overseas Bankers Club, on 6 February 1978', *Bank of England Quarterly Bulletin*, Vol. 18, No. 1, March.

Bank of England (1978b), 'Speech given at the Lord Mayor's dinner to the bankers and merchants of the City of London on 19 October 1978', *Bank of England Quarterly Bulletin*, Vol. 18, No. 4, December.

Berrel, R., Pain, N. and Cnossen, T. (1996), *Currency Regimes, Capital Controls and the Feldstein Horioka Puzzle: the Effects of Capital Market Liberalisation in Europe*, London: National Institute of Economic and Social Research.

Blake, D. (1978a), 'Treasury points out faults in "hurried" currency proposals', *The Times*, 11 July.

Blake, D. (1978b), 'UK moving away from European money plan', *The Times*, 22 September.

Blanden, M. (1978), 'Monetary system good for UK, says Morse', *Financial Times*, 1 November.

British Invisibles (1996a), *Invisibles Facts and Figures*, London: British Invisibles.

British Invisibles, 1996b), *The City Table 1995*, London: British Invisibles.

Brummer, A. (1978a), 'Midland Chairman: EMS is not worth a row of beans', *The Guardian*, 25 October.

Brummer, A. (1978b), 'Expenditure Committee says membership would lead to lower growth: more jobless warning over EMS', *The Guardian*, 23 November.

Buci-Glucksmann, C. (1980), *Gramsci and the State,* London: Lawrence & Wishart.

City Comment (1978), 'Euro Snake may cure rather than kill', *The Daily Telegraph*, 12 October.

Clark, G. (1978), 'Tories cautious on Bremen scheme', *The Times*, 10 July.

Coakley, J. and Harris, L. (1983), *The City of Capital: London's role as a financial center*, Oxford: Basil Blackwell.

Conservative Commonwealth and Overseas Council (1978), 'The City and Europe', *Financial Times*, 2 October.

Confederation of British Industry (1978), *Business Views on Exchange-rate Policy*, London: Confederation of British Industry, July.

Crawford, M. (1978), 'Treasury counter Euro-currency', *The Sunday Times*, 16 July.

Crouch, C., (ed) (1979), *State and Economy in Contemporary Capitalism*, London: Croom Helm.

De Cecco, M. (1982), *Credit Creation in the Eurocurrency Markets*, European University Institute, Working Paper No. 23.

De Jonquierers, G. and Riddel, P. (1978), 'Britain stays out of EMS', *Financial Times*, 6 December.

Deputy Chairman, Conservative Commonwealth and Overseas Council (1978), 'The City and Europe', *Financial Times*, 2 October.

Dornbush, R. and Layard, R (1987), *The Performance of the British Economy*, Oxford: Clarendon Press.

Emery, F. (1978), ' Heath says that Bremen plan is vital', *The Times*, 13 July.

Forrest, C. (1979), 'European Monetary System', *Barclays Review*, Vol. LIV, No. 1, February.

Goodman, E. (1978), 'Labour MPs to fight EMS', *Financial Times*, 10 November.

Hartfield, M. (1978), 'EMS against vital British interests, labour critics say', *The Times*, 28 November.

Hayek, F. (1976a), *Choice in Currencies: a way to stop inflation*, London: Institute of Economic Affairs, Occasional Papers, No. 48.

Hayek, F. (1976b), 'Denationalisation of money', *Hobart Paper Special*, No. 70, October, London: IEA.

Hayek, F. (1979), 'Toward a free market monetary system', *Journal of Libertarian Studies*, Vol. 3, No. 1.

Healey, D. (1989), *The Time of My Life*, London: Michael Joseph.

House of Commons (1980), *First Report from the Expenditure Committee Session 1978–79: The European Monetary System*, London: HMSO.

HM Treasury (1978), *Green Paper on European Monetary System presented to Parliament by the Chancellor of the Exchequer by Command of Her Majesty*, November , London: HMSO.

HM Treasury (1990a), 'Economic and Monetary Union', *HM Treasury Bulletin*, Summer.

HM Treasury (1990b), 'The UK proposal for a EMF and a hard ECU', *HM Treasury Bulletin*, Autumn.

Hornsby, M. (1978), 'Prospects of joining EMS fade', *The Times*, 8 November.

Hutber, P. (1978), 'Bremen pierrepoint and doctor Bray', *Sunday Telegraph*, 16 July.

Hutton, W. (1995), *The State We're In*, London: Jonathan Cape.

Ingham, G. (1984), *Capitalism Dived? The City and industry in British social development*, London: Macmillan Education Ltd.

Keegan, P.W. (1978), 'Euromoney jitters', *The Observer*, 15 October.

Langdom, J. (1978), 'MPs in new anti-EMS move', *The Guardian*, 30 October.

Lord Kaldor (1983), *The Economic Consequences of Mrs Thatcher*, London: Duckworth.

Lawson, N. (1992), *The View from No. 11: memoirs of a Tory radical*, London: Bentam Press.

Marsh, D. (1978), 'Britain and Italy in common ground on EMS', *Financial Times*, 23 November.

Moran, M. (1984), *The Politics of Banking*, London: Macmillan Press Ltd.

Gould, B., MP for Southampton, Test (Labour) (1978), 'Bremen currency initiative', *The Times*, 17 July 1978.

Nairn, T. (1977), 'The Twilight of British State', *New Left Review*, No. 101–102, February–April.

National Economic Development Council (1981), *Economic Considerations in British Foreign Policy*, NEDC (81) 37, 23 June.

Nott, J. (1978), 'Choosing your currency', *The Times*, 19 September.

Overbeek, H. (1980), 'Finance capital and the crisis in Britain', *Capital and Class*, 11, Summer.

Overbeek, H. (1990), *Global Capitalism and National Decline: the Thatcher decade in perspective*, London: Unwin Hyman.

Perkin, H. (1969), *The Origins of Modern English Society, 1780–1880*, London: Routledge.

Rawstorne, P. (1978a), 'Hint of Thatcher rift with Heath over Bremen', *Financial Times*, 13 July.

Rawstorne, P. (1978b), 'Biffen says EMS would clash with Tory policies', *Financial Times*, 31 October.

Rawstorne, P. and Riddel, P. (1978), 'CBI seeks monetary system safeguards', *Financial Times*, 19 October.

Riddel, P. (1978a), 'The pound in your pocket', in *Financial Times*, 20 September.

Riddel, P. (1978b), 'Unbelievers and enthusiasts', *Financial Times*, 2 October.

Riddel, P. (1978c), 'Ministers split as monetary system talks begin in Bonn', *Financial Times*, 18 October.

Riddel, P. (1978d), 'UK decision on European Monetary System delayed', *Financial Times*, 23 October.

Riddel, P. (1978e), 'Monetary system means big changes in policy', *Financial Times*, 30 October.

Riddel, P. (1978f), 'Fabian warning over jobs', *Financial Times*, 31 October.

Riddel P. (1978g), 'Big four split on European Monetary Plan', *Financial Times*, 8 November.

Riddel, P. (1978h), 'Caution on effects of EMS for Britain, *Financial Times*, 23 November.

Rose, H. (1979), 'The exchange rate puzzle', *Barclays Review*, Vol. LIV, No. 2, May.

Rubinstein, W.D. (1977), 'Wealth, elites and the class structure of modern Britain', *Past and Present*, No. 76, August.

Stanworth, P. and Giddens, A. (1974), *Elites and Power in British Society*, Cambridge: Cambridge University Press.

Strange, S. (1971), *Sterling and British Policy: a political study of an international currency in decline*, London: Oxford University Press.

Strange, S. (1986), *Casino Capitalism*, London: Basil Blackwell.

Tisdall, P. (1978), 'CBI's cautious support', *The Times*, 19 October.

Trade Union Congress (1980), *Report of the 111th Annual Trade Union Congress*, held in the Opera House, Blackpool, 3–7 September, London: Trade Union Congress.

Tyler, C. (1978a), 'Government asked to be wary over EMS plans', *Financial Times*, 30 October.

Tyler, C. (1978b), 'TUC leaders declare opposition to EMS', *The Times*, 31 October.

Waller, B. (1978), 'Callaghan to seek delay on currency', *Sunday Telegraph*, 29 October.

Walters, A. (1986), *Britain's Economic Renaissance: Margaret Thatcher's reforms 1979–1984*, London: Oxford University Press.

Walters, A. (1990), *Sterling in Danger: the economic consequences of pegged exchange rates*, London: Collins.

Whittam Smith, A. (1978), 'Pressure to link value of pound', *The Daily Telegraph*, 30 June.

Wood, D. (1978a), '2 pressing questions for party leaders', *The Times*, 16 October.

Wood, D. (1978b), 'Labour party facing crisis over joining European Monetary Pact', *The Times*, 17 October.

Young, H. (1978), 'Where the Unity has to stop', *The Sunday Times*, 29 October.

Zis, G. (1990), 'The international status of sterling', in Artis, M.J. and Cobham, D. (eds) (1990), *The Labour's Economic Policies, 1974–1979*, Manchester: Manchester University Press.

3 The UK and Entry into the ERM: Domestic Considerations and External Threats

Abrahams, P., Tomkins, R. and Thornhill, J. (1990), 'Business confidence expected to return', *Financial Times Weekend*, 6/7 October.

Arends, A. (1985), 'CBI in favour of Britain's full participation in EMS', *Financial Times*, 21 February.

Atkins, R. (1990), 'Labour shifts the attack to underlying problems', *Financial Times*, 8 October.

Bank of England (1982), 'Banking Act 1979: Annual Report by the Bank of England 1981–1982', *Reports and Accounts*, London: Hertford.

Bank of England (1988), *Banking Act 1987*, London: Bank of England.

Bank of England Quarterly Bulletin (1988), 'Recent economic and financial developments: General assessment', *Bank of England Quarterly Bulletin*, February, Vol. 28, No. 1.

Bank of England Quarterly Bulletin (1989a), 'The development of the European Monetary System', *Bank of England Quarterly Bulletin*, February, London: Bank of England.

Bank of England Quarterly Bulletin (1989b), 'The future of monetary arrangements in Europe', *Bank of England Quarterly Bulletin*, August, London: Bank of England.

Bank of England Quarterly Bulletin (1990a), 'Central Banking in Europe', *Bank of England Quarterly Bulletin,* February, London: Bank of England.

Bank of England Quarterly Bulletin (1990b), 'The United Kingdom's proposals for economic and monetary union', *Bank of England Quarterly Bulletin,* August, London: Bank of England.

Bank of England Quarterly Bulletin (1990c), 'Approaches to EMU', *Bank of England Quarterly Bulletin,* August, London: Bank of England.

Bank of England Quarterly Bulletin (1990d), 'Corporate finance, banking relationships and the London rules', *Bank of England Quarterly Bulletin,* November, London: Bank of England.

Bank of England Quarterly Bulletin (1990e), 'Approaches to monetary integration in Europe', *Bank of England Quarterly Bulletin,* November, London: Bank of England.

Bank of England Quarterly Bulletin (1991), 'The United Kingdom and Europe', *Bank of England Quarterly Bulletin,* 1 February, London: Bank of England.

Banham, J. (1990), 'A strategy for investment', *CBI News,* February.

Brittan, S. (1985), 'A start on job strategy', *Financial Times,* 20 March.

Brittan, S. (1987a), 'Better than the City expected', *Financial Times,* 18 March.

Brittan, S. (1987b), 'A budget policy for the world', *Financial Times,* 5 November.

Brittan, S. (1989), 'A dignified and necessary exit', *Financial Times,* 27 October.

Budd, A. (1989a), 'Macroeconomic policy and the ERM', *Barclays Economic Review,* February, London: Quarterly Barclays Bank.

Budd, A. (1989b), 'What went wrong?', *Barclays Economic Review,* May, London: Quarterly Barclays Bank.

Bush, J. (1987), 'City praises cautious approach to courting voters' approval', *Financial Times,* 19 March.

CBI/Price Waterhouse (1990), *The Exchange Rate Mechanism and manufacturing exports,* March, London: Confederation of British Industry.

Cianferotti, S. (1993), *La regolamentazione e l'operativita' del sistema bancario e finanziario inglese (1930–1993),* Firenze: Banca Toscana.

Commission of the European Communities (1989), *Delors Committee Report,* Brussels: CEC.

Confederation of British Industry (1986), *CBI Budget Recommendations 1986,* London: CBI.

Confederation of British Industry (1987a), *Survey of UK's Monetary Impact on Business: target exchange and interest rates,* August, London: CBI.

Confederation of British Industry (1987b), *Investing for Britain's future: Report of the CBI industry task force,* April, London: CBI.

Confederation of British Industry (1989a), *Building on business success: CBI economic priorities for 1989,* January, London: CBI.

Confederation of British Industry (1989b), *European Monetary Union: a business perspective,* November, London: CBI.

Confederation of British Industry (1990a), 'Britain's best way forward is in Europe', *CBI News*, January.

Confederation of British Industry (1990b), 'European Monetary Union', *Europe sans frontieres 1992: how it affects you*, Brief No. 22, February.

Conservative Party (1989), *Leading Europe into the 1990s: The Conservative Manifesto for Europe 1989*, London: The Conservative Party.

Corby, B. (1990a), 'Step by step to monetary union', *CBI News*, September.

Corby, B. (1990b), 'A boost to confidence', *CBI News*, November.

Currie, D. (1989), 'European Monetary Union or competing currencies: which way for monetary integration in Europe?', *Economic Viewpoint*, September.

Dawnay, I. (1990), 'Labour takes cautious line on fuller EC integration', *Financial Times*, 18 October.

De Cecco, M. (1992), *Monete in Concorrenza*, Bologna: Il Mulino.

Edmonds, K. and Shea, M. (1991), 'EMU and the ECU: the practitioner's viewpoint', *National Westminster Bank Quarterly Review*, November 1991.

Edwards, K. (1988), '1992: Setting the scene', in Confederation of British Industry, *1992: The New Europe,* London CBI.

Evans, R. (1986), 'Business leaders express delight', *Financial Times*, 19 March.

Evans, R. (1987), 'Praise, boos for tightrope act', *Financial Times*, 18 March.

Fidler, S. (1990), 'Financial markets hopes for billions of pounds inflows', *Financial Times Weekend*, 6/7 October.

Foley, P. (1989), '1992 Winners and losers', *Lloyds Bank Economic Bulletin*, Number 121, January.

Gamble, A. (1992), 'Labour party and macroeconomic management', in Smith, M.J. and Spear, J. (eds), *The Changing Labour Party*, London: Routledge.

Gapper, J. (1990), 'Long, hard road to wage restraint', *Financial Times*, 15 October.

George, S. and Rosamond, B. (1992), 'The European Community', in Smith, M.J. and Spear, J. (eds), *The Changing Labour Party*, London: Routledge.

Gill, K. (1990), 'An ERM rate to crucify industry', *Financial Times*, 13–14 October.

Goodhart, C. (1989), 'The Delors' Report: was Lawson reaction justifiable?', *LSE Financial Markets Group*, Special Paper No. 15, May, London.

Gowland, C. (1990), *The Regulation of the Financial Markets in the 1990s*, London: Edward Elgar.

HM Treasury (1989), *An Evolutionary Approach to Economic and Monetary Union*, November , London: HMSO.

HM Treasury (1990a), 'Economic and Monetary Union', *Treasury Bulletin*, Summer, London: HMSO.

HM Treasury (1990b), 'The UK proposals for a European Monetary Fund and hard ECU: making progress towards economic and monetary union in Europe', *Treasury Bulletin*, Autumn, London: HMSO.

Hayek, F.A. (1976a), 'Choice in currency: a way to stop inflation', *IEA Occasional Papers*, No. 48, London IEA.

Hayek, F.A. (1976b), 'Denationalisation of money', *Hobart Paper Special*, No. 70, October, London: IEA.

Hayek F.A. (1979), 'Towards a free market monetary system', *Journal of Libertarian Studies*, Vol. 3, No. 1.

Heseltine, M. (1989), *The challenge of Europe: can Britain win?*, London: Weidenfeld and Nicolson.

Holberton, S. (1988), 'Hesitant reaction reflected in the markets', *Financial Times*, 17 March.

Holberton, S. and Atkins, R. (1988), 'City backs Lawson but questions size of tax cuts', *Financial Times*, 16 March.

Holdsworth, T. (1990), 'My two years as president', *CBI News*, May.

Hollis, J. (1986), 'A monopoly broken by a series of accidents', *The Times*, 22 October.

House of Commons, Treasury and Civil Service Committee (1985), *The Financial and Economic Consequences of UK Membership of the European Communities. The European Monetary System, Volume 2: Minutes of Evidence*, London: Her Majesty's Stationery Office.

Howe, G. (1995), *Conflict of Loyalty*, London: Pan Books.

Hutton, W. (1990), 'Perfect time to shoot the fox', *The Guardian*, 6 October.

Johnson, C. (1989a), 'A tale of three cities', *Lloyds Bank Economic Bulletin*, No. 125, May.

Johnson, C. (1989b), 'Rest in peace MTFS', *The Banker*, June.

Johnson, C. (1989c), 'European Monetary Union: a view from the City', *De Pecunia: British views on EMU and miscellaneous*, Vol. 1, No. 2, October.

Johnson, C. (1989d), 'UK living on credit', *Lloyds Bank Economic Bulletin*, No. 131, November .

Johnson, C. (1990a), 'UK balancing acts collapses', *Lloyds Bank Economic Bulletin*, No. 142, October.

Johnson, C. (1990b), 'ERM: better late than never', *Lloyds Economic Bulletin*, No. 143, November.

Johnson, R. (1990), 'Kinnock loses economic aces from strong-looking hand', *Financial Times*, 8 October.

Labour Party (1988), *Social Justice and Economic Efficiency: First of Labour's Policy Review for the 1990s*, London: The Labour Party.

Labour Party (1989a), *Meet the challenge, make the change: A new agenda for Britain. Final Report of Labour's Policy Review for the 1990s*, London: The Labour Party.

Labour Party (1989b), *Conference Report*, Brighton.

Labour Party (1990), *Looking to the future: a dynamic economy, a decent society, strong in Europe,* London: The Labour Party.

Laidlaw, A. and Roberts, G. (1990), *Law Relating to Banking Services*, London: The Chartered Institute of Bankers.

Lascelles, D. (1989), 'Labour backs ERM entry for UK on reasonable terms', *Financial Times*, 1 December.

Lascelles, D. (1990), 'A source of relief from pain', *Financial Times Weekend*, 6/7 October.

Lawson, N. (1984a), 'The Budget: The Chancellor's Speech', *Financial Times*, 14 March.

Lawson, N. (1984b), 'The Budget: Details. Reduction of inflation remains aim of medium term strategy', *Financial Times*, 14 March.

Lawson, N. (1985), 'The Budget: The Chancellor's Speech', *Financial Times*, 20 March.

Lawson, N. (1986), 'The Budget: The Chancellor's Speech', *Financial Times*, 19 March.

Lawson, N. (1987a), 'The Budget: The Chancellor's Speech', *Financial Times*, 18 March.

Lawson, N. (1987b), 'Central aim of financial strategy is to reduce money growth', *Financial Times*, 18 March.

Lawson, N. (1989), 'The Budget: The Chancellor's speech', *Financial Times*, 15 March.

Lawson, N. (1992), *The View from No. 11*, London: Bentam Press.

Leadbeater, C. (1990), 'Business sees a guiding light', *Financial Times*, 8 October.

Lees, D. (1990), 'Investing for the new decade', *CBI News*, February.

Leigh-Pemberton, R. (1984), 'Domestic financial markets: progress and problems', in *Bank of England Quarterly Bulletin*, 24.

Leigh-Pemberton, R. (1989), 'Europe 1992: Some Monetary Policy Issues', *Economic Review, Federal Reserve Bank of Kansas City*, Vol. 74, No. 8, September/October.

Lewis, D. (1987), 'The Banking Bill: between Charybdis and Scylla', *The Journal of International Banking Law*, No. 2.

Lord Alexander of Weedon (1991), 'The vital UK role in Europe', *Natwest Quarterly Review*, February.

Major, J. (1990a), 'The Budget: the Chancellor's speech', *Financial Times*, 21 March.

Major, J. (1990b), 'Inflation pressures beginning to ease', *Financial Times Weekend*, 6/7 October.

Marsh, D. (1992), *The New Politics of British Trade Unionism: union power and the Thatcher legacy*, Ithaca, New York: ILR Press.

Mitchell, H. (1990), 'The Labour Party cannot be blamed for this mess', *Financial Times*, 9 October.

Moran, M. (1991), *The Politics of Financial Services Revolution*, London: Macmillan.

Norman, P. (1989a), 'Bankers agree on EC route to unity', *Financial Times*, 13 April.

Norman, P. (1989b), 'Major grilling substitutes charm for sarcasm', *Financial Times*, 5 December.

Norman, P. (1990), 'Britain to join the ERM on Monday', *The Financial Times*, 6/7 October.

Norman, P. and Marsh, P. (1990), 'Sanguine sterling is steady as she goes', *Financial Times*, 24/25 November.

O'Brien, L. (1973), 'EEC regulations', *The Banker*, No. 123.

Owen, I. (1984), 'Kinnock condemns "battering" of Britain', *Financial Times*, 14 March.

Owen, J. and Rutherford, M. (1987), 'Thinking about the year 2000: an interview with the Prime Minister', *Financial Times*, 23 November.

Pauley, R. (1984), '"Magic" of Lawson', *Financial Times*, 15 March.

Poeton, W. (1988), 'The small firm perspective', in Confederation of British Industry, *1992: The New Europe,* London: CBI.

Raisman, J. (1988), 'The way ahead', in Confederation of British Industry, *1992: The New Europe,* London: CBI.

Riddell, P. (1987), 'Thatcher stands firm against full EMS role', *Financial Times*, 23 November.

Ryder, F.R. (1979), *The Banking Act 1979*, London: Sweet and Maxwell.

Sheely, P. (1988), 'Making the most of 1992', in Confederation of British Industry, *1992: The New Europe,* London: CBI.

Skerrit, J. (1986), 'A systems approach for the City revolution', *The Banker*, March.

Smith, M. (1990), 'Pay bargaining structures face changes', *Financial Times*, 8 October.

Stephens, P. (1984), 'City dissects the pros and cons', *Financial Times*, 15 March.

Stephens, P. (1986), 'Ebullient Chancellor scoffs at strategy's critics', *Financial Times*, 20 March.

Stephens, P. (1987a), 'Lawson aims for steady L', *Financial Times*, 19 March.

Stephens, P. (1987b), 'Lawson reduces base rates to 9% to avert further market slide', *Financial Times*, 5 November.

Stephens, P. (1988), 'Top tax rate cut to 40% in "radical reforming" Budget', *Financial Times*, 16 March.

Stephens, P. (1989a), 'Thatcher ceases to thump the table over monetary union', *Financial Times*, 27 June.

Stephens, P. (1989b), 'Thatcher runs charmingly into an ambush', *Financial Times*, 28 June.

Stephens, P. (1989c), 'Thatcher seeks alternatives to Delors monetary union plan', *Financial Times*, 29 June.

Stephens, P. (1990a), 'Labour demands immediate talks on full EMS role', *Financial Times*, 24 September.

Stephens, P. (1990b), 'Ministers hope to cut Labour's lead', *Financial Times*, 6/7 October.

Stephens, P. (1996), *Politics and the Pound*, London: Macmillan.

Stephens, P. and Cassel, M. (1986), 'City warms the budget as leading banks cut base lending rate', *Financial Times*, 20 March.

Taylor, A. (1987), 'Industry and bankers see moves in right direction', *Financial Times*, 19 March.

Thatcher, M. (1993), *The Downing Street Years*, London: HarperCollins.

Trade Union Congress (1988), *Maximising the Benefits, Minimising the Costs: TUC Report on Europe 1992*, London: TUC.

Trade Union Congress (1989a), *Europe 1992: Progress Report on Trade Union Objectives. TUC Report on Europe 1992*, London: TUC.

Trade Union Congress (1989b), *Report of the 121st Annual Trade Union Congress*, Winter Gardens, Blackpool, 4–8 September.

Trade Union Congress (1990a), *TUC Budget Submission 1990*, London: TUC.

Trade Union Congress (1990b), *Managing the economy*, London: TUC.

Trade Union Congress (1990c), *Report of the 122nd Annual Trade Union Congress*, Winter Gardens, Blackpool, 3–7 September.

Trade Union Congress (1990d), *Europe 1992 and After: Challenges for Britain. Memorandum by the TUC*, London: TUC.

Walters, A. (1986), *Britain's Economic Renaissance: Margaret Thatcher's reforms 1979–1984*, London: Oxford University Press.

Walters, A. (1990), *Sterling in Danger: the economic consequences of pegged exchange rates*, London: Collins.

Wilkinson, M. (1985), 'The audience is getting restive', *Financial Times*, 16 March.

Williams, N. (1990), 'How much will the ERM save business?', *CBI News*, June.

Wintour, P. (1990), 'Kinnock to harden support for EMU', *The Guardian*, 17 October.

Woodford, M. (1990), 'Does competition between currencies lead to price level and exchange rate stability?', *Working Paper No. 3441, National Bureau of Economic Research*, September.

Young, J. (1989), 'Bridging the gap', *Lloyds Bank Economic Bulletin*, No. 127, July.

Part II: The Death of Consensus

4   Italy and the Departure from the ERM: Purely Economic Interests vs Political Economy Strategies

ABI (1992), *Relazioni pronunciate in occasione dell'assemblea ordinaria delle associate*, Rome, 24 June.

ABI (1993), *Relazione sull'attivita' svolta nel 1992*, Rome: ABI.

ABI (1994), *Relazione sull'attivita' svolta nel 1993*, Rome: ABI.

Arcucci, F. (1991), 'Una costellazione non favourevole di tassi di interesse', in *Banche e Banchieri*, Vol. XVIII, January.

Barucci, P. (1995), *L'isola italiana del tesoro*, Milan: Rizzoli.

Bianchi, T. (1991a), 'Dodici considerazioni sui saggi di interesse', *Banche e Banchieri*, Vol. XVIII, June.

Bianchi, T. (1991b), 'Inflazione, saggi di interesse, movimenti di capitali', *Banche e Banchieri*, Vol. XVIII, May.

Bianchi, T. (1992a), 'Due vie per i saggi di interesse?', *Banche e Banchieri*, Vol. XIX, January.

Bianchi, T. (1992b), *Relazione all'assemblea ordinaria delle associate*, Rome, 24 June.

Camozzini, S. (1992), 'Dini: difendiamo la lira', *Il Giornale d'Italia*, 20 June.

Ciampi, A. (1992a), *Relazione annuale Banca d'Italia*, Rome: Banca d'Italia.

Ciampi, A. (1992b), 'Intervento del Governatore della Banca d'Italia, Dr. Carlo Azeglio Ciampi', *Relazioni pronunciate in occasione dell'assemblea ordinaria delle associate*, 24 June.

Ciravegna, N. (1992), 'Battere l'inflazione, ricreare gli investimenti', *Il sole 24 ore*, 9 June.

CNEL (1990), *Rapporto CESOS 1989/90*, Rome: CNEL.

CNEL (1993), *Rapporto CESOS 1992/93*, Rome: CNEL.

Confindustria (1992), *XIV Rapporto del Csc*, May, Rome: SIPI.

Confindustria (1993), *L'industria in Europa: ristrutturazione, concorrenza, integrazione*, XV Rapporto CSC, May, Collana: L'industria Italiana, Rome: SIPI.

De Nardis, S. and Micossi, S. (1991), 'Dis-inflation and re-inflation in Italy and the problems for transition to monetary union', *BNL Quarterly Review*, No. 177, June.

Esposito M. (1992), 'Bianchi (ABI): sui tassi la tensione e' in calo', *Mercati Finanziari*, 24 June.

Falck, G. (1992), 'L'alternativa? Svalutare e stringere la cinghia', *Corriere della sera*, 20 July.

Ferrari, M. (1992), 'Quanto costa al Tesoro difendere la lira', *Italia Oggi*, 30 July.

Fossa, G. (1996), *Assembea annuale Confindustria. Relazione del Presidente*, Rome: Confindustria.

Lanzalaco, L. (1990), *Dall'impresa all'associazione*, Milan: Franco Angeli.

Marinelli, A. (1980), 'Organised business and Italian politics: Confindustria and the Christian Democrats in the post-war period', in Lange, P. and Tarrow, S. (eds), *Italy in Transition: conflict and consensus*, London: Frank Cass.

Mascini, M. (1992), 'La piccola impresa perde terreno. Grati lancia l'allarme competitivita', *Il sole 24 ore*, 18 June.

Mascini, M. (1993), 'Le organizzazioni imprenditoriali', in CNEL, *Rapporto CESOS 1992/1993*, Rome: CNEL.

Mattina, L. (1991), *Gli industriali e la democrazia: la Confindustria nella formazione dell'Italia repubblicana*, Bologna: Il Mulino.

Micossi, S. (1992), 'Previsioni Confindustria: un riequilibrio a costi crescenti', *Mondo Economico*, 4 July.

Micossi, S. and Padoan, P.C. (1994), 'Italy in the EMS: after crisis, salvation?', in Johnson, C. and Collignon, S. (eds), *The Monetary Economics of Europe: causes of the EMS crisis*, London: Pinter Publishers.

Monti, M. (1992), 'Perchè oggi non si può svalutare', *Il Corriere della sera*, 20 June.

Mucchetti, M. (1992), 'Da qui si puo' solo risalire', *L'Espresso*, 28 June.

Petrini, R. (1992), 'Il denaro e' sempre piu' salato', *La Repubblica*, 20 June.

Polsi, A. (1993), *Alle origini del capitalismo italiano*, Piccola Biblioteca Einaudi: Torino.

Riva, M. (1992), 'Signori, smettetela di dire che o si risana o si svaluta', *L'Espresso*, 28 June.

Schettino, G. (1992), 'Il rammarico di Spaventa: quel tabù del cambio', *La Repubblica*, 15 September.

Unnia, M. (1993), 'Imprenditori e partiti: verso un disegno politico-istituzionale?', *Rapporto CESOS 1992/1993*, Rome: CNEL.

Villari, L. (1992), *Il capitalismo italiano del novecento*, Biblioteca Universale Laterza: Rome.

5 The UK and the Departure from the ERM: Betting against EMU

Angus, M. (1991), 'Maastricht: too important to business to lose', *CBI News*, July/ August, London: CBI.

Balls, E. (1992), 'Why the case against devaluation is not clear cut', *Financial Times*, 20 January.

Banham, J. (1990), 'Investing in the new Europe: Extracts from John Banham's speech to the National Conference', *CBI News*, December.

Banham, J. (1991), 'Home thoughts from abroad', *CBI News*, April, London: CBI.

The Banker (1991a), 'Eurofed to the rescue', January.

The Banker (1991b), 'Two-tier EMU', January.

The Banker (1991c), '1992 Update', July.

The Banker (1991d), 'Everything up for grabs', December.

The Banker (1992), 'UK Banking', 21 November.

Blitz, J. (1992a), 'Bank under pressure to intervene as pound falls', *Financial Times*, 15–16 August.

Blitz, J. (1992b), 'Sterling falls to lowest ERM levels against D-Mark', *Financial Times*, 21 August .

Blitz, J., Marsh, P. and Marsh, D. (1992), 'Intervention steadies pound', *Financial Times*, 27 August.

Brittan, L. (1991), 'The home straight to EMU', *The Independent*, 13 September.

Brittan, S. (1992a), 'Sterling has many defences', *Financial Times*, 16 January.

Brittan, S. (1992b), 'Anatomy of the UK defeat', *Financial Times*, 24 September.

Brittan, S. (1992c), 'Early end to a puerile joy', *Financial Times*, 5 October.

Brittan, S. (1992d), 'The urgent need for a firm inner core', *Financial Times*, 26 November.

Brittan, S. (1992e), 'Devaluation defeat – how '92 differs', *Financial Times*, 17 September.

Brock, G. (1991), 'Lamont refuses to trade pound for the ECU', *The Times*, 24 September.

Buchan, D. (1991), 'Ministers unworried by the idea of two-speed EMU', *Financial Times*, 13 May.

Brummer, A. (1992), 'Lamont is off the hook, at least for the present', *The Guardian*, 14 September.

Cairncross, A. (1992), *The British Economy since 1945*, Oxford: Blackwell.

Confederation of British Industry (1990), A*genda Europe: completing the Single Market*, CBI, November 1990.

Confederation of British Industry (1991a), 'Taking the long view', *CBI News*, January, London: CBI.

Confederation of British Industry (1991b), *Priorities for Europe's Business: memorandum by the Confederation of British Industry*, NEDC (91) 23, 23 October.

Confederation of British Industry (1991c), *The Road to Recovery*, NEDC (92) 2, 20 December.

Confederation of British Industry (1991d), 'National Conference Report', *CBI News*, December 1991/January 1992, London: CBI.

Confederation of British Industry (1991e), *Competing in the New Europe: a business agenda for the 1990s*, London: CBI.

Confederation of British Industry (1992), *Making it in Britain*, London: CBI.

Congdom, T. (1992), 'Bank on a firm dollar, not on a dodgy DM', *The Daily Telegraph*, 13 August.

Corby, B. (1991), 'Creating the right Europe', *CBI News,* December 1991/January 1992, London: CBI.

Corby, B. (1992), 'Living with low inflation', *CBI News*, March, London: CBI.

Corrigan, T. and Tucker, E. (1992), 'Outflow of funds in day put at £10bn', *Financial Times*, 17 September.

Dawnay, I. (1991), 'Ministers tackle backbench worries on state economy', *Financial Times*, 24 December.

Dawnay, I. (1992a), 'Major stands firm on economic policy', *Financial Times,* 21 July.

Dawnay, I. (1992b), 'Cabinet divided over speed of re-entry to system', *Financial Times*, 19/20 September.

Dawnay, I. (1992c), 'ERM exit was sole option, says PM', *Financial Times*, 25 September.

Dawnay, I. and Smith, A. (1992), 'Lamont in calls to Tories', *Financial Times*, 16 July.

Davies, H. (1992a), 'A time for self-discipline', *CBI News*, September, London: CBI.

Davies, H. (1992b), 'Manufacturing: more needed', *CBI News*, November, London: CBI.

Dennis, P. (1992), 'Dangerous to believe no justification for UK to leave the ERM', *Financial Times*, 23 July.

Eberlie, D. (1991a), 'Timetable for EMU set out as EC debates political union', *CBI News*, July, London: CBI.

Eberlie, D. (1991b), 'A wider and deeper Europe', *CBI News*, October, London: CBI.

Eberlie, D. (1991c), 'All eyes on Maastricht', *CBI News*, December 1991/January 1992, London: CBI.

The Economist (1991a), 'What is phase 2?', 19 January.

The Economist (1991b), 'Hatching out', 18 May.

The Economist (1992), 'An end to the slippery slope', 18 July.

European Trade Union Confederation (1992), *Economic and Monetary Union after the Turmoil of September 1992*, Brussels: ETUC.

Financial Times (1992a), 'Marking time in the markets', 2 January.

Financial Times (1992b), 'Campaigning in earnest', 11/12 January.

Financial Times (1992c), 'Would leaving the ERM help Britain?', 17–18 July.

Financial Times (1992d), 'Extracts from the EC monetary Committee Communique', 14 September.

Financial Times (1992e), 'Alarm and disbelief in industry', 17 September.

The Guardian (1992a), 'Devalue pound, urges Thatcher', *The Guardian*, 7 January 1992.

The Guardian (1992b), 'Revaluing devaluation', 8 January.

The Guardian (1992c), 'The word can finally be spoken', 16 April.

The Guardian (1992c), 'Government comes under fire from industry despite cuts in interest rates', 23 September.

Gow, D. and Hutton, W. (1992), 'MPs to clear Lamont over ERM debacle', *The Guardian*, 3 November.

Harris, A. (1992), 'Panic and other kinds of policy', *Financial Times*, 6 January.

Hill, A. and Norman, P. (1991), 'The horse is back before the cart', *Financial Times*, 13 September.

Howe, M. (1993), *Maastricht and Social Europe: an escape or an entrapment?*, Oxford: Nelson & Pollard Publishing.

Huhne, C. (1992), 'Fundamental causes lie in world economy', *The Independent*, 17 September.

Hutton, W. (1992a), 'The case for devaluation', *The Guardian*, 13 January.

Hutton, W. (1992b), 'The Chancellor, the Banker and the death ears in Bath', *The Guardian*, 30 November.

Hutton, W. (1992c), 'Black Wednesday massacre', *The Guardian*, 1 December.

Ipsen, E. (1992a), 'Can devaluation cure Europe's slump?', *International Herald Tribune*, 8 January.

Ipsen, E. (1992b), 'Good-bye Delors, hello lower rates', *International Herald Tribune*, 3 September.

Ipsen, E. (1992c), 'Lamont is bearish on European Monetary Union', *International Herald Tribune*, 19–20 December.

Johnson, R. (1992), 'Most economists expect recession to end this year', *Financial Times*, 2 January.

Kaletsky, A. (1992), 'After the lira, how vulnerable is sterling?', *The Times*, 15 September.

Lamont, N. (1992a), 'Lamont spells out his strategy for recovery', *The Daily Telegraph*, 11 July.

Lamont, N. (1992b), 'Lamont denies shift in policy', *Financial Times*, 18 September.

Lamont, N. (1992c), 'How Britain can help itself out of the ERM', *The Daily Telegraph*, 9 October.

Lamont, N. (1992d), 'Priority is to restore policy framework', *Financial Times*, 30 October.

Leigh-Pemberton, R. (1992), 'How Britain can help itself out of the ERM', *The Daily Telegraph*, 9 October.

Marsh, D. (1991), 'In the shadow of the powerhouse', *Financial Times*, 12 March.

Marsh, D. (1992a), 'A fragile exchange', *Financial Times*, 17 January.

Marsh, D. (1992b), 'No place for bank to call home', *Financial Times*, 14 July.

Marsh, D. and Fisher, A. (1992), 'Race for Europe's central bank hots up', *Financial Times*, 5 May.

Marsh, P. (1991), 'Anniversary of what may be a marriage of convenience', *Financial Times*, 5/6 October.

Marsh, P. (1992a), 'Thoughts of devaluation gain currency', *Financial Times*, 10 July.

Marsh, P. (1992b), 'The case for a realignment', *Financial Times*, 27 August.

Marsh, P. and Blitz, J. (1992), 'Pound falls to new low in the ERM', *Financial Times*, 16 September.

Marshall, A. (1992), 'London stakes its claim for Europe's new bank', *The Independent*, 27 January.

Milne, I. (1993), *Maastricht: the case against economic and monetary union*, Oxford: Nelson & Pollard Publishing.

Minford, P. (1991), 'Monetary Union next in crisis queue', *The Daily Telegraph*, 21 January.

Minford, P. (1992), 'Liverpool Six launch fresh attack on monetary union', *The Daily Telegraph*, 10 January.

Mouthner, R. (1992), 'Domestic gales ruffle Major's EC outing', *Financial Times*, 17/18 October.

Narbrough, C. (1992), 'Schlesinger stands firm on stability for Europe', *The Times*, 1 January 1992.

Norman, P. (1991), 'Ingredients for recovery are in place: interview with Norman Lamont', *Financial Times*, 31 December.

Norman, P. (1992a), 'Indicators to guide UK policy', *Financial Times*, 21 September.

Norman, P. (1992b), 'Chancellor moves to plug economic policy gap', *Financial Times*, 9 October.

Norman, P. (1992c), 'ERM reform sidelined by need for unity', *Financial Times*, 16 October.

Norman, P. and Atkins, R. (1992), 'Lamont rules out "kickstart"', *Financial Times*, 13 October.

Norman, P. and Blitz, J. (1992), 'Treasury and Bank step up defence over sterling', *Financial Times*, 1/2 August.

Norman, P. and Peston, R. (1992), 'Credit where credit is due', *Financial Times*, 5/6 September.

Oakley, R. (1991), 'Delors sets Tory tongues wagging again on Europe', *The Times*, 16 May.

OECD (1991), *Economic Outlook*, No. 50, December.

Owen, I. (1992), 'Hurd rejects pound realignment in the ERM', *Financial Times*, 11–12 January.

Owen, D. (1992a), 'Tories join resignation chorus', *Financial Times*, 17 September.

Owen, D. (1992b), 'Lamont outlines post-crisis agenda', *Financial Times*, 25 September.

Owen, D. (1992c), 'Major in strongest denial yet on ERM', *Financial Times*, 21 October.

Palmer, J. (1992), 'Lamont sets up new ERM hurdle', *The Guardian*, 25 November.

Ridley, N. (1992), 'Float sterling, sink Labour', *The Times*, 8 January.

Sentance, A. (1991), 'Can the UK sustain low inflation?', *CBI News*, October, London: CBI.

Sentance, A. and Walsh, J. (1992), 'Britain inflation post ERM', *CBI News*, December 1992/ January, London: CBI.

Smith, A. (1992), 'Chancellor fails to sway critics', *Financial Times*, 27 August.

Smith, A. and Buchan, D. (1992), 'Major wins support on resisting two-speed EC', *Financial Times*, 1 October.

Smith,. A. and Norman, P. (1992), 'Bank warns on fall in pound', *Financial Times*, 30 September.

Stephens, P. (1990), 'Major moves to regain initiative over Euro-sceptics', *Financial Times*, 22 September.

Stephens, P. (1991), 'UK accepts it may have to boost Bank's independence', *Financial Times*, 23–24 November.

Stephens, P. (1992a), 'Major favours 9 April poll', *Financial Times*, 22 January.

Stephens (1992b), 'Major rules out a devaluation', *Financial Times*, 13 July.

Stephens, P. (1992c), 'Major faces the most serious test of his career', *Financial Times*, 17 September.

Stephens, P. and Tucker, E. (1992), 'Major stresses solid opposition to devaluation', *Financial Times*, 11 September.

Stephens, P. and Norman, P. (1992), 'Pound fall to post-poll low', *Financial Times*, 14 July.

The Times (1992), 'Letters', 7 January.

Trade Union Congress (1991a), *Building Links in Europe,* London: TUC.

Trade Union Congress (1991b), *Economic Integration in Europe: what 1992 and EMU mean for unions*, paper for a conference on 6 June at Congress House.

Trade Union Congress (1991c), *Report of the 123rd Annual Trade Union Congress*, London: TUC.

Trade Union Congress (1991d), *Economic policy options in the 1990s: memorandum by the TUC to the NEDC*, NEDC (92) 1, 18 December, London: NEDC.

Trade Union Congress (1992a), *Report of the 124th Annual Trade Union Congress*, London: TUC.

Trade Union Congress (1992b), *Unions after Maastricht: the challenge of social Europe, London: TUC Trade Union Congress*, London: TUC.

Trade Union Congress (1992c), *The Competitiveness of UK manufacturing industry*, submission to the Trade and Industry Select Committee by the Trade Union Congress.

Trade Union Congress (1992d), *Britain's New Manufacturing Partnership: a TUC discussion document*, London: TUC.

Trade Union Congress (1992e), *British Manufacturing Industry and the World Economy: an assessment of national performance*, London· TUC.

Trade Union Congress (1992f), *Industrial Partnership and Competitiveness: the trade union role*, London: TUC.

Trade Union Congress (1992g), *Call for Action: a programme for national recovery*, London: TUC.

Trade Union Congress (1992h), *Budget Submission 1993: strategy for full employment*, London: TUC.

Trade Union Congress (1992i), *Britain's New Manufacturing Partnership: a checklist for action*, London: TUC.

Trade Union Congress (1993a), *Report of the 125th Annual Trade Union Congress*, London: TUC.

Trade Union Congress (1993b), *The Maastricht Treaty: economic and employment issues*, London: TUC.

Webster, P. (1991), 'Labour wants Euro bank site in UK', *The Times*, 24 December.

Webster, P. and Leathley, A. (1992), 'Lamont backs ERM in face of Tory calls for interest rates cuts', *The Times*, 10 July.

Westaway, P. (1992), 'What price devaluation?', *The Guardian*, 31 August.

Williams, N. (1990), 'The ERM wait is over', *CBI News*, December.

Williams, N. (1991a), 'EMU update', *CBI News*, June.

Williams, N. (1991b), 'Are "real" interest rates high?', *CBI News*, June 1992, London: CBI.

Williams, N. (1992), 'EMU and Maastricht', *CBI News*, February, London: CBI.

Wolf, J. (1991), 'Britain offered monetary union opt-out', *The Guardian*, 11 May.

Wolf, M. (1992), '1992: the future imperfect', *Financial Times*, 2 January.

Urry, M. (1992), 'City finds new hopes amid apparent crisis', *Financial Times*, 18 September.

Part III: Future Consensus

6 *Italy and EMU: A Widespread Socioeconomic Consensus*

ABI (1991), 'Gli intermediari creditizi e la crisi del risparmio', *Bancaria*, Vol. 47, No. 12, December.

ABI (1992), 'Evitare le argomentazioni di comodo', *Bancaria*, Vol. 48, No. 5, May.

Agnelli, G. (1989a), 'The Association for the monetary union of Europe: why the association was set up', in *A single currency for Europe: political, economic and financial choices*, symposium promoted by AUME and organised by Confindustria, Rome, 21 February.

Agnelli, G. (1989b), 'L'Associazione per l'unione monetaria in Europa: le ragioni dell'iniziativa', *Rivista di Politica Economica*, March.

Banca d'Italia (1996), *Bollettino Economico*, October.

Barrel, R., Morgan, J. and Pain, N. (1995), 'The employment effects of the Maastricht fiscal criteria', *Niesr Discussion Papers*, No. 81, June.

Barrel, R. and Sefton, J. (1997), 'European unemployment macroeconomic aspects: fiscal policy, real exchange rate and monetary union', *EUI Working Papers*, RSC No. 97/40.

Bayoumi, T. and Eichengreen, B. (1992), 'Shocking aspects of European monetary unification', *CEPR Discussion Papers*, No. 643, May.

Benvenuto, G. (1990), 'Non vogliamo restare fuori dalla porta', *Lavorosocieta'* No. 12, December.

Bianchi, T. (1993), 'Che cosa ha inseganto il 1992', *Bancaria*, Vol. 49, No. 7–8, July–August.

Bianchi, T. (1996), 'Il cambiamento del sistema bancario e la sfida europea', *Bancaria*, No. 7–8, July–August.

CES (1991), 'Il sindacalismo europeo in un mondo che cambia', *Nuova Rassegna Sindacale*, No. 26, 15 July.

CGIL (1990), 'Le proposte di CGIL, CISL, e UIL per la presidenza italiana della Comunita', *Nuova Rassegna Sindacale*, No. 19, 14 May.

Calabresi, S. and Carnazza, P. (1995), 'La svalutazione della lira e la reazione delle imprese industriali: un'inchiesta ad hoc dell'ISCO', *Rassegna di Lavori dell'ISCO*, No. 1.

Calabresi, S. and Carnazza, P. (1996), 'La svalutazione della lira e la reazione delle imprese industriali: un'inchiesta ad hoc dell'ISCO', *Rivista di Politica Economica*, Vol. LXXXVI, Series III, April.

Confindustria (1992), *Confindustria per la modernizzazione. Proposte ed intese 1992–1995*, Rome: SIPI.

Confindustria (1995a), *XVII Rapporto CSC*, Rome: Confindustria.

Confindustria (1995b), *Conferenza intergovernativa europea 1996, posizione preliminare di Confindustria*, mimeo, October.

Confindustria (1996a), *Unione Europea 1996: una strategia per lo svilupo, l'occupazione' la presenza nel mondo, Contributo della Confindustria per il semestre italiano di Presidenza dell'Unione Europea (1 gennaio, 30 Giugno 1996)*, mimeo.

Confindustria (1996b), 'Un programma di finanza pubblica per restare in Europa', in Confindustria, *Confindustria per la modernizzazione. Volume II. Proposte ed intese*, October 1995–May 1996, Rome: SIPI.

EBF (1993), 'Le banche europee e l'unione economica e monetaria: passi verso un mercato integrato', *Bancaria*, Vol. 49, No. 7–8, July–August.

EBF (1995), 'Le banche europee e l'introduzione della moneta unica: un'indagine su tempi, costi e modalita', *Bancaria*, No. 5, May.

Fazio, A. (1997), 'Elogio della stabilita: la moneta', *Bancaria*, No. 2.

Gabaglio, E. (1990), 'Per ora vince il mercato', *Nuova Rassegna Sindacale*, No. 48, 24 December.

Gabaglio, E. (1992), 'Dopo la tempesta', *Nuova Rassegna Sindacale*, No. 35, 5 October.

Gnetti, C. (1990), 'Per ora vince il mercato', *Nuova Rassegna Sindacale*, No. 48, 24 December.

Gnetti, C. (1991a), 'Pensare Europeo', *Nuova Rassegna Sindacale*, No. 19, 27 May.

Gnetti, C. (1991b), 'Il grande salto', *Nuova Rassegna Sindacale*, No. 19, 27 May.

Lettieri, A. (1991), 'Un nuovo internazionalismo', *Nuova Rassegna Sindacale*, No. 26, 15 July.

Lettieri, A. (1992), 'Sindacati a due velocita', *Nuova Rassegna Sindacale*, No. 47, December.

Lettieri, A. (1993), 'Occhio all' Europa', *Nuova Rassegna Sindacale*, No. 25, 5 July.

Lipschitz, L. and McDonald (1991), 'Real exchange rate uncompetitiveness: a clarification of concepts and some measurement for Europe', *IMF working paper*, March.

Masucci, E. (1992), 'Il ruolo delle parti', *Nuova Rassegna Sindacale*, No. 10, 16 March.

Paruolo, S. (1991), 'Ostacoli sulla strada dell'integrazione', *Nuova Rassegna Sindacale*, No. 45, 16 December.

Pininfarina, S. (1989a), 'The Association for the monetary union of Europe: why the association was set up', in *A single currency for Europe: political, economic and financial choices*, symposium promoted by AUME and organised by Confindustria, Rome, 21 February.

Pininfarina, S. (1989b), 'La moneta unica, condizione per l'effettiva integrazione europea', *Rivista di Politica Economica*, March.

Scognamiglio, C. (1989), 'Cambi fissi o moneta unica', *Rivista di Politica Economica*, March.

Trentin, B. (1991), 'Verso un sindacato rappresentativo', *Nuova Rassegna Sindacale*, No. 26, 15 July.

Turner, P. and Van't dack, J. (1993), 'Measuring international price and cost competitiveness', *BIS economic papers*, No. 39, November.

Viñals, J. and Jimeno, J.F. (1996), 'Monetary Union and European unemployment', *CEPR Discussion Papers*, No. 1485.

7 *The UK and EMU: The City vs the Continent*

Artis, M.J. (1996), *The UK Economy*, 14th edn, Oxford: Oxford University Press.

Bank of England (1996), *Practical Issues Arising from the Introduction of the Euro*, London: Bank of England, 16 September.

Bank of England (1997), *Practical Issues Arising from the Introduction of the Euro*, Issue No. 6, 10 December.

British Banking Association, Association for Payment Clearing Services, London Investment Banking Association (1996), *Preparing for EMU: the implication of European Monetary Union for the banking and financial markets in the United Kingdom. Report of the EMU City Working Group*, London: BBA, APACS, LIBA, September 1996, Background Papers, Money Markets.

British Invisibles (1996a), *Key Facts about the City of London*, London: British Invisibles.

British Invisibles (1996b), *Invisibles Facts and Figures*, London: British Invisibles.

British Invisibles (1996c), *The City Table 1995*, London: British Invisibles.

Clarke, M.W. (1979), *Inside the City*, London: George Allen & Unwin.

Denton, N. (1997), 'European Monetary Union: Euro heralds an IT bonanza', *Financial Times*, 5 February.

Goacher, D.J. and Curwen, P.J. (1987), *British Non-bank Financial Intermediaries*, London: Allen & Unwin.

House of Lords, Select Committee on European Communities (1996), *An EMU of ins and outs*, London: HMSO.

Johnson, C. (forthcoming), 'La City de Londre face a l'Euro'.

Levitt, M. (1996a), *European Monetary Union – The Impact on Banking*, Royal Institute of International Affairs Conference, 13–14 March, London.

Levitt, M. (1996b), 'EMU: a view from the banking sector', *Journal of European Public Policy*, No. 3, Vol. 3, September.

LIBA (1996), *Non-participation in EMU: possible consequences for the City of London*, London: LIBA.

Moran, M. (1997), 'Planning for EMU: Banque Paribas forges ahead', *Financial Times*, 5 February.

Picchi, F. (1991), *Economics and Business: dizionario enciclopedico economico e commerciale inglese italiano, italiano inglese*, Bologna: Zanichelli.

Reid, M. (1988), *All-change in the City*, London: MacMillan Press.

Shaw, E.R. (1981), *The London Money Market*, London: Heineman.